ANSI C Programming

Yashavant P. Kanetkar

FIRST EDITION 2019
REPRINT 2025

ISBN : 978-93-89423-00-6

Distributors:

BPB PUBLICATIONS
20, Ansari Road, Darya Ganj
New Delhi-110002
Ph: 23254990/23254991

MICRO MEDIA
Shop No. 5, Mahendra Chambers, 150
DN Rd. Next to Capital Cinema, V.T.
(C.S.T.) Station,
MUMBAI-400 001
Ph: 22078296/22078297

DECCAN AGENCIES
4-3-329, Bank Street,
Hyderabad-500195
Ph: 24756967/24756400

Published by Manish Jain for BPB Publications, 20, Ansari Road, Darya Ganj, New Delhi-110002 and Printed by him at Manipal Technologies Limited, Manipal

Dedicated to baba

Who couldn't be here to see this day...

About the Author

Through his original works in the form of books and Quest Video courseware CDs on C, C++, Data Structures, VC++, .NET, Embedded Systems, etc. Yashavant Kanetkar has created, moulded and groomed lacs of IT careers in the last decade and half. In recognition of his immense contribution to IT education in India, he has been awarded the "Best .NET Technical Contributor" and "Most Valuable Professional" awards by Microsoft. His current passion includes Device Driver and Embedded System Programming. Yashavant has recently been honored with a "Distinguished Alumnus Award" by IIT Kanpur for his entrepreneurial, professional and academic excellence. Yashavant holds a BE from VJTI Mumbai and M.Tech. from IIT Kanpur. Yashavant's current affiliations include being a Director of KICIT and KSET.

Acknowledgments

Once I completed my first book, fifteen years ago, one person has continuously egged me on to write on newer and newer topics. He is Manish Jain of BPB. He has a way to motivate authors to produce better books. I hope every author gets a publisher who is as cooperative, knowledgeable and supportive as Manish.

I thank Seema, my wife, my parents and kids for supporting me throughout this book effort.

And finally my heartfelt gratitude to Monali Mohadikar for the countless hours she spent on formatting the text and the figures to make them appear just the way I wanted them to.

Preface

Writing C programs targeted for one compiler is one thing, but making the programs work under all compilers is what makes it portable and useful. In this heterogeneous world a program which is compiler dependant is simply unacceptable. In ANSI C programming I have attempted to teach C language in such a manner that you are able to write truly portable programs.

If you feel that I could have done certain things in this book better than what I have, or you have any suggestions about what you would like to see in the next edition, please drop a line to *sales@bpbonline.com*

All the best and happy programming!

Contents

0 Before We Begin...

- Detailed Compilation Steps
    - Compilation using TC / TC++
    - Problem of TC / TC++ with Windows Vista / Windows 7
    - Compilation using Visual Studio/Visual Studio Express
    - Compilation using gcc
- A Word of Caution

To understand C language and gain confidence in working with it you would be required to type programs in this book and then instruct the machine to execute them. To type any programs you need another program called Editor. Once the program has been typed it needs to be converted to machine language (0s and 1s) before the machine can execute it. To carry out this conversion we need another program called Compiler. Compiler vendors provide an Integrated Development Environment (IDE) which consists of an Editor as well as the Compiler.

There are several such IDEs available in the market targeted towards different operating systems. For example, Turbo C and Turbo C++ are popular compilers that work under MS-DOS; Visual Studio and Visual Studio Express Edition are the compilers that work under Windows, whereas gcc compiler works under Linux. Note that Turbo C, Turbo C++ and gcc compilers can also be installed on machines running Windows OS.

Of these, Visual Studio Express Edition and gcc compilers are available free of cost. They can be downloaded from the following sites:

http://www.microsoft.com/express/download

http://www.cygwin.com

You are free to use any of the compilers mentioned above for compiling programs in this book. If you wish to know my personal choice, I would prefer Visual Studio Express Edition for two simple reasons—it is a modern compiler with easy to use GUI and it is available free of cost.

To help you go through the installation process of Visual Studio Express Edition smoothly I have also recorded a video. You can watch the same at the following link:

http://www.youtube.com/asangdani

Detailed Compilation Steps

The compilation process with each of the compilers mentioned in the previous section is a bit different. So for your benefit I am giving below the detailed compilation and execution steps with each of these compilers.

Compilation using TC / TC++

Here are the steps that you need to follow to compile and execute programs using TC/TC++…

(a) Start the compiler at **C>** prompt. The compiler (TC.EXE) is usually present in **C:\TC\BIN** directory.

(b) Select **New** from the **File** menu.

(c) Type the program.

(d) Save the program using **F2** under a proper name (say Program1.c).

(e) Use **Ctrl + F9** to compile and execute the program.

(f) Use **Alt + F5** to view the output.

A word of caution! If you run this program in Turbo C++ compiler, you may get an error — "The function printf should have a prototype". To get rid of this error, perform the following steps and then recompile the program.

(a) Select 'Options' menu and then select 'Compiler | C++ Options'. In the dialog box that pops up, select 'CPP always' in the 'Use C++ Compiler' options.

(b) Again select 'Options' menu and then select 'Environment | Editor'. Make sure that the default extension is 'C' rather than 'CPP'.

Problem of TC with Windows Vista / Windows 7

The installation procedure of TC compiler is very simple. However, if you install TC compiler under Windows Vista, the window size becomes very small. So small is the screen size that you can hardly work with it. You can increase the size of TC window to occupy the entire screen. For this you will have to download an x86 emulator called DosBox from following link:

http://prdownloads.sourceforg.net/dosbox/dosbox0.72-win32-installer.exe?download

Once you have downloaded this emulator carry out the following steps:

(a) Install the DosBox software that you have downloaded.
(b) Create a folder called Turbo on your C: drive.

(c) Copy entire Turbo C / Turbo C++ software in this Turbo folder.

(d) Start DosBox by double clicking DosBox icon.

(e) You would be presented with two screens. You need to use the one which has a Z> prompt in it. Type the following command at Z> prompt.

```
mount  X  C:\Turbo
mount  D  C:\Turbo\TC
D:
cd  Bin
TC
```

By typing the last command "TC" you are executing the Turbo C / Turbo C++ software. This would bring up the normal blue colored TC window. To increase the window size just press Alt + Enter. Now the TC window will accommodate the entire screen.

(f) Go to the Options Menu (Alt O), select 'Directories' menu item and change the 'Include' and 'Library' directory such that they contain the following entries:

```
X:\TC\INCLUDE
X:\TC\LIB
```

(g) Once you have typed and saved program do not compile it using the usual Ctrl F9. Instead, compile it using the Compile Menu and execute it using Run Menu.

The following shortcut keys can be used while working in Turbo C / Turbo C++ environment. If you use them it will improve your productivity.

- Press Alt + F, N to open a new file
- Press F2 to save the current file
- Press Ctrl + F9 to compile and run the program
- Press Alt + F5 to view the output of the program
- Press Alt + F3 to close the currently opened file
- Press Alt + X to exit Turbo C

Compilation using Visual Studio / Visual Studio Express Edition

Carry out the following steps to compile and execute programs using any Visual Studio version:

(a) Start Visual Studio 2008 from Start | All Programs | Microsoft Visual Studio 2008 or start Visual Studio 2008 Express Edition from Start | All Programs | Microsoft Visual C++ 2008 Express Edition.

(b) Select File | New Project… from the File menu. Select Project Type as Visual C++ | Win32 Console Application from the dialog that pops up. Give a proper name of the project in Name TextBox (say Program1). Then click on OK and Finish.

(c) Type the program.

(d) Save the program using **Ctrl + S**.

(e) Use **Ctrl + F5** to compile and execute the program.

When you use Visual Studio to create a Win32 Console Application for the above program the wizard would insert the following code by default:

```
#include "stdafx.h"
int _tmain ( int argc, _TCHAR* argv[ ] )
{
    return 0 ;
}
```

You can delete this code and type your program in its place. If you now compile the program using Ctrl F5 you would get the following error:

```
Fatal error C1010:
unexpected end of file while looking for precompiled header.
Did you forget to add '#include "stdafx.h"' to your source?
```

If you add #include "stdafx.h" at the top of your program then it would compile and run successfully. However, including this file makes the program Visual Studio-centric and would not get compiled with TC / TC++ and gcc compilers. This is not good as the program no longer remains portable. To eliminate this error, you need to make a setting in Visual Studio. To make this setting carry out the following steps:

(a) Go to 'Solution Explorer'.

(b) Right click on the project name and select 'Properties' from the menu that pops up. On doing so, a dialog shown in Figure 0.1 would appear.

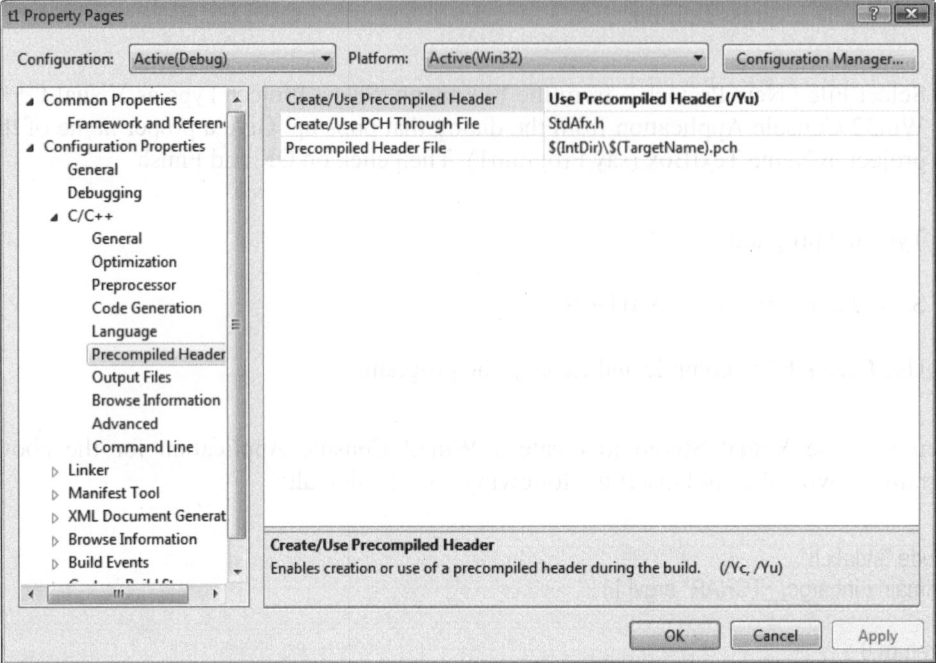

Figure 0.1

(c) From the left pane of this dialog first select 'Configuration Properties' followed by 'C/C++'.

(d) Select 'Precompiled Headers'

(e) From the right pane of the dialog click on 'Create/Use Precompiled Header'. On doing so in the value for this option a triangle would appear.

(f) Click on this triangle and a drop down list box would appear.

(g) From the list box select 'Not using Precompiled Header'.

(h) Click on OK button to make the setting effective.

In addition to this, you need to make one more setting. By default Visual Studio believes that your program is a C++ program and not a C program. So by making a setting you need to tell it that your program is a C program and not a C++ program. Carry out the following steps to make this setting:

(a) Go to 'Solution Explorer' window.

(b) Right click on the project name Right click on the project name and select 'Properties' from the menu that pops up. On doing so, a dialog shown in Figure 0.2 would appear.

(c) From the left pane of this dialog first select 'Configuration Properties' followed by 'C/C++'.

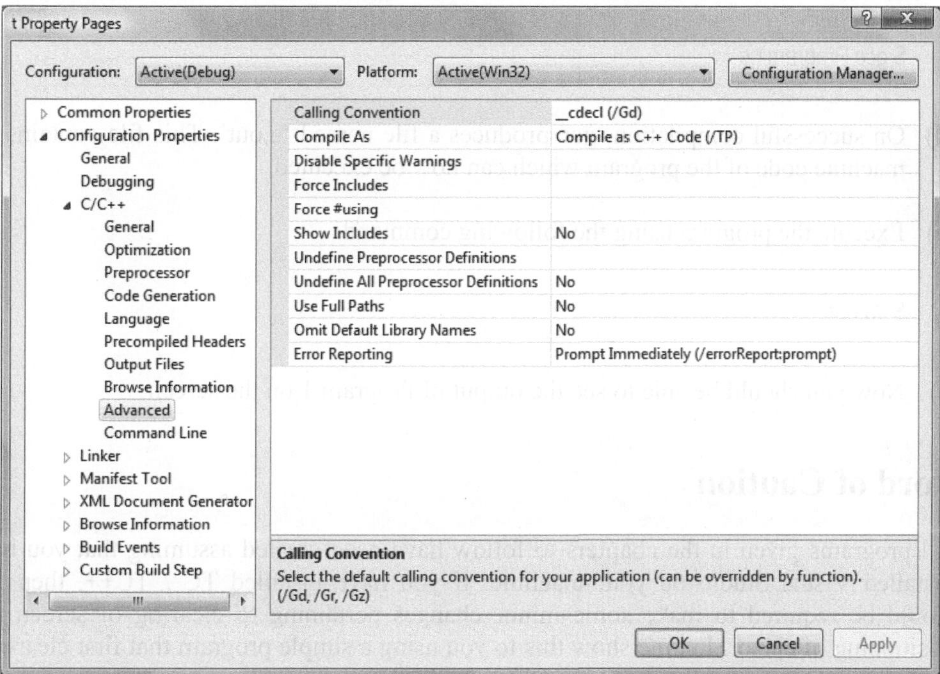

Figure 0.2

(d) In C/C++ options select 'Advanced'.

(e) Change the 'Compile As' option to 'Compile as C code (/TC)'.

Once this setting is made you can now compile the program using Ctrl F5. This time no error would be flagged and the program would compile and execute successfully.

Compilation using gcc

Carry out the following steps to compile and execute programs using gcc:

(a) Type the program using any editor like vi, vim or emacs and save it under the name 'Program1.c'.

(b) At the command prompt switch to the directory containing 'Program1.c' using the **cd** command.

(c) Now compile the program using the **gcc** compiler as shown below:

```
$ gcc Program1.c
```

(d) On successful compilation, **gcc** produces a file named 'a.out'. This file contains the machine code of the program which can now be executed.

(e) Execute the program using the following command.

```
$ ./a.out
```

(f) Now you should be able to see the output of Program 1 on the screen.

A Word of Caution

All programs given in the chapters to follow have been created assuming that you have installed Visual Studio on your machine. If you have installed TC / TC++, then you would be required to make some minor changes pertaining to clearing of screen and positioning of cursor. Let me show this to you using a simple program that first clears the screen then positions the cursor at 10th row, 20th column and prints a message at this location. If we were to use TC / TC++, the program would look like this...

```
#include <stdio.h>
#include <conio.h>
int main( )
```

```
{
    clrscr( ) ;  /* clear existing contents on screen */
    gotoxy ( 20, 10 ) ;  /* position cursor */
    printf ( "Hello" ) ;
    return 0 ;
}
```

A similar program in Visual Studio would take the following form:

```
#include <stdio.h>
#include <system.h>
void gotoxy ( short int col, short int row ) ;

int main( )
{
    system ( "cls" ) ;  /* clear existing contents on screen */
    gotoxy ( 20, 10 ) ;  /* position cursor */
    printf ( "Hello" ) ;
    return 0 ;
}

void gotoxy ( short int col, short int row )
{
    HANDLE hStdout = GetStdHandle ( STD_OUTPUT_HANDLE ) ;
    COORD position = { col, row } ;
    SetConsoleCursorPosition ( hStdout, position ) ;
}
```

So depending on whether you are using Turbo C / Turbo C++ compiler or Visual Studio compiler you will have to use the suitable form of **clrscr( )** and **gotoxy( )** shown above.

1 Introduction To Programming

- Basic Model of Computation
- Algorithms
- Flowchart
- Programming Languages
- Stages in the Development of a C Program
    - Developing the Program
    - Compiling the Program
    - Linking the Program
    - Testing the Program
    - Documenting the Program
- Summary
- Exercise

Attempting to learn C language before having any idea about the basic model of computation, the way to evolve a solution, the way to represent it and the overall program development process would be like putting a horse before the cart. Hence in this chapter we would focus on these topics and create a solid background before we venture into C programming. Let us begin with the computation model…

Basic Model of Computation

Really speaking, the idea of computing is not new to any of us. Each one of us have used mainly used pencil and paper to do fundamental computing operations like addition, subtraction, multiplication, division or slightly more complex operations like computing lengths, areas, volumes etc. While performing all these computations we follow some definite, unambiguous set of rules. Similarly when we do computation using a computer we follow a certain set of rules. The basic model of computation involves input, process and output. These are shown in Figure 1.1.

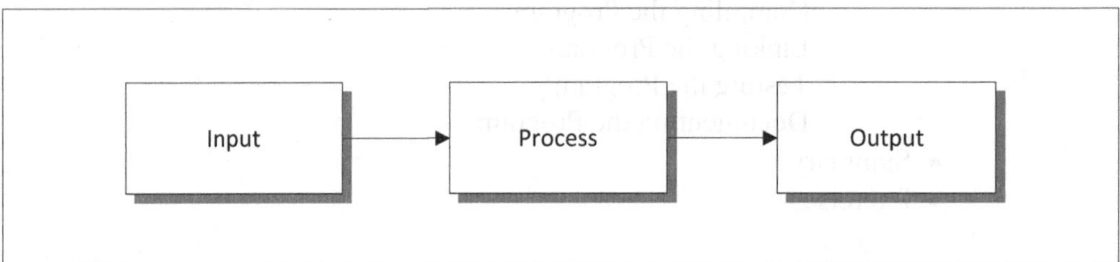

Figure 1.1

The input is received using input devices like keyboard, mouse, touch screen, etc. Once the input is received it is processed using the Central Processing Unit (CPU) of the computer and the result is then displayed using the output devices like VDU, printer, plotter, etc. The processing involves performing arithmetic operation and logical comparison operations (like a < b, c >= d, etc.). In addition to this the CPU also controls operations of input / output devices and memory. While solving any problem using a computer we need to explicitly write down the steps keeping the above model of computation in mind. These explicit steps for solving a given computing problem, is called an **Algorithm**. In Chapter 2 we would be studying and explicitly writing these steps for a variety of problems. For now, let us study the purpose of an algorithm in general.

Algorithms

As mentioned in the previous section, the explicit set of steps for solving a given computing problem is called an algorithm. Thus algorithms are used as a means of communication for specifying solutions to computational problems, unambiguously, so that others can understand the solutions. More precisely, an algorithm is a sequence of instructions that act on some input data to produce some output in a finite number of steps. An algorithm must have the following properties:

(a) Input – An algorithm must receive some input data supplied externally.

(b) Output – An algorithm must produce at least one output as the result.

(c) Finiteness – No matter what is the input, the algorithm must terminate after a finite number of steps. For example, a procedure which goes on performing a series of steps infinitely is not an algorithm.

(d) Definiteness – The steps to be performed in the algorithm must be clear and unambiguous.

(e) Effectiveness – One must be able to perform the steps in the algorithm without applying any intelligence. For example, the step—Select three numbers which form a Pythogorian triplet—is not effective.

While creating an algorithm it is important to choose an appropriate model of computation to describe an algorithm. Based on the choice we make, the type of computations that can be carried out in the model gets decided. For example, if our computational model contains only ruler and compass, then using these primitives we can write down explicit algorithms for drawing a line segment of specific length, bisecting it, drawing an angle, bisecting it, etc. However, using these primitives we would not be able to trisect an angle. For doing this we would need additional primitives like a protractor. For arithmetic computations we can use various computing models like calculators. As you can imagine, with each of these models of computing, the rules for specifying a solution (algorithms) are different. Therefore, it is important to first choose an appropriate model of computation while creating algorithms.

There are two ways in which we can describe an algorithm that is used for solving a problem:

(a) Describe it in the form of step by step procedure written in textual form
(b) Describe it in the form of a figure called **Flowchart**

We are quite habituated to describing a step by step procedure in textual form. However, when it comes to describing the procedure using a flowchart we need to understand the common rules followed for drawing it. Let us now try to understand them.

Flowchart

A flowchart describes an algorithm by showing the different steps in it as boxes of various shapes connected using arrows to indicate their order. Thus a flowchart gives a diagrammatic representation of a step-by-step solution to a given problem. Flowcharts are extensively used to describe an algorithm, as "a picture is worth a thousand words". A typical flowchart uses the symbols shown in Figure 1.2 to represent different tasks that are contained in an algorithm.

Symbol	Meaning
(rounded rectangle)	This symbol is used to signal the start or end of a process
(rectangle)	Represents a processing step, like "Add 1 to count"
(parallelogram)	Used to indicate input or output operation
(diamond)	Contains a Yes/No question or True/False test. This symbol has two arrows coming out of it, one corresponding to Yes or True, and another corresponding to No or False.
(arrows)	Indicate the "flow of control". An arrow coming from one symbol and ending at another represents that control passes to the symbol the arrow points to.
(circle)	Represent converging paths in the flowchart. They have more than one arrow coming into them but only one going out.
A	Off-page connectors are often used to signify a connection to a process described on another sheet

Figure 1.2

Let us now take some example and try to describe an algorithm for it in both forms—textual and flowchart. Suppose we wish to find out the biggest of three numbers. Given below is an algorithm and flowchart for it, both of which are self-explanatory. It would be a good idea to take any three numbers and try the algorithm and the flowchart on them.

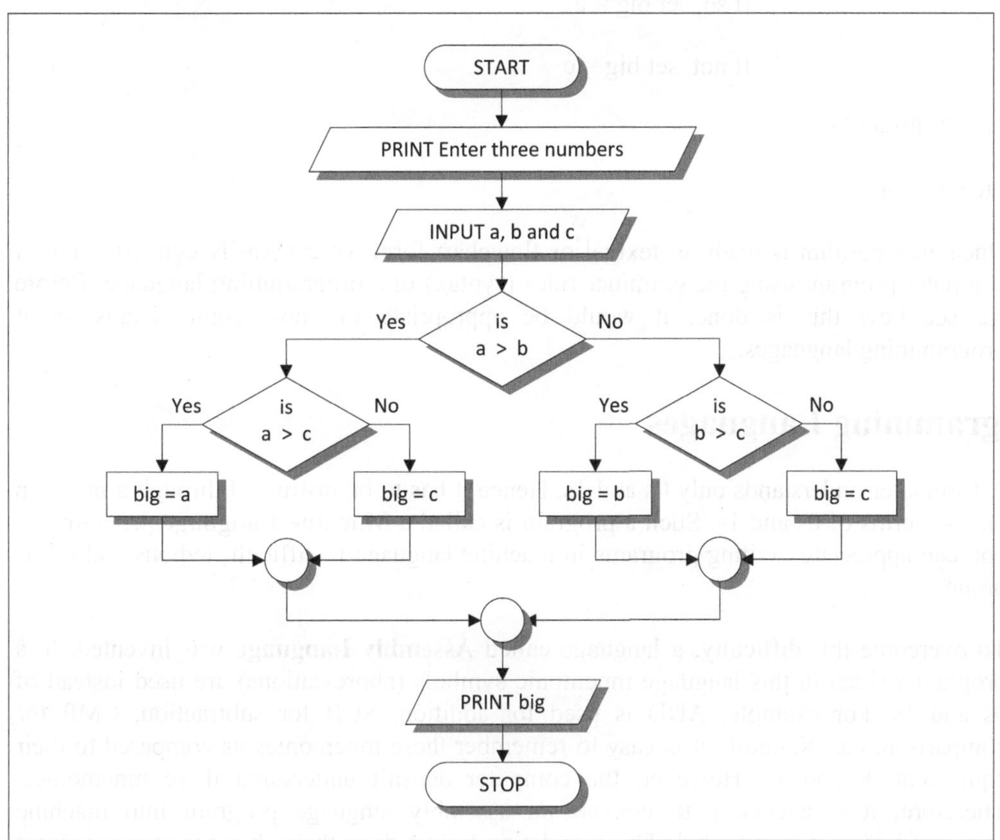

Figure 1.3

Algorithm:

Step 1: Enter three numbers, say a, b, c

Step 2: Check if a > b

If so, check if b > c

If so, set big = b

If not, set big = c

If not, check if a > c

If so, set big = a

If not, set big = c

Step 3: Print big

Step 4: Exit

Once an algorithm is ready in textual or flowchart form we can easily convert it into a computer program using the grammar rules (syntax) of a programming language. Before we see how this is done, it would be appropriate to know some details about programming languages.

Programming Languages

A Computer understands only 0s and 1s. Hence it has to be instructed through a program only in terms of 0s and 1s. Such a program is called a **Machine Language** program. As you can appreciate, writing programs in machine language is difficult, tedious and error-prone.

To overcome this difficulty, a language called **Assembly Language** was invented. In a program written in this language mnemonic symbols (abbreviations) are used instead of 0s and 1s. For example, ADD is used for addition, SUB for subtraction, CMP for comparison, etc. Naturally it is easy to remember these mnemonics as compared to their equivalent 0s and 1s. However, the computer doesn't understand these mnemonics. Therefore, it is necessary to convert an assembly language program into machine language before it is executed. This translation task is done through a converter program called **Assembler**.

A language in which each statement or an instruction is directly translated into a single machine instruction is known as a **Low-level** language. Each mnemonic of an assembly language has a unique machine code. Hence Assembly language is a low-level language. Machine language is also a low-level language. The instructions that one Microprocessor (CPU) can understand are different than those understood by another. This is because internal architecture of each microprocessor is different. Hence the machine language and correspondingly the assembly language for each microprocessor are different. Thus, machine language and assembly language for Intel Pentium microprocessor are different than those for Atmel ATmega32 microprocessor. This means assembly language program written for one microprocessor cannot be used on another microprocessor. In other words it is not portable. Hence, to write an assembly language program, a programmer must have detailed knowledge of the instruction set of the particular microprocessor, its internal architecture, registers, and connection of peripherals to ports etc.

To overcome these difficulties associated with assembly language, **High-level** languages have been developed. In a high level language instead of mnemonics English-like instructions are used. Instructions in these languages permit programmers to describe tasks in the forms that are problem-oriented rather than machine-oriented. Moreover, one does not have to possess knowledge of the architecture of the microprocessor to be able write programs in these languages. Some of the popular high-level languages include BASIC, FORTRAN, Pascal, COBOL, C, C++, Java, C#, etc. The differences that exist between these languages are beyond the scope of this book. In this book we would be concentrating only on learning one of the most popular and widely used high-level language, namely C.

A program written in a high level language is converted into machine language program using software called **Compiler**. These compilers are targeted for different microprocessors. For example, the **Visual Studio** compiler can convert a C language program into machine language instructions that can be understood by Intel microprocessors. Similarly, the **gcc** complier can convert a C language program into machine language instructions that can be understood by ATmega32.

Stages in the Development of a C Program

One has to go through several stages before a program gets ready to be used on a computer. These stages are discussed below. The entire process is also shown in Figure 1.4 in the form of a flowchart to help understand the process better.

Developing the Program

The task of developing a program for a particular problem involves a careful study of the problem with an aim to clearly identify the output desired from the program and input that would be provided to it. For example, while developing a program to solve a quadratic equation, input would be the coefficients and output would be the roots of the quadratic equation. Once this is done the next task is to prepare an algorithm or a flowchart (or both) that details the steps to be carried out to obtain the desired output from the input provided. Finally we need to convert this algorithm / flowchart into a C language program. Once the program is ready, we need to type it into a computer and store in a file on the disk.

Compiling the Program

The next step is to translate the C language program into machine language. This is done using a C compiler. The converted code in machine language is often called object code. If there are any errors in your program, then the compiler prints the appropriate messages pointing out these errors and the compilation process terminates. We now need to identify the error prone portion of the program and make the necessary corrections and repeat the compilation process.

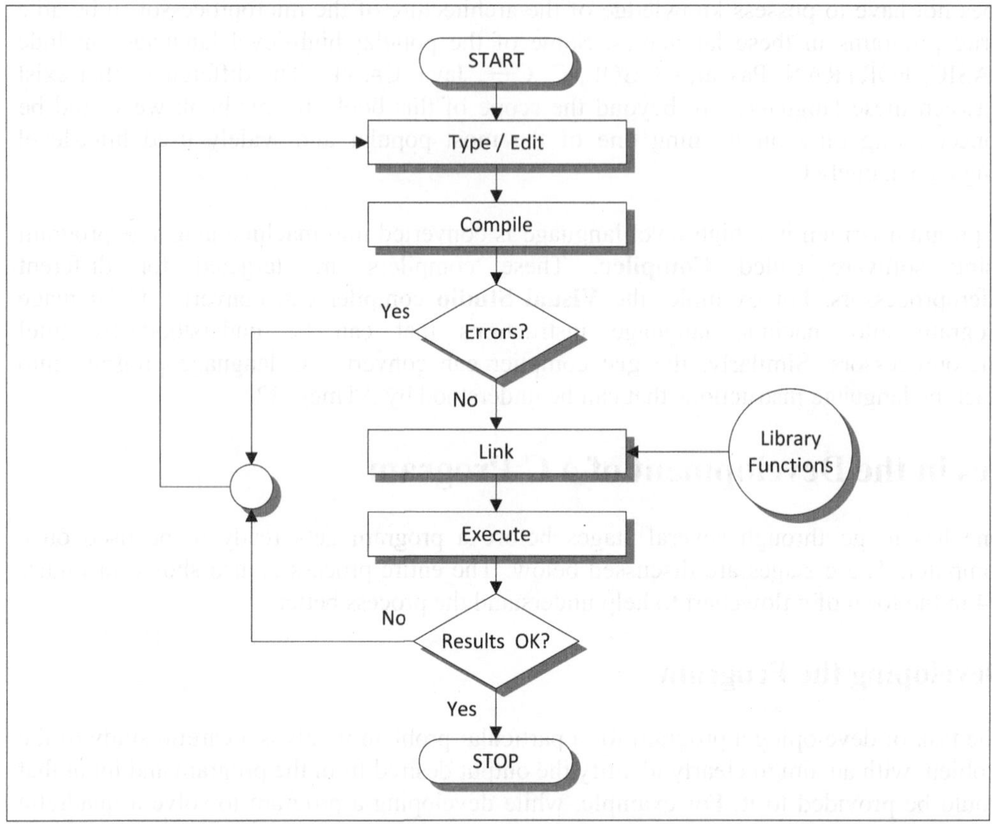

Figure 1.4

Linking the Program

Once the program is successfully compiled, the machine language version of our C program is ready. However, it is not in the form in which we can execute it. This is because in our program we may have used certain ready-made instructions (called **Library Functions**). These functions are usually provided by companies that create compilers. These companies develop these functions, compile them separately and make them available to us in machine language form. So now there is a need to combine our program's machine language code with library functions' machine language code. This is done using a program called **Linker**. The combined code is called executable code and is in a form which can be executed on a machine.

Testing the Program

The next stage in the development of a program is called **Testing**. In this stage the program is thoroughly tested for its correctness. For this the program is executed with all possible values of input data for which results are known. If the program's output matches with the known results then the program is declared as correct. If not, then the program is scanned thoroughly to locate the logical errors and is duly rectified. At times, the algorithm and flowchart are also reviewed to locate the errors.

Documenting the Program

The final stage in the development of a program is **Documentation**. In this stage all the relevant and important information about the program is recorded in such a manner that anyone who is later on required to upgrade or modify this program would be able to understand its intended purpose and the logic used to achieve this purpose.

Summary

(a) Basic model of computation involves input, process and output.
(b) The explicit steps for solving a given computing problem are called an Algorithm.
(c) Every algorithm must have the properties - Input, Output, Finiteness, Definiteness and Effectiveness.
(d) The pictorial way of representing an algorithm is called a Flowchart.
(e) Flowchart is drawn using standard symbols.
(f) Programming languages are used to represent an algorithm in the form of a program.
(g) Machine language and Assembly language are Low-level languages.
(h) C, C++, Java, C# are High-level languages.
(i) All programs have to be converted into machine language before execution.
(j) Different stages in the development of a C program are Development, Compilation, Linking, Testing and Documentation.

Exercise

[A] State whether the following statements are True or False:

(a) A linker is used to combine two different C programs.

(b) A compiler converts an assembly language program into a machine language program.

(c) An assembly language program is converted into a machine language program using an assembler.

(d) An algorithm is developed on the basis of a C program.

(e) An algorithm and a flowchart are different ways of representing the same solution.

(f) Linking precedes the compilation operation.

(g) A C program uses mnemonics to represent instructions.

(h) Whether we write a program in assembly language or in a C language it has to be converted into machine language before it can get executed.

(i) An algorithm need not have the scalability property.

(j) An algorithm must terminate after a finite number of steps.

(k) An algorithm must receive some input data and must produce at least one output as the result.

(l) While creating an algorithm an appropriate model of computation must be chosen to describe it.

(m) In a flowchart, a processing step is represented using a Parallelogram.

(n) In a flowchart, the Input or Output operation is represented using a Rhombus.

(o) Instructions in a low-level language get translated into multiple machine instructions.

(p) Assembly language instructions for all microprocessors are same.

(q) Assembly language program written for one microprocessor can be used on another microprocessor.

[B] Match the following pairs of flowchart symbols and their purpose:

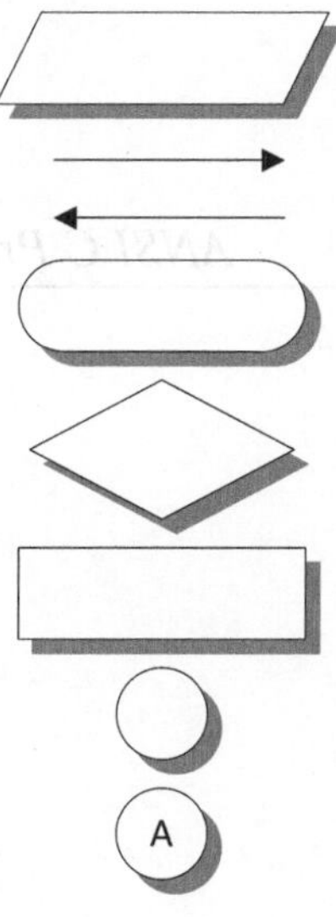

Processing symbol

Start symbol

Decision symbol

Input or Output operation symbol

Arrows

Off-page connector

Connector

2 Algorithms For Problem Solving

- Exchanging values of two variables
- Summation of a set of numbers
- Decimal to Binary Conversion
- Reversing digits of an integer
- GCD of two numbers
- Testing whether a number is prime
- Organizing numbers in ascending order
- Square root of a number
- Factorial computation
- Evaluation of 'sin x'
- Fibonacci sequence
- Reversal of array elements
- Finding largest number in an array
- Printing elements of upper triangular matrix
- Multiplication of two matrices
- Exercise

In the last chapter we saw what are algorithms and flowcharts and how they can be used as aids for describing and depicting a solution to any programming problem. However, just understanding the purpose of algorithms and flowcharts is not enough. We must be able to actually use them to solve programming problems. Best way to do this is to go ahead and use them in solving some problems. This is what we intend to do in this chapter. We would take several problems and write algorithms and draw flowcharts for solution to each of them. So let us begin…

Exchanging values of two variables

If values of two variables are input through the keyboard, draw a flowchart and write an algorithm for exchanging the contents of two variables.

Flowchart:

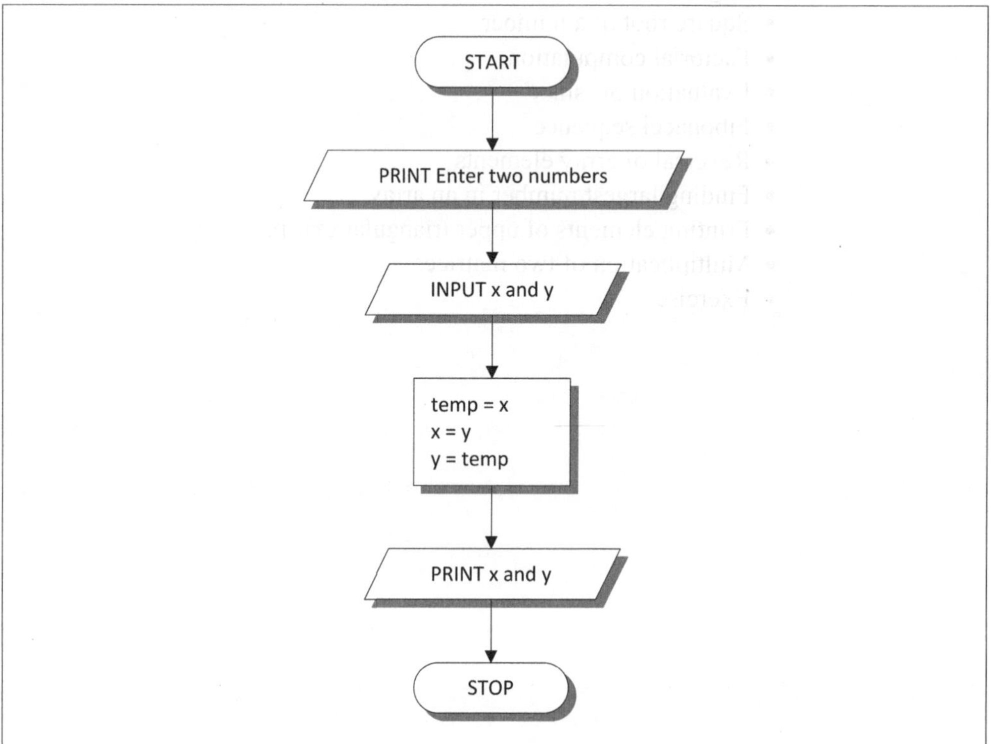

Figure 2.1

Algorithm:

Step 1: Declare x, y and temp as integer variables

Step 2: Enter values of two variables i.e. x and y

Step 3: Exchange values of two variables

Step 4: Print values of variables x and y

Summation of a set of numbers

If values of 'n' number of variables are input through the keyboard, draw a flowchart and write an algorithm for finding summation of a set of 'n' numbers.

Flowchart:

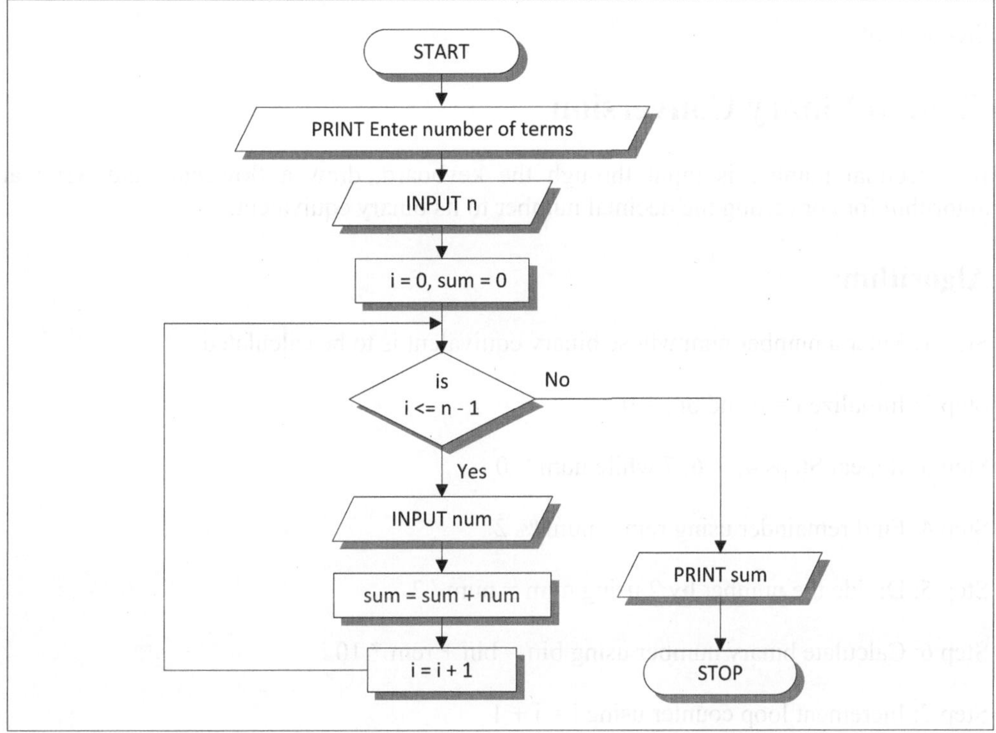

Figure 2.2

Algorithm:

Step 1: Enter number of terms (say n) whose sum is to be calculated

Step 2: Initialize i = 0 and sum = 0

Step 3: Repeat steps 4, 5, 6 while i <= n – 1

Step 4: Enter each number i.e. num

Step 5: Calculate sum using sum = sum + num

Step 6: Increment loop counter using i = i + 1

[End of Step 3 Loop]

Step 7: Print sum

Step 8: Exit

Decimal to Binary Conversion

If a decimal number is input through the keyboard, draw a flowchart and write an algorithm for converting the decimal number to its binary equivalent.

Algorithm:

Step 1: Enter a number num whose binary equivalent is to be calculated

Step 2: Initialize i = 0 and bin = 0

Step 3: Repeat Steps 4, 5, 6, 7 while num > 0

Step 4: Find remainder using rem = num % 2

Step 5: Divide the number by 2 using num = num / 2

Step 6: Calculate binary number using bin = bin + rem * 10 i

Step 7: Increment loop counter using i = i + 1

[End of Step 3 Loop]

Step 8: Print bin

Step 9: Exit

Flowchart:

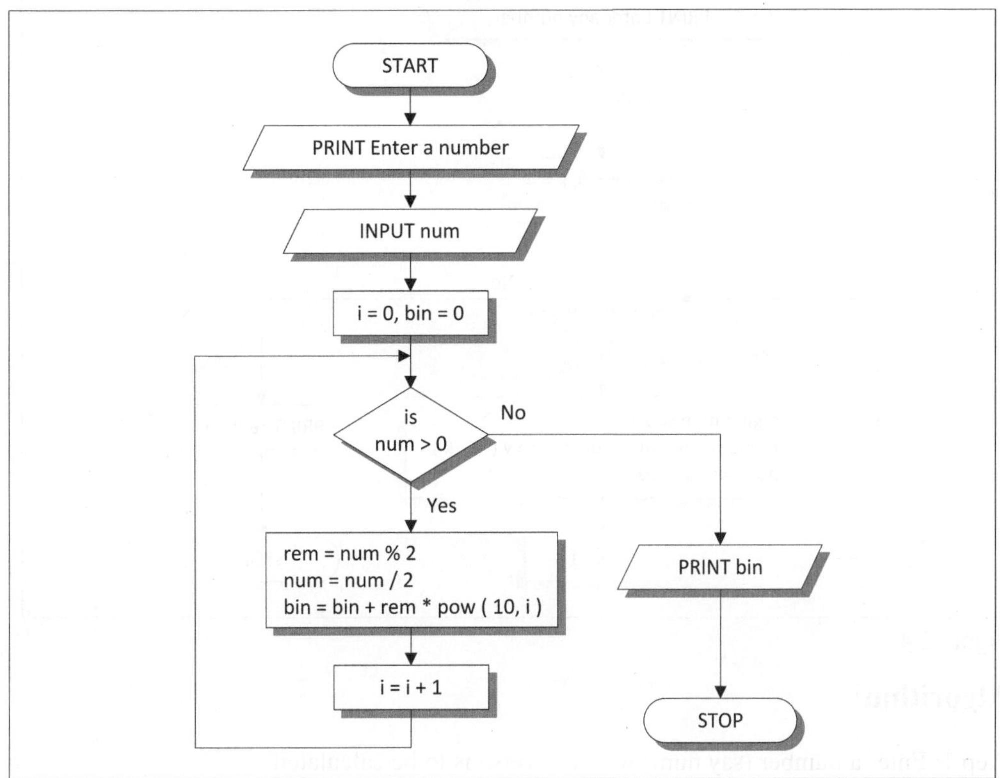

Figure 2.3

Reversing digits of an integer

If a 5-digit number is input through the keyboard, draw a flowchart and write an algorithm to calculate reverse of that number.

Flowchart:

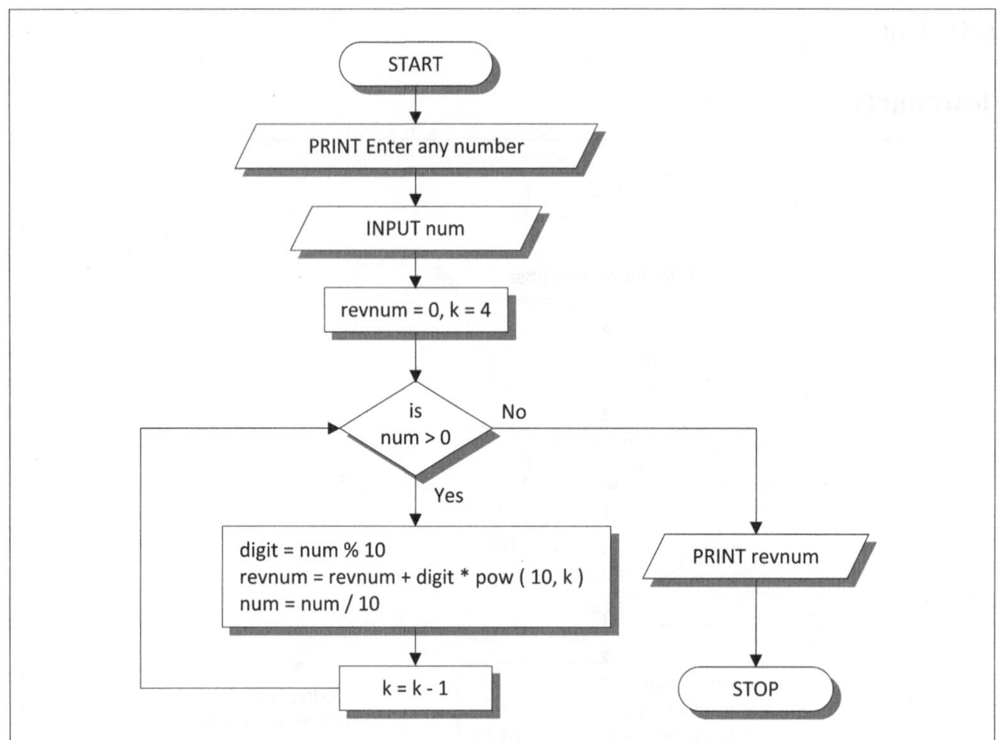

Figure 2.4

Algorithm:

Step 1: Enter a number (say num) whose reverse is to be calculated

Step 2: Initialize revnum = 0, k = 4

Step 3: Repeat Steps 4, 5, 6, 7 while num > 0

Step 4: Find last digit using digit = num % 10

Step 5: Update revnum using revnum = revnum + digit * 10 raised to k

Step 6: Reduce the number using num = num / 10

Step 7: Increment k using k = k - 1

[End of Step 3 Loop]

Step 7: Print revnum

Step 8: Exit

GCD of two numbers

If two numbers are input through the keyboard, draw a flowchart and write an algorithm to calculate Greatest Common Divisor (GCD) of the two numbers.

Algorithm:

Step 1: Enter two numbers whose gcd is to be calculated, say, x and y

Step 2: Check if x < y, if it is true then set small = x, otherwise set small = y

Step 3: Initialize gcd = 1, i = 1

Step 4: Repeat Steps 5, 6 while i <= small

Step 5: Check whether x % i == 0 && y % i == 0, and if both are true then assign gcd = i

Step 6: Increment i using i = i + 1

[End of Step 3 Loop]

Step 7: Print gcd

Step 8: Exit

Flowchart:

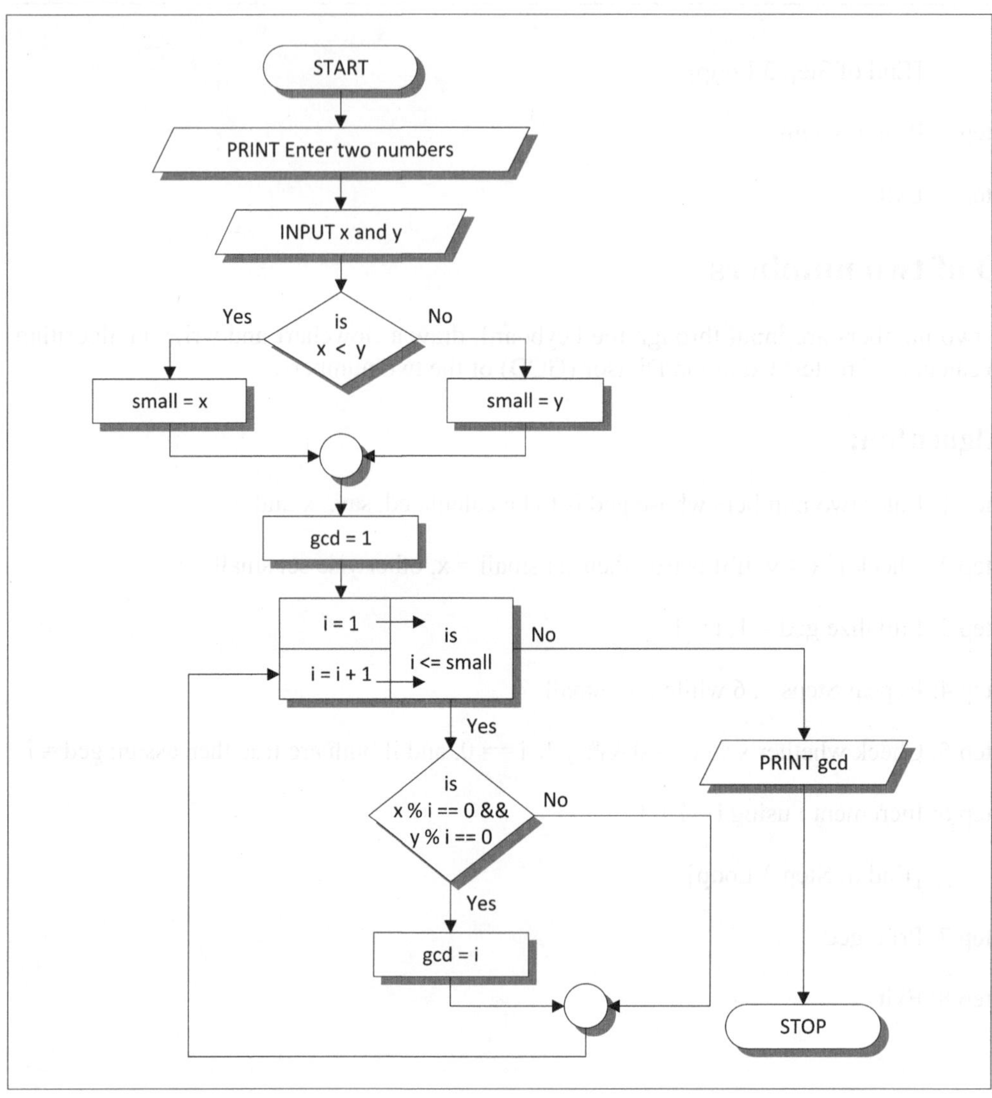

Figure 2.5

Testing whether a number is prime

If a number is input through the keyboard, draw a flowchart and write an algorithm to determine whether the number entered is Prime or not.

Flowchart:

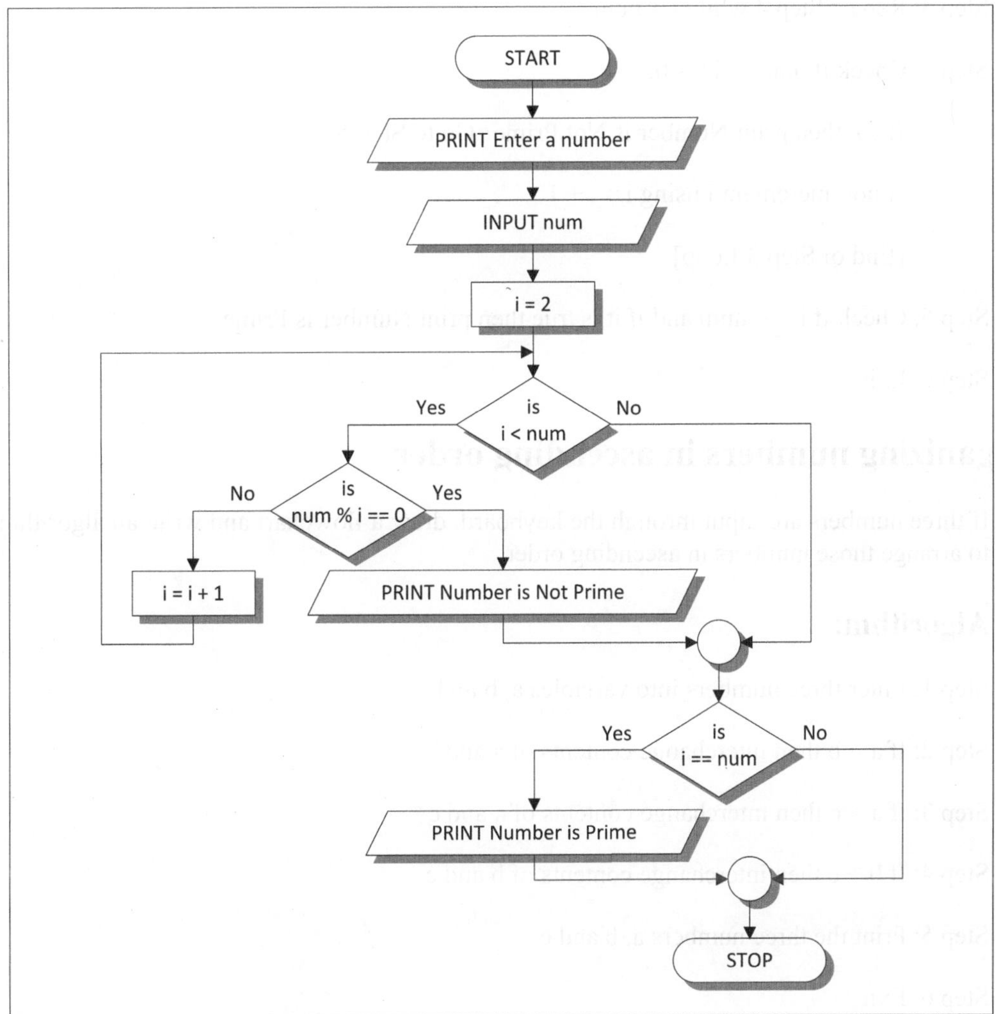

Figure 2.6

Algorithm:

Step 1: Enter a number, say num

Step 2: Initialize i = 2

Step 3: Repeat Step 4 while i < num

Step 4: Check if num % i == 0,

If so, then print Number is Not Prime, Go to Step 5

If not, increment i using i = i + 1

[End of Step 3 Loop]

Step 5: Check if i = = num and if it is true then print Number is Prime

Step 6: Exit

Organizing numbers in ascending order

If three numbers are input through the keyboard, draw a flowchart and write an algorithm to arrange those numbers in ascending order.

Algorithm:

Step 1: Enter three numbers into variables a, b and c

Step 2: If a > b then interchange contents of a and b

Step 3: If a > c then interchange contents of a and c

Step 4: If b > c then interchange contents of b and c

Step 5: Print the three numbers a, b and c

Step 6: Exit

Flowchart:

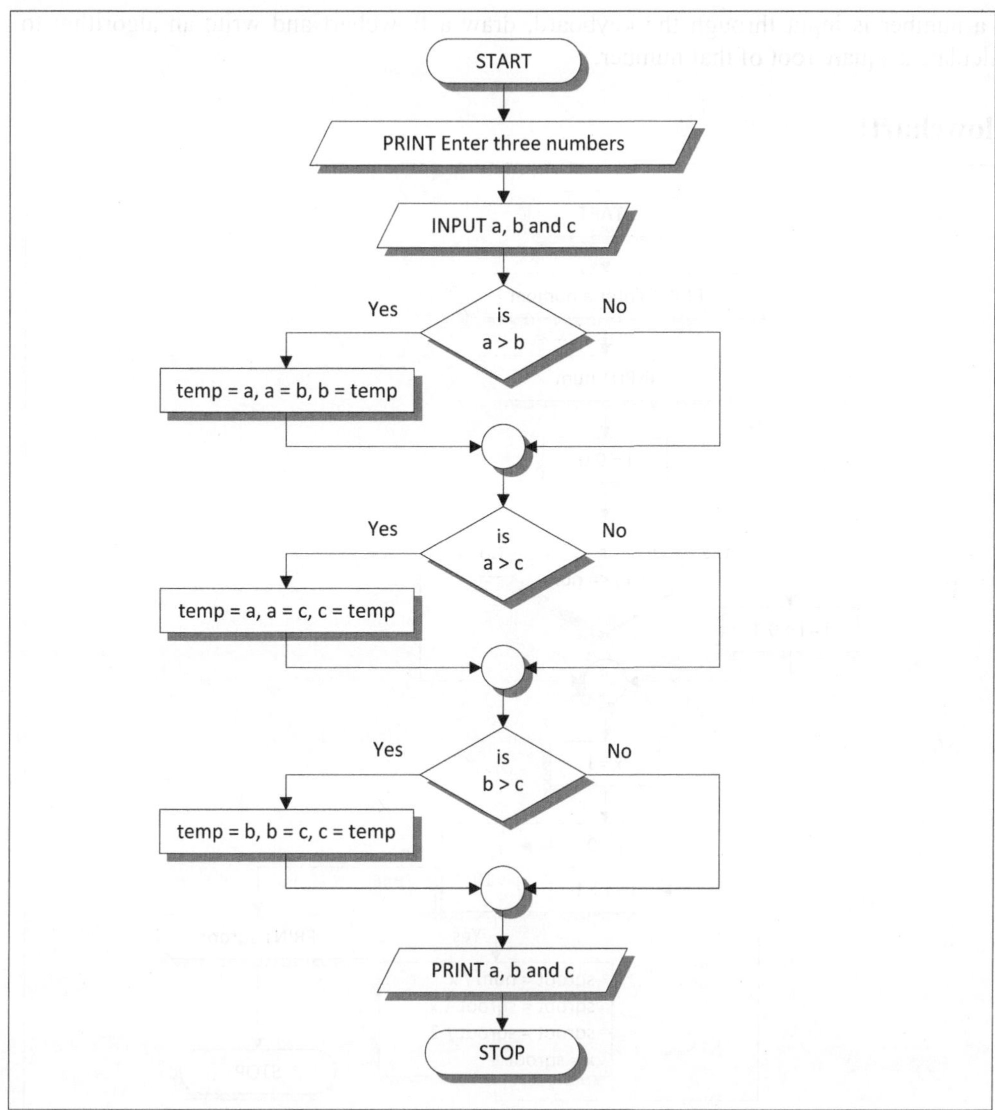

Figure 2.7

Square root of a number

If a number is input through the keyboard, draw a flowchart and write an algorithm to calculate a square root of that number.

Flowchart:

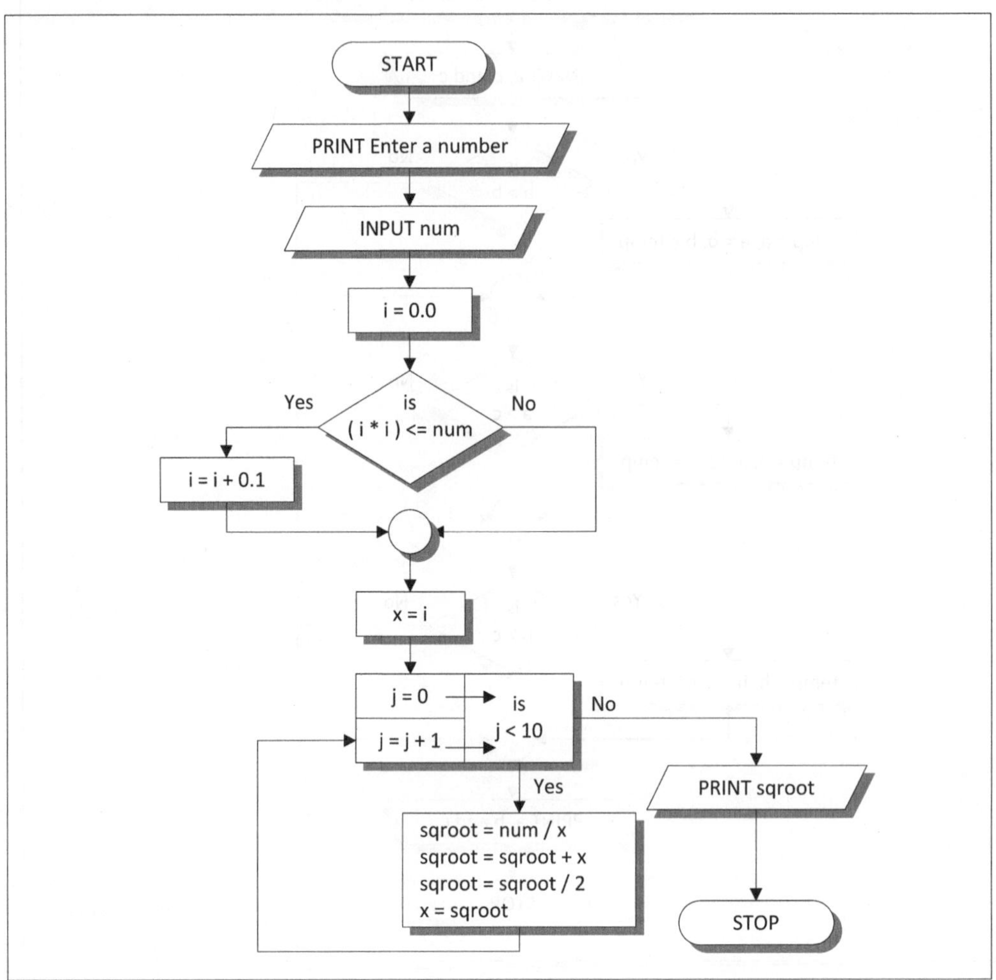

Figure 2.8

Algorithm:

Step 1: Enter a number, say num, whose square root is to be calculated

Step 2: Initialize i = 0.0

Step 3: Repeat Step 4 while (i * i) <= num

Step 4: Increment i using i = i + 0.1

[End of Step 3 Loop]

Step 5: Initialize x = i

Step 6: Initialize j = 0

Step 7: Repeat Steps 8, 9 while j < 10

Step 8: Set

sqroot = num / x

sqroot = sqroot + x

sqroot = sqroot / 2

x = sqroot

Step 9: Increment j using j = j + 1

[End of Step 7 Loop]

Step 10: Print sqroot

Step 11: Exit

Factorial computation

If a number is input through the keyboard, draw a flowchart and write an algorithm to calculate a factorial value of that number.

Flowchart:

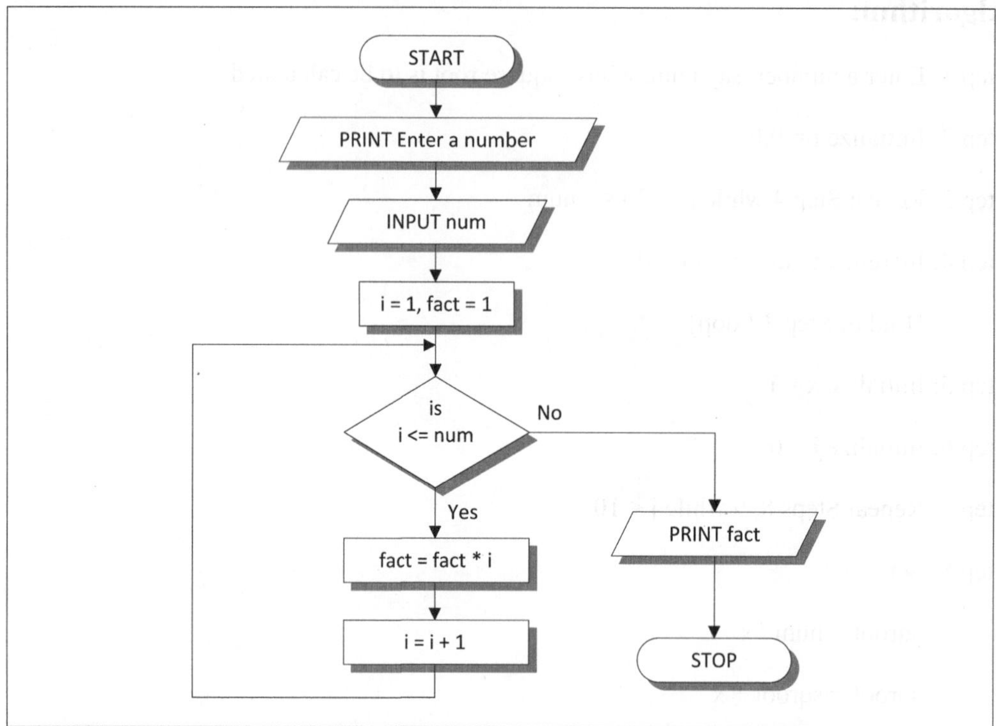

Figure 2.9

Algorithm:

Step 1: Enter a number, say num, whose factorial value is to be calculated

Step 2: Initialize i = 1 and fact = 1

Step 3: Repeat Steps 4 and 5 while i <= num

Step 4: Calculate factorial using fact = fact * i

Step 5: Increment loop counter using i = i + 1

[End of Step 3 Loop]

Step 6: Print fact

Step 7: Exit

Evaluation of 'sin x'

Draw a flowchart and write an algorithm to calculate a sine series where value of 'x' is input through the keyboard.

Algorithm:

Step 1: Enter the value of x

Step 2: Initialize sum = 0.0

Step 3: Initialize i =1, j = 1

Step 3: Repeat Steps 4, 5 while j <= 19

Step 4: Calculate numerator, denominator and term using:

a = numerator (x, j)

b = denominator (j)

t = a / b

Step 5: Check whether i % 2 == 0

If it is true then calculate sum as sum = sum – t

If it is false then calculate sum as sum = sum + t

Step 6: Increment i and j using i = i +1 and j = j + 2

[End of Step 3 Loop]

Step 8: Print sum

Step 9: Exit

Flowchart:

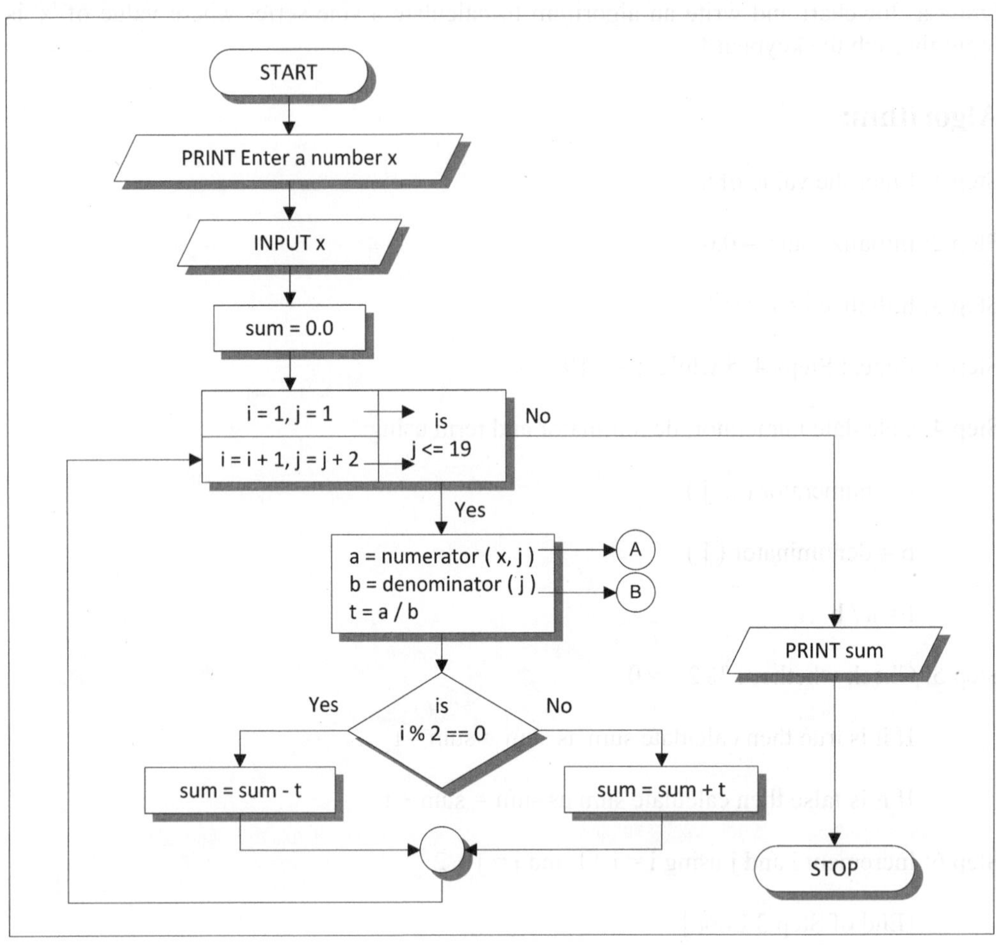

Figure 2.10

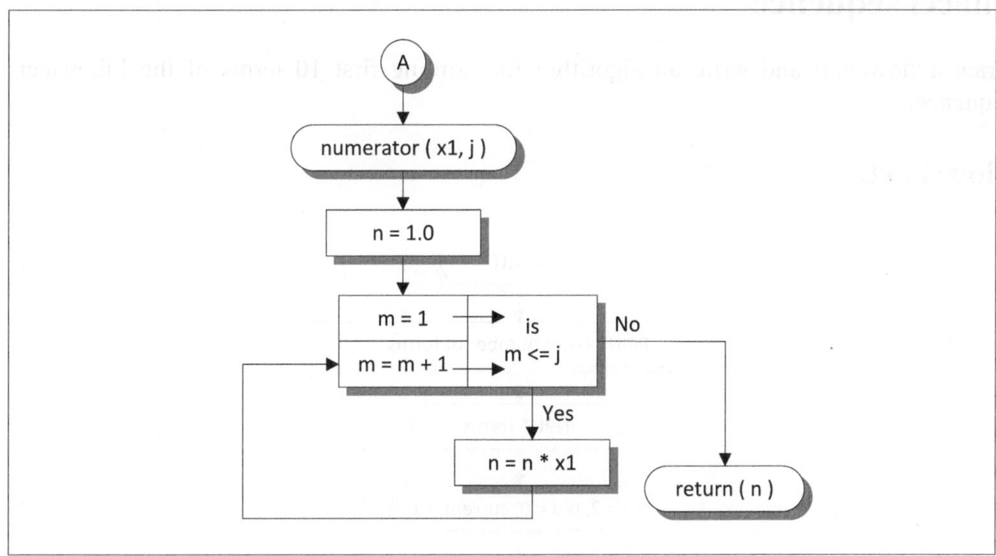

Figure 2.11(a)

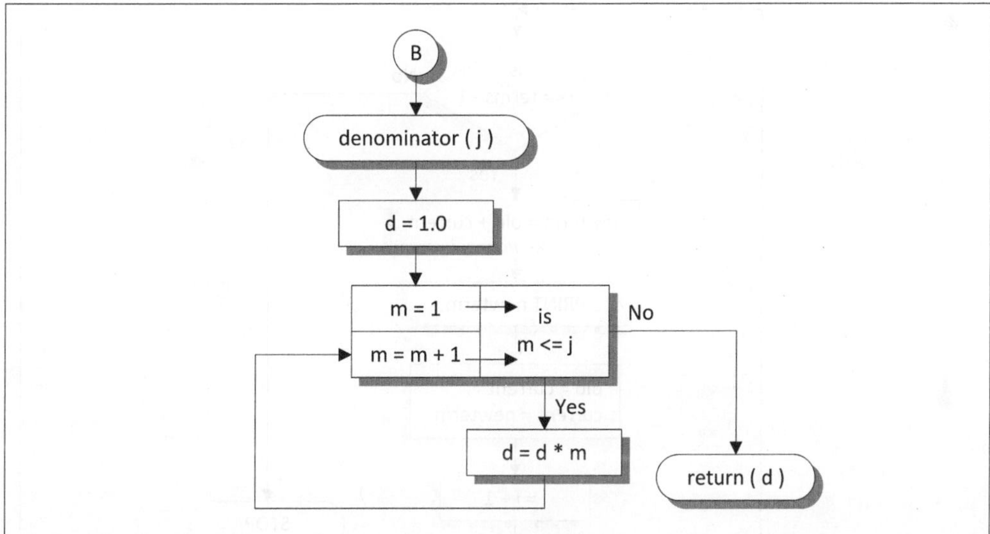

Figure 2.11(b)

Fibonacci sequence

Draw a flowchart and write an algorithm for printing first 10 terms of the Fibonacci sequence.

Flowchart:

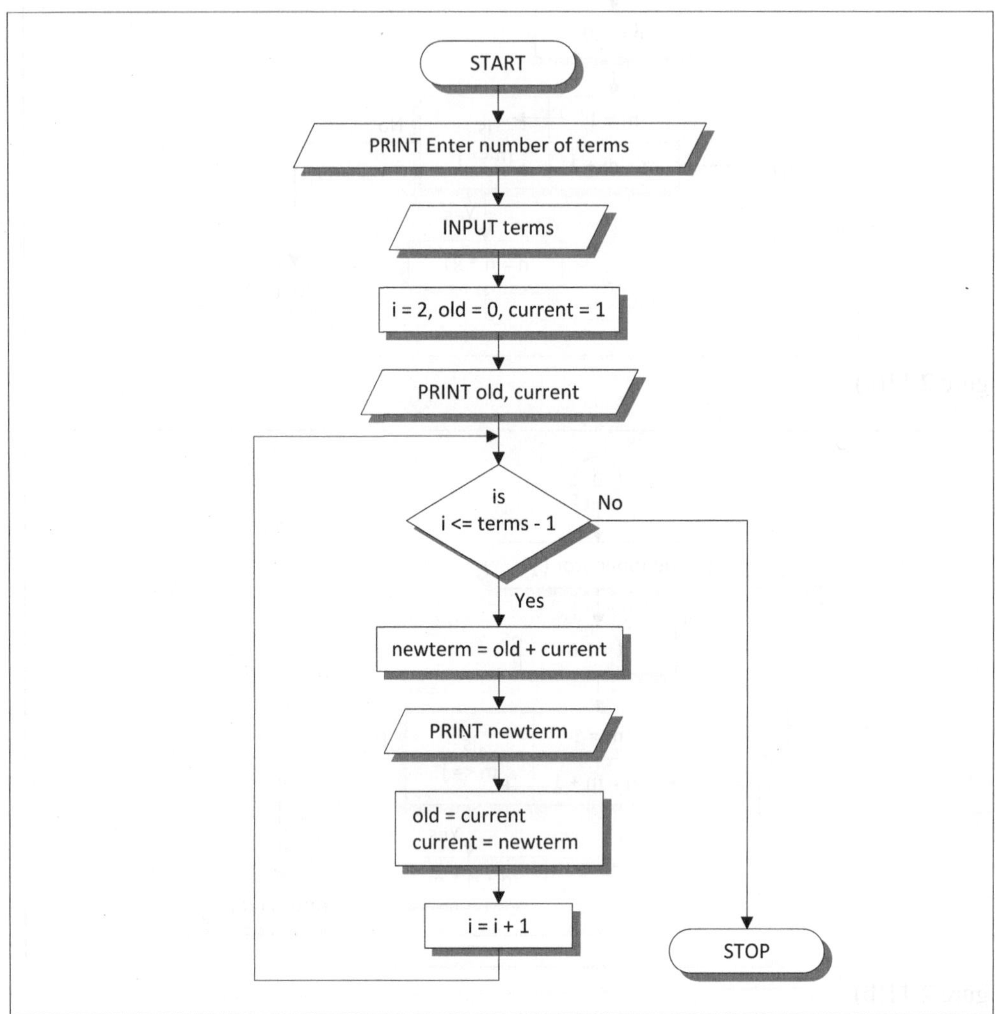

Figure 2.12

Algorithm:

Step 1: Enter number of terms i.e. terms

Step 2: Initialize i = 2, old = 0 and current = 1

Step 3: Print old and current

Step 4: Repeat Steps 5, 6, 7, 8 while i <= terms - 1

Step 5: Calculate new term using newterm = old + current

Step 6: Print newterm

Step 7: Assign old = current and current = newterm

Step 8: Increment the loop counter using i = i + 1

[End of Step 4 Loop]

Step 9 : Exit

Reversal of array elements

If 25 elements of an array are entered through the keyboard, draw a flowchart and write an algorithm to reverse order of elements of an array.

Algorithm:

Step 1: Declare array arr[25]

Step 2: Enter 25 elements of an array arr

Step 3: Initialize i using i = 0

Step 4: Repeat Steps 5, 6 while i < 25 / 2

Step 5: Set

temp = arr[i]

arr[i] = arr[25 - i - 1]

arr[25 - i - 1] = temp

Step 6: Increment i using i = i + 1

[End of Step 4 Loop]

Step 7: Print elements of array arr

Step 8: Exit

Flowchart:

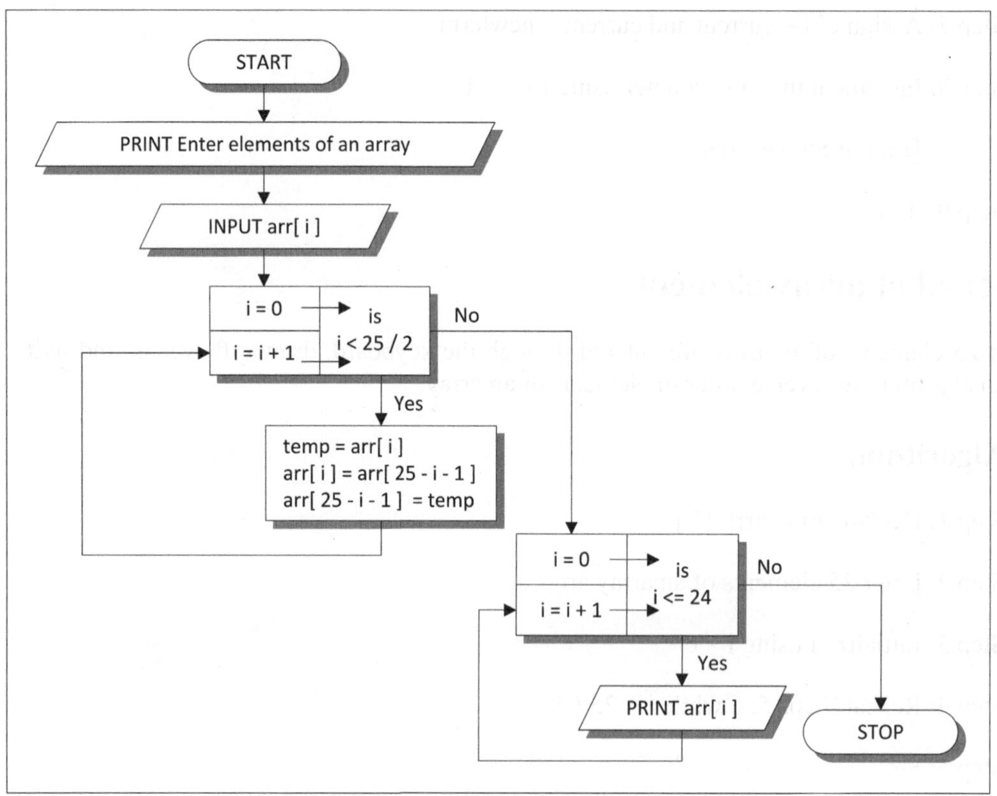

Figure 2.13

Finding largest number in an array

If 25 elements of an array are entered through the keyboard, draw a flowchart and write an algorithm to find largest number in an array.

Flowchart:

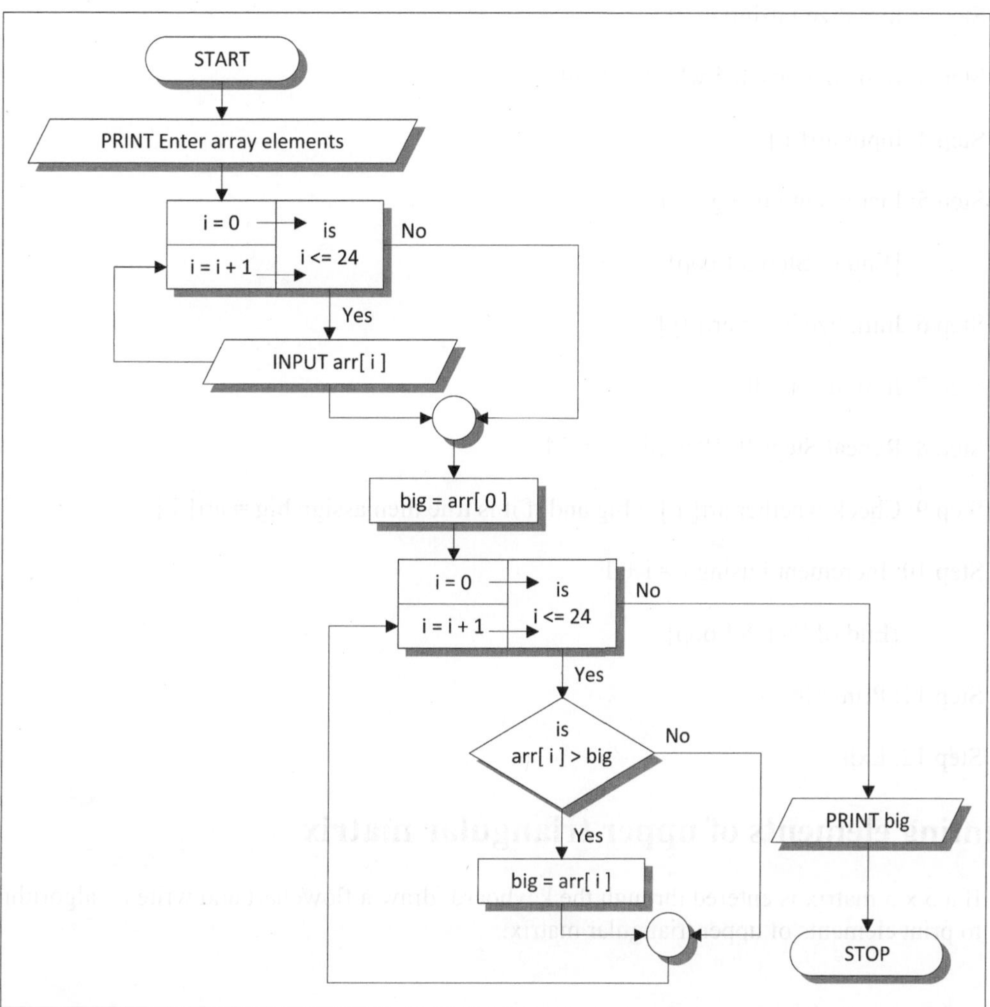

Figure 2.14

Algorithm:

Step 1: Declare array arr[25]

Step 2: Initialize i using i = 0

Step 3: Repeat Steps 4, 5 while i <= 24

Step 4: Input arr[i]

Step 5: Increment i using i = i + 1

[End of Step 3 Loop]

Step 6: Initialize big = arr[0]

Step 7: Initialize i = 0

Step 8: Repeat Steps 9, 10 while i <= 24

Step 9: Check whether arr[i] > big and if it is true then assign big = arr[i]

Step 10: Increment i using i = i + 1

[End of Step 8 Loop]

Step 11: Print big

Step 12: Exit

Printing elements of upper triangular matrix

If a 5 x 5 matrix is entered through the keyboard, draw a flowchart and write an algorithm to print elements of upper triangular matrix.

Flowchart:

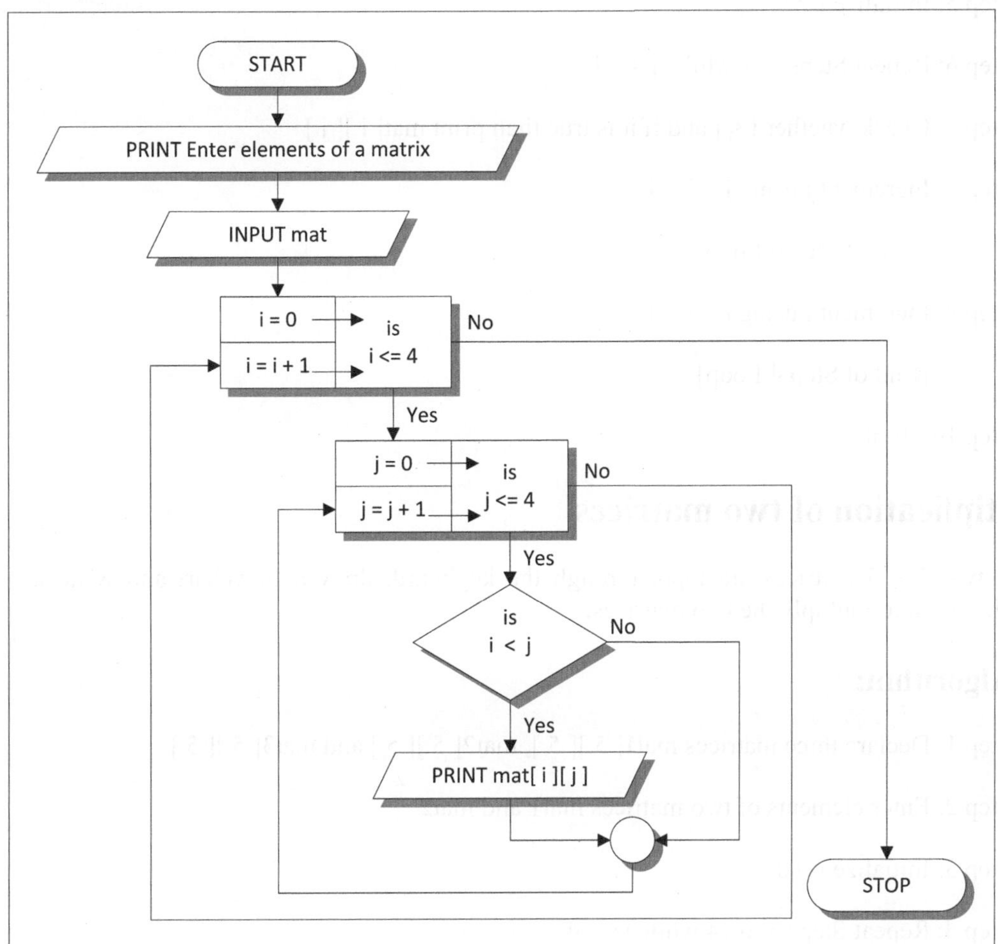

Figure 2.15

Algorithm:

Step 1: Declare a matrix of 5 rows and 5 columns mat[5][5]

Step 2: Enter elements of matrix mat

Step 3: Initialize i = 0

Step 4: Repeat Steps 5, 6, 7, 8, 9 while i <= 4

Step 5: Initialize j = 0

Step 6: Repeat Steps 7, 8 while j <= 4

Step 7: Check whether i < j and if it is true then print mat[i][j]

Step 8: Increment j using j = j + 1

[End of Step 6 Loop]

Step 9: Increment i using i = i + 1

[End of Step 4 Loop]

Step 10 : Exit

Multiplication of two matrices

If two 5 x 5 matrices are input through the keyboard, draw a flowchart and write an algorithm to multiply the two matrices.

Algorithm:

Step 1: Declare three matrices mat1[5][5], mat2[5][5] and mat3[5][5]

Step 2: Enter elements of two matrices mat1 and mat2

Step 3: Initialize i = 0

Step 4: Repeat Steps 5 to 14 while i <= 4

Step 5: Initialize j = 0

Step 6: Repeat Steps 7 to 13 while j <= 4

Step 7: Initialize sum = 0

Step 8: Initialize k = 0

Step 9: Repeat Steps 10, 11 while k <= 4

Step 10: Calculate sum as sum = sum + mat1[i][k] * mat2[k][j]

Step 11: Increment k using k = k + 1

[End of Step 9 Loop]

Step 12: Assign mat3[i][j] = sum

Step 13: Increment j using j = j + 1

[End of Step 6 Loop]

Step 14: Increment i using i = i + 1

[End of Step 4 Loop]

Step 15: Print the elements of matrix mat3

Step 16: Exit

Flowchart:

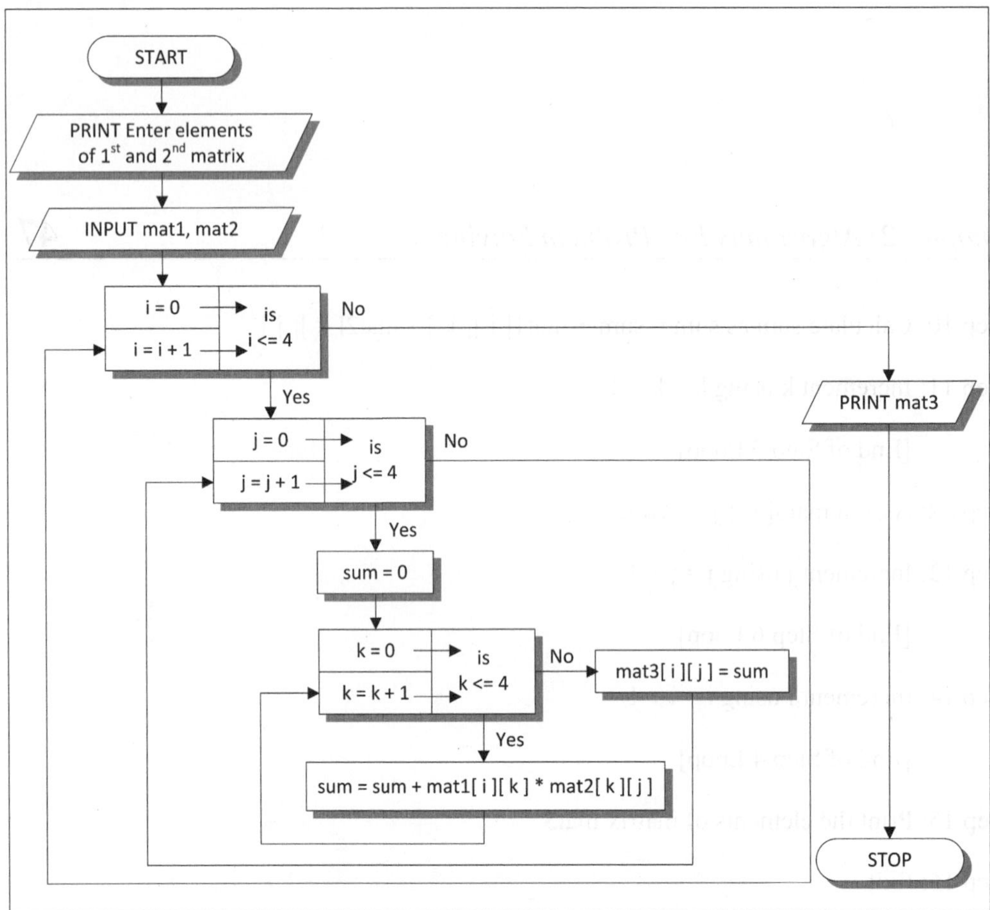

Figure 2.16

Exercise

[A] Attempt the following:

(a) If three numbers are input through the keyboard, draw a flowchart and write an algorithm for finding the minimum of these three numbers.

(b) If a number is input through the keyboard, draw a flowchart and write an algorithm for finding out whether the number is odd or even.

(c) Draw a flowchart and write an algorithm for calculating and printing out a table of 15.

(d) Draw a flowchart and write an algorithm for finding out squares and cubes of all numbers from 1 to 20.

(e) If a number is input through the keyboard, draw a flowchart and write an algorithm to check whether a number is divisible by 2 and 5.

(f) If two numbers are input through the keyboard, draw a flowchart and write an algorithm to find the absolute value of difference between the two numbers.

(g) Draw a flowchart and write an algorithm to find the sum of first 25 natural numbers.

(h) Draw a flowchart and write an algorithm to print first 20 odd numbers and their squares.

(i) If coefficients of a quadratic equation are input through the keyboard, draw a flowchart and write an algorithm to obtain the roots of the quadratic equation.

(j) If a number is input through the keyboard then draw a flowchart and write an algorithm to check whether any digit is repeated in that number. If so then display that digit, otherwise report that there is no repetition of digit.

(k) If an array of 25 characters is input through the keyboard then draw a flowchart and write an algorithm to check whether the characters form a palindrome or not. A set of characters form a palindrome if they read same left to right and right to left.

(l) If a 5 x 5 matrix is input through the keyboard, draw a flowchart and write an algorithm to find the sum of elements of the matrix below the main diagonal.

(m) The number 145 is said to be well-ordered because the digits in the number (1, 4, 5) increase from left to right. If a number is input through the keyboard, draw a flowchart and write an algorithm to check whether it is well-ordered or not.

(n) Suppose the rates of a courier company called mailing letters are as follows:

Rs. 4 per 10 grams for the first 50 grams,
Rs. 3 per 10 grams for the next 100 grams,
Rs. 2 per 10 grams for the next 250 grams and

Rs. 25 per kilogram for letters weighing more than 400 grams.

If weight of the letter is input through the keyboard then draw a flowchart and write an algorithm to print the courier charges to be paid.

(o) The monthly mobile phone bill is to be computed as follows:

Minimum Rs. 75 for up to 100 calls
Rs. 0.75 per call for the next 50 calls
Rs. 0.50 per call for the next 50 calls
Rs. 0.40 per call for any call beyond 200 calls

Draw a flowchart and write an algorithm to compute the monthly mobile bill for the given number of calls.

(p) A character array contains an English sentence terminated by a special character '\0'. Draw a flowchart and write an algorithm to count number of characters, vowels and words present in the array.

3 Introduction To C Language

Before we can begin to write serious programs in C, it would be interesting to find out what really is C, how it came into existence and how does it compare with other computer languages. In this chapter, we would briefly outline these issues.

Four important aspects of any language are the way it stores data, the way it operates upon this data, how it accomplishes input and output and how it lets you control the sequence of execution of instructions in a program. We would discuss the first three of these building blocks in this chapter.

What is C

C is a programming language developed at AT & T's Bell Laboratories of USA in 1972. It was designed and written by a man named Dennis Ritchie. In the late seventies C began to replace the more familiar languages of that time like PL/I, ALGOL, etc. No one pushed C. It wasn't made the 'official' Bell Labs language. Thus, without any advertisement, C's reputation spread and its pool of users grew. Ritchie seems to have been rather surprised that so many programmers preferred C to older languages like FORTRAN or PL/I, or the newer ones like Pascal and APL. But, that's what happened.

Possibly why C seems so popular is because it is reliable, simple and easy to use. Moreover, in an industry where newer languages, tools and technologies emerge and vanish day in and day out, a language that has survived for more than three decades has to be really good.

An opinion that is often heard today is – "C has been already superceded by languages like C++, C# and Java, so why bother to learn C today". I seriously beg to differ with this opinion. There are several reasons for this:

(a) I believe that nobody can learn C++ or Java directly. This is because while learning these languages you have things like classes, objects, inheritance, polymorphism, templates, exception handling, references, etc. do deal with apart from knowing the actual language elements. Learning these complicated concepts when you are not even comfortable with the basic language elements is like putting the cart before the horse. Hence one should first learn all the language elements very thoroughly using C language before migrating to C++, C# or Java. Though this two-step learning process may take more time, but at the end of it you will definitely find it worth the trouble.

(b) C++, C# or Java make use of a principle called Object Oriented Programming (OOP) to organize the program. This organizing principle has lots of advantages to offer. But even while using this organizing principle you would still need a good hold over the language elements of C and the basic programming skills.

(c) Though many C++ and Java based programming tools and frameworks have evolved over the years the importance of C is still unchallenged because knowingly or unknowingly while using these frameworks and tools you would be still required to use the core C language elements—another good reason why one should learn C before C++, C# or Java.

(d) Major parts of popular operating systems like Windows, UNIX, Linux are still written in C. This is because even today when it comes to performance (speed of execution) nothing beats C. Moreover, if one is to extend the operating system to work with new devices one needs to write device driver programs. These programs are exclusively written in C.

(e) Mobile devices like cellular phones and palmtops have become rage of today. Also, common consumer devices like microwave ovens, washing machines and digital cameras are getting smarter by the day. This smartness comes from a microprocessor, an operating system and a program embedded in these devices. These programs not only have to run fast but also have to work in limited amount of memory. No wonder that such programs are written in C. With these constraints on time and space, C is the language of choice while building such operating systems and programs.

(f) You must have seen several professional 3D computer games where the user navigates some object, like say a spaceship and fires bullets at the invaders. The essence of all such games is speed. Needless to say, such games won't become popular if they takes a long time to move the spaceship or to fire a bullet. To match the expectations of the player the game has to react fast to the user inputs. This is where C language scores over other languages. Many popular gaming frameworks have been built using C language.

(g) At times one is required to very closely interact with the hardware devices. Since C provides several language elements that make this interaction feasible without compromising the performance it is the preferred choice of the programmer.

I hope that these are very convincing reasons why you should adopt C as the first and the very important step in your quest for learning programming languages.

What is ANSI C

Once a C program is written it has to be converted into machine language using another program called Compiler. This complier is created by different software companies. At times these companies provide extensions to the C language. If you use these extended features in your program, your program may compile using that vendor's compiler, but may not compile successfully using another vendor's compiler. This makes the program compiler dependant.

Also, when a program is written to run on one type of machine (say Intel Pentium), it should be possible to run the same program on another machine (say Apple) just by recompiling the same program for the new machine. This may not happen if the program is written in a non-standard way.

To avoid such issues, a standard for C language has evolved. This standard has been published by the American National Standards Institute and is known as ANSI C. If software developers write C programs as per this standard then their programs would become portable across compilers and across machines. The ANSI C standard was adopted by International Organization for Standardization (ISO) and subsequent revisions published by ISO have been adopted by ANSI. This standard is known as ANSI C, ISO C or just Standard C.

In 1983 ANSI set up a committee called X3J11 to establish a standard specification of C. This committee released the standard specification in 1989, which came to be known as ANSI C or simply as C89. Later on ISO adopted this standard, corrected some details and released an updated standard in 1999. This is known popularly as C99. This standard was adopted as an ANSI standard in May 2000.

Almost all widely used compilers now support ANSI C. Any program written in ANSI C is guaranteed to compile correctly with any ANSI C compliant compiler.

Getting Started with C

Communicating with a computer involves speaking the language the computer understands, which immediately rules out English as the language of communication with computer. However, there is a close analogy between learning English language and learning C language. The classical method of learning English is to first learn the alphabets used in the language, then learn to combine these alphabets to form words, which, in turn, are combined to form sentences and sentences are combined to form paragraphs. Learning C is similar and easier. Instead of straight-away learning how to write programs, we must first know what alphabets, numbers and special symbols are used in C, then how using them, constants, variables and keywords are constructed, and finally, how are these combined to form an instruction. A group of instructions would be combined later on to form a program. This is illustrated in the Figure 3.1.

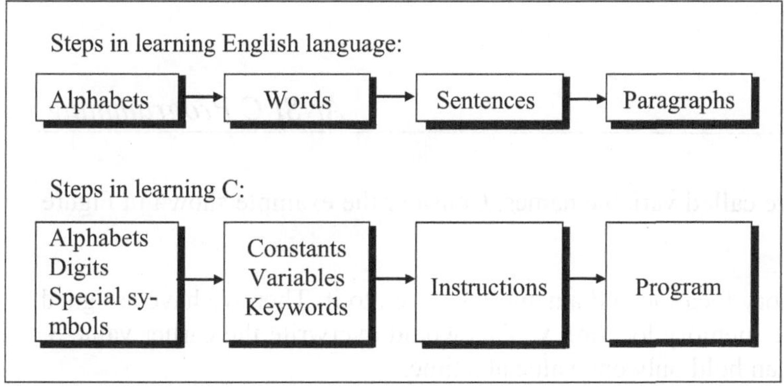

Figure 3.1

The C Character Set

A character denotes any alphabet, digit or special symbol used to represent information. Figure 3.2 shows the valid alphabets, numbers and special symbols allowed in C.

<table>
<tr><td>Alphabets</td><td>A, B, ….., Y, Z
a, b, ……, y, z</td></tr>
<tr><td>Digits</td><td>0, 1, 2, 3, 4, 5, 6, 7, 8, 9</td></tr>
<tr><td>Special symbols</td><td>~ ‘ ! @ # % ^ & * ( ) _ - + = | \ { }
[ ] : ; " ' <> , . ? /</td></tr>
</table>

Figure 3.2

Constants, Variables and Keywords

The alphabets, numbers and special symbols when properly combined form constants, variables and keywords. Let us see what are ‘constants’ and ‘variables’ in C. A constant is an entity that doesn’t change, whereas, a variable is an entity that may change.

In any program we typically do lots of calculations. The results of these calculations are stored in computer’s memory. Like human memory, the computer’s memory also consists of millions of cells. The calculated values are stored in these memory cells. To make the retrieval and usage of these values easy these memory cells (also called memory locations) are given names. Since the value stored in each location may change the names given to these locations are called variable names. Consider the example shown in Figure 3.3.

Here 3 is stored in a memory location and a name **x** is given to it. Then we have assigned a new value 5 to the same memory location **x**. This would overwrite the earlier value 3, since a memory location can hold only one value at a time.

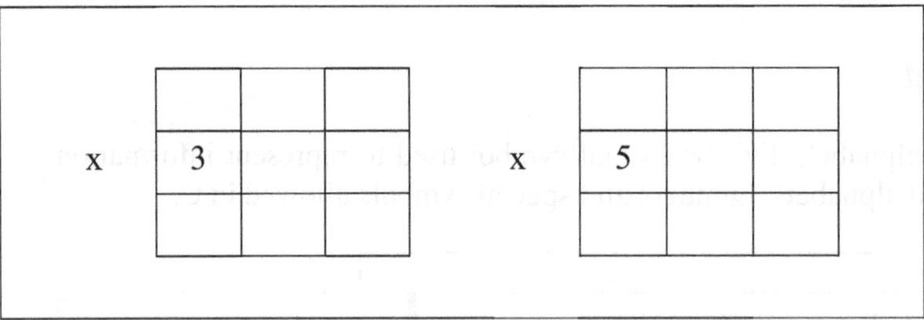

Figure 3.3

Since the location whose name is **x** can hold different values at different times **x** is known as a variable. As against this, 3 or 5 do not change, hence are known as constants.

Types of C Constants

C constants can be divided into two major categories:

(a) Primary Constants
(b) Secondary Constants

These constants are further categorized as shown in Figure 3.4.

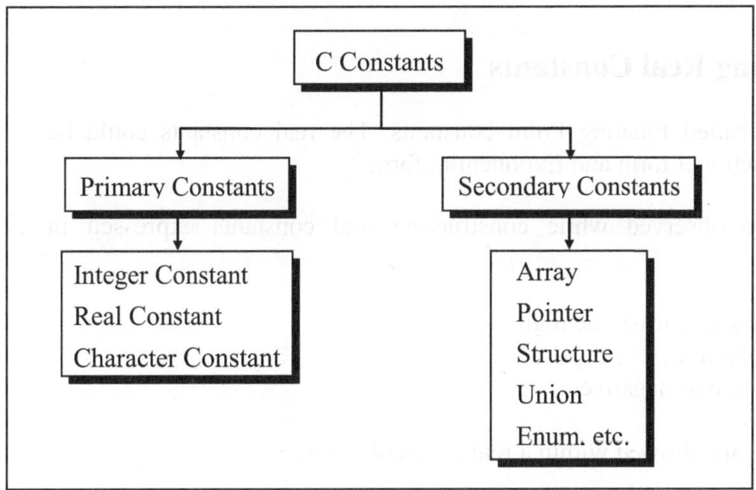

Figure 3.4

At this stage, we would restrict our discussion to only Primary constants, namely, Integer, Real and Character constants. Let us see the details of each of these constants. For constructing these different types of constants, certain rules have been laid down. These rules are as under:

Rules for Constructing Integer Constants

(a) An integer constant must have at least one digit.
(b) It must not have a decimal point.
(c) It can be either positive or negative.
(d) If no sign precedes an integer constant, it is assumed to be positive.
(e) No commas or blanks are allowed within an integer constant.
(f) The allowable range for integer constants is -32768 to 32767.

Truly speaking, the range of an Integer constant depends upon the compiler. For a 16-bit compiler like Turbo C or Turbo C++ the range is –32768 to 32767. For a 32-bit compiler, the range would be even greater. Questions like what exactly do you mean by a 16-bit or a 32-bit compiler, what range of an Integer constant has to do with the type of compiler, etc. are discussed in detail in Chapter 16. Till that time it would be assumed that we are working with a 16-bit compiler.

Ex.: 426
+782
-8000
-7605

Rules for Constructing Real Constants

Real constants are often called Floating Point constants. The real constants could be written in two forms—Fractional form and Exponential form.

Following rules must be observed while constructing real constants expressed in fractional form:

(a) A real constant must have at least one digit.
(b) It must have a decimal point.
(c) It could be either positive or negative.
(d) Default sign is positive.
(e) No commas or blanks are allowed within a real constant.

```
Ex.: +325.34
     426.0
     -32.76
     -48.5792
```

The exponential form of representation of real constants is usually used if the value of the constant is either too small or too large. It, however, doesn't restrict us in any way from using exponential form of representation for other real constants.

In exponential form of representation, the real constant is represented in two parts. The part appearing before 'e' is called mantissa, whereas the part following 'e' is called exponent. Thus 0.000342 can be represented in exponential form as 3.42e-4.

Following rules must be observed while constructing real constants expressed in exponential form:

(a) The mantissa part and the exponential part should be separated by a letter e or E.
(b) The mantissa part may have a positive or negative sign.
(c) Default sign of mantissa part is positive.
(d) The exponent must have at least one digit, which must be a positive or negative integer. Default sign is positive.
(e) Range of real constants expressed in exponential form is -3.4e38 to 3.4e38.

```
Ex.: +3.2e-5
     4.1e8
```

```
-0.2E+3
-3.2e-5
```

Rules for Constructing Character Constants

(a) A character constant is a single alphabet, a single digit or a single special symbol enclosed within single inverted commas. Both the inverted commas should point to the left. For example, 'A' is a valid character constant whereas 'A' is not.

(b) The maximum length of a character constant can be 1 character.

```
Ex.: 'A'
     'I'
     '5'
     '='
```

Types of C Variables

As we saw earlier, an entity that may vary during program execution is called a variable. Variable names are names given to locations in memory. These locations can contain integer, real or character constants. In any language, the types of variables that it can support depend on the types of constants that it can handle. This is because a particular type of variable can hold only the same type of constant. For example, an integer variable can hold only an integer constant, a real variable can hold only a real constant and a character variable can hold only a character constant.

The rules for constructing different types of constants are different. However, for constructing variable names of all types, the same set of rules applies. These rules are given below.

Rules for Constructing Variable Names

(a) A variable name is any combination of 1 to 31 alphabets, digits or underscores. Some compilers allow variable names whose length could be up to 247 characters. Still, it would be safer to stick to the rule of 31 characters. Do not create unnecessarily long variable names as it adds to your typing effort.

(b) The first character in the variable name must be an alphabet or underscore.

(c) No commas or blanks are allowed within a variable name.

(d) No special symbol other than an underscore (as in **gross_sal**) can be used in a variable name.

```
Ex.: si_int
     m_hra
```

```
pop_e_89
```

These rules remain same for all the types of primary and secondary variables. Naturally, the question follows... how is C able to differentiate between these variables? This is a rather simple matter. C compiler is able to distinguish between the variable names by making it compulsory for you to declare the type of any variable name that you wish to use in a program. This type declaration is done at the beginning of the program. Following are the examples of type declaration statements:

```
Ex.: int  si, m_hra ;
     float  bassal ;
     char  code ;
```

Since, the maximum allowable length of a variable name is 31 characters, an enormous number of variable names can be constructed using the above-mentioned rules. It is a good practice to exploit this enormous choice in naming variables by using meaningful variable names.

Thus, if we want to calculate simple interest, it is always advisable to construct meaningful variable names like **prin**, **roi**, **noy** to represent Principle, Rate of interest and Number of years rather than using the variables **a**, **b**, **c**.

C Keywords

Keywords are the words whose meaning has already been explained to the C compiler (or in a broad sense to the computer). The keywords **cannot** be used as variable names because if we do so, we are trying to assign a new meaning to the keyword, which is not allowed by the computer. Some C compilers allow you to construct variable names that exactly resemble the keywords. However, it would be safer not to mix up the variable names and the keywords. The keywords are also called 'Reserved words'.

There are only 32 keywords available in C. Figure 3.5 gives a list of these keywords for your ready reference. A detailed discussion of each of these keywords would be taken up in later chapters wherever their use is relevant.

auto	double	int	struct
break	else	long	switch
case	enum	register	typedef
char	extern	return	union
const	float	short	unsigned
continue	for	signed	void
default	goto	sizeof	volatile
do	if	static	while

Figure 3.5

Note that compiler vendors (like Microsoft, Borland, etc.) provide their own keywords apart from the ones mentioned above. These include extended keywords like **near**, **far**, **asm**, etc. Though it has been suggested by the ANSI committee that every such compiler specific keyword should be preceded by two underscores (as in **__asm**), not every vendor follows this rule.

The First C Program

Armed with the knowledge about the types of variables, constants & keywords the next logical step is to combine them to form instructions. However, instead of this, we would write our first C program now. Once we have done that we would see in detail the instructions that it made use of.

Before we begin with our first C program do remember the following rules that are applicable to all C programs:

(a) Each instruction in a C program is written as a separate statement. Therefore, a complete C program would comprise a series of statements.

(b) The statements in a program must appear in the same order in which we wish them to be executed; unless of course the logic of the problem demands a deliberate 'jump' or transfer of control to a statement, which is out of sequence.

(c) Blank spaces may be inserted between two words to improve the readability of the statement. However, no blank spaces are allowed within a variable, constant or keyword.

(d) All statements are entered in small case letters.

(e) C has no specific rules for the position at which a statement is to be written. That's why it is often called a free-form language.

(f) Every C statement must end with a ;. Thus ; acts as a statement terminator.

Let us now write down our first C program. It would simply calculate simple interest for a set of values representing principle, number of years and rate of interest.

```
/* Calculation of simple interest */
/* Author gekay  Date: 25/08/2009 */
# include <stdio.h>

int main( )
{
    int  p, n ;
    float  r, si ;
    p = 1000 ;
    n = 3 ;
    r = 8.5 ;

    /* formula for simple interest */
    si = p * n * r / 100 ;

    printf ( "%f\n" , si ) ;
    return 0 ;
}
```

Now a few useful tips about the program...

- Comment about the program should be enclosed within /* */. For example, the first two statements in our program are comments.

- Though comments are not necessary, it is a good practice to begin a program with a comment indicating the purpose of the program, its author and the date on which the program was written.

- Any number of comments can be written at any place in the program. For example, a comment can be written before the statement, after the statement or within the statement as shown below:

```
/* formula */ si = p * n * r / 100 ;
si = p * n * r / 100 ; /* formula */
si = p * n * r / /* formula */ 100 ;
```

- Sometimes it is not very obvious as to what a particular statement in a program accomplishes. At such times it is worthwhile mentioning the purpose of the statement (or a set of statements) using a comment. For example:

```
/* formula for simple interest */
si = p * n * r / 100 ;
```

- Often programmers seem to ignore writing of comments. But when a team is building big software well commented code is almost essential for other team members to understand it.

- Although a lot of comments are probably not necessary in this program, it is usually the case that programmers tend to use too few comments rather than too many. An adequate number of comments can save hours of misery and suffering when you later try to figure out what the program does.

- The normal language rules do not apply to text written within /* .. */. Thus we can type this text in small case, capital or a combination. This is because the comments are solely given for the understanding of the programmer or the fellow programmers and are completely ignored by the compiler.

- Comments cannot be nested. For example,

```
/* Cal of SI /* sam date 01/05/2005 */ */
```

  is invalid.

- A comment can be split over more than one line, as in,

```
/* This is
   a jazzy
   comment */
```

  Such a comment is often called a multi-line comment.

- **main( )** is a function. A function is nothing but a set of statements. In a C program there can be multiple functions. To begin with, we would concentrate on only those programs which have only one function. The name of this function has to be **main( )**, it cannot be anything else. All statements that belong to **main( )** are enclosed within a pair of braces { } as shown below.

```
int main( )
{
    statement 1 ;
    statement 2 ;
    statement 3 ;
}
```

- The way functions in a calculator return a value, similarly, functions in C also return a value. **main( )** function always returns an integer value, hence there is an **int** before **main( )**. The integer value that we are returning is 0. Some compilers even permit us to return nothing from **main( )**. In such a case we should precede it with the keyword **void**. We would discuss functions and their working in great detail in Chapter 5.

- Any variable used in the program must be declared before using it. For example,

```
int  p, n ;             /* declaration */
float  r, si ;          /* declaration */
si = p * n * r / 100 ;  /* usage */
```

- Any C statement always ends with a ;

  For example,

```
float  r, si ;
r = 8.5 ;
```

- In the statement,

```
si = p * n * r / 100 ;
```

  * and / are the arithmetic operators. The arithmetic operators available in C are **+**, **-**, ***** and **/**. C is very rich in operators. There are about 45 operators available in C. Surprisingly there is no operator for exponentiation... a slip, which can be forgiven considering the fact that C has been developed by an individual, not by a committee.

- Once the value of **si** is calculated it needs to be displayed on the screen. Unlike other languages, C does not contain any instruction to display output on the screen. All output to screen is achieved using readymade library functions. One such function is **printf( )**. We have used it display on the screen the value contained in **si**.

- For us to be able to use the **printf( )** function, it is necessary to use **#include <stdio.h>** at the beginning of the program. **#include** is a preprocessor directive. Its purpose will be clarified in Chapter 7. For now, use it whenever you use **printf( )**.
- The general form of **printf( )** function is,

```
printf ( "<format string>", <list of variables> ) ;
```

<format string> can contain,

```
%f for printing real values
%d for printing integer values
%c for printing character values
```

In addition to format specifiers like **%f**, **%d** and **%c**, the format string may also contain any other characters. These characters are printed as they are when the **printf( )** is executed.

Following are some examples of usage of **printf( )** function:

```
printf ( "%f", si ) ;
printf ( "%d %d %f %f", p, n, r, si ) ;
printf ( "Simple interest = Rs. %f", si ) ;
printf ( "Principal = %d \nRate = %f", p, r ) ;
```

The output of the last statement would look like this...

```
Principal = 1000
Rate = 8.500000
```

What is '\n' doing in this statement? It is called newline and it takes the cursor to the next line. Therefore, you get the output split over two lines. '\n' is one of the several Escape Sequences available in C. These are discussed in detail in Chapter 11. Right now, all that we can say is '\n' comes in handy when we want to format the output properly on separate lines.

printf( ) can not only print values of variables, it can also print the result of an expression. An expression is nothing but a valid combination of constants, variables and operators. Thus, 3, 3 + 2, c and a + b * c – d all are valid expressions. The results of these expressions can be printed as shown below:

```
printf ( "%d %d %d %d", 3, 3 + 2, c, a + b * c - d ) ;
```

Note that **3** and **c** also represent valid expressions.

Compilation and Execution

Once you have written the program you need to type it and instruct the machine to execute it. To type your C program you need another program called Editor. Once the program has been typed it needs to be converted to machine language (0s and 1s) before the machine can execute it. To carry out this conversion we need another program called Compiler. Compiler vendors provide an Integrated Development Environment (IDE) which consists of an Editor as well as the Compiler.

There are several such IDEs available in the market targeted towards different operating systems. For example, Turbo C, Turbo C++ and Microsoft C are some of the popular compilers that work under MS-DOS; Visual Studio and Borland C++ are the compilers that work under Windows, whereas gcc compiler works under Linux. Note that Turbo C++, Microsoft C++ and Borland C++ software also contain a C compiler bundled with them. If you are a beginner you would be better off using a simple compiler like Turbo C or Turbo C++. Once you have mastered the language elements you can then switch over to more sophisticated compilers like Visual Studio under Windows or gcc under Linux. Most of the programs in this book would work with all the compilers. Wherever there is a deviation I would point it out at that time.

Assuming that you are using a Turbo C or Turbo C++ compiler here are the steps that you need to follow to compile and execute your first C program…

(a) Start the compiler at **C>** prompt. The compiler (TC.EXE is usually present in **C:\TC\BIN** directory).
(b) Select **New** from the **File** menu.
(c) Type the program.
(d) Save the program using **F2** under a proper name (say Program1.c).
(e) Use **Ctrl + F9** to compile and execute the program.
(f) Use **Alt + F5** to view the output.

Note that on compiling the program its machine language equivalent is stored as an EXE file (Program1.EXE) on the disk. This file is called an executable file. If we copy this file to another machine we can execute it there without being required to recompile it. In fact the other machine need not even have a compiler to be able to execute the file.

A word of caution! If you run this program in Turbo C++ compiler, you may get an error — "The function printf should have a prototype". To get rid of this error, perform the following steps and then recompile the program.

(a) Select 'Options' menu and then select 'Compiler | C++ Options'. In the dialog box that pops up, select 'CPP always' in the 'Use C++ Compiler' options.
(b) Again select 'Options' menu and then select 'Environment | Editor'. Make sure that the default extension is 'C' rather than 'CPP'.

Receiving Input

In the program discussed above we assumed the values of **p**, **n** and **r** to be 1000, 3 and 8.5. Every time we run the program we would get the same value for simple interest. If we want to calculate simple interest for some other set of values then we are required to make the relevant change in the program, and again compile and execute it. Thus the program is not general enough to calculate simple interest for any set of values without being required to make a change in the program. Moreover, if you distribute the EXE file of this program to somebody he would not even be able to make changes in the program. Hence it is a good practice to create a program that is general enough to work for any set of values.

To make the program general, the program itself should ask the user to supply the values of **p**, **n** and **r** through the keyboard during execution. This can be achieved using a function called **scanf( )**. This function is a counter-part of the **printf( )** function. **printf( )** outputs the values to the screen whereas **scanf( )** receives them from the keyboard. This is illustrated in the program given below.

```
/* Calculation of simple interest */
/* Author gekay Date 25/07/2008 */
# include <stdio.h>
int main( )
{
    int  p, n ;
    float  r, si ;

    printf ( "Enter values of p, n, r" ) ;
    scanf ( "%d %d %f", &p, &n, &r ) ;

    si = p * n * r / 100 ;
    printf ( "%f\n" , si ) ;
    return 0 ;
}
```

The first **printf( )** outputs the message 'Enter values of p, n, r' on the screen. Here we have not used any expression in **printf( )** which means that using expressions in **printf( )** is optional.

Note that the ampersand (**&**) before the variables in the **scanf( )** function is a must. **&** is an 'Address of' operator. It gives the location number used by the variable in memory. When we say **&a**, we are telling **scanf( )** at which memory location should it store the value supplied by the user from the keyboard. The detailed working of the **&** operator would be taken up in Chapter 5.

Note that a blank, a tab or a new line must separate the values supplied to **scanf( )**. Note that a blank is creating using a spacebar, tab using the Tab key and new line using the Enter key. This is shown below:

Ex.: The three values separated by blank

```
1000 5 15.5
```

Ex.: The three values separated by tab.

```
1000	5	15.5
```

Ex.: The three values separated by newline.

```
1000
5
15.5
```

So much for the tips. How about another program to give you a feel of things...

```
/* Just for fun. Author: Bozo */
# include <stdio.h>
int main( )
{
    int  num ;

    printf ( "Enter a number" ) ;
    scanf ( "%d", &num ) ;

    printf ( "Now I am letting you on a secret...\n" ) ;
    printf ( "You have just entered the number %d\n", num ) ;
    return 0 ;
```

}

C Instructions

Now that we have written a few programs let us look at the instructions that we used in these programs. There are basically three types of instructions in C:

(a) Type Declaration Instruction
(b) Arithmetic Instruction
(c) Control Instruction

The purpose of each of these instructions is given below:

(a) Type declaration instruction	–	To declare the type of variables used in a C program.
(b) Arithmetic instruction	–	To perform arithmetic operations between constants and variables.
(c) Control instruction	–	To control the sequence of execution of various statements in a C program.

Since, the elementary C programs would usually contain only the type declaration and the arithmetic instructions; we would discuss only these two instructions at this stage. The other types of instructions would be discussed in detail in the subsequent chapters.

Type Declaration Instruction

This instruction is used to declare the type of variables being used in the program. Any variable used in the program must be declared before using it in any statement. The type declaration statement is written at the beginning of **main( )** function.

Ex.:
```
int  bas ;
float  rs, grosssal ;
char  name, code ;
```

There are several subtle variations of the type declaration instruction. These are discussed below:

(a) While declaring the type of variable we can also initialize it as shown below.

```
int i = 10, j = 25 ;
float a = 1.5, b = 1.99 + 2.4 * 1.44 ;
```

(b) The order in which we define the variables is sometimes important sometimes not. For example,

```
int i = 10, j = 25 ;
```

is same as

```
int j = 25, i = 10 ;
```

However,

```
float a = 1.5, b = a + 3.1 ;
```

is alright, but

```
float  b = a + 3.1, a = 1.5 ;
```

is not. This is because here we are trying to use **a** even before defining it.

(c) The following statements would work

```
int a, b, c, d ;
a = b = c = 10 ;
```

However, the following statement would not work

```
int a = b = c = d = 10 ;
```

Once again we are trying to use **b** (to assign to **a**) before defining it.

Arithmetic Instruction

A C arithmetic instruction consists of a variable name on the left hand side of = and variable names & constants on the right hand side of =. The variables and constants appearing on the right hand side of = are connected by arithmetic operators like **+**, **-**, *****, and **/**.

```
Ex.: int ad ;
     float kot, deta, alpha, beta, gamma ;
     ad = 3200 ;
     kot = 0.0056 ;
     deta = alpha * beta / gamma + 3.2 * 2 / 5 ;
```

Here,

***, /, -, +** are the arithmetic operators.
= is the assignment operator.
2, 5 and 3200 are integer constants.
3.2 and 0.0056 are real constants.
ad is an integer variable.
kot, deta, alpha, beta, gamma are real variables.

The variables and constants together are called 'operands' that are operated upon by the 'arithmetic operators' and the result is assigned, using the assignment operator, to the variable on left-hand side.

A C arithmetic statement could be of three types. These are as follows:

(a) Integer mode arithmetic statement - This is an arithmetic statement in which all operands are either integer variables or integer constants.

```
Ex.: int i, king, issac, noteit ;
     i = i + 1 ;
     king = issac * 234 + noteit - 7689 ;
```

(b) Real mode arithmetic statement - This is an arithmetic statement in which all operands are either real constants or real variables.

```
Ex.: float qbee, antink, si, prin, anoy, roi ;
     qbee = antink + 23.123 / 4.5 * 0.3442 ;
     si = prin * anoy * roi / 100.0 ;
```

(c) Mixed mode arithmetic statement - This is an arithmetic statement in which some of the operands are integers and some of the operands are real.

```
Ex.: float si, prin, anoy, roi, avg ;
     int a, b, c, num ;
     si = prin * anoy * roi / 100.0 ;
     avg = ( a + b + c + num ) / 4 ;
```

It is very important to understand how the execution of an arithmetic statement takes place. Firstly, the right hand side is evaluated using constants and the numerical values stored in the variable names. This value is then assigned to the variable on the left-hand side.

Though Arithmetic instructions look simple to use, one often commits mistakes in writing them. Let us take a closer look at these statements. Note the following points carefully.

(a) C allows only one variable on left-hand side of **=**. That is, **z = k * l** is legal, whereas **k * l = z** is illegal.

(b) In addition to the division operator C also provides a modular division operator. This operator returns the remainder on dividing one integer with another. Thus the expression 10 / 2 yields 5, whereas, 10 % 2 yields 0. Note that the modulus operator (%) cannot be applied on a float. Also note that on using % the sign of the remainder is always same as the sign of the numerator. Thus –5 % 2 yields –1, whereas, 5 % -2 yields 1.

(c) An arithmetic instruction is at times used for storing character constants in character variables.

```
char  a, b, d ;
a = 'F' ;
b = 'G' ;
d = '+' ;
```

When we do this the ASCII values of the characters are stored in the variables. ASCII values are used to represent any character in memory. The ASCII values of ‘F’ and ‘G’ are 70 and 71 (refer to the ASCII Table in Appendix E).

(d) Arithmetic operations can be performed on **int**s, **float**s and **char**s.

Thus the statements,

```
char  x, y ;
int  z ;
x = 'a' ;
y = 'b' ;
z = x + y ;
```

are perfectly valid, since the addition is performed on the ASCII values of the characters and not on characters themselves. The ASCII values of ‘a’ and ‘b’ are 97 and 98, and hence can definitely be added.

(e) No operator is assumed to be present. It must be written explicitly. In the following example, the multiplication operator after b must be explicitly written.

```
a = c.d.b(xy)                    usual arithmetic statement
b = c * d * b * ( x * y )        C statement
```

(f) Unlike other high level languages, there is no operator for performing exponentiation operation. Thus following statements are invalid.

```
a = 3 ** 2 ;
b = 3 ^ 2 ;
```

If we want to do the exponentiation we can get it done this way:

```
# include <math.h>
# include <stdio.h>

int main( )
{
    int a ;
    a = pow ( 3, 2 ) ;
    printf ( "%d", a ) ;
}
```

Here **pow( )** function is a standard library function. It is being used to raise 3 to the power of 2. **#include <math.h>** is a preprocessor directive. It is being used here to ensure that the **pow( )** function works correctly. We would learn more about standard library functions in Chapter 5 and about preprocessor in Chapter 7.

(g) In addition to +, -, * and /, there exists one more arithmetic operator in C. It is called a modular division operator, and it is represented using the symbol %. Unlike /, which returns the quotient, % returns the remainder. Thus 5 % 3 yields 2 as the remainder.

Integer and Float Conversions

In order to effectively develop C programs, it will be necessary to understand the rules that are used for the implicit conversion of floating point and integer values in C. These are mentioned below. Note them carefully.

(a) An arithmetic operation between an integer and integer always yields an integer result.

(b) An operation between a real and real always yields a real result.

(c) An operation between an integer and real always yields a real result. In this operation the integer is first promoted to a real and then the operation is performed. Hence the result is real.

I think a few practical examples shown in Figure 3.6 would put the issue beyond doubt.

Operation	Result	Operation	Result
5 / 2	2	2 / 5	0
5.0 / 2	2.500000	2.0 / 5	0.400000
5 / 2.0	2.500000	2 / 5.0	0.400000
5.0 / 2.0	2.500000	2.0 / 5.0	0.400000

Figure 3.6

Type Conversion in Assignments

It may so happen that the type of the expression and the type of the variable on the left-hand side of the assignment operator may not be the same. In such a case, the value of the expression is promoted or demoted depending on the type of the variable on left-hand side of =.

For example, consider the following assignment statements.

```
int i ;
float b ;
i = 3.5 ;
b = 30 ;
```

Here in the first assignment statement, though the expression's value is a **float** (3.5), it cannot be stored in **i** since it is an **int**. In such a case, the **float** is demoted to an **int** and then its value is stored. Hence what gets stored in **i** is 3. Exactly opposite happens in the next statement. Here, 30 is promoted to 30.000000 and then stored in **b**, since **b** being a **float** variable cannot hold anything except a **float** value.

Instead of a simple expression used in the above examples, if a complex expression occurs, still the same rules apply. For example, consider the following program fragment.

```
float  a, b, c ;
int  s ;
s = a * b * c / 100 + 32 / 4 - 3 * 1.1 ;
```

Here, in the assignment statement, some operands are **ints** whereas others are **floats**. As we know, during evaluation of the expression, the **ints** would be promoted to **floats** and the result of the expression would be a **float**. But when this **float** value is assigned to **s** it is again demoted to an **int** and then stored in **s**.

Observe the results of the arithmetic statements shown in Figure 3.7. It has been assumed that **k** is an integer variable and **a** is a real variable.

Arithmetic Instruction	Result	Arithmetic Inst.	Result
k = 2 / 9	0	a = 2 / 9	0.000000
k = 2.0 / 9	0	a = 2.0 / 9	0.222222
k = 2 / 9.0	0	a = 2 / 9.0	0.222222
k = 2.0 / 9.0	0	a = 2.0 / 9.0	0.222222
k = 9 / 2	4	a = 9 / 2	4.000000
k = 9.0 / 2	4	a = 9.0 / 2	4.500000
k = 9 / 2.0	4	a = 9 / 2.0	4.500000
k = 9.0 / 2.0	4	a = 9.0 / 2.0	4.500000

Figure 3.7

Note that though the following statements give the same result, 0, the results are obtained differently.

```
k = 2 / 9 ;
k = 2.0 / 9 ;
```

In the first statement, since both 2 and 9 are integers, the result is an integer, i.e. 0. This 0 is then assigned to **k**. In the second statement 9 is promoted to 9.0 and then the division is performed. Division yields 0.222222. However, this cannot be stored in **k**, **k** being an **int**. Hence it gets demoted to 0 and then stored in **k**.

Hierarchy of Operations

While executing an arithmetic statement, which has two or more operators, we may have some problems as to how exactly does it get executed. For example, does the expression 2 * x - 3 * y correspond to (2x)-(3y) or to 2(x-3y)? Similarly, does A / B * C correspond to A / (B * C) or to (A / B) * C? To answer these questions satisfactorily, one has to understand the 'hierarchy' of operations. The priority or precedence in which the operations in an arithmetic statement are performed is called the hierarchy of operations. The hierarchy of commonly used operators is shown in Figure 3.8.

Priority	Operators	Description
1st	* / %	multiplication, division, modular division
2nd	+ -	addition, subtraction
3rd	=	Assignment

Figure 3.8

Now a few tips about usage of operators in general.

(a) Within parentheses the same hierarchy as mentioned in Figure 3.11 is operative. Also, if there are more than one set of parentheses, the operations within the innermost parentheses would be performed first, followed by the operations within the second innermost pair and so on.

(b) We must always remember to use pairs of parentheses. A careless imbalance of the right and left parentheses is a common error. Best way to avoid this error is to type ( ) and then type an expression inside it.

A few examples would clarify the issue further.

Example 3.1: Determine the hierarchy of operations and evaluate the following expression, assuming that **i** is an integer variable:

```
i = 2 * 3 / 4 + 4 / 4 + 8 - 2 + 5 / 8
```

Stepwise evaluation of this expression is shown below:

```
i = 2 * 3 / 4 + 4 / 4 + 8 - 2 + 5 / 8
i = 6 / 4 + 4 / 4 + 8 - 2 + 5 / 8          operation: *
i = 1 + 4 / 4 + 8 - 2 + 5 / 8              operation: /
```

```
i = 1 + 1+ 8 - 2 + 5 / 8            operation: /
i = 1 + 1 + 8 - 2 + 0               operation: /
i = 2 + 8 - 2 + 0                   operation: +
i = 10 - 2 + 0                      operation: +
i = 8 + 0                           operation : -
i = 8                               operation: +
```

Note that 6 / 4 gives 1 and not 1.5. This so happens because 6 and 4 both are integers and therefore would evaluate to only an integer constant. Similarly 5 / 8 evaluates to zero, since 5 and 8 are integer constants and hence must return an integer value.

Example 3.2: Determine the hierarchy of operations and evaluate the following expression, assuming that **kk** is a float variable:

```
kk = 3 / 2 * 4 + 3 / 8 + 3
```

Stepwise evaluation of this expression is shown below:

```
kk = 3 / 2 * 4 + 3 / 8 + 3
kk = 1 * 4 + 3 / 8 + 3              operation: /
kk = 4 + 3 / 8 + 3                  operation: *
kk = 4 + 0 + 3                      operation: /
kk = 4 + 3                          operation: +
kk = 7                              operation: +
```

Note that 3 / 8 gives zero, again for the same reason mentioned in the previous example.

All operators in C are ranked according to their precedence. And mind you, there are as many as 45 odd operators in C, and these can affect the evaluation of an expression in subtle and unexpected ways if we aren't careful. Unfortunately, there are no simple rules that one can follow, such as "BODMAS" that tells algebra students in which order does an expression evaluate. We have not encountered many out of these 45 operators, so we won't pursue the subject of precedence any further here. However, it can be realized at this stage that it would be almost impossible to remember the precedence of all these operators. So a full-fledged list of all operators and their precedence is given in Appendix A. This may sound daunting, but when its contents are absorbed in small bites, it becomes more palatable.

So far we have seen how the computer evaluates an arithmetic statement written in C. But our knowledge would be incomplete unless we know how to convert a general arithmetic statement to a C statement. C can handle any complex expression with ease. Some of the examples of C expressions are shown in Figure 3.9.

Algebric Expression	C Expression
$a \times b - c \times d$	a * b – c * d
$(m + n)(a + b)$	(m + n) * (a + b)
$3x^2 + 2x + 5$	3 * x * x + 2 * x + 5
$\frac{a+b+c}{d+e}$	(a + b + c) / (d + e)
$\left[\frac{2BY}{d+1} - \frac{x}{3(z+y)}\right]$	2 * b * y / (d + 1) – x / 3 * (z + y)

Figure 3.9

Associativity of Operators

When an expression contains two operators of equal priority the tie between them is settled using the associativity of the operators. Associativity can be of two types—Left to Right or Right to Left. Left to Right associativity means that the left operand must be unambiguous. Unambiguous in what sense? It must not be involved in evaluation of any other sub-expression. Similarly, in case of Right to Left associativity the right operand must be unambiguous. Let us understand this with an example. Consider the expression

```
a = 3 / 2 * 5 ;
```

Here there is a tie between operators of same priority, that is between / and *. This tie is settled using the associativity of / and *. But both enjoy Left to Right associativity. Figure 3.10 shows for each operator which operand is unambiguous and which is not.

Operator	Left	Right	Remark
/	3	2 or 2 * 5	Left operand is unambiguous, Right is not
*	3 / 2 or 2	5	Right operand is unambiguous, Left is not

Figure 3.10

Since both / and * have L to R associativity and only / has unambiguous left operand (necessary condition for L to R associativity) it is performed earlier.

Consider one more expression

```
a = b = 3 ;
```

Here both assignment operators have the same priority and same associativity (Right to Left). Figure 3.11 shows for each operator which operand is unambiguous and which is not.

Operator	Left	Right	Remark
=	a	b or b = 3	Left operand is unambiguous, Right is not
=	b or a = b	3	Right operand is unambiguous, Left is not

Figure 3.11

Since both = have R to L associativity and only the second = has unambiguous right operand (necessary condition for R to L associativity) the second = is performed earlier.

Consider yet another expression

```
z = a * b + c / d ;
```

Here * and / enjoys same priority and same associativity (Left to Right). Figure 3.12 shows for each operator which operand is unambiguous and which is not.

Operator	Left	Right	Remark
*	a	B	Both operands are unambiguous
/	c	D	Both operands are unambiguous

Figure 3.12

Here since left operands for both operators are unambiguous Compiler is free to perform * or / operation as per its convenience, since no matter which is performed earlier, the result would be same.

Appendix A gives the associativity of all the operators available in C.

Control Instructions in C

As the name suggests, the 'Control Instructions' enable us to specify the order in which the various instructions in a program are to be executed by the computer. In other words, the control instructions determine the 'flow of control' in a program. There are four types of control instructions in C. They are:

(a) Sequence Control Instruction
(b) Selection or Decision Control Instruction
(c) Repetition or Loop Control Instruction
(d) Case Control Instruction

The Sequence control instruction ensures that the instructions are executed in the same order in which they appear in the program. Decision and Case control instructions allow the computer to take a decision as to which instruction is to be executed next. The Loop control instruction helps computer to execute a group of statements repeatedly. In the following chapters, we are going to learn these instructions in detail. Try your hand at the Exercise presented on the following pages before proceeding to the next chapter, which discusses the decision control instruction.

Summary

(a) The three primary constants and variable types in C are integer, float and character.
(b) A variable name can be of maximum 31 characters.
(c) Do not use a keyword as a variable name.
(d) An expression may contain any sequence of constants, variables and operators.

(e) Operators having equal precedence are evaluated using associativity.

(f) Left to right associativity means that the left operand of a operator must be unambiguous whereas right to left associativity means that the right operand of a operator must be unambiguous.

(g) Input/output in C can be achieved using **scanf( )** and **printf( )** functions.

Exercise

[A] Which of the following are invalid variable names and why?

BASICSALARY	_basic	basic-hra
#MEAN	group.	422
population in 2006	over time	mindovermatter
FLOAT	hELLO	queue.
team'svictory	Plot # 3	2015_DDay

[B] Point out the errors, if any, in the following C statements:

(a) int = 314.562 * 150 ;

(b) name = 'Ajay' ;

(c) varchar = '3' ;

(d) 3.14 * r * r * h = vol_of_cyl ;

(e) k = (a * b) (c + (2.5a + b) (d + e) ;

(f) m_inst = rate of interest * amount in rs ;

(g) si = principal * rateofinterest * numberofyears / 100 ;

(h) area = 3.14 * r ** 2 ;

(i) volume = 3.14 * r ^ 2 * h ;

(j) k = ((a * b) + c) (2.5 * a + b) ;

(k) a = b = 3 = 4 ;

(l) count = count + 1 ;

(m) date = '2 Mar 04' ;

[C] Evaluate the following expressions and show their hierarchy.

(a) g = big / 2 + big * 4 / big - big + abc / 3 ;
(abc = 2.5, big = 2, assume **g** to be a float)

(b) on = ink * act / 2 + 3 / 2 * act + 2 + tig ;
(ink = 4, act = 1, tig = 3.2, assume **on** to be an int)

(c) s = qui * add / 4 - 6 / 2 + 2 / 3 * 6 / god ;
(qui = 4, add = 2, god = 2, assume **s** to be an int)

(d) s = 1 / 3 * a / 4 - 6 / 2 + 2 / 3 * 6 / g ;
(a = 4, g = 3, assume **s** to be an int)

[D] Fill the following table for the expressions given below and then evaluate the result. A sample entry has been filled in the table for expression (a).

Operator	Left	Right	Remark
/	10	5 or 5 / 2 / 1	Left operand is unambiguous, Right is not
..	..	..	..

(a) g = 10 / 5 /2 / 1 ;

(b) b = 3 / 2 + 5 * 4 / 3 ;

(c) a = b = c = 3 + 4 ;

[E] Convert the following equations into corresponding C statements.

(a) $$Z = \frac{8.8(a+b)2/c-0.5+2a/(q+r)}{(a+b)*(1/m)}$$

(b) $X = \dfrac{-b + (b * b) + 2\ 4ac}{2a}$

(c) $R = \dfrac{2v + 6.22\ (c + d)}{g + v}$

(d) $A = \dfrac{7.7b\ (xy + a) / c - 0.8 + 2b}{(x + a)\ (1 / y)}$

[F] What will be the output of the following programs:

(a)
```
# include <stdio.h>
int main( )
{
    int  i = 2, j = 3, k, l ;
    float  a, b ;
    k = i / j * j ;
    l = j / i * i ;
    a = i / j * j ;
    b = j / i * i ;
    printf ( "%d %d %f %f\n", k, l, a, b ) ;
    return 0 ;
}
```

(b)
```
# include <stdio.h>
int main( )
{
    int  a, b ;
    a = -3 - - 3 ;
    b = -3 - - ( - 3 ) ;
    printf ( "a = %d b = %d\n", a, b ) ;
    return 0 ;
}
```

(c)
```
# include <stdio.h>
int main( )
{
    float a = 5,  b = 2 ;
    int c ;
    c = a % b ;
    printf ( "%d\n", c ) ;
    return 0 ;
```

```
}
```

(d)
```
# include <stdio.h>
int main( )
{
    printf ( "nn \n\n nn\n" ) ;
    printf ( "nn /n/n nn/n" ) ;
    return 0 ;
}
```

(e)
```
# include <stdio.h>
int main( )
{
    int a, b ;
    printf ( "Enter values of a and b" ) ;
    scanf ( " %d %d ", &a, &b ) ;
    printf ( "a = %d b = %d", a, b ) ;
    return 0 ;
}
```

(f)
```
# include <stdio.h>
int main( )
{
    int abc56 = 65, abC, Abc, _aBc = 65 ;
    printf ( "%d %d %d %d\n", abc56, abC, Abc, _aBc ) ;
    return 0 ;
}
```

(g)
```
# include <stdio.h>
int main( )
{
    char a = 4 ;
    a = a == '2' / '5' * '6' + '9' - '3' + '1' + '8' / '0' ;
    printf ( "%d\n", a ) ;
    return 0 ;
}
```

(h)
```
# include <stdio.h>
int main( )
{
    int k, j ;
    printf ( "%d %d\n", k, j ) ;
    return 0 ;
```

```
    }
```

(i)
```
# include <stdio.h>
int main( )
{
    int x ;
    x = 4 + 5 / 2 % -8 ;
    printf ( "x = %d\n", x ) ;
    return 0 ;
}
```

[G] Pick up the correct alternative for each of the following questions:

(a) C language has been developed by
  (1) Ken Thompson
  (2) Dennis Ritchie
  (3) Peter Norton
  (4) Martin Richards

(b) C can be used on
  (1) Only MS-DOS operating system
  (2) Only Linux operating system
  (3) Only Windows operating system
  (4) All the above

(c) C programs are converted into machine language with the help of
  (1) An Editor
  (2) A compiler
  (3) An operating system
  (4) None of the above

(d) The real constant in C can be expressed in which of the following forms
  (1) Fractional form only
  (2) Exponential form only
  (3) ASCII form only
  (4) Both Fractional and Exponential forms

(e) A character variable can at a time store
  (1) 1 character
  (2) 8 characters
  (3) 254 characters
  (4) None of the above

(f) The statement **char ch = 'Z'** would store in **ch**
  (1) The character Z
  (2) ASCII value of Z
  (3) Z along with the single inverted commas
  (4) Both (1) and (2)

(g) Which of the following is NOT a character constant
  (1) 'Thank You'
  (2) 'Enter values of P, N, R'
  (3) '23.56E-03'
  (4) All the above

(h) The maximum value that an integer constant can have is
  (1) -32767
  (2) 32767
  (3) 1.7014e+38
  (4) –1.7014e+38

(i) A C variable cannot start with
  (1) An alphabet
  (2) A number
  (3) A special symbol other than underscore
  (4) Both (2) & (3) above

(j) Which of the following statements is wrong
  (1) mes = 123.56 ;
  (2) con = 'T' * 'A' ;
  (3) this = 'T' * 20 ;
  (4) 3 + a = b ;

(k) Which of the following shows the correct hierarchy of arithmetic operators in C
  (1) **, * or /, + or -
  (2) **, *, /, +, -
  (3) **, /, *, +, -
  (4) / or *, - or +

(l) In b = 6.6 / a + 2 * n ; which operation will be performed first?
  (1) 6.6 / a
  (2) a + 2
  (3) 2 * n
  (4) Depends upon compiler

(m) Which of the following is allowed in a C Arithmetic instruction
  (1) [ ]
  (2) { }
  (3) ( )
  (4) None of the above

(n) Which of the following statements is FALSE
  (1) Each new C instruction has to be written on a separate line
  (2) Usually all C statements are entered in small case letters
  (3) Blank spaces may be inserted between two words in a C statement
  (4) Blank spaces cannot be inserted within a variable name

(o) If a is an integer variable, a = 5 / 2 ; will return a value
  (1) 2.5
  (2) 3
  (3) 2
  (4) 0

(p) The expression, a = 7 / 22 * (3.14 + 2) * 3 / 5 ; evaluates to
  (1) 8.28
  (2) 6.28
  (3) 3.14
  (4) 0

(q) The expression, a = 30 * 1000 + 2768 ; evaluates to
  (1) 32768
  (2) -32768
  (3) 113040
  (4) 0

(r) The expression x = 4 + 2 % - 8 evaluates to
  (1) -6
  (2) 6
  (3) 4
  (4) None of the above

(s) Hierarchy decides which operator
  (1) is most important
  (2) is used first
  (3) is fastest
  (4) operates on largest numbers

(t) An integer constant in C must have
(1) At least one digit
(2) At least one decimal point
(3) A comma along with digits
(4) Digits separated by commas

(u) In C a variable cannot contain
(1) Blank spaces
(2) Hyphen
(3) Decimal point
(4) All the above

(v) Which of the following is FALSE in C
(1) Keywords can be used as variable names
(2) Variable names can contain a digit
(3) Variable names do not contain a blank space
(4) Capital letters can be used in variable names

(w) In C, Arithmetic instruction cannot contain
(1) variables
(2) constants
(3) variable names on right side of =
(4) constants on left side of =

(x) Which of the following is odd one out
(1) +
(2) -
(3) /
(4) **

(y) What will be the value of **d** (assume **d** to be a **float**) after the operation **d = 2 / 7.0**?
(1) 0
(2) 0.2857
(3) Cannot be determined
(4) None of the above

[H] Write C programs for the following:

(a) Ramesh's basic salary is input through the keyboard. His dearness allowance is 40% of basic salary, and house rent allowance is 20% of basic salary. Write a program to calculate his gross salary.

(b) The distance between two cities (in km.) is input through the keyboard. Write a program to convert and print this distance in meters, feet, inches and centimeters.

(c) If the marks obtained by a student in five different subjects are input through the keyboard, find out the aggregate marks and percentage marks obtained by the student. Assume that the maximum marks that can be obtained by a student in each subject is 100.

(d) Temperature of a city in Fahrenheit degrees is input through the keyboard. Write a program to convert this temperature into Centigrade degrees.

(e) The length & breadth of a rectangle and radius of a circle are input through the keyboard. Write a program to calculate the area & perimeter of the rectangle, and the area & circumference of the circle.

(f) Two numbers are input through the keyboard into two locations C and D. Write a program to interchange the contents of C and D.

(g) If a five-digit number is input through the keyboard, write a program to calculate the sum of its digits.

(Hint: Use the modulus operator '%')

(h) If a five-digit number is input through the keyboard, write a program to reverse the number.

(i) If a four-digit number is input through the keyboard, write a program to obtain the sum of the first and last digit of this number.

(j) In a town, the percentage of men is 52. The percentage of total literacy is 48. If total percentage of literate men is 35 of the total population, write a program to find the total number of illiterate men and women if the population of the town is 80,000.

(k) A cashier has currency notes of denominations 10, 50 and 100. If the amount to be withdrawn is input through the keyboard in hundreds, find the total number of currency notes of each denomination the cashier will have to give to the withdrawer.

(l) If the total selling price of 15 items and the total profit earned on them is input through the keyboard, write a program to find the cost price of one item.

(m) If a five-digit number is input through the keyboard, write a program to print a new number by adding one to each of its digits. For example, if the number that is input is 12391, then the output should be displayed as 23502.

(n) Suppose a five digit number is entered through the keyboard. Write a program to print the sum of the ASCII values of individual digits of the number.

(o) You have already written a program to reverse a five digit number. Modify it suitably so that the user can supply any number between -99999999 to 99999999.

(p) Consider a currency system in which there are notes of seven denominations, namely, Re 1, Rs 2, Rs 5, Rs 10, Rs 20, Rs 50 and Rs 100

A sum of Rs. N is entered through the keyboard, write a program to compute the smallest number of notes that will combine to give Rs. N.

4 The Decision Control Structure

We all need to alter our actions in the face of changing circumstances. If the weather is fine, then I will go for a stroll. If the highway is busy, I would take a diversion. If the pitch takes spin, we would win the match. If she says no, I would look elsewhere. If you like this book, I would write the next edition. You can notice that all these decisions depend on some condition being met.

C language too must be able to perform different sets of actions depending on the circumstances. In fact, this is what makes it worth its salt. C has three major decision making instructions—the **if** statement, the **if-else** statement, and the **switch** statement. A fourth, somewhat less important structure is the one that uses conditional operators. In this chapter, we will explore all these ways (except **switch**, which has a separate chapter devoted to it, later) in which a C program can react to changing circumstances.

Decisions! Decisions!

In the programs written in Chapter 1, we have used sequence control structure in which the various steps are executed sequentially, i.e. in the same order in which they appear in the program. In fact, to execute the instructions sequentially, we don't have to do anything at all. By default, the instructions in a program are executed sequentially. However, in serious programming situations, seldom do we want the instructions to be executed sequentially. Many a time, we want a set of instructions to be executed in one situation, and an entirely different set of instructions to be executed in another situation. This kind of situation is dealt with in C programs using a decision control instruction. As mentioned earlier, a decision control instruction can be implemented in C using:

(a) The **if** statement
(b) The **if-else** statement
(c) The conditional operators

Now let us learn each of these and their variations in turn.

The *if* Statement

Like most languages, C uses the keyword **if** to implement the decision control instruction. The general form of **if** statement looks like this:

```
if ( this condition is true )
    execute this statement ;
```

The keyword **if** tells the compiler that what follows is a decision control instruction. The condition following the keyword **if** is always enclosed within a pair of parentheses. If the condition, whatever it is, is true, then the statement is executed. If the condition is not true, then the statement is not executed; instead the program skips past it. But how do we express the condition itself in C? And how do we evaluate its truth or falsity? As a general rule, we express a condition using C's 'relational' operators. The relational operators allow us to compare two values to see whether they are equal to each other, unequal, or whether one is greater than the other. Here's how they look and how they are evaluated in C.

this expression	**is true if**
x == y	x is equal to y
x != y	x is not equal to y
x < y	x is less than y
x > y	x is greater than y
x <= y	x is less than or equal to y
x >= y	x is greater than or equal to y

Figure 4.1

The relational operators should be familiar to you except for the equality operator == and the inequality operator **!=**. Note that = is used for assignment, whereas, **==** is used for comparison of two quantities. Here is a simple program, which demonstrates the use of **if** and the relational operators.

```
/* Demonstration of if statement */
# include <stdio.h>
int main( )
{
    int  num ;

    printf ( "Enter a number less than 10 " ) ;
    scanf ( "%d", &num ) ;

    if ( num < 10 )
        printf ( "What an obedient servant you are !\n" ) ;

    return 0 ;
}
```

On execution of this program, if you type a number less than 10, you get a message on the screen through **printf( )**. If you type some other number the program doesn't do anything. The flowchart given in Figure 4.2 would help you understand the flow of control in the program.

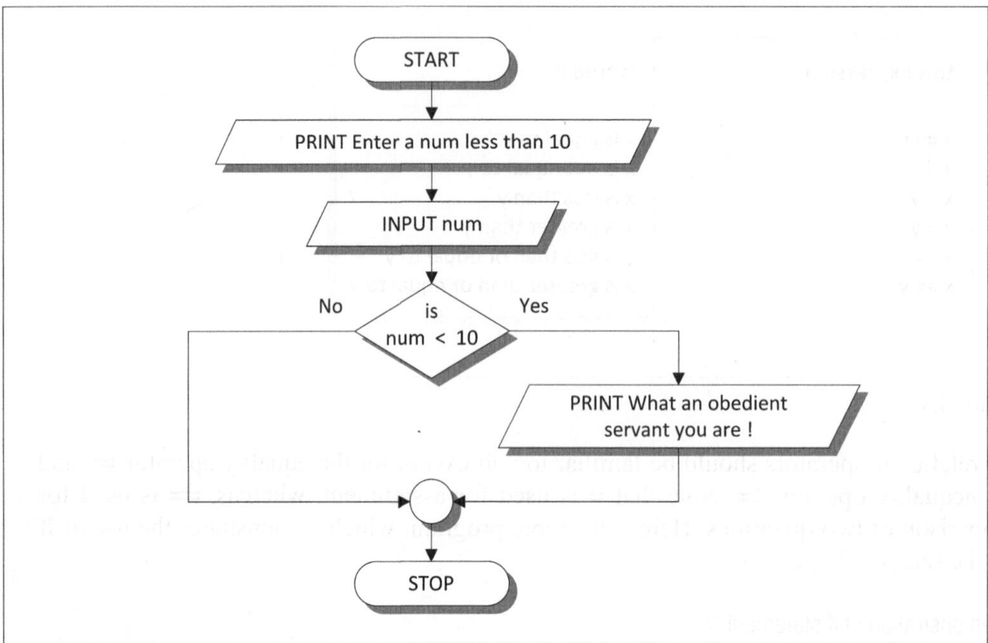

Figure 4.2

To make you comfortable with the decision control instruction, one more example has been given below. Study it carefully before reading further. To help you understand it easily, the program is accompanied by an appropriate flowchart.

Example 4.1: While purchasing certain items, a discount of 10% is offered if the quantity purchased is more than 1000. If quantity and price per item are input through the keyboard, write a program to calculate the total expenses.

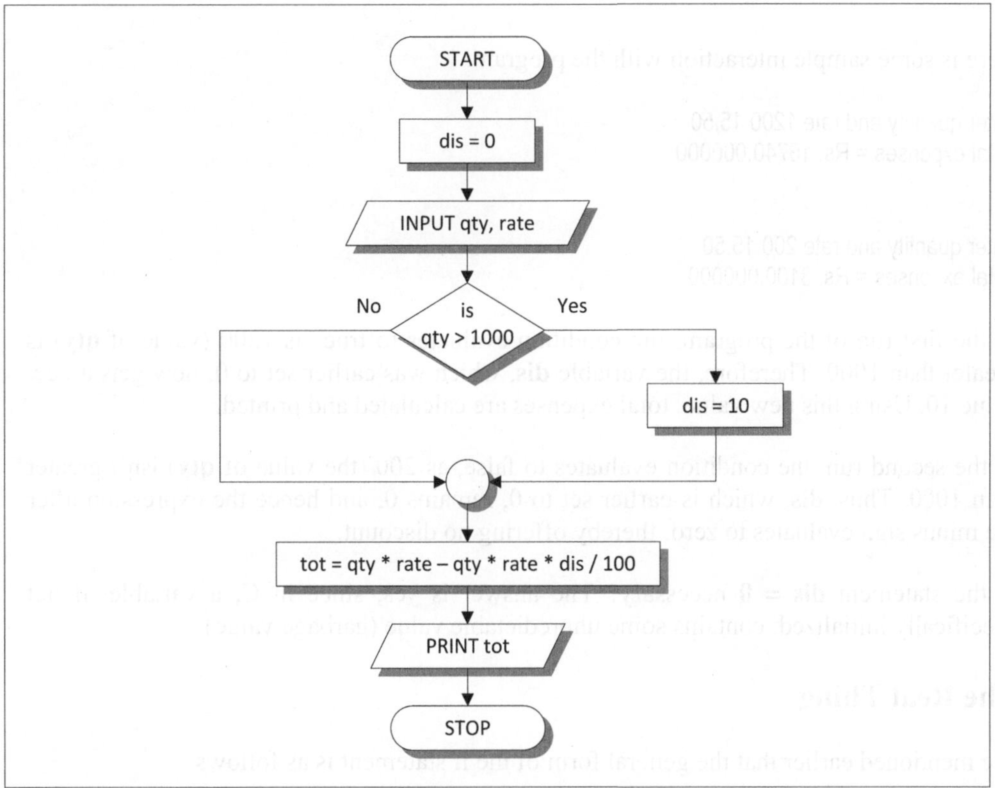

Figure 4.3

```
/* Calculation of total expenses */
# include <stdio.h>
int main( )
{
    int  qty, dis = 0 ;
    float  rate, tot ;
    printf ( "Enter quantity and rate " ) ;
    scanf ( "%d %f", &qty, &rate) ;

    if ( qty > 1000 )
        dis = 10 ;

    tot = ( qty * rate ) - ( qty * rate * dis / 100 ) ;
    printf ( "Total expenses = Rs. %f\n", tot ) ;
    return 0 ;
}
```

Here is some sample interaction with the program.

```
Enter quantity and rate 1200 15.50
Total expenses = Rs. 16740.000000
```

```
Enter quantity and rate 200 15.50
Total expenses = Rs. 3100.000000
```

In the first run of the program, the condition evaluates to true, as 1200 (value of **qty**) is greater than 1000. Therefore, the variable **dis**, which was earlier set to 0, now gets a new value 10. Using this new value, total expenses are calculated and printed.

In the second run, the condition evaluates to false, as 200 (the value of **qty**) isn't greater than 1000. Thus, **dis**, which is earlier set to 0, remains 0, and hence the expression after the minus sign evaluates to zero, thereby offering no discount.

Is the statement **dis = 0** necessary? The answer is yes, since in C, a variable, if not specifically initialized, contains some unpredictable value (garbage value).

The Real Thing

We mentioned earlier that the general form of the if statement is as follows

```
if ( condition )
    statement ;
```

Truly speaking the general form is as follows:

```
if ( expression )
    statement ;
```

Here the expression can be any valid expression including a relational expression. We can even use arithmetic expressions in the **if** statement. For example all the following **if** statements are valid

```
if ( 3 + 2 % 5 )
    printf ( "This works" ) ;

if ( a = 10 )
    printf ( "Even this works" ) ;
```

```
if ( -5 )
    printf ( "Surprisingly even this works" ) ;
```

Note that in C a non-zero value is considered to be true, whereas a 0 is considered to be false. In the first **if**, the expression evaluates to **5** and since **5** is non-zero it is considered to be true. Hence the **printf( )** gets executed.

In the second **if**, 10 gets assigned to **a** so the **if** is now reduced to **if (a)** or **if (10)**. Since 10 is non-zero, it is true hence again **printf( )** goes to work.

In the third **if**, -5 is a non-zero number, hence true. So again **printf( )** goes to work. In place of -5 even if a float like 3.14 were used it would be considered to be true. So the issue is not whether the number is integer or float, or whether it is positive or negative. Issue is whether it is zero or non-zero.

Multiple Statements within *if*

It may so happen that in a program we want more than one statement to be executed if the expression following **if** is satisfied. If such multiple statements are to be executed, then they must be placed within a pair of braces, as illustrated in the following example.

Example 4.2: The current year and the year in which the employee joined the organization are entered through the keyboard. If the number of years for which the employee has served the organization is greater than 3, then a bonus of Rs. 2500/- is given to the employee. If the years of service are not greater than 3, then the program should do nothing.

```
/* Calculation of bonus */
# include <stdio.h>
int main( )
{
    int  bonus, cy, yoj, yos ;

    printf ( "Enter current year and year of joining " ) ;
    scanf ( "%d %d", &cy, &yoj ) ;

    yos = cy - yoj ;

    if ( yos > 3 )
    {
        bonus = 2500 ;
```

```
        printf ( "Bonus = Rs. %d\n", bonus ) ;
    }
    return 0 ;
}
```

Observe that here the two statements to be executed on satisfaction of the condition have been enclosed within a pair of braces. If a pair of braces is not used, then the C compiler assumes that the programmer wants only the immediately next statement after the **if** to be executed on satisfaction of the condition. In other words, we can say that the default scope of the **if** statement is the immediately next statement after it.

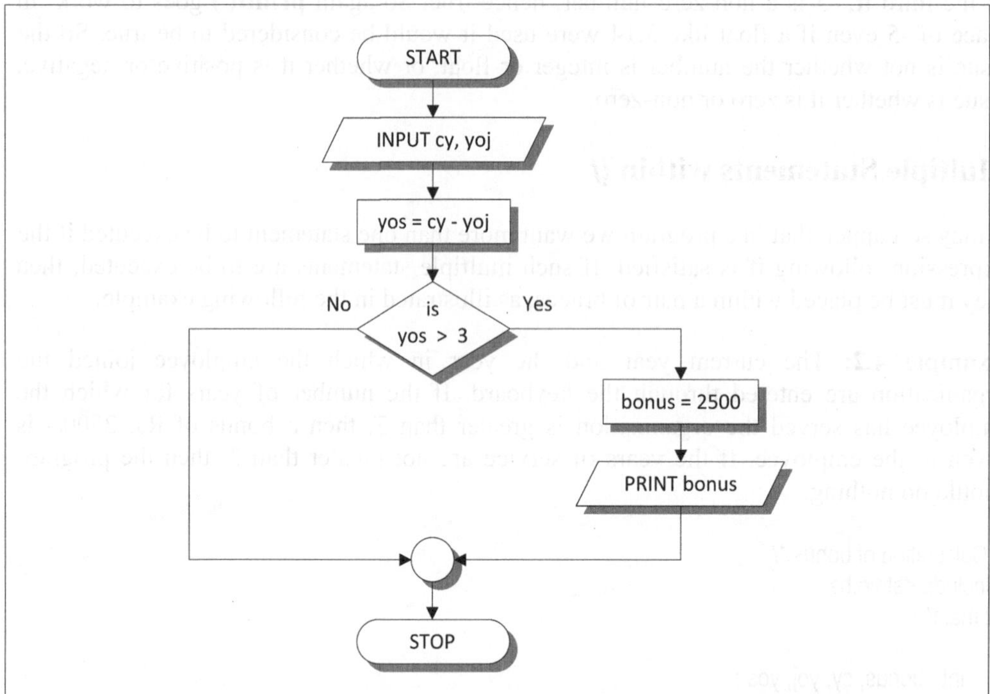

Figure 4.4

The *if-else* Statement

The **if** statement by itself will execute a single statement, or a group of statements, when the expression following **if** evaluates to true. It does nothing when the expression evaluates to false. Can we execute one group of statements if the expression evaluates to true and another group of statements if the expression evaluates to false? Of course! This is what is the purpose of the **else** statement that is demonstrated in the following example:

Example 4.3: In a company an employee is paid as under:

If his basic salary is less than Rs. 1500, then HRA = 10% of basic salary and DA = 90% of basic salary. If his salary is either equal to or above Rs. 1500, then HRA = Rs. 500 and DA = 98% of basic salary. If the employee's salary is input through the keyboard write a program to find his gross salary.

```
/* Calculation of gross salary */
# include <stdio.h>
int main( )
{
    float  bs, gs, da, hra ;

    printf ( "Enter basic salary " ) ;
    scanf ( "%f", &bs ) ;

    if ( bs < 1500 )
    {
        hra = bs * 10 / 100 ;
        da = bs * 90 / 100 ;
    }
    else
    {
        hra = 500 ;
        da = bs * 98 / 100 ;
    }

    gs = bs + hra + da ;
    printf ( "gross salary = Rs. %f\n", gs ) ;
    return 0 ;
}
```

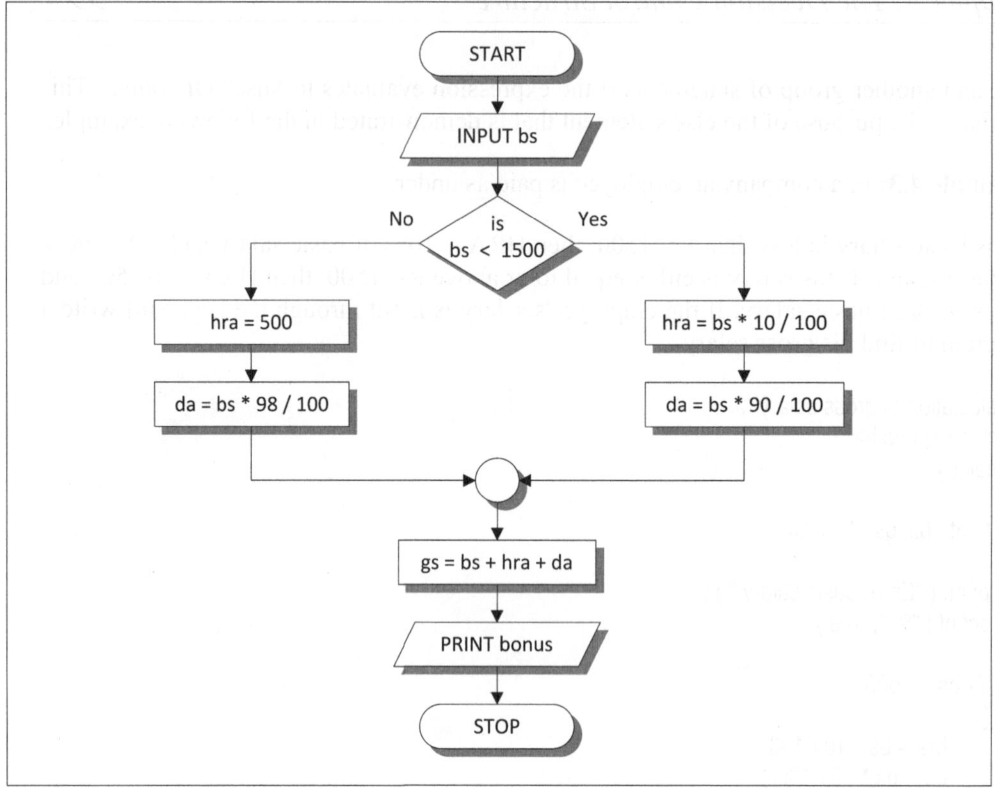

Figure 4.5

A few points worth noting...

(a) The group of statements after the **if** upto and not including the **else** is called an 'if block'. Similarly, the statements after the **else** form the 'else block'.

(b) Notice that the **else** is written exactly below the **if**. The statements in the if block and those in the else block have been indented to the right. This formatting convention is followed throughout the book to enable you to understand the working of the program better.

(c) Had there been only one statement to be executed in the if block and only one statement in the else block we could have dropped the pair of braces.

(d) As with the **if** statement, the default scope of **else** is also the statement immediately after the **else**. To override this default scope, a pair of braces, as shown in the above example, must be used.

Nested *if-elses*

It is perfectly all right if we write an entire **if-else** construct within either the body of the **if** statement or the body of an **else** statement. This is called 'nesting' of **if**s. This is shown in the following program.

```
/* A quick demo of nested if-else */
# include <stdio.h>
int main( )
{
    int  i ;

    printf ( "Enter either 1 or 2 " ) ;
    scanf ( "%d", &i ) ;

    if ( i == 1 )
        printf ( "You would go to heaven !\n" ) ;
    else
    {
        if ( i == 2 )
            printf ( "Hell was created with you in mind\n" ) ;
        else
            printf ( "How about mother earth !\n" ) ;
    }
    return 0 ;
}
```

Note that the second **if-else** construct is nested in the first **else** statement. If the condition in the first **if** statement is false, then the condition in the second **if** statement is checked. If it is false as well, then the final **else** statement is executed.

You can see in the program how each time a **if-else** construct is nested within another **if-else** construct, it is also indented to add clarity to the program. Inculcate this habit of indentation; otherwise, you would end up writing programs which nobody (you included) can understand easily at a later date. Note that whether we indent or do not indent the program, it doesn't alter the flow of execution of instructions in the program.

In the above program, an **if-else** occurs within the **else** block of the first **if** statement. Similarly, in some other program, an **if-else** may occur in the **if** block as well. There is no limit on how deeply the **ifs** and the **elses** can be nested.

Forms of *if*

The **if** statement can take any of the following forms:

(a)
```
if ( condition )
    do this ;
```

(b)
```
if ( condition )
{
    do this ;
    and this ;
}
```

(c)
```
if ( condition )
    do this ;
else
    do this ;
```

(d)
```
if ( condition )
{
    do this ;
    and this ;
}
else
{
    do this ;
    and this ;
}
```

(e)
```
if ( condition )
    do this ;
else
{
    if ( condition )
        do this ;
    else
    {
        do this ;
        and this ;
```

```
        }
    }
```

```
(f)  if ( condition )
     {
         if ( condition )
             do this ;
         else
         {
             do this ;
             and this ;
         }
     }
     else
         do this ;
```

Use of Logical Operators

C allows usage of three logical operators, namely, &&, || and !. These are to be read as 'AND' 'OR' and 'NOT' respectively.

There are several things to note about these logical operators. Most obviously, two of them are composed of double symbols: **||** and **&&**. Don't use the single symbol **|** and **&**. These single symbols also have a meaning. They are bitwise operators, which we would examine in Chapter 14.

The first two operators, **&&** and **||**, allow two or more conditions to be combined in an **if** statement. Let us see how they are used in a program. Consider the following example.

Example 4.4: The marks obtained by a student in 5 different subjects are input through the keyboard. The student gets a division as per the following rules:

Percentage above or equal to 60 - First division
Percentage between 50 and 59 - Second division
Percentage between 40 and 49 - Third division
Percentage less than 40 - Fail

Write a program to calculate the division obtained by the student.

There are two ways in which we can write a program for this example. These methods are given below.

```
/* Method – I */
# include <stdio.h>
int main( )
{
    int  m1, m2, m3, m4, m5, per ;

    printf ( "Enter marks in five subjects " ) ;
    scanf ( "%d %d %d %d %d", &m1, &m2, &m3, &m4, &m5 ) ;
    per = ( m1 + m2 + m3 + m4 + m5 ) / 500 * 100 ;

    if ( per >= 60 )
        printf ( "First division\n" ) ;
    else
    {
        if ( per >= 50 )
            printf ( "Second division\n" ) ;
        else
        {
            if ( per >= 40 )
                printf ( "Third division\n" ) ;
            else
                printf ( "Fail\n" ) ;
        }
    }
    return 0 ;
}
```

This is a straight forward program. Observe that the program uses nested **if-elses**. This leads to three disadvantages:

(a) As the number of conditions go on increasing the level of indentation also goes on increasing. As a result, the whole program creeps to the right.
(b) Care needs to be exercised to match the corresponding **if**s and **else**s.
(c) Care needs to be exercised to match the corresponding pair of braces.

All these three problems can be eliminated by usage of 'Logical operators'. The following program illustrates this.

```
/* Method – II */
# include <stdio.h>
int main( )
{
    int  m1, m2, m3, m4, m5, per ;
```

```
    printf ( "Enter marks in five subjects " ) ;
    scanf ( "%d %d %d %d %d", &m1, &m2, &m3, &m4, &m5 ) ;
    per = ( m1 + m2 + m3 + m4 + m5 ) / 500 * 100 ;

    if ( per >= 60 )
        printf ( "First division\n" ) ;

    if ( ( per >= 50 ) && ( per < 60 ) )
        printf ( "Second division\n" ) ;

    if ( ( per >= 40 ) && ( per < 50 ) )
        printf ( "Third division\n" ) ;

    if ( per < 40 )
        printf ( "Fail\n" ) ;

    return 0 ;
}
```

As can be seen from the second **if** statement, the **&&** operator is used to combine two conditions. 'Second division' gets printed if both the conditions evaluate to true. If one of the conditions evaluate to false then the whole thing is treated as false.

Two distinct advantages can be cited in favour of this program:

(a) The matching (or do I say mismatching) of the **if**s with their corresponding **else**s gets avoided, since there are no **else**s in this program.

(b) In spite of using several conditions, the program doesn't creep to the right. In the previous program the statements went on creeping to the right. This effect becomes more pronounced as the number of conditions goes on increasing. This would make the task of matching the **if**s with their corresponding **else**s and matching of opening and closing braces much more difficult.

There is a negative side to the program too. Even if the first condition turns out to be true, still all other conditions are checked. This will increase the time of execution of the program. This can be avoided using the **else if** clause discussed in the next section.

The *else if* Clause

There is one more way in which we can write program for Example 4.4. This involves usage of **else if** blocks as shown below:

```
/* else if ladder demo */
# include <stdio.h>
int main( )
{
    int  m1, m2, m3, m4, m5, per ;

    per = ( m1+ m2 + m3 + m4+ m5 ) /  500 * 100 ;

    if ( per >= 60 )
        printf ( "First division\n" ) ;
    else if ( per >= 50 )
        printf ( "Second division\n" ) ;
    else if ( per >= 40 )
        printf ( "Third division\n" ) ;
    else
        printf ( "fail\n" ) ;

    return 0 ;
}
```

You can note that this program reduces the indentation of the statements. In this case, every **else** is associated with its previous **if**. The last **else** goes to work only if all the conditions fail. Also, if the first condition is satisfied, other conditions are not checked. Even in **else if** ladder, the last **else** is optional.

Note that the **else if** clause is nothing different. It is just a way of rearranging the **else** with the **if** that follows it. This would be evident if you look at the following code:

```
if ( i == 2 )
    printf (  "With you..." ) ;
else
{
    if ( j == 2 )
        printf ( "...All the time" ) ;
}
```

```
if ( i == 2 )
    printf (  "With you..." ) ;
else if ( j == 2 )
    printf ( "...All the time " ) ;
```

Another place where logical operators are useful is when we want to write programs for complicated logics that ultimately boil down to only two answers. For example, consider the following example:

Example 4.5: A company insures its drivers in the following cases:

- If the driver is married.
- If the driver is unmarried, male & above 30 years of age.
- If the driver is unmarried, female & above 25 years of age.

In all other cases, the driver is not insured. If the marital status, sex and age of the driver are the inputs, write a program to determine whether the driver is to be insured or not.

Here after checking a complicated set of instructions the final output of the program would be one of the two—Either the driver should be ensured or the driver should not be ensured. As mentioned above, since these are the only two outcomes this problem can be solved using logical operators. But before we do that let us write a program that does not make use of logical operators.

```
/* Insurance of driver - without using logical operators */
# include <stdio.h>
int main( )
{
    char  sex, ms ;
    int  age ;

    printf ( "Enter age, sex, marital status " ) ;
    scanf ( "%d %c %c", &age, &sex, &ms ) ;

    if ( ms == 'M' )
        printf ( "Driver is insured\n" ) ;
    else
    {
        if ( sex == 'M' )
        {
            if ( age > 30 )
                printf ( "Driver is insured\n" ) ;
            else
                printf ( "Driver is not insured\n" ) ;
        }
        else
        {
            if ( age > 25 )
                printf ( "Driver is insured\n" ) ;
```

```
        else
            printf ( "Driver is not insured\n" ) ;
        }
    }
    return 0 ;
}
```

From the program it is evident that we are required to match several **if**s and **else**s and several pairs of braces. In a more real-life situation there would be more conditions to check leading to the program creeping to the right. Let us now see how to avoid these problems by using logical operators.

As mentioned above, in this example, we expect the answer to be either 'Driver is insured' or 'Driver is not insured'. If we list down all those cases in which the driver is insured, then they would be:

(a) Driver is married.
(b) Driver is an unmarried male above 30 years of age.
(c) Driver is an unmarried female above 25 years of age.

Since all these cases lead to the driver being insured, they can be combined together using **&&** and **||** as shown in the program below:

```
/* Insurance of driver - using logical operators */
# include <stdio.h>
int main( )
{
    char  sex, ms ;
    int  age ;

    printf ( "Enter age, sex, marital status " ) ;
    scanf ( "%d %c %c" &age, &sex, &ms ) ;

    if ( ( ms == 'M') || ( ms == 'U' && sex == 'M' && age > 30 ) ||
                ( ms == 'U' && sex == 'F' && age > 25 ) )
        printf ( "Driver is insured\n" ) ;
    else
        printf ( "Driver is not insured\n" ) ;
    return 0 ;
}
```

In this program, it is important to note that:

- The driver will be insured only if one of the conditions enclosed in parentheses evaluates to true.

- For the second pair of parentheses to evaluate to true, each condition in the parentheses separated by **&&** must evaluate to true.

- Even if one of the conditions in the second parentheses evaluates to false, then the whole of the second parentheses evaluates to false.

- The last two of the above arguments apply to third pair of parentheses as well.

Thus, we can conclude that the **&&** and **||** are useful in the following programming situations:

(a) When it is to be tested whether a value falls within a particular range or not.
(b) When after testing several conditions, the outcome is only one of the two answers (This problem is often called yes/no problem).

There can be one more situation other than checking ranges or yes/no problem, where you might find logical operators useful. The following program demonstrates it.

Example 4.6: Write a program to calculate the salary as per the following table:

Gender	Years of Service	Qualifications	Salary
Male	>= 10	Post-Graduate	15000
	>= 10	Graduate	10000
	< 10	Post-Graduate	10000
	< 10	Graduate	7000
Female	>= 10	Post-Graduate	12000
	>= 10	Graduate	9000
	< 10	Post-Graduate	10000
	< 10	Graduate	6000

Figure 4.6

```
# include <stdio.h>
int main( )
{
    char  g ;
    int  yos, qual, sal = 0 ;

    printf ( "Enter Gender, Years of Service and
              Qualifications ( 0 = G, 1 = PG ):" ) ;
    scanf ( "%c%d%d", &g, &yos, &qual ) ;

    if ( g == 'm' && yos >= 10 && qual == 1 )
        sal = 15000 ;
    else if ( ( g == 'm' && yos >= 10 && qual == 0 ) ||
        ( g == 'm' && yos < 10 && qual == 1 ) )
        sal = 10000 ;
    else if ( g == 'm' && yos < 10 && qual == 0 )
        sal = 7000 ;
    else if ( g == 'f' && yos >= 10 && qual == 1 )
        sal = 12000 ;
    else if ( g == 'f' && yos >= 10 && qual == 0 )
        sal = 9000 ;
    else if ( g == 'f' && yos < 10 && qual == 1 )
        sal = 10000 ;
    else if ( g == 'f' && yos < 10 && qual == 0 )
        sal = 6000 ;

    printf ( "\nSalary of Employee = %d\n", sal ) ;
    return 0 ;
}
```

The ! Operator

So far we have used only the logical operators **&&** and **||**. The third logical operator is the NOT operator, written as **!**. This operator reverses the result of the expression it operates on. For example, if the expression evaluates to a non-zero value, then applying **!** operator to it results into a 0. Vice versa, if the expression evaluates to zero then on applying **!** operator to it makes it 1, a non-zero value. The final result (after applying **!**) 0 or 1 is considered to be false or true respectively. Here is an example of the NOT operator applied to a relational expression.

```
! ( y < 10 )
```

This means "not **y** less than 10". In other words, if **y** is less than 10, the expression will be false, since **(y < 10)** is true. We can express the same condition as **(y >= 10)**.

The NOT operator is often used to reverse the logical value of a single variable, as in the expression

```
if ( ! flag )
```

This is another way of saying

```
if ( flag == 0 )
```

Does the NOT operator sound confusing? Avoid it if you want, as the same thing can be achieved without using the NOT operator.

Hierarchy of Operators Revisited

Since we have now added the logical operators to the list of operators we know, it is time to review these operators and their priorities. Figure 4.7 summarizes the operators we have seen so far. The higher the position of an operator is in the table, higher is its priority. (A full-fledged precedence table of operators is given in Appendix A.)

Operators	**Type**
!	Logical NOT
* / %	Arithmetic and modulus
+ -	Arithmetic
< > <= >=	Relational
== !=	Relational
&&	Logical AND
||	Logical OR
=	Assignment

Figure 4.7

A Word of Caution

What will be the output of the following program:

```
# include <stdio.h>
int main( )
{
    int i ;
    printf ( "Enter value of i " ) ;
    scanf ( "%d", &i ) ;
    if ( i = 5 )
        printf ( "You entered 5\n" ) ;
    else
        printf ( "You entered something other than 5\n" ) ;

    return 0 ;
}
```

And here is the output of two runs of this program...

```
Enter value of i 200
You entered 5
Enter value of i 9999
You entered 5
```

Surprising? You have entered 200 and 9999, and still you find in either case the output is 'You entered 5'. This is because we have written the condition wrongly. We have used the assignment operator = instead of the relational operator ==. As a result, the condition gets reduced to **if (5)**, irrespective of what you supply as the value of **i**. And remember that in C, 'truth' is always non-zero, whereas, 'falsity' is always zero. Therefore, **if (5)** always evaluates to true and hence the result.

Another common mistake while using the **if** statement is to write a semicolon (;) after the condition, as shown below:

```
# include <stdio.h>
int main( )
{
    int i ;

    printf ( "Enter value of i " ) ;
    scanf ( "%d", &i ) ;

    if ( i == 5 ) ;
        printf ( "You entered 5\n" ) ;
    return 0 ;
```

```
}
```

The ; makes the compiler to interpret the statement as if you have written it in following manner:

```
if ( i == 5 )
    ;
printf ( "You entered 5\n" ) ;
```

Here, if the condition evaluates to true, the ; (null statement, which does nothing on execution) gets executed, following which the **printf( )** gets executed. If the condition fails, then straightaway the **printf( )** gets executed. Thus, irrespective of whether the condition evaluates to true or false, the **printf( )** is bound to get executed. Remember that the compiler would not point out this as an error, since as far as the syntax is concerned, nothing has gone wrong, but the logic has certainly gone awry. Moral is, beware of such pitfalls.

The following figure summarizes the working of all the three logical operators.

Operands		Results			
x	y	!x	!y	x && y	x || y
0	0	1	1	0	0
0	non-zero	1	0	0	1
non-zero	0	0	1	0	1
non-zero	non-zero	0	0	1	1

Figure 4.8

The Conditional Operators

The conditional operators **?** and **:** are sometimes called ternary operators since they take three arguments. In fact, they form a kind of foreshortened if-then-else. Their general form is,

```
expression 1 ? expression 2 : expression 3
```

What this expression says is: "if **expression 1** is true (that is, if its value is non-zero), then the value returned will be **expression 2**, otherwise the value returned will be **expression 3**". Let us understand this with the help of a few examples:

(a)
```
int x, y ;
scanf ( "%d", &x ) ;
y = ( x > 5 ? 3 : 4 ) ;
```

This statement will store 3 in **y** if **x** is greater than 5, otherwise it will store 4 in y.

The equivalent **if** statement will be,

```
if ( x > 5 )
    y = 3 ;
else
    y = 4 ;
```

(b)
```
char a ;
int y ;
scanf ( "%c", &a ) ;
y = ( a >= 65 && a <= 90 ? 1 : 0 ) ;
```

Here 1 would be assigned to **y** if **a >=65 && a <=90** evaluates to true, otherwise 0 would be assigned.

The following points may be noted about the conditional operators:

(a) It's not necessary that the conditional operators should be used only in arithmetic statements. This is illustrated in the following examples:

Ex.:
```
int i ;
scanf ( "%d", &i ) ;
( i == 1 ? printf ( "Amit" ) : printf ( "All and sundry" ) ) ;
```

Ex.:
```
char a = 'z' ;
printf ( "%c" , ( a >= 'a' ? a : '!' ) ) ;
```

(b) The conditional operators can be nested as shown below.

```
int big, a, b, c ;
big = ( a > b ? ( a > c ? 3: 4 ) : ( b > c ? 6: 8 ) ) ;
```

(c) Check out the following conditional expression:

```
a > b ? g = a : g = b ;
```

This will give you an error 'Lvalue Required'. The error can be overcome by enclosing the statement in the **:** part within a pair of parenthesis. This is shown below:

```
a > b ? g = a : ( g = b ) ;
```

In absence of parentheses, the compiler believes that **b** is being assigned to the result of the expression to the left of second **=**. Hence it reports an error.

The limitation of the conditional operators is that after the **?** or after the **:** , only one C statement can occur. In practice, rarely is this the requirement. Therefore, in serious C programming, conditional operators aren't as frequently used as the **if-else**.

Summary

(a) There are three ways for taking decisions in a program. First way is to use the **if-else** statement, second way is to use the conditional operators and third way is to use the **switch** statement.
(b) The default scope of the **if** statement is only the next statement. So, to execute more than one statement they must be written in a pair of braces.
(c) An **if** block need not always be associated with an **else** block. However, an **else** block is always associated with an **if** statement.
(d) If the outcome of an **if-else** ladder is only one of two answers then the ladder should be replaced either with an **else-if** clause or by logical operators.
(e) **&&** and **||** are binary operators, whereas, **!** is a unary operator.
(f) In C every test expression is evaluated in terms of zero and non-zero values. A zero value is considered to be false and a non-zero value is considered to be true.
(g) Assignment statements used with conditional operators must be enclosed within a pair of parenthesis.

Exercise

if, if-else, Nested *if-elses*

[A] What will be the output of the following programs:

(a)
```
# include <stdio.h>
int main( )
{
```

```
    int  a = 300, b, c ;
    if ( a >= 400 )
        b = 300 ;
        c = 200 ;
            printf ( "%d %d\n", b, c ) ;
    return 0 ;
}
```

(b)
```
# include <stdio.h>
int main( )
{
    int  a = 500, b, c ;
    if ( a >= 400 )
        b = 300 ;
        c = 200 ;
    printf ( "%d %d\n", b, c ) ;
    return 0 ;
}
```

(c)
```
# include <stdio.h>
int main( )
{
    int  x = 10, y = 20 ;
    if ( x == y ) ;
        printf ( "%d %d\n", x, y ) ;
    return 0 ;
}
```

(d)
```
# include <stdio.h>
int main( )
{
    int  x = 3, y = 5 ;
    if ( x == 3 )
        printf ( "%d\n", x ) ;
    else ;
        printf ( "\n%d\n", y ) ;
    return 0 ;
}
```

(e)
```
# include <stdio.h>
int main( )
{
    int  x = 3 ;
    float  y = 3.0 ;
```

```
    if ( x == y )
        printf ( "x and y are equal\n" ) ;
    else
        printf ( "x and y are not equal\n" ) ;
    return 0 ;
}
```

(f)
```
# include <stdio.h>
int main( )
{
    int  x = 3, y, z ;
    y = x = 10 ;
    z = x < 10 ;
    printf ( "x = %d y = %d z = %d\n", x, y, z ) ;
    return 0 ;
}
```

(g)
```
# include <stdio.h>
int main( )
{
    int  k = 35 ;
    printf ( "%d %d %d\n", k == 35, k = 50, k > 40 ) ;
    return 0 ;
}
```

(h)
```
# include <stdio.h>
int main( )
{
    int i = 65 ;
    char j = 'A' ;
    if ( i == j )
        printf ( "C is WOW\n" ) ;
    else
        printf ( "C is a headache\n" ) ;
    return 0 ;
}
```

(i)
```
# include <stdio.h>
int main( )
{
    int  a = 5, b, c ;
    b = a = 15 ;
    c = a < 15 ;
```

```
        printf ( "a = %d b = %d c = %d\n", a, b, c ) ;
        return 0 ;
    }
```

(j)
```
    # include <stdio.h>
    int main( )
    {
        int  x = 15 ;
        printf ( "%d %d %d\n", x != 15, x = 20, x < 30 ) ;
        return 0 ;
    }
```

(k)
```
    # include <stdio.h>
    int main( )
    {
        int i = 9, j = 0 ;
        printf ( "%d %d %d %d %d\n", i < 99, i > 99, i = 999, i == 0, i = 0 ) ;
        return 0 ;
    }
```

(l)
```
    # include <stdio.h>
    int main( )
    {
        int c = 32768 ;
        if ( c == 32768 )
            printf ( "Common mistakes Beginners make\n" ) ;
        else
            if ( c == -32768 )
                printf ( "Common Sense is Very Uncommon\n" ) ;
            else
                printf ( "Common starts with C\n" ) ;
        return 0 ;
    }
```

(m)
```
    # include <stdio.h>
    int main( )
    {
        int x, y, z ;
        x = y = z = 0 ;
        x = ++x + x++ + x ;
        y = y++ + ++x + y ;
        z = z * 90 == z * 9 ;
        printf ( "x = %d y = %d z = %d\n", y, z, x ) ;
```

```
    return 0 ;
}
```

(n)
```
# include <stdio.h>
int main( )
{
    int count = count == count ;
    printf ( "%d\n", count ) ;
    return 0 ;
}
```

(o)
```
# include <stdio.h>
int main( )
{
    int v = 3 ;
    v = ++v * ++v / ++v ;
    printf ( "%d\n", v-- ) ;
    return 0 ;
}
```

(p)
```
# include <stdio.h>
int main( )
{
    int a = 500, b, c = 10 ;
    if ( ! a >= 400 )
        b = 300 ;
        c = 200 ;
        printf ( "%d %d\n", b, c ) ;
    return 0 ;
}
```

(q)
```
# include <stdio.h>
int main( )
{
    int x = 10, y = 100 % 90 ;
    if ( x != y ) ;
        printf ( "%d %d\n", x, y ) ;
    return 0 ;
}
```

[B] Point out the errors, if any, in the following programs:

(a)
```
# include <stdio.h>
```

```
    int main( )
    {
        float  a = 12.25, b = 12.52 ;
        if ( a = b )
            printf ( "\na and b are equal" ) ;
        return 0 ;
    }
```

(b)
```
    # include <stdio.h>
    int main( )
    {
        int  j = 10, k = 12 ;
        if ( k >= j )
        {
            {
                k = j ;
                j = k ;
            }
        }
        return 0 ;
    }
```

(c)
```
    # include <stdio.h>
    int main( )
    {
        if ( 'X' < 'x' )
            printf ( "ascii value of X is smaller than that of x\n" ) ;
    }
```

(d)
```
    # include <stdio.h>
    int main( )
    {
        int  x = 10 ;
        if ( x >= 2 ) then
            printf ( "%d\n", x ) ;
        return 0 ;
    }
```

(e)
```
    # include <stdio.h>
    int main( )
    {
        int  x = 10, y = 15 ;
        if ( x % 2 = y % 3 )
```

```
        printf ( "Carpathians\n" ) ;
}
```

(f)
```
# include <stdio.h>
int main( )
{
    int x = 30 , y = 40 ;
    if ( x == y )
        printf ( "x is equal to y\n" ) ;
    elseif ( x > y )
        printf ( "x is greater than y\n" ) ;
    elseif ( x < y )
        printf ( "x is less than y\n" ) ;
    return 0 ;
}
```

(g)
```
# include <stdio.h>
int main( )
{
    int a, b ;
    scanf ( "%d %d", a, b ) ;
    if ( a > b ) ;
        printf ( "This is a game\n" ) ;
    else
            printf ( "You have to play it\n" ) ;
    return 0 ;
}
```

[C] Attempt the following:

(a) If cost price and selling price of an item is input through the keyboard, write a program to determine whether the seller has made profit or incurred loss. Also determine how much profit he made or loss he incurred.

(b) Any integer is input through the keyboard. Write a program to find out whether it is an odd number or even number.

(c) Any year is input through the keyboard. Write a program to determine whether the year is a leap year or not.
(Hint: Use the % (modulus) operator)

(d) According to the Gregorian calendar, it was Monday on the date 01/01/01. If any year is input through the keyboard write a program to find out what is the day on 1st January of this year.

(e) A five-digit number is entered through the keyboard. Write a program to obtain the reversed number and to determine whether the original and reversed numbers are equal or not.

(f) If the ages of Ram, Shyam and Ajay are input through the keyboard, write a program to determine the youngest of the three.

(g) Write a program to check whether a triangle is valid or not, when the three angles of the triangle are entered through the keyboard. A triangle is valid if the sum of all the three angles is equal to 180 degrees.

(h) Find the absolute value of a number entered through the keyboard.

(i) Given the length and breadth of a rectangle, write a program to find whether the area of the rectangle is greater than its perimeter. For example, the area of the rectangle with length = 5 and breadth = 4 is greater than its perimeter.

(j) Given three points **(x1, y1)**, **(x2, y2)** and **(x3, y3)**, write a program to check if all the three points fall on one straight line.

(k) Given the coordinates **(x, y)** of a center of a circle and it's radius, write a program which will determine whether a point lies inside the circle, on the circle or outside the circle.

(Hint: Use **sqrt( )** and **pow( )** functions)

(l) Given a point **(x, y)**, write a program to find out if it lies on the x-axis, y-axis or on the origin, viz. (0, 0).

Logical Operators

[D] If a = 10, b = 12, c = 0, find the values of the expressions in the following table:

Expression	Value
a != 6 && b > 5 a == 9 || b < 3 ! (a < 10) ! (a > 5 && c) 5 && c != 8 || !c	1

[E] What will be the output of the following programs:

(a)
```
# include <stdio.h>
int main( )
{
    int  i = 4, z = 12 ;
    if ( i = 5 || z > 50 )
        printf ( "Dean of students affairs\n" ) ;
    else
        printf ( "Dosa\n" ) ;
    return 0 ;
}
```

(b)
```
# include <stdio.h>
int main( )
{
    int  i = 4, z = 12 ;
    if ( i = 5 && z > 5 )
        printf ( "Let us C\n" ) ;
    else
        printf ( "Wish C was free !\n" ) ;
    return 0 ;
}
```

(c)
```
#include <stdio.h>
int main( )
{
    int  i = 4, j = -1, k = 0, w, x, y, z ;
    w = i || j || k ;
    x = i && j && k ;
```

```
    y = i || j && k ;
    z = i && j || k ;
    printf ( "w = %d x = %d y = %d z = %d\n", w, x, y, z ) ;
    return 0 ;
}
```

(d)
```
# include <stdio.h>
int main( )
{
    int  i = 4, j = -1, k = 0, y, z ;
    y = i + 5 && j + 1 || k + 2 ;
    z = i + 5 || j + 1 && k + 2 ;
    printf ( "y = %d z = %d\n", y, z ) ;
    return 0 ;
}
```

(e)
```
# include <stdio.h>
int main( )
{
    int  i = -3, j = 3 ;
    if ( !i + !j * 1 )
        printf ( "Massaro\n" ) ;
    else
        printf ( "Bennarivo\n" ) ;
    return 0 ;
}
```

(f)
```
# include <stdio.h>
int main( )
{
    int  a = 40 ;
    if ( a > 40 && a < 45 )
        printf ( "a is greater than 40 and less than 45\n" ) ;
    else
        printf ( "%d\n", a ) ;
    return 0 ;
}
```

(g)
```
# include <stdio.h>
int main( )
{
    int  p = 8, q = 20 ;
    if ( p == 5 && q > 5 )
```

```
        printf ( "Why not C\n" ) ;
    else
        printf ( "Definitely C !\n" ) ;
    return 0 ;
}
```

(h)
```
# include <stdio.h>
int main( )
{
    int i = -1, j = 1, k , l ;
    k = i && j ;
    l = i || j ;
    printf ( "%d %d\n", l, j ) ;
    return 0 ;
}
```

(i)
```
# include <stdio.h>
int main( )
{
    int x = 20 , y = 40 , z = 45 ;
    if ( x > y && x > z )
        printf ( "x is big\n" ) ;
    else if ( y > x && y > z )
        printf ( "y is big\n" ) ;
    else if ( z > x && z > y )
        printf ( "z is big\n" ) ;
    return 0 ;
}
```

(j)
```
# include <stdio.h>
int main( )
{
    int i = -1, j = 1, k, l ;
    k = !i && j ;
    l = !i  ||  j ;
    printf ( "%d %d\n", i, j ) ;
    return 0 ;
}
```

(k)
```
# include <stdio.h>
int main( )
{
    int  j = 4, k ;
```

```
    k = !5 && j ;
    printf ( "k = %d\n", k ) ;
    return 0 ;
}
```

(l)
```
# include <stdio.h>
int main( )
{
    if ( 1 != 1 || ! ( 0 || 1 ) && ( 1 && -1 ) )
        printf ( "If you have nothing to do\n" ) ;
    else
        printf ( "don't do it here\n" ) ;
    return 0 ;
}
```

(m)
```
# include <stdio.h>
int main( )
{
    int s = 20, y = 100 ;
    printf ( "Is salary > 1000 %d\n", s > 10 && !y ) ;
    return 0 ;
}
```

(n)
```
# include <stdio.h>
int main( )
{
    int x = 10, y = 20 ;
    x = !x ;
    y = !x && !y ;
    printf ( "x = %d y = %d\n", x, y ) ;
    return 0 ;
}
```

(o)
```
# include <stdio.h>
int main( )
{
    int x = -1, y = -2, z = -3, a, b, c, d ;
    a = ++x || ++y && ++z ;
    b = x++ || y++ && z++ ;
    c = ++x && ++y || ++z ;
    d = x++ && y++ || z++ ;
    printf ( "%d %d %d %d\n", a, b, c, d ) ;
    return 0 ;
```

```
}
```

[F] Point out the errors, if any, in the following programs:

(a)
```
/* This program
/* is an example of
/* using Logical operators */
# include <stdio.h>
int main( )
{
    int  i = 2, j = 5 ;
    if ( i == 2 && j == 5 )
        printf ( "Satisfied at last\n" ) ;
    return 0 ;
}
```

(b)
```
# include <stdio.h>
int main( )
{
    int  code, flag ;
    if ( code == 1 & flag == 0 )
        printf ( "The eagle has landed\n" ) ;
    return 0 ;
}
```

(c)
```
# include <stdio.h>
int main( )
{
    char  spy = 'a', password = 'z' ;
    if ( spy == 'a' or password == 'z' )
        printf ( "All the birds are safe in the nest\n" ) ;
    return 0 ;
}
```

(d)
```
# include <stdio.h>
int main( )
{
    int  i = 10, j = 20 ;
    if ( i = 5 ) && if ( j = 10 )
        printf ( "Have a nice day\n" ) ;
    return 0 ;
}
```

(e)
```
# include <stdio.h>
int main( )
{
    int  x = 10 , y = 20;
    if ( x >= 2 and y <=50 )
        printf ( "%d\n", x ) ;
}
```

(f)
```
# include <stdio.h>
int main( )
{
    int  a, b ;
    if ( a == 1 & b == 0 )
        printf ( "God is Great\n" ) ;
    return 0 ;
}
```

(g)
```
# include <stdio.h>
int main( )
{
    int x = 2;
    if ( x == 2 && x != 0 ) ;
    {
        printf ( "Hi\n" ) ;
        printf ( "Hello\n" ) ;
    }
    else
        printf ( "Bye\n" ) ;
    return 0 ;
}
```

(h)
```
# include <stdio.h>
int main( )
{
    int  i = 10, j = 10 ;
    if ( i && j == 10)
        printf ( "Have a nice day\n" ) ;
    return 0 ;
}
```

[G] Attempt the following:

(a) Any year is entered through the keyboard, write a program to determine whether the year is leap or not. Use the logical operators **&&** and **||**.

(b) Any character is entered through the keyboard, write a program to determine whether the character entered is a capital letter, a small case letter, a digit or a special symbol.

The following table shows the range of ASCII values for various characters.

Characters	**ASCII Values**
A – Z	65 – 90
a – z	97 – 122
0 – 9	48 – 57
special symbols	0 - 47, 58 - 64, 91 - 96, 123 - 127

(c) A certain grade of steel is graded according to the following conditions:

(i) Hardness must be greater than 50
(ii) Carbon content must be less than 0.7
(iii) Tensile strength must be greater than 5600

The grades are as follows:

Grade is 10 if all three conditions are met
Grade is 9 if conditions (i) and (ii) are met
Grade is 8 if conditions (ii) and (iii) are met
Grade is 7 if conditions (i) and (iii) are met
Grade is 6 if only one condition is met
Grade is 5 if none of the conditions are met

Write a program, which will require the user to give values of hardness, carbon content and tensile strength of the steel under consideration and output the grade of the steel.

(d) A library charges a fine for every book returned late. For first 5 days the fine is 50 paise, for 6-10 days fine is one rupee and above 10 days fine is 5 rupees. If you return the book after 30 days your membership will be cancelled. Write a program to accept the number of days the member is late to return the book and display the fine or the appropriate message.

(e) If the three sides of a triangle are entered through the keyboard, write a program to check whether the triangle is valid or not. The triangle is valid if the sum of two sides is greater than the largest of the three sides.

(f) If the three sides of a triangle are entered through the keyboard, write a program to check whether the triangle is isosceles, equilateral, scalene or right angled triangle.

(g) In a company, worker efficiency is determined on the basis of the time required for a worker to complete a particular job. If the time taken by the worker is between 2 – 3 hours, then the worker is said to be highly efficient. If the time required by the worker is between 3 – 4 hours, then the worker is ordered to improve speed. If the time taken is between 4 – 5 hours, the worker is given training to improve his speed, and if the time taken by the worker is more than 5 hours, then the worker has to leave the company. If the time taken by the worker is input through the keyboard, write a program to find the efficiency of the worker.

(h) The policy followed by a company to process customer orders is given by the following rules:

(a) If a customer order quantity is less than or equal to that in stock and his credit is OK, supply his requirement.

(a) If his credit is not OK do not supply. Send him an intimation.

(b) If his credit is Ok but the item in stock is less than his order, supply what is in stock. Intimate to him the date on which the balance will be shipped.

Write a C program to implement the company policy.

(i) Write a program to implement the following game. You select a number between 0 to 100. The computer should be able to guess the number chosen by you in seven tries or less.

1. The computer will show a number on the screen.

2. You tell it if the number is higher, lower or equal to the number that you have guessed.

3. If equal, the number is found hence the game ends. Otherwise the computer should repeat steps 1 and 2 till the number is not found.

(j) Any three numbers are entered through the keyboard. Write a program to determine whether they form a Pythagorean triplet or not. For example, 3, 4 and 5 form a Pythagorean triplet.

Conditional operators

[H] What will be the output of the following programs:

(a)
```
# include <stdio.h>
int main( )
{
    int  i = -4, j, num ;
    j = ( num < 0 ? 0 : num * num ) ;
    printf ( "%d\n", j ) ;
    return 0 ;
}
```

(b)
```
# include <stdio.h>
int main( )
{
    int  k, num = 30 ;
    k = ( num > 5 ? ( num <= 10 ? 100 : 200 ) : 500 ) ;
    printf ( "%d\n", num ) ;
    return 0 ;
}
```

(c)
```
# include <stdio.h>
int main( )
{
    int  j = 4 ;
    ( !j != 1 ? printf ( "Welcome\n" ) : printf ( "Good Bye\n") ) ;
    return 0 ;
}
```

(d)
```
# include <stdio.h>
int main( )
{
    int a, c = 0, d = 5, e = 10 ;
    a = c > 1 ? d > 1 || e > 1 ? 100 : 200 : 300 ;
    printf ( "%d\n", a ) ;
    return 0 ;
```

```
}
```

[I] Point out the errors, if any, in the following programs:

(a)
```
# include <stdio.h>
int main( )
{
    int  tag = 0, code = 1 ;
    if ( tag == 0 )
        ( code > 1 ? printf ( "Hello\n" ) ? printf ( "Hi\n" ) ) ;
    else
        printf ( "Hello Hi !!\n" ) ;
    return 0 ;
}
```

(b)
```
# include <stdio.h>
int main( )
{
    int  ji = 65 ;
    printf ( "ji >= 65 ? %d : %c\n", ji ) ;
    return 0 ;
}
```

(c)
```
# include <stdio.h>
int main( )
{
    int  i = 10, j ;
    i >= 5 ? ( j = 10 ) : ( j = 15 ) ;
    printf ( "%d %d\n", i, j ) ;
    return 0 ;
}
```

(d)
```
# include <stdio.h>
int main( )
{
    int a = 5 , b = 6 ;
    ( a == b ? printf ( "%d\n",a ) ) ;
    return 0 ;
}
```

(e)
```
# include <stdio.h>
int main( )
```

```
{
    int n = 9 ;
    ( n == 9 ? printf ( "You're correct\n" ) ; : printf ( "You"re wrong\n" ) ; );
    return 0 ;
}
```

(f)
```
# include <stdio.h>
int main( )
{
    int  kk = 65 ,ll ;
    ll = ( kk == 65 : printf ( "kk == 65\n" ) : printf ( "kk != 65\n" ) ) ;
    printf ( "%d\n", ll ) ;
    return 0 ;
}
```

(g)
```
# include <stdio.h>
int main( )
{
    int  x = 10, y = 20 ;
    x == 20 && y != 10 ? printf ( "True\n" ) : printf ( "False\n" ) ;
    return 0 ;
}
```

[J] Rewrite the following programs using conditional operators.

(a)
```
# include <stdio.h>
int main( )
{
    int  x, min, max ;
    scanf ( "%d %d", &max, &x ) ;
    if ( x > max )
        max = x ;
    else
        min = x ;
    return 0 ;
}
```

(b)
```
# include <stdio.h>
int main( )
{
    int  code ;
    scanf ( "%d", &code ) ;
    if ( code > 1 )
```

```
        printf ( "Jerusalem\n" ) ;
    else
        if ( code < 1 )
            printf ( "Eddie\n" ) ;
        else
            printf ( "C Brain\n" ) ;
    return 0 ;
}
```

(c)
```
# include <stdio.h>
int main( )
{
    float sal ;
    printf ( "Enter the salary" ) ;
    scanf ( "%f", &sal ) ;
    if ( sal < 40000 && sal > 25000 )
        printf ( "Manager\n" ) ;
    else
        if ( sal < 25000 && sal > 15000 )
            printf ( "Accountant\n" ) ;
        else
            printf ( "Clerk\n" ) ;
    return 0 ;
}
```

[K] Attempt the following:

(a) Using conditional operators determine:

(1) Whether the character entered through the keyboard is a lower case alphabet or not.
(2) Whether a character entered through the keyboard is a special symbol or not.

(b) Write a program using conditional operators to determine whether a year entered through the keyboard is a leap year or not.

(c) Write a program to find the greatest of the three numbers entered through the keyboard using conditional operators.

5 The Loop Control Structure

- Loops
- The *while* Loop
    - Tips and Traps
    - More Operators
- The *for* Loop
    - Nesting of Loops
    - Multiple Initialisations in the *for* Loop
- The Odd Loop
- The *break* Statement
- The *continue* Statement
- The *do-while* Loop
- Summary
- Exercise

The programs that we have developed so far used either a sequential or a decision control instruction. In the first one, the calculations were carried out in a fixed order, while in the second, an appropriate set of instructions were executed depending upon the outcome of the condition being tested (or a logical decision being taken).

These programs were of limited nature, because when executed, they always performed the same series of actions, in the same way, exactly once. Almost always, if something is worth doing, it's worth doing more than once. You can probably think of several examples of this from real life, such as eating a good dinner or going for a movie. Programming is the same; we frequently need to perform an action over and over, often with variations in the details each time. The mechanism, which meets this need, is the 'loop', and loops are the subject of this chapter.

Loops

The versatility of the computer lies in its ability to perform a set of instructions repeatedly. This involves repeating some portion of the program either a specified number of times or until a particular condition is being satisfied. This repetitive operation is done through a loop control instruction.

There are three methods by way of which we can repeat a part of a program. They are:

(a) Using a **for** statement
(b) Using a **while** statement
(c) Using a **do-while** statement

Each of these methods is discussed in the following pages.

The *while* Loop

It is often the case in programming that you want to do something a fixed number of times. Perhaps you want to calculate gross salaries of ten different persons, or you want to convert temperatures from Centigrade to Fahrenheit for 15 different cities. The **while** loop is ideally suited for this. Let us look at a simple example, which uses a **while** loop. The flowchart shown below would help you to understand the operation of the **while** loop.

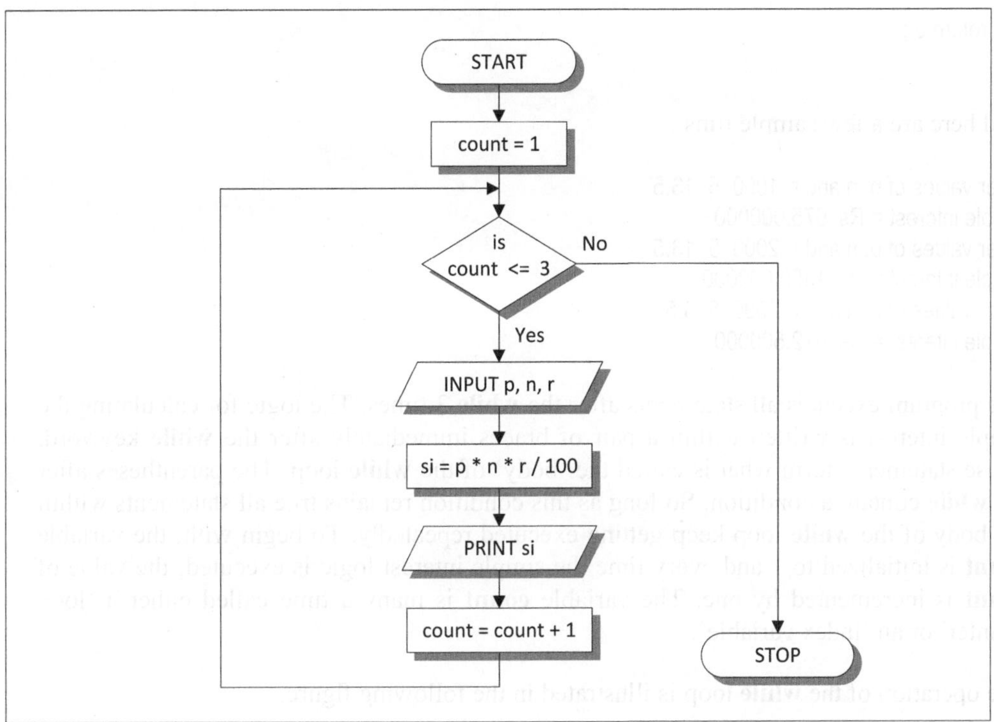

Figure 5.1

```
/* Calculation of simple interest for 3 sets of p, n and r */
# include <stdio.h>
int main( )
{
    int  p, n, count ;
    float  r, si ;

    count = 1 ;
    while ( count <= 3 )
    {
        printf ( "\nEnter values of p, n and r " ) ;
        scanf ( "%d %d %f", &p, &n, &r ) ;
        si = p * n * r / 100 ;
        printf ( "Simple interest = Rs. %\nf", si ) ;

        count = count + 1 ;
    }
```

```
    return 0 ;
}
```

And here are a few sample runs...

```
Enter values of p, n and r  1000  5  13.5
Simple interest = Rs. 675.000000
Enter values of p, n and r  2000  5  13.5
Simple interest = Rs. 1350.000000
Enter values of p, n and r  3500  5  3.5
Simple interest = Rs. 612.500000
```

The program executes all statements after the **while** 3 times. The logic for calculating the simple interest is written within a pair of braces immediately after the **while** keyword. These statements form what is called the 'body' of the **while** loop. The parentheses after the **while** contain a condition. So long as this condition remains true all statements within the body of the **while** loop keep getting executed repeatedly. To begin with, the variable **count** is initialized to 1 and every time the simple interest logic is executed, the value of **count** is incremented by one. The variable **count** is many a time called either a 'loop counter' or an 'index variable'.

The operation of the **while** loop is illustrated in the following figure.

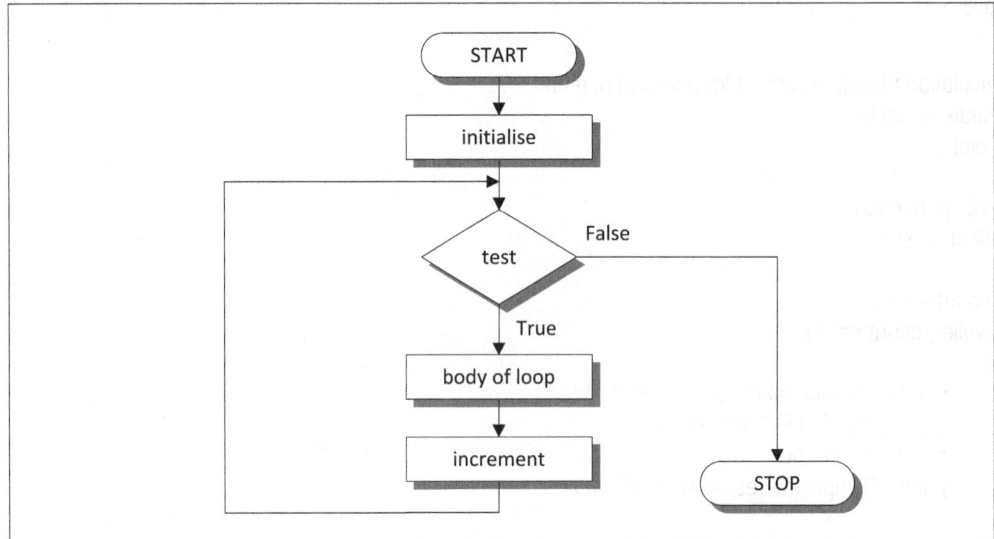

Figure 5.2

Tips and Traps

The general form of **while** is as shown below:

```
initialise loop counter ;
while ( test loop counter using a condition )
{
    do this ;
    and this ;
    increment loop counter ;
}
```

Note the following points about **while...**

- The statements within the **while** loop would keep on getting executed till the condition being tested remains true. When the condition becomes false, the control passes to the first statement that follows the body of the **while** loop.

  In place of the condition there can be any other valid expression. So long as the expression evaluates to a non-zero value the statements within the loop would get executed.

- The condition being tested may use relational or logical operators as shown in the following examples:

```
while ( i <= 10 )
while ( i >= 10 && j <= 15 )
while ( j > 10 && ( b < 15 || c < 20 ) )
```

- The statements within the loop may be a single line or a block of statements. In the first case, the braces are optional. For example,

```
while ( i <= 10 )
    i = i + 1 ;
```

  is same as

```
while ( i <= 10 )
{
    i = i + 1 ;
```

```
}
```

– Almost always, the while must test a condition that will eventually become false, otherwise the loop would be executed forever, indefinitely.

```
# include <stdio.h>
int main( )
{
    int  i = 1 ;
    while ( i <= 10 )
        printf ( "%d\n", i ) ;
    return 0 ;
}
```

This is an indefinite loop, since **i** remains equal to 1 forever. The correct form would be as under:

```
# include <stdio.h>
int main( )
{
    int  i = 1 ;
    while ( i <= 10 )
    {
        printf ( "%d\n", i ) ;
        i = i + 1 ;
    }
    return 0 ;
}
```

– Instead of incrementing a loop counter, we can even decrement it and still manage to get the body of the loop executed repeatedly. This is shown below:

```
# include <stdio.h>
int main( )
{
    int  i = 5 ;
    while ( i >= 1 )
    {
        printf ( "Make the computer literate!\n" ) ;
        i = i - 1 ;
    }
}
```

– It is not necessary that a loop counter must only be an int. It can even be a float.

```
# include <stdio.h>
int main( )
{
    float  a = 10.0 ;
    while ( a <= 10.5 )
    {
        printf ( "Raindrops on roses..." ) ;
        printf ( "...and whiskers on kittens\n" ) ;
        a = a + 0.1 ;
    }
    return 0 ;
}
```

– Even floating point loop counters can be decremented. Once again, the increment and decrement could be by any value, not necessarily 1.

What do you think would be the output of the following program?

```
# include <stdio.h>
int main( )
{
    int  i = 1 ;
    while ( i <= 32767 )
    {
        printf ( "%d\n", i ) ;
        i = i + 1 ;
    }
    return 0 ;
}
```

No, it doesn't print numbers from 1 to 32767. It's an indefinite loop. To begin with, it prints out numbers from 1 to 32767. After that, value of **i** is incremented by 1, therefore it tries to become 32768, which falls outside the valid integer range, so it goes to other side and becomes -32768 which would certainly satisfy the condition in the **while**. This process goes on indefinitely.

– What will be the output of the following program?

```
# include <stdio.h>
int main( )
{
```

```
    int  i = 1 ;
    while ( i <= 10 ) ;
    {
        printf ( "%d\n", i ) ;
        i = i + 1 ;
    }
    return 0 ;
}
```

This is another indefinite loop, and it doesn't give any output at all. The reason is, we have carelessly given a **;** after the **while**. This would make the loop work like this...

```
while ( i <= 10 )
    ;
{
    printf ( "%d\n", i ) ;
    i = i + 1 ;
}
```

Since the value of **i** is not getting incremented, the control would keep rotating within the loop, eternally. Note that enclosing **printf( )** and **i = i +1** within a pair of braces is not an error. In fact we can put a pair of braces around any individual statement or set of statements without affecting the execution of the program.

More Operators

There are varieties of operators that are frequently used with **while**. To illustrate their usage, let us consider a problem wherein numbers from 1 to 10 are to be printed on the screen. The program for performing this task can be written using **while** in the following different ways:

(a)
```
# include <stdio.h>
int main( )
{
    int  i = 1 ;
    while ( i <= 10 )
    {
        printf ( "%d\n", i ) ;
        i = i + 1 ;
    }
    return 0 ;
}
```

(b)
```
# include <stdio.h>
int main( )
{
    int i = 1 ;
    while ( i <= 10 )
    {
        printf ( "%d\n", i ) ;
        i++ ;
    }
    return 0 ;
}
```

Note that the increment operator **++** increments the value of **i** by 1, every time the statement **i++** gets executed. Similarly, to reduce the value of a variable by 1, a decrement operator **--** is also available.

However, never use **n+++** to increment the value of **n** by 2, since C doesn't recognize the operator **+++**.

(c)
```
# include <stdio.h>
int main( )
{
    int i = 1 ;
    while ( i <= 10 )
    {
        printf ( "%d\n", i ) ;
        i += 1 ;
    }
    return 0 ;
}
```

Note that **+=** is a compound assignment operator. It increments the value of **i** by 1. Similarly, **j = j + 10** can also be written as **j += 10**. Other compound assignment operators are **-=**, ***=**, **/=** and **%=**.

(d)
```
# include <stdio.h>
int main( )
{
    int i = 0 ;
    while ( i++ < 10 )
```

```
        printf ( "%d\n", i ) ;
    return 0 ;
}
```

In the statement **while (i++ < 10)**, first the comparison of value of **i** with 10 is performed, and then the incrementation of **i** takes place. Since the incrementation of **i** happens after its usage, here the **++** operator is called a post-incrementation operator. When the control reaches **printf( )**, **i** has already been incremented, hence **i** must be initialized to 0.

(e)
```
# include <stdio.h>
int main( )
{
    int i = 0 ;
    while ( ++i <= 10 )
        printf ( "%d\n", i ) ;
    return 0 ;
}
```

In the statement **while (++i <= 10)**, first incrementation of **i** takes place, then the comparison of valuc of **i** with 10 is performed. Since the incrementation of **i** happens before its usage, here the **++** operator is called a pre-incrementation operator.

The *for* Loop

Perhaps one reason why few programmers use **while** is that they are too busy using the **for**, which is probably the most popular looping instruction. The **for** allows us to specify three things about a loop in a single line:

(a) Setting a loop counter to an initial value.
(b) Testing the loop counter to determine whether its value has reached the number of repetitions desired.
(c) Increasing the value of loop counter each time the program segment within the loop has been executed.

The general form of **for** statement is as under:

```
for ( initialise counter ; test counter ; increment counter )
{
    do this ;
    and this ;
    and this ;
```

}

Let us write down the simple interest program using **for**. Compare this program with the one, which we wrote using **while**. The flowchart is also given below for a better understanding.

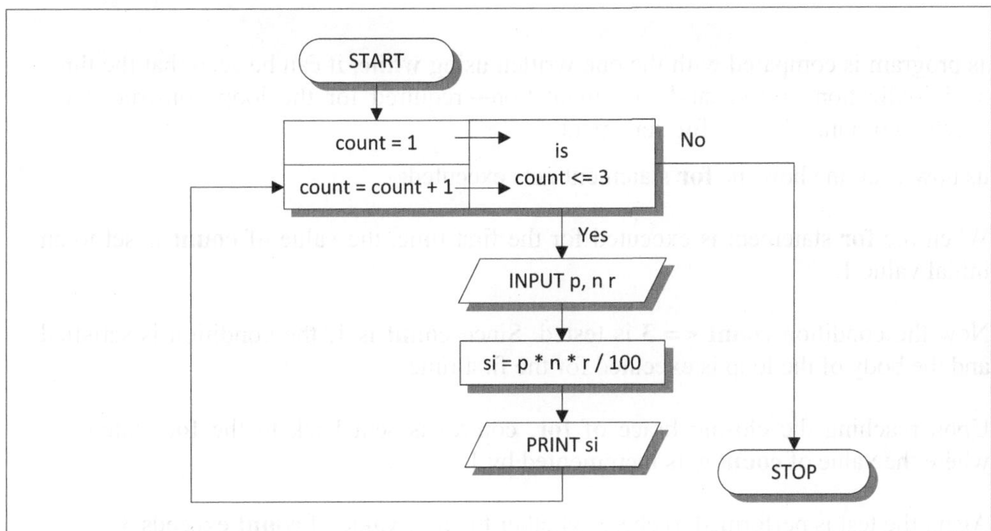

Figure 5.3

```
/* Calculation of simple interest for 3 sets of p, n and r */
# include <stdio.h>
int main( )
{
    int  p, n, count ;
    float  r, si ;

    for ( count = 1 ; count <= 3 ; count = count + 1 )
    {
        printf ( "Enter values of p, n, and r " ) ;
        scanf ( "%d %d %f", &p, &n, &r ) ;

        si = p * n * r / 100 ;
        printf ( "Simple Interest = Rs.%f\n", si ) ;
        return 0 ;
    }
}
```

If this program is compared with the one written using **while**, it can be seen that the three steps—initialization, testing and incrementation—required for the loop construct have now been incorporated in the **for** statement.

Let us now examine how the **for** statement gets executed:

- When the **for** statement is executed for the first time, the value of **count** is set to an initial value 1.
- Now the condition **count <= 3** is tested. Since **count** is 1, the condition is satisfied and the body of the loop is executed for the first time.
- Upon reaching the closing brace of **for**, control is sent back to the **for** statement, where the value of **count** gets incremented by 1.
- Again the test is performed to check whether the new value of **count** exceeds 3.
- If the value of **count** is less than or equal to 3, the statements within the braces of **for** are executed again.
- The body of the **for** loop continues to get executed till **count** doesn't exceed the final value 3.
- When **count** reaches the value 4, the control exits from the loop and is transferred to the statement (if any) immediately after the body of **for**.

The following figure would help in further clarifying the concept of execution of the **for** loop.

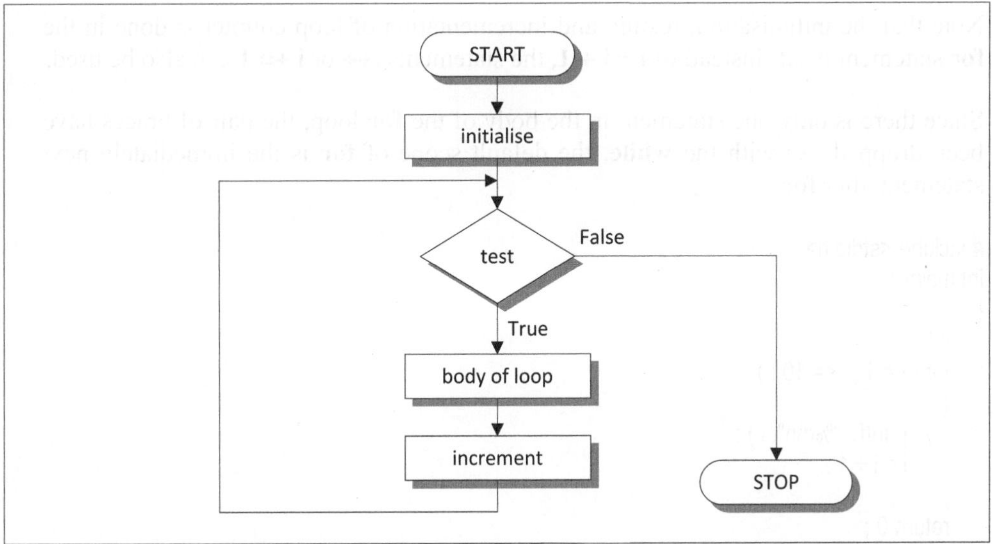

Figure 5.4

It is important to note that the initialization, testing and incrementation part of a **for** loop can be replaced by any valid expression. Thus the following **for** loops are perfectly ok.

```
for ( i = 10 ; i ; i -- )
    printf ( "%d ", i ) ;
for ( i < 4 ; j = 5 ; j = 0 )
    printf ( "%d ", i ) ;
for ( i = 1; i <=10 ; printf ( "%d ",i++ )
    ;
for ( scanf ( "%d", &i ) ; i <= 10 ; i++ )
    printf ( "%d", i ) ;
```

Let us now write down the program to print numbers from 1 to 10 in different ways. This time we would use a **for** loop instead of a **while** loop.

```
(a)  # include <stdio.h>
     int main( )
     {
        int  i ;
        for ( i = 1 ; i <= 10 ; i = i + 1 )
                  printf ( "%d\n", i ) ;
        return 0 ;
     }
```

Note that the initialisation, testing and incrementation of loop counter is done in the **for** statement itself. Instead of **i = i + 1**, the statements **i++** or **i += 1** can also be used.

Since there is only one statement in the body of the **for** loop, the pair of braces have been dropped. As with the **while**, the default scope of **for** is the immediately next statement after **for**.

(b)
```
# include <stdio.h>
int main( )
{
    int  i ;
    for ( i = 1 ; i <= 10 ; )
    {
        printf ( "%d\n", i ) ;
        i = i + 1 ;
    }
    return 0 ;
}
```

Here, the incrementation is done within the body of the **for** loop and not in the **for** statement. Note that, in spite of this, the semicolon after the condition is necessary.

(c)
```
# include <stdio.h>
int main( )
{
    int  i = 1 ;
    for ( ; i <= 10 ; i = i + 1 )
        printf ( "%d\n", i ) ;
    return 0 ;
}
```

Here the initialisation is done in the declaration statement itself, but still the semicolon before the condition is necessary.

(d)
```
# include <stdio.h>
int main( )
{
    int  i = 1 ;
    for ( ; i <= 10 ; )
    {
        printf ( "%d\n", i ) ;
        i = i + 1 ;
```

```
    }
    return 0 ;
}
```

Here, neither the initialisation, nor the incrementation is done in the **for** statement, but still the two semicolons are necessary.

(e)
```
# include <stdio.h>
int main( )
{
    int i ;
    for ( i = 0 ; i++ < 10 ; )
        printf ( "%d\n", i ) ;
    return 0 ;
}
```

Here, the comparison as well as the incrementation is done through the same statement, **i++ < 10**. Since the **++** operator comes after **i**, first comparison is done, followed by incrementation. Note that it is necessary to initialize **i** to 0.

(f)
```
# include <stdio.h>
int main( )
{
    int i ;
    for ( i = 0 ; ++i <= 10 ; )
        printf ( "%d\n", i ) ;
    return 0 ;
}
```

Here again, both, the comparison and the incrementation are done through the same statement, **++i <= 10**. Since **++** precedes **i** first incrementation is done, followed by comparison. Note that it is necessary to initialize **i** to 0.

Nesting of Loops

The way **if** statements can be nested, similarly **while**s and **for**s can also be nested. To understand how nested loops work, look at the program given below:

```
/* Demonstration of nested loops */
# include <stdio.h>
int main( )
{
```

```
    int  r, c, sum ;
    for ( r = 1 ; r <= 3 ; r++ )  /* outer loop */
    {
        for ( c = 1 ; c <= 2 ; c++ )  /* inner loop */
        {
            sum = r + c ;
            printf ( "r = %d c = %d sum = %d\n", r, c, sum ) ;
        }
    }
    return 0 ;
}
```

When you run this program, you will get the following output:

```
r = 1 c = 1 sum = 2
r = 1 c = 2 sum = 3
r = 2 c = 1 sum = 3
r = 2 c = 2 sum = 4
r = 3 c = 1 sum = 4
r = 3 c = 2 sum = 5
```

Here, for each value of **r**, the inner loop is cycled through twice, with the variable **c** taking values from 1 to 2. The inner loop terminates when the value of **c** exceeds 2, and the outer loop terminates when the value of **r** exceeds 3.

As you can see, the body of the outer **for** loop is indented, and the body of the inner **for** loop is further indented. These multiple indentations make the program easier to understand.

Instead of using two statements, one to calculate **sum** and another to print it out, we can compact this into one single statement by saying:

```
printf ( "r = %d c = %d sum = %d\n", r, c, r + c ) ;
```

The way **for** loops have been nested here, similarly, two **while** loops can also be nested. Not only this, a **for** loop can occur within a **while** loop, or a **while** within a **for**.

Multiple Initialisations in the *for* Loop

The initialisation expression of the **for** loop can contain more than one statement separated by a comma. For example,

```
for ( i = 1, j = 2 ; j <= 10 ; j++ )
```

Multiple statements can also be used in the incrementation expression of **for** loop; i.e., you can increment (or decrement) two or more variables at the same time. However, only one statement is allowed in the test expression. This expression may contain several conditions linked together using logical operators.

Use of multiple statements in the initialisation expression also demonstrates why semicolons are used to separate the three expressions in the **for** loop. If commas had been used, they could not also have been used to separate multiple statements in the initialisation expression, without confusing the compiler.

The Odd Loop

The loops that we have used so far executed the statements within them a finite number of times. However, in real life programming, one comes across a situation when it is not known beforehand how many times the statements in the loop are to be executed. This situation can be programmed as shown below:

```
/* Execution of a loop an unknown number of times */
# include <stdio.h>
int main( )
{
    char another ;
    int num ;
    do
    {
        printf ( "Enter a number " ) ;
        scanf ( "%d", &num ) ;
        printf ( "square of %d is %d\n", num, num * num ) ;
        printf ( "Want to enter another number y/n " ) ;
        scanf ( " %c", &another ) ;
    } while ( another == 'y' ) ;

    return 0 ;
}
```

And here is the sample output...

```
Enter a number 5
square of 5 is 25
Want to enter another number y/n y
```

```
Enter a number 7
square of 7 is 49
Want to enter another number y/n n
```

In this program, the **do-while** loop would keep getting executed till the user continues to answer y. The moment he answers n, the loop terminates, since the condition (**another == 'y'**) fails. Note that this loop ensures that statements within it are executed at least once even if **n** is supplied first time itself.

Though it is simpler to program such a requirement using a **do-while** loop, the same functionality if required, can also be accomplished using **for** and **while** loops as shown below:

```
/* odd loop using a for loop */
# include <stdio.h>
int main( )
{
    char another = 'y' ;
    int num ;
    for ( ; another == 'y' ; )
    {
        printf ( "Enter a number " ) ;
        scanf ( "%d", &num ) ;
        printf ( "square of %d is %d\n", num, num * num ) ;
        printf ( "Want to enter another number y/n " ) ;
        scanf ( "%c", &another ) ;
    }
    return 0 ;
}
```

```
/* odd loop using a while loop */
# include <stdio.h>
int main( )
{
    char another = 'y' ;
    int num ;

    while ( another == 'y' )
    {
        printf ( "Enter a number " ) ;
        scanf ( "%d", &num ) ;
        printf ( "square of %d is %d\n", num, num * num ) ;
        printf ( "Want to enter another number y/n " ) ;
```

```
        scanf ( " %c", &another ) ;
    }
    return 0 ;
}
```

The *break* Statement

We often come across situations where we want to jump out of a loop instantly, without waiting to get back to the conditional test. The keyword **break** allows us to do this. When **break** is encountered inside any loop, control automatically passes to the first statement after the loop. A **break** is usually associated with an **if**. As an example, let's consider the following example.

Example: Write a program to determine whether a number is prime or not. A prime number is one, which is divisible only by 1 or itself.

All we have to do to test whether a number is prime or not, is to divide it successively by all numbers from 2 to one less than itself. If remainder of any of these divisions is zero, the number is not a prime. If no division yields a zero then the number is a prime number. Following program implements this logic.

```
# include <stdio.h>
int main( )
{
    int  num, i ;

    printf ( "Enter a number " ) ;
    scanf ( "%d", &num ) ;

    i = 2 ;
    while ( i <= num - 1 )
    {
        if ( num % i == 0 )
        {
            printf ( "Not a prime number\n" ) ;
            break ;
        }
        i++ ;
    }

    if ( i == num )
        printf ( "Prime number\n" ) ;
```

```
}
```

In this program, the moment **num % i** turns out to be zero, (i.e. **num** is exactly divisible by **i**), the message "Not a prime number" is printed and the control breaks out of the **while** loop. Why does the program require the **if** statement after the **while** loop at all? Well, there are two ways the control could have reached outside the **while** loop:

(a) It jumped out because the number proved to be not a prime.
(b) The loop came to an end because the value of **i** became equal to **num**.

When the loop terminates in the second case, it means that there was no number between 2 to **num - 1** that could exactly divide **num**. That is, **num** is indeed a prime. If this is true, the program should print out the message "Prime number".

The keyword **break**, breaks the control only from the **while** in which it is placed. Consider the following program, which illustrates this fact.

```
# include <stdio.h>
int main( )
{
    int i = 1 , j = 1 ;

    while ( i++ <= 100 )
    {
        while ( j++ <= 200 )
        {
            if ( j == 150 )
                break ;
            else
                printf ( "%d %d\n", i, j ) ;
        }
    }
    return 0 ;
}
```

In this program when **j** equals 150, **break** takes the control outside the inner **while** only, since it is placed inside the inner **while**.

The *continue* Statement

In some programming situations, we want to take the control to the beginning of the loop, bypassing the statements inside the loop, which have not yet been executed. The keyword

continue allows us to do this. When **continue** is encountered inside any loop, control automatically passes to the beginning of the loop.

A **continue** is usually associated with an **if**. As an example, let's consider the following program.

```
# include <stdio.h>
int main( )
{
    int  i, j ;

    for ( i = 1 ; i <= 2 ; i++ )
    {
        for ( j = 1 ; j <= 2 ; j++ )
        {
            if ( i == j )
                continue ;

            printf ( "%d %d\n", i, j ) ;
        }
    }
    return 0 ;
}
```

The output of the above program would be...

```
1 2
2 1
```

Note that when the value of **i** equals that of **j**, the **continue** statement takes the control to the **for** loop (inner) bypassing the rest of the statements pending execution in the **for** loop (inner).

The *do-while* Loop

The **do-while** loop looks like this:

```
do
{
    this ;
    and this ;
    and this ;
```

```
    and this ;
} while ( this condition is true ) ;
```

There is a minor difference between the working of **while** and **do-while** loops. This difference is the place where the condition is tested. The **while** tests the condition before executing any of the statements within the **while** loop. As against this, the **do-while** tests the condition after having executed the statements within the loop. Figure 5.5 would clarify the execution of **do-while** loop still further.

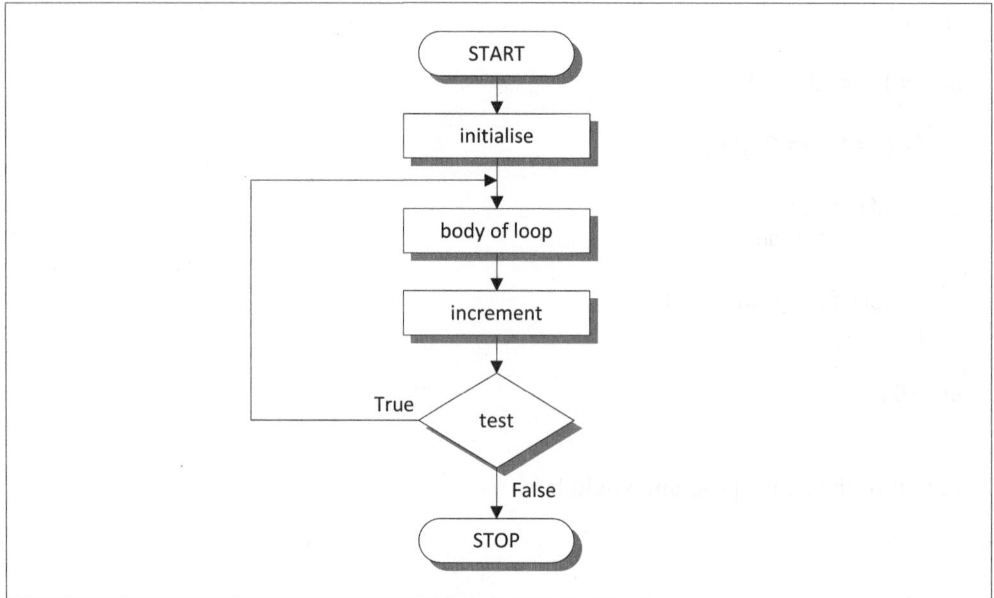

Figure 5.5

This means that **do-while** would execute its statements at least once, even if the condition fails for the first time. The **while**, on the other hand will not execute its statements if the condition fails for the first time. This difference is brought about more clearly by the following program.

```
# include <stdio.h>
int main( )
{
    while ( 4 < 1 )
        printf ( "Hello there \n" ) ;
    return 0 ;
}
```

Here, since the condition fails the first time itself, the **printf( )** will not get executed at all. Let's now write the same program using a **do-while** loop.

```
# include <stdio.h>
int main( )
{
    do
    {
        printf ( "Hello there \n" ) ;
    } while ( 4 < 1 ) ;

    return 0 ;
}
```

In this program, the **printf( )** would be executed once, since first the body of the loop is executed and then the condition is tested.

There are some occasions when we want to execute a loop at least once no matter what. This is illustrated in the following example:

break and **continue** are used with **do-while** just as they would be in a **while** or a **for** loop. A **break** takes you out of the **do-while** bypassing the conditional test. A **continue** sends you straight to the test at the end of the loop.

Summary

(a) The three type of loops available in C are **for**, **while**, and **do-while**.
(b) A **break** statement takes the execution control out of the loop.
(c) A **continue** statement skips the execution of the statements after it and takes the control to the beginning of the loop.
(d) A **do-while** loop is used to ensure that the statements within the loop are executed at least once.
(e) The **++** operator increments the operand by 1, whereas, the -- operator decrements it by 1.
(f) The operators +=, -=, *=, /=, %= are compound assignment operators. They modify the value of the operand to the left of them.

Exercise

while Loop

[A] What will be the output of the following programs:

(a)
```
# include <stdio.h>
int main( )
{
    int i = 1 ;
    while ( i <= 10 ) ;
    {
        printf ( "%d\n", i ) ;
        i++ ;
    }
    return 0 ;
}
```

(b)
```
# include <stdio.h>
int main( )
{
    int x = 4 ;
    while ( x == 1 )
    {
        x = x - 1 ;
        printf ( "%d\n", x ) ;
        - - x ;
    }
    return 0 ;
}
```

(c)
```
# include <stdio.h>
int main( )
{
    int x = 4, y, z ;
    y = --x ;
    z = x-- ;
    printf ( "%d %d %d\n", x, y, z ) ;
    return 0 ;
}
```

(d)
```
# include <stdio.h>
int main( )
{
    int x = 4, y = 3, z ;
    z = x-- -y ;
    printf ( "%d %d %d\n", x, y, z ) ;
    return 0 ;
```

```
}
```

(e)
```
# include <stdio.h>
int main( )
{
    while ( 'a' < 'b' )
        printf ( "malyalam is a palindrome\n" ) ;
    return 0 ;
}
```

(f)
```
# include <stdio.h>
int main( )
{
    int  i ;
    while ( i = 10 )
    {
        printf ( "%d\n", i ) ;
        i = i + 1 ;
    }
    return 0 ;
}
```

(g)
```
# include <stdio.h>
int main( )
{
    float  x = 1.1 ;
    while ( x == 1.1 )
    {
        printf ( "%f\n", x ) ;
        x = x - 0.1 ;
    }
    return 0 ;
}
```

(h)
```
# include <stdio.h>
int main( )
{
    int  x = 4, y = 0, z ;
    while ( x >= 0 )
    {
        x-- ;
        y++ ;
        if ( x == y )
            continue ;
```

```
        else
            printf ( "%d %d\n", x, y ) ;
    }
    return 0 ;
}
```

(i)
```
# include <stdio.h>
int main( )
{
    int  x = 4, y = 0, z ;
    while ( x >= 0 )
    {
        if ( x == y )
            break ;
        else
            printf ( "%d %d\n", x, y ) ;
        x-- ;
        y++ ;
    }
    return 0 ;
}
```

(j)
```
# include <stdio.h>
int main( )
{
    long no = 04 ;
    int i = 1 ;

    while ( no = no / 10 )
            i++ ;

    printf ( "%d\n", i ) ;
    return 0 ;
}
```

[B] Attempt the following:

(a) Write a program to calculate overtime pay of 10 employees. Overtime is paid at the rate of Rs. 12.00 per hour for every hour worked above 40 hours. Assume that employees do not work for fractional part of an hour.

(b) Write a program to find the factorial value of any number entered through the keyboard.

(c) Two numbers are entered through the keyboard. Write a program to find the value of one number raised to the power of another.

(d) Write a program to print all the ASCII values and their equivalent characters using a **while** loop. The ASCII values vary from 0 to 255.

(e) Write a program to print out all Armstrong numbers between 1 and 500. If sum of cubes of each digit of the number is equal to the number itself, then the number is called an Armstrong number. For example, 153 = (1 * 1 * 1) + (5 * 5 * 5) + (3 * 3 * 3)

(f) Write a program for a matchstick game being played between the computer and a user. Your program should ensure that the computer always wins. Rules for the game are as follows:

- There are 21 matchsticks.
- The computer asks the player to pick 1, 2, 3, or 4 matchsticks.
- After the person picks, the computer does its picking.
- Whoever is forced to pick up the last matchstick loses the game.

(g) Write a program to enter the numbers till the user wants and at the end it should display the count of positive, negative and zeros entered.

(h) Write a program to receive an integer and find its octal equivalent.

(i) Write a program to find the range of a set of numbers. Range is the difference between the smallest and biggest number in the list.

for, break, continue, do-while

[C] What will be the output of the following programs:

(a)
```
# include <stdio.h>
int main( )
{
    int i = 0 ;
    for ( ; i ; )
        printf ( "Here is some mail for you\n" ) ;
    return 0 ;
}
```

(b)
```
# include <stdio.h>
int main( )
{
    int i ;
    for ( i = 1 ; i <= 5 ; printf ( "%d\n", i ) ) ;
        i++ ;
    return 0 ;
}
```

(c)
```
# include <stdio.h>
int main( )
{
    int i = 1, j = 1 ;
    for ( ; ; )
    {
        if ( i > 5 )
            break ;
        else
            j += i ;
        printf ( "%d\n", j ) ;
        i += j ;
        return 0 ;
    }
}
```

(d)
```
# include <stdio.h>
int main( )
{
    char j, i ;
    for ( j = 3, i = 3 ; j < 4 && i > 2 ; j--, i = 2 )
        printf ( "jack %c jill\n", j ) ;
    return 0 ;
}
```

(e)
```
# include <stdio.h>
int main( )
{
    int i, j, k ;
    for ( i = 1 ; i <= 3 ; i++ )
    {
        for ( j = 1 ; j <= 3 ; j++ )
        {
            for ( k = 1 ; k <= 3 ; k++ )
```

```
            {
                if ( i == j || j == k || k == i )
                    break ;
                printf ( "%d %d %d\n", i, j, k ) ;
            }
        }
    }
    return 0 ;
}
```

(f)
```
# include <stdio.h>
int main( )
{
    int i ;
    for ( i = 0 ; i <= 255 ; i++ ) ;
        printf ( "%d %c\n", i, i ) ;
    return 0 ;
}
```

(g)
```
# include <stdio.h>
int main( )
{
    int count = 0 ;
    do
    { }
    while ( count-- < 0 ) ;
    printf ( "%d\n", count ) ;
    return 0 ;
}
```

[D] Answer the following:

(a) The three parts of the loop expression in the **for** loop are:

the i____________ expression
the t____________ expression
the i____________ expression

(b) An expression contains relational operators, assignment operators, and arithmetic operators. In the absence of parentheses, they will be evaluated in which of the following order:

1. assignment, relational, arithmetic
2. arithmetic, relational, assignment

3. relational, arithmetic, assignment
4. assignment, arithmetic, relational

(c) The **break** statement is used to exit from:

1. an **if** statement
2. a **for** loop
3. a program
4. the **main( )** function

(d) A **do-while** loop is useful when we want that the statements within the loop must be executed:

1. Only once
2. At least once
3. More than once
4. None of the above

(e) In what sequence the initialization, testing and execution of body is done in a **do-while** loop

1. Initialization, execution of body, testing
2. Execution of body, initialization, testing
3. Initialization, testing, execution of body
4. None of the above

(f) Which of the following is not an infinite loop?

1.
```
int i = 1 ;
while ( 1 )
{
    i++ ;
}
```

2.
```
for ( ; ; ) ;
```

3.
```
int True = 0, false ;
while ( True )
{
    False = 1 ;
}
```

4.
```
int y, x = 0 ;
do
{
    y = x ;
} while ( x == 0 ) ;
```

(g) Which of the following statement is used to take the control to the beginning of the loop?

1. exit

2. break
3. continue
4. None of the above

(h) How many times the **while** loop in the following Ansi C code will get executed?

```
# include <stdio.h>
int main( )
{
    int j = 1 ;
    while ( j <= 255 ) ;
    {
        printf ( "%c %d ", j, j ) ;
        j++;
    }
    return 0 ;
}
```

(i) Which of the following statements are true for the following program?

```
# include <stdio.h>
int main( )
{
    int x=10, y = 100%90 ;
    for ( i = 1 ; i <= 10 ; i++ ) ;
    if ( x != y ) ;
        printf ( "x = %d y = %d\n", x, y ) ;
    return 0 ;
}
```

(1) The **printf( )** function is called 10 times.
(2) The program will produce the output x=10 y=10.
(3) The ; after the **if (x!=y)** would NOT produce an error.
(4) The program will not produce any output.
(5) The **printf( )** function is called infinite times.

(j) Which of the following statement is true about a for loop used in a ANSI C program?

(1) **for** loop works faster than a **while** loop.
(2) All things that can be done using a **for** loop can also be done using a **while** loop.
(3) **for (; ;)** implements an infinite loop.
(4) **for** loop can be used if we want statements in a loop to

get executed at least once.

(5) **for** loop works faster than a **do-while** loop.

[E] Attempt the following:

(a) Write a program to print all prime numbers from 1 to 300. (Hint: Use nested loops, **break** and **continue**)

(b) Write a program to fill the entire screen with a smiling face. The smiling face has an ASCII value 1.

(c) Write a program to add first seven terms of the following series using a **for** loop:

$$\frac{1}{1!} + \frac{2}{2!} + \frac{3}{3!} + \quad \ldots$$

(d) Write a program to generate all combinations of 1, 2 and 3 using **for** loop.

(e) According to a study, the approximate level of intelligence of a person can be calculated using the following formula:

i = 2 + (y + 0.5 x)

Write a program that will produce a table of values of **i**, **y** and **x**, where **y** varies from 1 to 6, and, for each value of **y**, **x** varies from 5.5 to 12.5 in steps of 0.5.

(f) Write a program to produce the following output:

```
A B C D E F G F E D C B A
A B C D E F   F E D C B A
A B C D E       E D C B A
A B C D           D C B A
A B C               C B A
A B                   B A
A                       A
```

(g) Write a program to produce the following output:

```
            1
        2       3
    4       5       6
7       8       9       10
```

(h) Write a program to produce the following output:

```
                1
            1       1
        1       2       1
    1       3       3       1
1       4       6       4       1
```

(i) Write a program to print the multiplication table of the number entered by the user. The table should get displayed in the following form:

29 * 1 = 29
29 * 2 = 58
...

(j) A machine is purchased which will produce earning of Rs. 1000 per year while it lasts. The machine costs Rs. 6000 and will have a salvage value of Rs. 2000 when it is condemned. If 12 percent per annum can be earned on alternate investments What will be the minimum life of the machine to make it a more attractive investment compared to alternative investment?

(k) When interest compounds **q** times per year at an annual rate of **r** % for **n** years, the principle **p** compounds to an amount **a** as per the following formula

$$a = p (1 + r / q) ^{nq}$$

Write a program to read 10 sets of **p, r, n & q** and calculate the corresponding **a**s.

(l) The natural logarithm can be approximated by the following series.

$$\frac{x-1}{x} + \frac{1}{2}\left(\frac{x-1}{x}\right)^2 + \frac{1}{2}\left(\frac{x-1}{x}\right)^3 + \frac{1}{2}\left(\frac{x-1}{x}\right)^4 + \ldots.$$

If **x** is input through the keyboard, write a program to calculate the sum of first seven terms of this series.

(m) Write a program to calculate the sum of the following series:

1! + 2! + 3! + 4! + ... + 10!

(n) Write a program to generate the following pattern on the screen. Do not use cursor movement function like **gotoxy( )**.

```
1  1  1  1  1  a
1  1  1  1  a  1
1  1  1  a  1  1
1  1  a  1  1  1
1  a  1  1  1  1
a  1  1  1  1  1
```

(o) You have already written a program to print ASCII values and their corresponding characters on the screen. Modify it suitably so that the program at a time displays only 20 characters, then waits for the user to hit a key, then displays the next 20 characters and so on till the end of the ASCII table.

6 The Case Control Structure

- Decisions Using *switch*
  - The Tips and Traps
- *switch* Versus *if-else* Ladder
- The *goto* Keyword
- Summary
- Exercise

In real life, we are often faced with situations where we are required to make a choice between a number of alternatives rather than only one or two. For example, which school to join or which hotel to visit or still harder which girl to marry (you almost always end up making a wrong decision is a different matter altogether!). Serious C programming is same; the choice we are asked to make is more complicated than merely selecting between two alternatives. C provides a special control statement that allows us to handle such cases effectively; rather than using a series of **if** statements. This control instruction is, in fact, the topic of this chapter. Towards the end of the chapter, we would also study a keyword called **goto**, and understand why we should avoid its usage in C programming.

Decisions Using *switch*

The control statement that allows us to make a decision from the number of choices is called a **switch**, or more correctly a **switch-case-default**, since these three keywords go together to make up the control statement. They most often appear as follows:

```
switch ( integer expression )
{
    case constant 1 :
        do this ;
    case constant 2 :
        do this ;
    case constant 3 :
        do this ;
    default :
        do this ;
}
```

The integer expression following the keyword **switch** is any C expression that will yield an integer value. It could be an integer constant like 1, 2 or 3, or an expression that evaluates to an integer. The keyword **case** is followed by an integer or a character constant. Each constant in each **case** must be different from all the others. The "do this" lines in the above form of **switch** represent any valid C statement.

What happens when we run a program containing a **switch**? First, the integer expression following the keyword **switch** is evaluated. The value it gives is then matched, one by one, against the constant values that follow the **case** statements. When a match is found, the program executes the statements following that **case**, and all subsequent **case** and **default** statements as well. If no match is found with any of the **case** statements, only the statements following the **default** are executed. A few examples will show how this control structure works.

Consider the following program:

```
# include <stdio.h>
int main( )
{
    int  i = 2 ;

    switch ( i )
    {
        case 1 :
            printf ( "I am in case 1 \n" ) ;
        case 2 :
            printf ( "I am in case 2 \n" ) ;
        case 3 :
            printf ( "I am in case 3 \n" ) ;
        default :
            printf ( "I am in default \n" ) ;
    }
    return 0 ;
}
```

The output of this program would be:

```
I am in case 2
I am in case 3
I am in default
```

The output is definitely not what we expected! We didn't expect the second and third line in the above output. The program prints case 2 and 3 and the default case. Well, yes. We said the **switch** executes the case where a match is found and all the subsequent **cases** and the **default** as well.

If you want that only case 2 should get executed, it is upto you to get out of the **switch** then and there by using a **break** statement. The following example shows how this is done. Note that there is no need for a **break** statement after the **default**, since the control comes out of the **switch** anyway.

```
# include <stdio.h>
int main( )
{
    int  i = 2 ;
    switch ( i )
    {
```

```
        case 1 :
            printf ( "I am in case 1 \n" ) ;  break ;
        case 2 :
            printf ( "I am in case 2 \n" ) ;  break ;
        case 3 :
            printf ( "I am in case 3 \n" ) ;  break ;
        default :
            printf ( "I am in default \n" ) ;
    }
    return 0 ;
}
```

The output of this program would be:

```
I am in case 2
```

The operation of **switch** is shown below in the form of a flowchart for a better understanding.

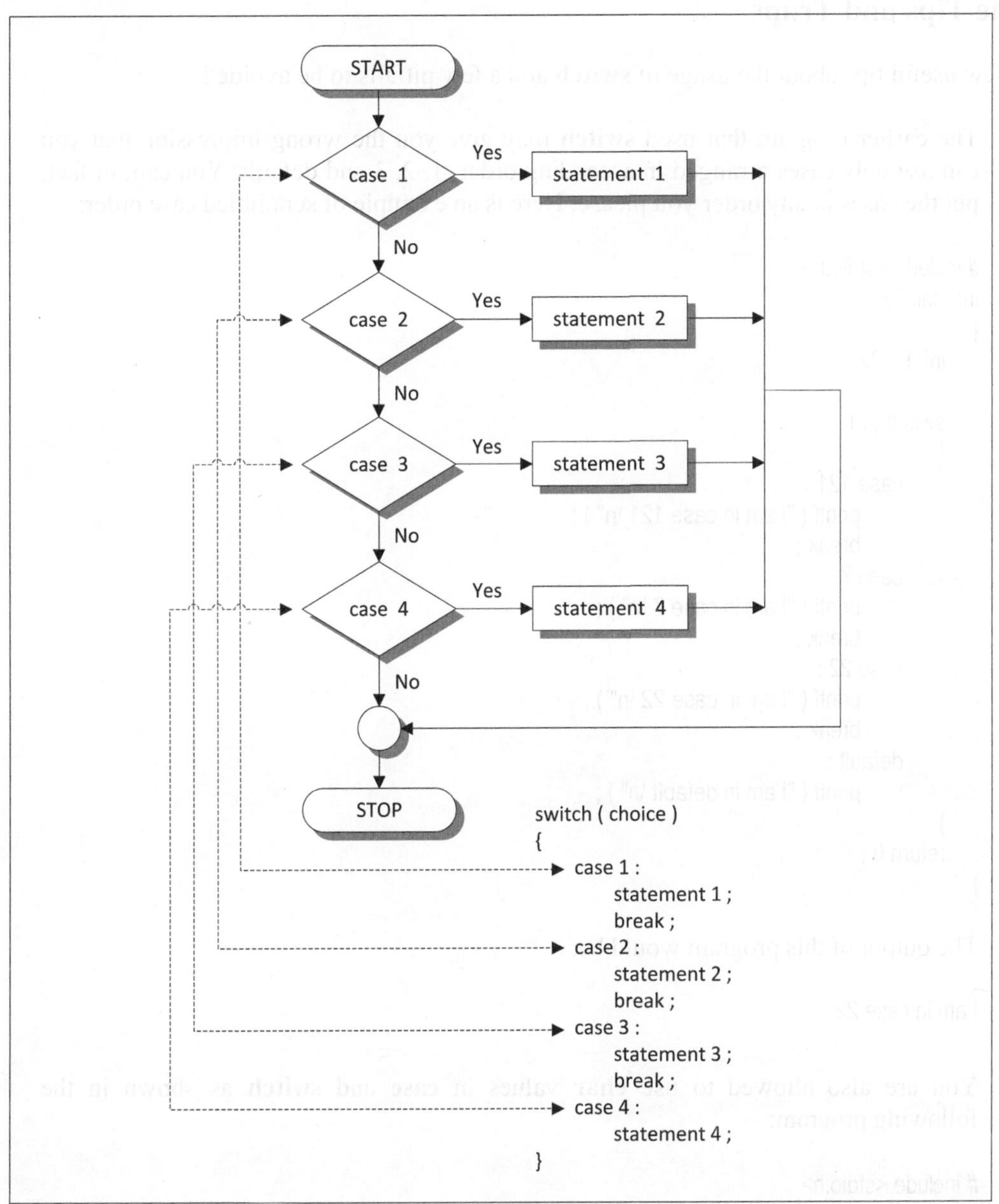
START
case 1
Yes
statement 1
No
case 2
Yes
statement 2
No
case 3
Yes
statement 3
No
case 4
Yes
statement 4
No
STOP
switch (choice)
{
case 1 :
statement 1 ;
break ;
case 2 :
statement 2 ;
break ;
case 3 :
statement 3 ;
break ;
case 4 :
statement 4 ;
}

Figure 6.1

The Tips and Traps

A few useful tips about the usage of **switch** and a few pitfalls to be avoided:

(a) The earlier program that used **switch** may give you the wrong impression that you can use only cases arranged in ascending order, 1, 2, 3 and default. You can, in fact, put the cases in any order you please. Here is an example of scrambled case order:

```
# include <stdio.h>
int main( )
{
    int i = 22 ;

    switch ( i )
    {
        case 121 :
            printf ( "I am in case 121 \n" ) ;
            break ;
        case 7 :
            printf ( "I am in case 7 \n" ) ;
            break ;
        case 22 :
            printf ( "I am in case 22 \n" ) ;
            break ;
        default :
            printf ( "I am in default \n" ) ;
    }
    return 0 ;
}
```

The output of this program would be:

```
I am in case 22
```

(b) You are also allowed to use **char** values in **case** and **switch** as shown in the following program:

```
# include <stdio.h>
int main( )
{
    char c = 'x' ;
```

```
    switch ( c )
    {
        case 'v' :
            printf ( "I am in case v \n" ) ;
            break ;
        case 'a' :
            printf ( "I am in case a \n" ) ;
            break ;
        case 'x' :
            printf ( "I am in case x \n" ) ;
            break ;
        default :
            printf ( "I am in default \n" ) ;
    }
    return 0 ;
}
```

The output of this program would be:

```
I am in case x
```

In fact here when we use 'v', 'a', 'x' they are actually replaced by the ASCII values (118, 97, 120) of these character constants.

(c) At times we may want to execute a common set of statements for multiple **cases**. How this can be done is shown in the following example.

```
# include <stdio.h>
int main( )
{
    char ch ;

    printf ( "Enter any one of the alphabets a, b, or c " ) ;
    scanf ( "%c", &ch ) ;

    switch ( ch )
    {
        case 'a' :
        case 'A' :
            printf ( "a as in ashar\n" ) ;
            break ;
        case 'b' :
        case 'B' :
```

```
            printf ( "b as in brain\n" ) ;
            break ;
        case 'c' :
        case 'C' :
            printf ( "c as in cookie\n" ) ;
            break ;
        default :
            printf ( "wish you knew what are alphabets\n" ) ;

        return 0 ;
    }
}
```

Here, we are making use of the fact that once a **case** is satisfied; the control simply falls through the **case** till it doesn't encounter a **break** statement. That is why if an alphabet **a** is entered, the **case 'a'** is satisfied and since there are no statements to be executed in this **case**, the control automatically reaches the next **case** i.e. **case 'A'** and executes all the statements in this **case**.

(d) Even if there are multiple statements to be executed in each **case**, there is no need to enclose them within a pair of braces (unlike **if**, and **else**).

(e) Every statement in a **switch** must belong to some **case** or the other. If a statement doesn't belong to any **case**, the compiler won't report an error. However, the statement would never get executed. For example, in the following program, the **printf( )** never goes to work.

```
# include <stdio.h>
int main( )
{
    int i, j ;

    printf ( "Enter value of i" ) ;
    scanf ( "%d", &i ) ;

    switch ( i )
    {
        printf ( "Hello\n" ) ;
        case 1 :
            j = 10 ;
            break ;
        case 2 :
            j = 20 ;
```

```
            break ;
    }
    return 0 ;
}
```

(f) If we have no **default** case, then the program simply falls through the entire **switch** and continues with the next instruction (if any,) that follows the closing brace of **switch**.

(g) Is **switch** a replacement for **if**? Yes and no. Yes, because it offers a better way of writing programs as compared to **if**, and no, because, in certain situations, we are left with no choice but to use **if**. The disadvantage of **switch** is that one cannot have a case in a **switch** which looks like:

```
case i <= 20 :
```

All that we can have after the case is an **int** constant or a **char** constant or an expression that evaluates to one of these constants. Even a **float** is not allowed.

The advantage of **switch** over **if** is that it leads to a more structured program and the level of indentation is manageable, more so, if there are multiple statements within each **case** of a **switch**.

(h) We can check the value of any expression in a **switch**. Thus, the following **switch** statements are legal.

```
switch ( i + j * k )
switch ( 23 + 45 % 4 * k )
switch ( a < 4 && b > 7 )
```

Expressions can also be used in cases provided they are constant expressions. Thus **case 3 + 7** is correct, however, **case a + b** is incorrect.

(i) The **break** statement when used in a **switch** takes the control outside the **switch**. However, use of **continue** will not take the control to the beginning of **switch** as one is likely to believe. This is because **switch** is not a looping statement unlike **while**, **for** or **do-while**.

(j) In principle, a **switch** may occur within another, but in practice, it is rarely done. Such statements would be called nested **switch** statements.

(k) The **switch** statement is very useful while writing menu driven programs. This aspect of **switch** is discussed in the exercise at the end of this chapter.

switch Versus *if-else* Ladder

There are some things that you simply cannot do with a **switch**. These are:

(a) A float expression cannot be tested using a **switch**

(b) Cases can never have variable expressions (for example it is wrong to say **case a +3 :**)

(c) Multiple cases cannot use same expressions. Thus the following **switch** is illegal:

```
switch ( a )
{
    case 3 :
        ...
    case 1 + 2 :
        ...
}
```

(a), (b) and (c) above may lead you to believe that these are obvious disadvantages with a **switch**, especially since there weren't any such limitations with **if-else**. Then why use a **switch** at all? For speed—**switch** works faster than an equivalent **if-else** ladder. How come? This is because the compiler generates a jump table for a **switch** during compilation. As a result, during execution it simply refers the jump table to decide which case should be executed, rather than actually checking which case is satisfied. As against this, **if-else**s are slower because the conditions in them are evaluated at execution time. Thus a **switch** with 10 cases would work faster than an equivalent **if-else** ladder. If the 10th **case** is satisfied then jump table would be referred and statements for the 10th **case** would be executed. As against this, in an **if-else** ladder 10 conditions would be evaluated at execution time, which makes it slow. Note that a lookup in the jump table is faster than evaluation of a condition, especially if the condition is complex.

If on the other hand the conditions in the **if-else** were simple and less in number then **if-else** would work out faster than the lookup mechanism of a **switch**. Hence a **switch** with two **case**s would work slower than an equivalent **if-else**. Thus, you as a programmer should take a decision which of the two should be used when.

The *goto* Keyword

Avoid **goto** keyword! They make a C programmer's life miserable. There is seldom a legitimate reason for using **goto**, and its use is one of the reasons that programs become unreliable, unreadable, and hard to debug. And yet many programmers find **goto** seductive.

In a difficult programming situation, it seems so easy to use a **goto** to take the control where you want. However, almost always, there is a more elegant way of writing the same program using **if**, **for**, **while** and **switch**. These constructs are far more logical and easy to understand.

The big problem with **goto**s is that when we do use them we can never be sure how we got to a certain point in our code. They obscure the flow of control. So as far as possible skip them. You can always get the job done without them. Trust me, with good programming skills **goto** can always be avoided. This is the first and last time that we are going to use **goto** in this book. However, for sake of completeness of the book, the following program shows how to use **goto**.

```
# include <stdio.h>
int main( )
{
    int  goals ;

    printf ( "Enter the number of goals scored against India" ) ;
    scanf ( "%d", &goals ) ;

    if ( goals <= 5 )
        goto sos ;
    else
    {
        printf ( "About time soccer players learnt C\n" ) ;
        printf ( "and said goodbye! adieu! to soccer\n" ) ;
        exit( ) ; /* terminates program execution */
    }

    sos :
        printf ( "To err is human!\n" ) ;

    return 0 ;
}
```

And here are two sample runs of the program...

```
Enter the number of goals scored against India 3
To err is human!
Enter the number of goals scored against India 7
```

```
About time soccer players learnt C
and said goodbye! adieu! to soccer
```

A few remarks about the program would make the things clearer.

- If the condition is satisfied the **goto** statement transfers control to the label 'sos', causing **printf( )** following **sos** to be executed.
- The label can be on a separate line or on the same line as the statement following it, as in,

```
sos : printf ( "To err is human!\n" ) ;
```

- Any number of **goto**s can take the control to the same label.
- The **exit( )** function is a standard library function which terminates the execution of the program. It is necessary to use this function since we don't want the statement

```
printf ( "To err is human!\n" )
```

  to get executed after execution of the **else** block.

- The only programming situation in favour of using **goto** is when we want to take the control out of the loop that is contained in several other loops. The following program illustrates this.

```
# include <stdio.h>
int main( )
{
    int i, j, k ;

    for ( i = 1 ; i <= 3 ; i++ )
    {
        for ( j = 1 ; j <= 3 ; j++ )
        {
            for ( k = 1 ; k <= 3 ; k++ )
            {
                if ( i == 3 && j == 3 && k == 3 )
                    goto out ;
                else
```

```
                    printf ( "%d %d %d\n", i, j, k ) ;
                }
            }
        }
        out :
            printf ( "Out of the loop at last!\n" ) ;

        return 0 ;
    }
```

Go through the program carefully and find out how it works. Also write down the same program without using **goto**.

Summary

(a) When we need to choose one among number of alternatives, a **switch** statement is used.
(b) The **switch** keyword is followed by an integer or an expression that evaluates to an integer.
(c) The **case** keyword is followed by an integer or a character constant.
(d) The control falls through all the cases unless the **break** statement is given.
(e) The usage of the **goto** keyword should be avoided as it usually violets the normal flow of execution.

Exercise

[A] What will be the output of the following programs:

(a)
```
# include <stdio.h>
int main( )
{
    char suite = 3 ;
    switch ( suite )
    {
        case 1 :
            printf ( "Diamond\n" ) ;
        case 2 :
            printf ( "Spade\n" ) ;
        default :
            printf ( "Heart\n" ) ;
    }
    printf ( "I thought one wears a suite\n" ) ;
```

```
        return 0 ;
    }
```

(b)
```
# include <stdio.h>
int main( )
{
    int c = 3 ;
    switch ( c )
    {
        case '3' :
            printf ( "You never win the silver prize\n" ) ;
            break ;
        case 3 :
            printf ( "You always lose the gold prize\n" ) ;
            break ;
        default :
            printf ( "Of course provided you win a prize\n" ) ;
    }
    return 0 ;
}
```

(c)
```
# include <stdio.h>
int main( )
{
    int i = 3 ;
    switch ( i )
    {
        case 0 :
            printf ( "Customers are dicey\n" ) ;
        case 1 + 0 :
            printf ( "Markets are pricey\n" ) ;
        case 4 / 2 :
            printf ( "Investors are moody\n" ) ;
        case 8 % 5 :
            printf ( "At least employees are good\n" ) ;
    }
    return 0 ;
}
```

(d)
```
# include <stdio.h>
int main( )
{
    int k ;
```

```
        float j = 2.0 ;
        switch ( k = j + 1 )
        {
            case 3 :
                printf ( "Trapped\n" ) ;
                break ;
            default :
                printf ( "Caught!\n" ) ;
        }
        return 0 ;
    }
```

(e)
```
    # include <stdio.h>
    int main( )
    {
        int  ch = 'a' + 'b' ;
        switch ( ch )
        {
            case 'a' :
            case 'b' :
                printf ( "You entered b\n" ) ;
            case 'A' :
                printf ( "a as in ashar\n" ) ;
            case 'b' + 'a' :
                printf ( "You entered a and b\n" ) ;
        }
        return 0 ;
    }
```

(f)
```
    # include <stdio.h>
    int main( )
    {
        int  i = 1 ;
        switch ( i - 2 )
        {
            case -1 :
                printf ( "Feeding fish\n" ) ;
            case 0 :
                printf ( "Weeding grass\n" ) ;
            case 1 :
                printf ( "Mending roof\n" ) ;
            default :
                printf ( "Just to survive\n" ) ;
```

```
    }
    return 0 ;
}
```

(g)
```
# include <stdio.h>
int main( )
{
    int escape_sequence = '\r' ;
    switch ( escape_sequence )
    {
        case '\r':
            printf ( "Praise in public\rCriticise in private" ) ;
        case '\n':
            printf ( "\n" ) ;
        default:
            printf ( "We like to do it so" ) ;
        case '\b':
            printf ( "#\b!" ) ;
            break ;
        case '\t':
            printf ( "\tWe hate, when it happens to us" ) ;
    }
    return 0 ;
}
```

(h)
```
# include <stdio.h>
int main( )
{
    int i = 3, j = 2 / i, k, x = 0 ;
    for ( k = j ; k <= 3 ; k++ )
    {
        switch ( k - i )
        {
            default :
                printf ( "%d", x ) ;
            case -1 :
            case -2 :
                printf ( "\nCAPITALISTS" ) ;
            case 1 :
            case 2 :
                printf ( "\nwe are not capitalists" ) ;
                goto here ;
        }
    }
```

```
    here :
        ;
    return 0 ;
}
```

[B] Point out the errors, if any, in the following programs:

(a)
```
# include <stdio.h>
int main( )
{
    int  suite = 1 ;
    switch ( suite ) ;
    {
        case 0 ;
            printf ( "Club\n" ) ;
        case 1 ;
            printf ( "Diamond\n" ) ;
    }
    return 0 ;
}
```

(b)
```
# include <stdio.h>
int main( )
{
    int  temp ;
    scanf ( "%d", &temp ) ;
    switch ( temp )
    {
        case ( temp <= 20 ) :
            printf ( "Ooooooohhhh! Damn cool!\n" ) ;
        case ( temp > 20 && temp <= 30 ) :
            printf ( "Rain rain here again!\n" ) ;
        case ( temp > 30 && temp <= 40 ) :
            printf ( "Wish I am on Everest\n" ) ;
        default :
            printf ( "Good old nagpur weather\n" ) ;
    }
    return 0 ;
}
```

(c)
```
# include <stdio.h>
int main( )
{
```

```
        float  a = 3.5 ;
        switch ( a )
        {
            case 0.5 :
                printf ( "The art of C\n" ) ;
                break ;
            case 1.5 :
                printf ( "The spirit of C\n" ) ;
                break ;
            case 2.5 :
                printf ( "See through C\n" ) ;
                break ;
            case 3.5 :
                printf ( "Simply c\n" ) ;
        }
        return 0 ;
    }
```

(d)
```
    # include <stdio.h>
    int main( )
    {
        int a = 3, b = 4, c ;
        c = b – a ;
        switch ( c )
        {
            case 1 || 2 :
                printf ( "God give me an opportunity to change things\n" ) ;
                break ;

            case a || b :
                printf ( "God give me an opportunity to run my show\n" ) ;
                break ;
        }
        return 0 ;
    }
```

[C] Write a menu driven program which has following options:

1. Factorial of a number.
2. Prime or not
3. Odd or even
4. Exit

Once a menu item is selected the appropriate action should be taken and once this action is finished, the menu should reappear. Unless the user selects the 'Exit' option the program should continue to work.

Hint: Make use of an infinite **while** and a **switch** statement.

[D] Write a program which to find the grace marks for a student using **switch**. The user should enter the class obtained by the student and the number of subjects he has failed in. Use the following logic:

- If the student gets first class and the number of subjects he failed in is greater than 3, then he does not get any grace. If the number of subjects he failed in is less than or equal to 3, then the grace is of 5 marks per subject.

- If the student gets second class and the number of subjects he failed in is greater than 2, then he does not get any grace. If the number of subjects he failed in is less than or equal to 2, then the grace is of 4 marks per subject.

- If the student gets third class and the number of subjects he failed in is greater than 1, then he does not get any grace. If the number of subjects he failed in is equal to 1, then the grace is of 5 marks per subject.

7 Functions & Pointers

Knowingly or unknowingly we rely on so many persons for so many things. Man is an intelligent species, but still cannot perform all of life's tasks all alone. He has to rely on others. You may call a mechanic to fix up your bike, hire a gardener to mow your lawn, or rely on a store to supply you groceries every month. A computer program (except for the simplest one) finds itself in a similar situation. It cannot handle all the tasks by itself. Instead, it requests other program-like entities—called 'functions' in C—to get its tasks done. In this chapter we will study these functions. We will look at a variety of features of these functions, starting with the simplest one and then working towards those that demonstrate the power of C functions.

What is a Function

A function is a self-contained block of statements that perform a coherent task of some kind. Every C program can be thought of as a collection of these functions. As we noted earlier, using a function is something like hiring a person to do a specific job for you. Sometimes the interaction with this person is very simple; sometimes it's complex.

Suppose you have a task that is always performed exactly in the same way—say a bimonthly servicing of your motorbike. When you want it to be done, you go to the service station and say, "It's time, do it now". You don't need to give instructions, because the mechanic knows his job. You don't need to be told how the job is done. You assume the bike would be serviced in the usual way, the mechanic does it and that's that.

Let us now look at a simple C function that operates in much the same way as the mechanic. Actually, we will be looking at two things—a function that calls or activates the function and the function itself.

```
# include <stdio.h>
void message( ) ;  /* function prototype declaration */
int main( )
{
    message( ) ;  /* function call */
    printf ( "Cry, and you stop the monotony!\n" ) ;
    return 0 ;
}
void message( )  /* function definition */
{
    printf ( "Smile, and the world smiles with you...\n" ) ;
}
```

And here's the output...

```
Smile, and the world smiles with you...
Cry, and you stop the monotony!
```

Here, we have defined two functions—**main( )** and **message( )**. In fact we have used the word **message** at three places in the program. Let us understand the meaning of each.

The first is the function prototype and is written as:

```
void message( ) ;
```

This prototype declaration indicates that **message( )** is a function which after completing its execution does not return anything. This 'does not return anything' is indicated using the keyword **void**. It is necessary to mention the prototype of every function that we intend to define in the program.

The second usage of **message** is...

```
void message( )
{
    printf ( "Smile, and the world smiles with you...\n" ) ;
}
```

This is the function definition. In this definition right now we are having only **printf( )**, but we can also use **if**, **for**, **while**, **switch**, etc. within this function definition.

The third usage is...

```
message( ) ;
```

Here the function **message( )** if being called by **main( )**. What do we mean when we say that **main( )** 'calls' the function **message( )**? We mean that the control passes to the function **message( )**. The activity of **main( )** is temporarily suspended; it falls asleep while the **message( )** function wakes up and goes to work. When the **message( )** function runs out of statements to execute, the control returns to **main( )**, which comes to life again and begins executing its code at the exact point where it left off. Thus, **main( )** becomes the 'calling' function, whereas **message( )** becomes the 'called' function.

If you have grasped the concept of 'calling' a function you are prepared for a call to more than one function. Consider the following example:

```
# include <stdio.h>
void italy( ) ;
```

```
void brazil( ) ;
void argentina( ) ;
int main( )
{
    printf ( "I am in main\n" ) ;
    italy( ) ;
    brazil( ) ;
    argentina( ) ;
    return 0 ;
}
void italy( )
{
    printf ( "I am in italy\n" ) ;
}
void brazil( )
{
    printf ( "I am in brazil\n" ) ;
}
void argentina( )
{
    printf ( "I am in argentina\n" ) ;
}
```

The output of the above program when executed would be as under:

```
I am in main
I am in italy
I am in brazil
I am in argentina
```

A number of conclusions can be drawn from this program:

- A C program is a collection of one or more functions.
- If a C program contains only one function, it must be **main( )**.
- If a C program contains more than one function, then one (and only one) of these functions must be **main( )**, because program execution always begins with **main( )**.
- There is no limit on the number of functions that might be present in a C program.
- Each function in a program is called in the sequence specified by the function calls in **main( )**.

– After each function has done its thing, control returns to **main( )**.When **main( )** runs out of statements and function calls, the program ends.

As we have noted earlier, the program execution always begins with **main( ).** Except for this fact, all C functions enjoy a state of perfect equality. No precedence, no priorities, nobody is nobody's boss. One function can call another function it has already called but has in the meantime left temporarily in order to call a third function which will sometime later call the function that has called it, if you understand what I mean. No? Well, let's illustrate with an example.

```
# include <stdio.h>
void italy( ) ;
void brazil( ) ;
void argentina( ) ;
int main( )
{
    printf ( "I am in main\n" ) ;
    italy( ) ;
    printf ( "I am finally back in main\n" ) ;
    return 0 ;
}
void italy( )
{
    printf ( "I am in italy\n" ) ;
    brazil( ) ;
    printf ( "I am back in italy\n" ) ;
}
void brazil( )
{
    printf ( "I am in brazil\n" ) ;
    argentina( ) ;
}
void argentina( )
{
    printf ( "I am in argentina\n" ) ;
}
```

And the output would look like...

```
I am in main
I am in italy
I am in brazil
I am in argentina
```

```
I am back in italy
I am finally back in main
```

Here, **main( )** calls other functions, which in turn call still other functions. Trace carefully the way control passes from one function to another. Since the compiler always begins the program execution with **main( )**, every function in a program must be called directly or indirectly by **main( )**. In other words, the **main( )** function drives other functions.

Let us now summarize what we have learnt so far.

(a) A function gets called when the function name is followed by a semicolon. For example,

```
int main( )
{
    argentina( ) ;
}
```

(b) A function is defined when function name is followed by a pair of braces in which one or more statements may be present. For example,

```
void argentina( )
{
    statement 1 ;
    statement 2 ;
    statement 3 ;
}
```

(c) Any function can be called from any other function. Even **main( )** can be called from other functions. For example,

```
# include <stdio.h>
void message( ) ;
int main( )
{
    message( ) ;
    return 0 ;
}
void message( )
{
    printf ( "Can't imagine life without C\n" ) ;
```

```
    main( ) ;
}
```

(d) A function can be called any number of times. For example,

```
# include <stdio.h>
void message( ) ;
int main( )
{
    message( ) ;
    message( ) ;
    return 0 ;
}
void message( )
{
    printf ( "Jewel Thief!!\n" ) ;
}
```

(e) The order in which the functions are defined in a program and the order in which they get called need not necessarily be same. For example,

```
# include <stdio.h>
void message1( ) ;
void message2( ) ;
int main( )
{
    message1( ) ;
    message2( ) ;
    return 0 ;
}
void message2( )
{
    printf ( "But the butter was bitter\n" ) ;
}
void message1( )
{
    printf ( "Mary bought some butter\n" ) ;
}
```

Here, even though **message1( )** is getting called before **message2( )**, still, **message1( )** has been defined after **message2( )**. However, it is advisable to define the functions in the same order in which they are called. This makes the program easier to understand.

(f) A function can call itself. Such a process is called 'recursion'. We would discuss this aspect of C functions later in this chapter.

(g) A function can be called from another function, but a function cannot be defined in another function. Thus, the following program code would be wrong, since **argentina( )** is being defined inside another function, **main( )**.

```
int main( )
{
    printf ( "I am in main\n" ) ;
    void argentina( )
    {
        printf ( "I am in argentina\n" ) ;
    }
}
```

(h) There are basically two types of functions:

Library functions Ex. **printf( )**, **scanf( )**, etc.
User-defined functions Ex. **argentina( )**, **brazil( )**, etc.

As the name suggests, library functions are nothing but commonly required functions grouped together and stored in what is called a Library. This library of functions is present on the disk and is written for us by people who write compilers for us. Almost always, a compiler comes with a library of standard functions. The procedure of calling both types of functions is exactly same.

Why Use Functions

Why write separate functions at all? Why not squeeze the entire logic into one function, **main( )**? Two reasons:

(a) Writing functions avoids rewriting the same code over and over. Suppose you have a section of code in your program that calculates area of a triangle. If later in the program you want to calculate the area of a different triangle, you won't like it if you are required to write the same instructions all over again. Instead, you would prefer to jump to a 'section of code' that calculates area and then jump back to the place from where you left off. This section of code is nothing but a function.

(b) By using functions it becomes easier to write programs and keep track of what they are doing. If the operation of a program can be divided into separate activities, and each activity placed in a different function, then each could be written and checked more or less independently. Separating the code into modular functions also makes the program easier to design and understand.

What is the moral of the story? Don't try to cram the entire logic in one function. It is a very bad style of programming. Instead, break a program into small units and write functions for each of these isolated subdivisions. Don't hesitate to write functions that are called only once. What is important is that these functions perform some logically isolated task.

Passing Values between Functions

The functions that we have used so far haven't been very flexible. We call them and they do what they are designed to do. Like our mechanic who always services the motorbike in exactly the same way, we haven't been able to influence the functions in the way they carry out their tasks. It would be nice to have a little more control over what functions do, in the same way it would be nice to be able to tell the mechanic, "Also change the engine oil, I am going for an outing". In short, now we want to communicate between the 'calling' and the 'called' functions.

The mechanism used to convey information to the function is the 'argument'. You have unknowingly used the arguments in the **printf( )** and **scanf( )** functions; the format string and the list of variables used inside the parentheses in these functions are arguments. The arguments are sometimes also called 'parameters'.

Consider the following program. In this program, in **main( )** we receive the values of **a**, **b** and **c** through the keyboard and then output the sum of **a**, **b** and **c**. However, the calculation of sum is done in a different function called **calsum( )**. If sum is to be calculated in **calsum( )** and values of **a**, **b** and **c** are received in **main( )**, then we must pass on these values to **calsum( )**, and once **calsum( )** calculates the sum, we must return it from **calsum( )** back to **main( )**.

```
/* Sending and receiving values between functions */
# include <stdio.h>
int calsum ( int x, int y, int z ) ;
int main( )
{
    int a, b, c, sum ;
```

```
    printf ( "Enter any three numbers " ) ;
    scanf ( "%d %d %d", &a, &b, &c ) ;
    sum = calsum ( a, b, c ) ;
    printf ( "Sum = %d\n", sum ) ;
    return 0 ;
}
int calsum ( int x, int y, int z )
{
    int d ;

    d = x + y + z ;
    return ( d ) ;
}
```

And here is the output...

```
Enter any three numbers 10 20 30
Sum = 60
```

There are a number of things to note about this program:

(a) In this program, from the function **main( )**, the values of **a**, **b** and **c** are passed on to the function **calsum( )**, by making a call to the function **calsum( )** and mentioning **a**, **b** and **c** in the parentheses:

```
sum = calsum ( a, b, c ) ;
```

In the **calsum( )** function these values get collected in three variables **x**, **y** and **z**:

```
int calsum ( int x, int y, int z )
```

(b) The variables **a**, **b** and **c** are called 'actual arguments', whereas the variables **x**, **y** and **z** are called 'formal arguments'. Any number of arguments can be passed to a function being called. However, the type, order and number of the actual and formal arguments must always be same.

Instead of using different variable names **x**, **y** and **z**, we could have used the same variable names **a**, **b** and **c**. But the compiler would still treat them as different variables since they are in different functions.

(c) Note the function prototype declaration of **calsum( )**. Instead of the usual **void**, we are using **int**. This indicates that **calsum( )** is going to return a value of the type **int**.

It is not compulsory to use variable names in the prototype declaration. Hence we could as well have written the prototype as

```
int calsum ( int, int, int ) ;
```

In the definition of **calsum** too, **void** has been replaced by **int**.

(d) In the earlier programs, the moment closing brace (}) of the called function was encountered, the control returned to the calling function. No separate **return** statement was necessary to send back the control.

This approach is fine if the called function is not going to return any meaningful value to the calling function. In the above program, however, we want to return the sum of **x**, **y** and **z**. Therefore, it is necessary to use the **return** statement.

The **return** statement serves two purposes:

(1) On executing the **return** statement, it immediately transfers the control back to the calling function.

(2) It returns the value present in the parentheses after **return**, to the calling function. In the above program, the value of sum of three numbers is being returned.

(e) There is no restriction on the number of **return** statements that may be present in a function. Also, the **return** statement need not always be present at the end of the called function. The following program illustrates these facts.

```
int fun( )
{
    int n ;
    printf ( "Enter any number " ) ;
    scanf ( "%d", &n ) ;
    if ( n >= 10 && n <= 90 )
        return ( n ) ;
    else
        return ( n + 32 ) ;
}
```

In this function, different **return** statements will be executed depending on whether **ch** is capital or not.

(f) Whenever the control returns from a function, the sum being returned is collected in the calling function by equating the called function to some variable. For example,

```
sum = calsum ( a, b, c ) ;
```

(g) All the following are valid **return** statements.

```
return ( a ) ;
return ( 23 ) ;
return ;
```

In the last statement, a garbage value is returned to the calling function since we are not returning any specific value. Note that, in this case, the parentheses after **return** are dropped. In the other **return** statements too, the parentheses can be dropped.

(h) A function can return only one value at a time. Thus, the following statements are invalid.

```
return ( a, b ) ;
return ( x, 12 ) ;
```

There is a way to get around this limitation, which would be discussed later in this chapter, when we learn pointers.

(i) If the value of a formal argument is changed in the called function, the corresponding change does not take place in the calling function. For example,

```
# include <stdio.h>
void fun ( int ) ;
int main( )
{
    int  a = 30 ;
    fun ( a ) ;
    printf ( "%d\n", a ) ;
    return 0 ;
}
void fun ( int  b )
{
    b = 60 ;
    printf ( "%d\n", b ) ;
}
```

The output of the above program would be:

```
60
30
```

Thus, even though the value of **b** is changed in **fun( ),** the value of **a** in **main( )** remains unchanged. This means that when values are passed to a called function, the values present in actual arguments are not physically moved to the formal arguments; just a photocopy of values in actual argument is made into formal arguments.

Scope Rule of Functions

Look at the following program:

```
# include <stdio.h>
void display ( int ) ;
int main( )
{
    int i = 20 ;
    display ( i ) ;
    return 0 ;
}
void display ( int j )
{
    int k = 35 ;
    printf ( "%d\n", j ) ;
    printf ( "%d\n", k ) ;
}
```

In this program, is it necessary to pass the value of the variable **i** to the function **display( )**? Will it not become automatically available to the function **display( )**? No. Because, by default, the scope of a variable is local to the function in which it is defined. The presence of **i** is known only to the function **main( )** and not to any other function. Similarly, the variable **k** is local to the function **display( )** and hence it is not available to **main( )**. That is why to make the value of **i** available to **display( )**, we have to explicitly pass it to **display( )**. Likewise, if we want **k** to be available to **main( )**, we will have to return it to **main( )** using the **return** statement. In general, we can say that the scope of a variable is local to the function in which it is defined.

Calling Convention

Calling convention indicates two things:

(a) The order in which the arguments are passed to the function.
(b) Which function (calling function or called function) performs the cleanup of variables when the control returns from the function.

When a function call is encountered and the arguments are to be passed to a function two possibilities exist:

(a) Arguments can be passed from left to right.
(b) Arguments can be passed from right to left.

The formal arguments and the local variables defined inside a function are created at a place in memory called 'Stack'. When the control returns from the function the stack is cleaned up. Either the calling function or the called function clears the stack. Which function would do this is decided by the calling convention.

There are different calling conventions available. The most common amongst them is a convention called standard calling convention. In this convention the arguments are passed to a function in right to left order and the stack is cleaned up by the called function.

Consider the following function call:

```
fun (a, b, c, d ) ;
```

In this call, it doesn't matter whether the arguments are passed from left to right or from right to left. However, in some function call, the order of passing arguments becomes an important consideration. For example:

```
int a = 1 ;
printf ( "%d %d %d\n", a, ++a, a++ ) ;
```

It appears that this **printf( )** would output 1 2 2.

This however is not the case. Surprisingly, it outputs 3 3 1. This is because, C's calling convention is from right to left. That is, firstly 1 is passed through the expression **a++** and then **a** is incremented to 2. Then result of **++a** is passed. That is, **a** is incremented to 3 and then passed. Finally, latest value of **a**, i.e. 3, is passed. Thus in right to left order, 1, 3, 3 get passed. Once **printf( )** collects them, it prints them in the order in which we have asked it to get them printed (and not the order in which they were passed). Thus 3 3 1 gets printed.

One Dicey Issue

Consider the following program:

```
# include <conio.h>
int main( )
{
    clrscr( ) ;
    gotoxy ( 10, 20 ) ;
    ch = getch ( a ) ;
    return 0 ;
}
```

Here we are calling three standard library functions. As we know, before calling any function, we must declare its prototype. This helps the compiler in checking whether the values being passed and returned are as per the prototype declaration. But since we don't define the library functions (we merely call them), we may not know the prototypes of library functions. Hence, when the library of functions is provided, a set of '.h' files is also provided. These files contain the prototypes of library functions. But why multiple files? Because the library functions are divided into different groups and one file is provided for each group. For example, prototypes of all input/output functions are provided in the file 'stdio.h', prototypes of all mathematical functions are provided in the file 'math.h', etc.

Prototypes of functions **clrscr( )**, **gotoxy( )** and **getch( )** are declared in the file 'conio.h'. To make these prototypes available to our program we need to **#include** the file 'conio.h'. You can even open this file and look at the prototypes. They would appear as shown below:

```
void clrscr( ) ;
void gotoxy ( int, int ) ;
int getch( ) ;
```

Now consider the following program:

```
# include <stdio.h>
int main( )
{
    int  i = 10, j = 20 ;
```

```
    printf ( "%d %d %d\n", i, j ) ;
    printf ( "%d\n", i, j ) ;
    return 0 ;
}
```

This program gets successfully compiled, even though there is a mismatch in the format specifiers and the variables in the list used in **printf( )**. This is because, **printf( )** accepts *variable* number of arguments (sometimes 2 arguments, sometimes 3 arguments, etc.), and even with the mismatch above, the call still matches with the prototype of **printf( )** present in 'stdio.h'. At run-time, when the first **printf( )** is executed, since there is no variable matching with the last specifier **%d**, a garbage integer gets printed. Similarly, in the second **printf( )**, since the format specifier for **j** has not been mentioned, its value does not get printed.

Advanced Features of Functions

With a sound basis of the preliminaries of C functions, let us now get into their intricacies. Following advanced topics would be considered here.

(a) Return type of function
(b) Calling functions by value or by reference
(c) Recursion

Let us understand these features one by one.

Return Type of Function

Suppose we want to find out square of a floating point number using a function. This is how this simple program would look like:

```
# include <stdio.h>
float square ( float ) ;
int main( )
{
    float  a, b ;
    printf ( "Enter any number " ) ;
    scanf ( "%f", &a ) ;
    b = square ( a ) ;
    printf ( "Square of %f is %f\n", a, b ) ;
    return 0 ;
}
float square ( float  x )
```

```
{
    float y ;
    y = x * x ;
    return ( y ) ;
}
```

And here are three sample runs of this program...

```
Enter any number 3
Square of 3 is 9.000000
Enter any number 1.5
Square of 1.5 is 2.250000
Enter any number 2.5
Square of 2.5 is 6.250000
```

Since we are returning a **float** value from this function we have indicated the return type of the **square( )** function as **float** in the prototype declaration as well as in the function definition. Had we dropped **float** from the prototype and the definition, the compiler would have assumed that **square( )** is supposed to return an integer value.

Call by Value and Call by Reference

By now, we are well familiar with how to call functions. But, if you observe carefully, whenever we called a function and passed something to it we have always passed the 'values' of variables to the called function. Such function calls are called 'calls by value'. By this what we mean is, on calling a function, we are passing values of variables to it. The examples of call by value are shown below:

```
sum = calsum ( a, b, c ) ;
f = factr ( a ) ;
```

We have also learnt that variables are stored somewhere in memory. So instead of passing the value of a variable, can we not pass the location number (also called address) of the variable to a function? If we were able to do so, it would become a 'call by reference'. What purpose a 'call by reference' serves we would find out a little later. First we must equip ourselves with knowledge of how to make a 'call by reference'. This feature of C functions needs at least an elementary knowledge of a concept called 'pointers'. So let us first acquire the basics of pointers after which we would take up this topic once again.

An Introduction to Pointers

Which feature of C do beginners find most difficult to understand? The answer is easy: pointers. Other languages have pointers but few use them so frequently as C does. And why not? It is C's clever use of pointers that makes it the excellent language it is.

The difficulty beginners have with pointers has much to do with C's pointer terminology than the actual concept. For instance, when a C programmer says that a certain variable is a "pointer", what does that mean? It is hard to see how a variable can point to something, or in a certain direction.

It is hard to get a grip on pointers just by listening to programmer's jargon. In our discussion of C pointers, therefore, we will try to avoid this difficulty by explaining pointers in terms of programming concepts we already understand. The first thing we want to do is explain the rationale of C's pointer notation.

Pointer Notation

Consider the declaration,

```
int i = 3 ;
```

This declaration tells the C compiler to:

(a) Reserve space in memory to hold the integer value.
(b) Associate the name **i** with this memory location.
(c) Store the value 3 at this location.

We may represent **i**'s location in memory by the following memory map.

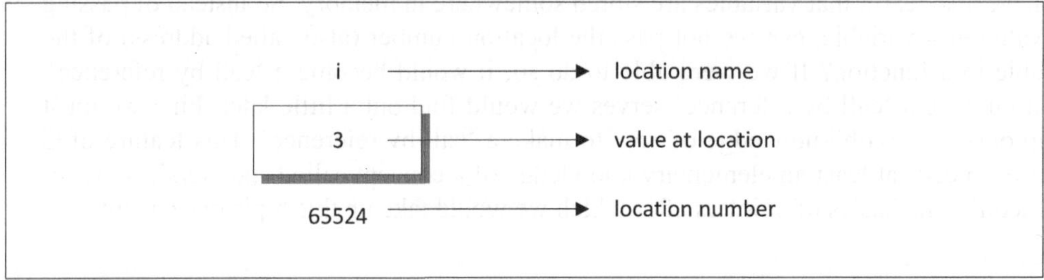

Figure 7.1

We see that the computer has selected memory location 65524 as the place to store the value 3. The location number 65524 is not a number to be relied upon, because some other time the computer may choose a different location for storing the value 3. The important point is, **i**'s address in memory is a number.

We can print this address number through the following program:

```
# include <stdio.h>
int main( )
{
    int i = 3 ;
    printf ( "Address of i = %u\n", &i ) ;
    printf ( "Value of i = %d\n", i ) ;
    return 0 ;
}
```

The output of the above program would be:

```
Address of i = 65524
Value of i = 3
```

Look at the first **printf( )** statement carefully. '&' used in this statement is C's 'address of' operator. The expression **&i** returns the address of the variable **i**, which in this case happens to be 65524. Since 65524 represents an address, there is no question of a sign being associated with it. Hence it is printed out using **%u**, which is a format specifier for printing an unsigned integer. We have been using the '&' operator all the time in the **scanf( )** statement.

The other pointer operator available in C is '*', called 'value at address' operator. It gives the value stored at a particular address. The 'value at address' operator is also called 'indirection' operator.

Observe carefully the output of the following program:

```
# include <stdio.h>
int main( )
{
    int i = 3 ;
    printf ( "Address of i = %u\n", &i ) ;
    printf ( "Value of i = %d\n", i ) ;
    printf ( "Value of i = %d\n", *( &i ) ) ;
    return 0 ;
}
```

The output of the above program would be:

```
Address of i = 65524
Value of i = 3
Value of i = 3
```

Note that printing the value of ***(&i)** is same as printing the value of **i**.

The expression **&i** gives the address of the variable **i**. This address can be collected in a variable, by saying,

```
j = &i ;
```

But remember that **j** is not an ordinary variable like any other integer variable. It is a variable that contains the address of other variable (**i** in this case). Since **j** is a variable, the compiler must provide it space in the memory. Once again, the following memory map would illustrate the contents of **i** and **j**.

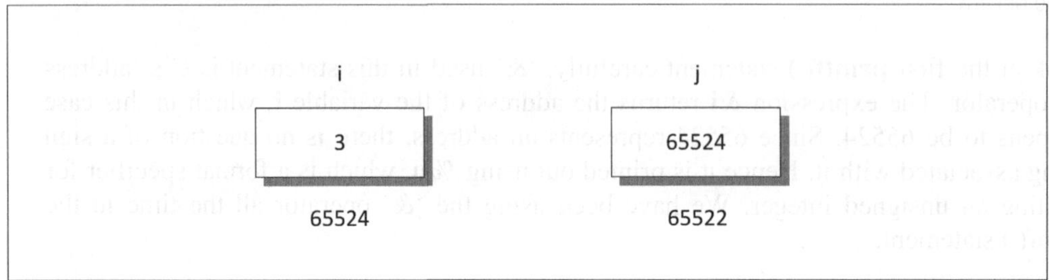

Figure 7.2

As you can see, **i**'s value is 3 and **j**'s value is **i**'s address.

But wait, we can't use **j** in a program without declaring it. And since **j** is a variable that contains the address of **i**, it is declared as,

```
int *j ;
```

This declaration tells the compiler that **j** will be used to store the address of an integer value. In other words, **j** points to an integer. How do we justify the usage of * in the declaration,

```
int *j ;
```

Let us go by the meaning of *. It stands for 'value at address'. Thus, **int *j** would mean, the value at the address contained in **j** is an **int**.

Here is a program that demonstrates the relationships we have been discussing.

```
# include <stdio.h>
int main( )
{
    int i = 3 ;
    int *j ;

    j = &i ;
    printf ( "Address of i = %u\n", &i ) ;
    printf ( "Address of i = %u\n", j ) ;
    printf ( "Address of j = %u\n", &j ) ;
    printf ( "Value of j = %u\n", j ) ;
    printf ( "Value of i = %d\n", i ) ;
    printf ( "Value of i = %d\n", *( &i ) ) ;
    printf ( "Value of i = %d\n", *j ) ;
    return 0 ;
}
```

The output of the above program would be:

```
Address of i = 65524
Address of i = 65524
Address of j = 65522
Value of j = 65524
Value of i = 3
Value of i = 3
Value of i = 3
```

Work through the above program carefully, taking help of the memory locations of **i** and **j** shown earlier. This program summarizes everything that we have discussed so far. If you don't understand the program's output, or the meanings of **&i**, **&j**, ***j** and ***(&i)**, re-read the last few pages. Everything we say about pointers from here onwards will depend on your understanding these expressions thoroughly.

Look at the following declarations:

```
int *alpha ;
char *ch ;
float *s ;
```

Here, **alpha, ch** and **s** are declared as pointer variables, i.e. variables capable of holding addresses. Remember that, addresses (location nos.) are always going to be whole numbers, therefore pointers always contain whole numbers. Now we can put these two facts together and say—pointers are variables that contain addresses, and since addresses are always whole numbers, pointers would always contain whole numbers.

The declaration **float *s** does not mean that **s** is going to contain a floating-point value. What it means is, **s** is going to contain the address of a floating-point value. Similarly, **char *ch** means that **ch** is going to contain the address of a char value. Or in other words, the value at address stored in **ch** is going to be a **char**.

The concept of pointers can be further extended. Pointer, we know is a variable that contains address of another variable. Now this variable itself might be another pointer. Thus, we now have a pointer that contains another pointer's address. The following example should make this point clear.

```
# include <stdio.h>
int main( )
{
    int i = 3, *j, **k ;

    j = &i ;
    k = &j ;
    printf ( "Address of i = %u\n", &i ) ;
    printf ( "Address of i = %u\n ", j ) ;
    printf ( "Address of i = %u\n ", *k ) ;
    printf ( "Address of j = %u\n ", &j ) ;
    printf ( "Address of j = %u\n ", k ) ;
    printf ( "Address of k = %u\n ", &k ) ;
    printf ( "Value of j  = %u\n ", j ) ;
    printf ( "Value of k  = %u\n ", k ) ;
    printf ( "Value of i  = %d\n ", i ) ;
    printf ( "Value of i  = %d\n ", * ( &i ) ) ;
    printf ( "Value of i  = %d\n ", *j ) ;
    printf ( "Value of i  = %d\n ", **k ) ;
    return 0 ;
}
```

The output of the above program would be:

```
Address of i = 65524
Address of i = 65524
```

```
Address of i = 65524
Address of j = 65522
Address of j = 65522
Address of k = 65520
Value of j  = 65524
Value of k  = 65522
Value of i  = 3
Value of i  = 3
Value of i  = 3
Value of i  = 3
```

Figure 7.3 would help you in tracing out how the program prints the above output.

Remember that when you run this program, the addresses that get printed might turn out to be something different than the ones shown in the figure. However, with these addresses too, the relationship between **i**, **j** and **k** can be easily established.

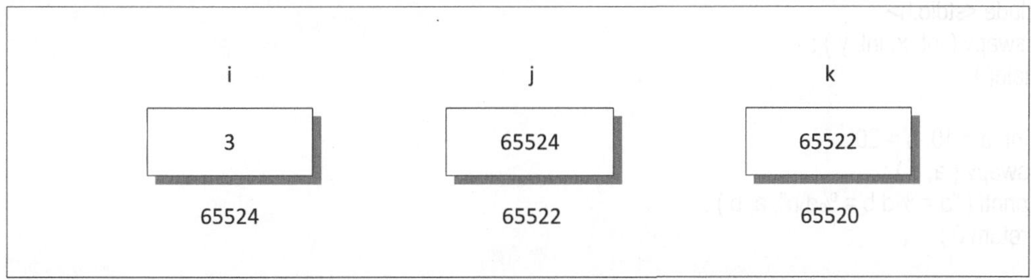

Figure 7.3

Observe how the variables **j** and **k** have been declared,

```
int  i, *j, **k ;
```

Here, **i** is an ordinary **int**, **j** is a pointer to an **int** (often called an integer pointer), whereas **k** is a pointer to an integer pointer. We can extend the above program still further by creating a pointer to a pointer to an integer pointer. In principle, you would agree that likewise there could exist a pointer to a pointer to a pointer to a pointer to a pointer. There is no limit on how far can we go on extending this definition. Possibly, till the point we can comprehend it. And that point of comprehension is usually a pointer to a pointer. Beyond this, one rarely requires to extend the definition of a pointer. But just in case...

Back to Function Calls

Having had the first tryst with pointers, let us now get back to what we had originally set out to learn—the two types of function calls—call by value and call by reference. Arguments can generally be passed to functions in one of the two ways:

(a) sending the values of the arguments
(b) sending the addresses of the arguments

In the first method, the 'value' of each of the actual arguments in the calling function is copied into corresponding formal arguments of the called function. With this method, the changes made to the formal arguments in the called function have no effect on the values of actual arguments in the calling function. The following program illustrates the 'Call by Value'.

```
# include <stdio.h>
void swapv ( int  x, int  y ) ;
int main( )
{
    int  a = 10, b = 20 ;
    swapv ( a, b ) ;
    printf ( "a = %d b = %d\n", a, b ) ;
    return 0 ;
}
void swapv ( int  x, int  y )
{
    int  t ;
    t = x ;
    x = y ;
    y = t ;
    printf ( "x = %d y = %d\n", x, y ) ;
}
```

The output of the above program would be:

```
x = 20 y = 10
a = 10 b = 20
```

Note that values of **a** and **b** remain unchanged even after exchanging the values of **x** and **y**.

In the second method (call by reference), the addresses of actual arguments in the calling function are copied into the formal arguments of the called function. This means that, using these addresses, we would have an access to the actual arguments and hence we would be able to manipulate them. The following program illustrates this fact.

```
# include <stdio.h>
void swapr ( int *, int * ) ;
int main( )
{
    int a = 10, b = 20 ;
    swapr ( &a, &b ) ;
    printf ( "a = %d b = %d\n", a, b ) ;
    return 0 ;
}
void swapr ( int *x, int *y )
{
    int t ;
    t = *x ;
    *x = *y ;
    *y = t ;
}
```

The output of the above program would be:

```
a = 20 b = 10
```

Note that this program manages to exchange the values of **a** and **b** using their addresses stored in **x** and **y**.

Usually, in C programming, we make a call by value. This means that, in general, you cannot alter the actual arguments. But if desired, it can always be achieved through a call by reference.

Using a call by reference intelligently, we can make a function return more than one value at a time, which is not possible ordinarily. This is shown in the program given below.

```
# include <stdio.h>
void areaperi ( int, float *, float * ) ;
int main( )
{
    int radius ;
    float area, perimeter ;
```

```
    printf ( "Enter radius of a circle " ) ;
    scanf ( "%d", &radius ) ;
    areaperi ( radius, &area, &perimeter ) ;

    printf ( "Area = %f\n", area ) ;
    printf ( "Perimeter = %f\n", perimeter ) ;
    return 0 ;
}
void areaperi ( int  r, float  *a, float  *p )
{
    *a = 3.14 * r * r ;
    *p = 2 * 3.14 * r ;
}
```

And here is the output...

```
Enter radius of a circle 5
Area = 78.500000
Perimeter = 31.400000
```

Here, we are making a mixed call, in the sense, we are passing the value of **radius** but, addresses of **area** and **perimeter**. And since we are passing the addresses, any change that we make in values stored at addresses contained in the variables **a** and **p**, would make the change effective in **main( )**. That is why, when the control returns from the function **areaperi( )**, we are able to output the values of **area** and **perimeter**.

Thus, we have been able to indirectly return two values from a called function, and hence, have overcome the limitation of the **return** statement, which can return only one value from a function at a time.

Conclusions

From the programs that we discussed here, we can draw the following conclusions:

(a) If we want that the value of an actual argument should not get changed in the function being called, pass the actual argument by value.

(b) If we want that the value of an actual argument should get changed in the function being called, pass the actual argument by reference.

(c) If a function is to be made to return more than one value at a time, then return these values indirectly by using a call by reference.

Recursion

In C, it is possible for the functions to call themselves. A function is called 'recursive' if a statement within the body of a function calls the same function. Sometimes called 'circular definition', recursion is thus the process of defining something in terms of itself.

Let us now see a simple example of recursion. Suppose we want to calculate the factorial value of an integer. As we know, the factorial of a number is the product of all the integers between 1 and that number. For example, 4 factorial is 4 * 3 * 2 * 1. This can also be expressed as 4! = 4 * 3! where '!' stands for factorial. Thus factorial of a number can be expressed in the form of itself. Hence this can be programmed using recursion. However, before we try to write a recursive function for calculating factorial let us take a look at the non-recursive function for calculating the factorial value of an integer.

```
# include <stdio.h>
int factorial ( int ) ;
int main( )
{
    int a, fact ;

    printf ( "Enter any number " ) ;
    scanf ( "%d", &a ) ;

    fact = factorial ( a ) ;
    printf ( "Factorial value = %d\n", fact ) ;\
    return 0 ;
}

int factorial ( int x )
{
    int f = 1, i ;

    for ( i = x ; i >= 1 ; i-- )
        f = f * i ;

    return ( f ) ;
}
```

And here is the output...

```
Enter any number 3
Factorial value = 6
```

Work through the above program carefully, till you understand the logic of the program properly. Recursive factorial function can be understood only if you are thorough with the above logic.

Following is the recursive version of the function to calculate the factorial value.

```
# include <stdio.h>
int rec ( int ) ;
int main( )
{
    int a, fact ;

    printf ( "Enter any number " ) ;
    scanf ( "%d", &a ) ;

    fact = rec ( a ) ;
    printf ( "Factorial value = %d\n", fact ) ;
    return 0 ;
}
int rec ( int x )
{
    int f ;

    if ( x == 1 )
        return ( 1 ) ;
    else
        f = x * rec ( x - 1 ) ;

    return ( f ) ;
}
```

And here is the output for four runs of the program

```
Enter any number 1
Factorial value = 1
Enter any number 2
Factorial value = 2
Enter any number 3
Factorial value = 6
Enter any number 5
Factorial value = 120
```

Let us understand this recursive factorial function thoroughly. In the first run when the number entered through **scanf( )** is 1, let us see what action does **rec( )** take. The value of **a** (i.e. 1) is copied into **x**. Since **x** turns out to be 1, the condition **if (x == 1)** is satisfied and hence 1 (which indeed is the value of 1 factorial) is returned through the **return** statement.

When the number entered through **scanf( )** is 2, the **(x == 1)** test fails, so we reach the statement,

```
f = x * rec ( x - 1 ) ;
```

And here is where we meet recursion. How do we handle the expression **x * rec (x - 1)**? We multiply **x** by **rec (x - 1)**. Since the current value of **x** is 2, it is same as saying that we must calculate the value (2 * rec (1)). We know that the value returned by **rec (1)** is 1, so the expression reduces to (2 * 1), or simply 2. Thus the statement,

```
x * rec ( x - 1 ) ;
```

evaluates to 2, which is stored in the variable **f**, and is returned to **main( )**, where it is duly printed as

```
Factorial value = 2
```

Now perhaps you can see what would happen if the value of **a** is 3, 4, 5 and so on.

In case the value of **a** is 5, **main( )** would call **rec( )** with 5 as its actual argument, and **rec( )** will send back the computed value. But before sending the computed value, **rec( )** calls **rec( )** and waits for a value to be returned. It is possible for the **rec( )** that has just been called to call yet another **rec( )**, the argument **x** being decreased in value by 1 for each of these recursive calls. We speak of this series of calls to **rec( )** as being different invocations of **rec( )**. These successive invocations of the same function are possible because the C compiler keeps track of which invocation calls which. These recursive invocations end finally when the last invocation gets an argument value of 1, which the preceding invocation of **rec( )** now uses to calculate its own **f** value and so on up the ladder. So we might say what happens is,

```
rec ( 5 ) returns ( 5 times rec ( 4 ),
    which returns ( 4 times rec ( 3 ),
        which returns ( 3 times rec ( 2 ),
            which returns ( 2 times rec ( 1 ),
                which returns ( 1 ) ) ) ) )
```

Foxed? Well, that is recursion for you in its simplest garbs. I hope you agree that it's difficult to visualize how the control flows from one function call to another. Possibly Figure 7.4 would make things a bit clearer.

Assume that the number entered through **scanf( )** is 3. Using Figure 7.4 let's visualize what exactly happens when the recursive function **rec( )** gets called. Go through the figure carefully. The first time when **rec( )** is called from **main( )**, **x** collects 3. From here, since **x** is not equal to 1, the **if** block is skipped and **rec( )** is called again with the argument (**x – 1**), i.e. 2. This is a recursive call. Since **x** is still not equal to 1, **rec( )** is called yet another time, with argument (2 - 1). This time as **x** is 1, control goes back to previous **rec( )** with the value 1, and **f** is evaluated as 2.

Similarly, each **rec( )** evaluates its **f** from the returned value, and finally 6 is returned to **main( )**. The sequence would be grasped better by following the arrows shown in Figure 7.4. Let it be clear that while executing the program, there do not exist so many copies of the function **rec( )**. These have been shown in the figure just to help you keep track of how the control flows during successive recursive calls.

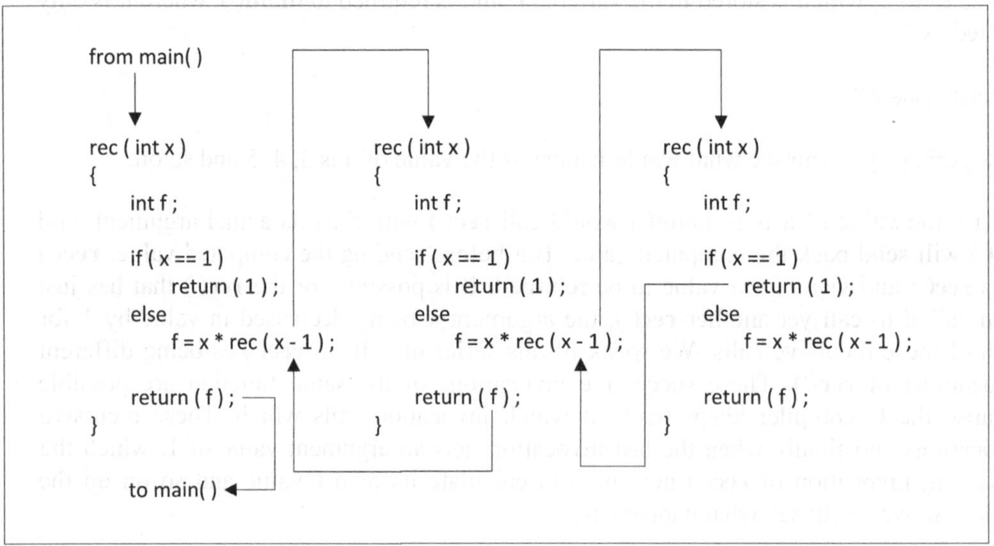

Figure 7.4

Recursion may seem strange and complicated at first glance, but it is often the most direct way to code an algorithm, and once you are familiar with recursion, the clearest way of doing so.

Recursion and Stack

There are different ways in which data can be organized. For example, if you are to store five numbers then we can store them in five different variables, an array, a linked list, a binary tree, etc. All these different ways of organizing the data are known as data structures. The compiler uses one such data structure called stack for implementing normal as well as recursive function calls.

A stack is a Last In First Out (LIFO) data structure. This means that the last item to get stored on the stack (often called Push operation) is the first one to get out of it (often called as Pop operation). You can compare this to the stack of plates in a cafeteria—the last plate that goes on the stack is the first one to get out of it. Now let us see how the stack works in case of the following program.

```
# include <stdio.h>
int add ( int, int ) ;
int main( )
{
    int a = 5, b = 2, c ;
    c = add ( a, b ) ;
    printf ( "sum = %d\n", c ) ;
    return 0 ;
}
int add ( int i, int j )
{
    int sum ;
    sum = i + j ;
    return sum ;
}
```

In this program, before transferring the execution control to the function **add( )**, the values of parameters **a** and **b** are pushed on the stack. Following this, the address of the statement **printf( )** is pushed on the stack and the control is transferred to **add( )**. It is necessary to push this address on the stack. In **add( )**, the values of **a** and **b** that were pushed on the stack are referred as **i** and **j**. Once inside **add( )**, the local variable **sum** gets pushed on the stack. When value of **sum** is returned, **sum** is popped off from the stack. Next, the address of the statement where the control should be returned, is popped off from the stack. Using this address, the control returns to the **printf( )** statement in **main( )**. Before execution of **printf( )** begins, the two integers that were earlier pushed on the stack are now popped off.

How the values are being pushed and popped even though we didn't write any code to do so? Simple—the compiler, on encountering the function call, would generate code to push the parameters and the address. Similarly, it would generate code to clear the stack when the control returns back from **add( )**. Figure 7.5 shows the contents of the stack at different stages of execution.

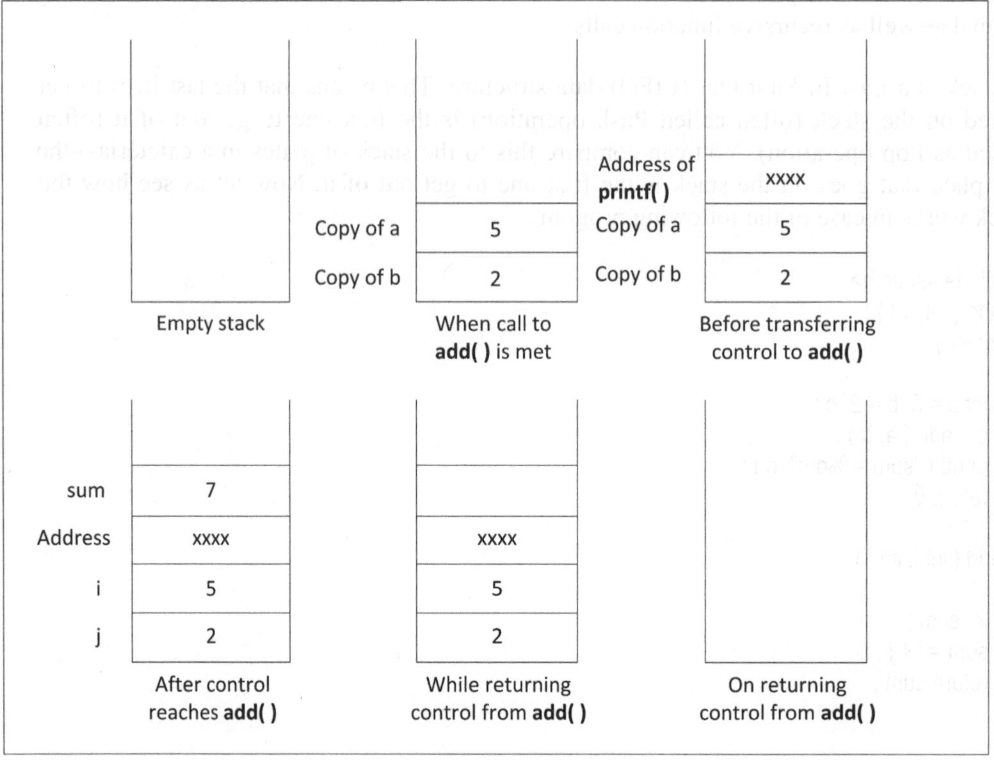

Figure 7.5

Note that in this program, popping of **sum** and address is done by **add( )**, whereas, popping of the two integers is done by **main( )**. When it is done this way, it is known as 'CDecl Calling Convention'. There are other calling conventions as well, where instead of **main( )**, **add( )** itself clears the two integers. The calling convention also decides whether the parameters being passed to the function are pushed on the stack in left-to-right or right-to-left order. The standard calling convention always uses the right-to-left order. Thus, during the call to **add( )** firstly value of **b** is pushed to the stack, followed by the value of **a**.

The recursive calls are no different. Whenever we make a recursive call the parameters and the return address gets pushed on the stack. The stack gets unwound when the control returns from the called function. Thus during every recursive function call we are working with a fresh set of parameters.

Also, note that while writing recursive functions, you must have an **if** statement somewhere in the recursive function to force the function to return without recursive call being executed. If you don't do this and you call the function, you will fall in an indefinite loop, and the stack will keep on getting filled with parameters and the return address each time there is a call. Soon the stack would become full and you would get a run-time error indicating that the stack has become full. This is a very common error while writing recursive functions. My advice is to use **printf( )** statement liberally during the development of recursive function, so that you can watch what is going on and can abort execution if you see that you have made a mistake.

Adding Functions to the Library

Most of the times, we either use the functions present in the standard library or we define our own functions and use them. Can we not add our functions to the standard library? And would it make any sense in doing so? We can add user-defined functions to the library. It makes sense in doing so as the functions that are to be added to the library are first compiled and then added. When we use these functions (by calling them), we save on their compilation time as they are available in the library in the compiled form.

Let us now see how to add user-defined functions to the library. Different compilers provide different utilities to add/delete/modify functions in the standard library. For example, Turbo C/C++ compilers provide a utility called 'tlib.exe' (Turbo Librarian). Let us use this utility to add a function **factorial( )** to the library.

Given below are the steps to do so:

(a) Write the function definition of **factorial( )** in some file, say 'fact.c'.

```
int factorial ( int num )
{
    int i, f = 1 ;
    for ( i = 1 ; i <= num ; i++ )
        f = f * i ;
    return ( f ) ;
}
```

(b) Compile the 'fact.c' file using Alt F9. A new file called 'fact.obj' will get created containing the compiled code in machine language.

(c) Add the function to the library 'maths.lib' by issuing the command

```
C:\>tlib maths.lib + c:\fact.obj
```

Here, 'maths.lib' is a library filename, + is a switch, which means we want to add a new function to library and 'c:\fact.obj' is the path of the '.obj' file.

(d) Declare the prototype of the **factorial( )** function in the header file, say 'fact.h'. This file should be included while calling the function.

(e) To use the function present inside the library, create a program as shown below:

```
# include "c:\fact.h"
# include <stdio.h>
int main( )
{
    int f ;
    f = factorial ( 5 ) ;
    printf ( "%d\n", f ) ;
    return 0 ;
}
```

(f) Compile and execute the program using Ctrl F9.

If we wish we can delete the existing functions present in the library using the minus (-) switch.

Instead of modifying the existing libraries, we can create our own library. Let's see how to do this. Let us assume that we wish to create a library containing the functions **factorial( )**, **prime( )** and **fibonacci( )**. As their names suggest, **factorial( )** calculates and returns the factorial value of the integer passed to it, **prime( )** reports whether the number passed to it is a prime number or not and **fibonacci( )** prints the first **n** terms of the Fibonacci series, where **n** is the number passed to it. Here are the steps that need to be carried out to create this library. Note that, these steps are specific to Turbo C/C++ compiler and would vary for other compilers.

(a) Define the functions **factorial( )**, **prime( )** and **fibonacci( )** in a file, say 'myfuncs.c'. Do not define **main( )** in this file.

(b) Create a file 'myfuncs.h' and declare the prototypes of **factorial( )**, **prime( )** and **fibonacci( )** in it as shown below:

```
int factorial ( int ) ;
int prime ( int ) ;
void fibonacci ( int ) ;
```

(c) From the Options menu select the menu-item 'Application'. From the dialog that pops us select the option 'Library'. Select OK.

(d) Compile the program using Alt F9. This would create the library file called 'myfuncs.lib'.

That's it. The library now stands created. Now we have to use the functions defined in this library. Here is how it can be done.

(a) Create a file, say 'sample.c' and type the following code in it.

```
# include "myfuncs.h"
# include <stdio.h>
int main( )
{
    int f, result ;
    f = factorial ( 5 ) ;
    result = prime ( 13 ) ;
    fibonacci ( 6 ) ;
    printf ( "%d %d\n", f, result ) ;
    return 0 ;
}
```

Note that the file 'myfuncs.h' should be in the same directory as the file 'sample.c'. If not, then while including 'myfuncs.h' mention the appropriate path.

(b) Go to the 'Project' menu and select 'Open Project…' option. On doing so a dialog would pop up. Give the name of the project, say 'sample.prj' and select OK.

(c) From the 'Project' menu select 'Add Item'. On doing so a file dialog would appear. Select the file 'sample.c' and then select 'Add'. Also add the file 'myfuncs.lib' in the same manner. Finally select 'Done'.

(d) Compile and execute the project using Ctrl F9.

Summary

(a) To avoid repetition of code and bulky programs functionally related statements are isolated into a function.

(b) Function declaration specifies the return type of the function and the types of parameters it accepts.

(c) Function definition defines the body of the function.

(d) Variables declared in a function are not available to other functions in a program. So, there won't be any clash even if we give same name to the variables declared in different functions.

(e) Pointers are variables which hold addresses of other variables.

(f) A function can be called either by value or by reference.

(g) Pointers can be used to make a function return more than one value simultaneously.

(h) Recursion is difficult to understand, but in some cases offer a better solution than loops.

(i) Adding too many functions and calling them frequently may slow down the program execution.

Exercise

Simple functions, Passing values between functions

[A] What will be the output of the following programs:

(a)
```
# include <stdio.h>
void display( ) ;
int main( )
{
    printf ( "Only stupids use C?\n" ) ;
    display( ) ;
    return 0 ;
}
void display( )
{
    printf ( "Fools too use C!\n" ) ;
    main( ) ;
}
```

(b)
```
# include <stdio.h>
int main( )
```

```
    {
        printf ( "C to it that C survives\n" ) ;
        main( ) ;
        return 0 ;
    }
```

(c)
```
    # include <stdio.h>
    int check ( int ) ;
    int main( )
    {
        int  i = 45, c ;
        c = check ( i ) ;
        printf ( "%d\n", c ) ;
        return 0 ;
    }
    int check ( int  ch )
    {
        if ( ch >= 45 )
            return ( 100 ) ;
        else
            return ( 10 * 10 ) ;
    }
```

(d)
```
    # include <stdio.h>
    int check ( int ) ;
    int main( )
    {
        int  i = 45, c ;
        c = multiply ( i * 1000 ) ;
        printf ( "%d\n", c ) ;
        return 0 ;
    }
    int check ( int  ch )
    {
        if ( ch >= 40000 )
            return ( ch / 10 ) ;
        else
            return ( 10 ) ;
    }
```

(e)
```
    # include <stdio.h>
    int rec ( int ) ;
    int main( )
    {
```

```
    int k, j ;
    j = 12121 ;
    k = rec ( j ) ;
    printf ( "%d\n", k ) ;
    return 0 ;
}
int rec ( int n )
{
    int dig, sum = 0 ;
    if ( n == 0 )
        return ( sum ) ;
    else
    {
        dig = n % 10 ;
        sum = sum + dig ;
        n = ( n - dig ) / 10 ;
        rec ( n ) ;
    }
}
```

(f)
```
# include <stdio.h>
int fact ( int ) ;
int main( )
{
    int f, i = 10 ;
    f = fact ( i ) ;
    printf ( "%d\n", f ) ;
    return 0 ;
}
int fact ( int n )
{
    int k = 1, fact = 1 ;
    for ( k = 1 ; k <= n ; k++ )
        fact = fact * k ;
    return ( fact ) ;
}
```

(g)
```
# include <stdio.h>
float product ( float, int ) ;
int main( )
{
    float a = 3.5, b = 2 ;
    printf ( "%f\n", product ( a, b ) ) ;
```

```
    return 0 ;
}
float product ( float a, int b )
{
    return ( a * b ) ;
}
```

(h)
```
# include <stdio.h>
int funct ( int ) ;
int main( )
{
    printf ( "%d\n", funct ( 5 - funct ( 5 ) ) ) ;
    return 0 ;
}
int funct ( int accept )
{
    return accept *= 5 ;
}
```

(i)
```
# include <stdio.h>
int main( )
{
    printf ( "0" ) ? printf ( "confused completely" ) : printf ( "incredible C" ) ;
    return 0 ;
}
```

[B] Point out the errors, if any, in the following programs:

(a)
```
# include <stdio.h>
int addmult ( int, int )
int main( )
{
    int i = 3, j = 4, k, l ;
    k = addmult ( i, j ) ;
    l = addmult ( i, j ) ;
    printf ( "%d %d\n", k, l ) ;
    return 0 ;
}
int addmult ( int ii, int jj )
{
    int kk, ll ;
    kk = ii + jj ;
    ll = ii * jj ;
```

```
        return ( kk, ll ) ;
    }
```

(b)
```
# include <stdio.h>
void message( ) ;
int main( )
{
    int  a ;
    a = message( ) ;
    return 0 ;
}
void message( )
{
    printf ( "Viruses are written in C\n" ) ;
    return ;
}
```

(c)
```
# include <stdio.h>
int main( )
{
    float  a = 15.5 ;
    char  ch = 'C' ;
    printit ( a, ch ) ;
    return 0 ;
}
printit ( a, ch )
{
    printf ( "%f %c\n", a, ch ) ;
}
```

(d)
```
# include <stdio.h>
void message( ) ;
int main( )
{
    message( ) ;
    message( ) ;
    return 0 ;
}
void message( ) ;
{
    printf ( "Praise worthy and C worthy are synonyms\n" ) ;
}
```

(e)
```
# include <stdio.h>
```

```
int main( )
{
    let_us_c( )
    {
        printf ( "C is a Cimple minded language !\n" ) ;
        printf ( "Others are of course no match !\n" ) ;
    }
    return 0 ;
}
```

(f)
```
# include <stdio.h>
void message( ) ;
int main( )
{
    message ( message( ) ) ;
    return 0 ;
}
void message( )
{
    printf ( "It's a small world after all...\n" ) ;
}
```

(g)
```
# include <stdio.h>
int main( )
{
    int i ;
    cls( ) ;
    for ( i = 0 ; i <= 255 ; i++ )
        printf ( "%d %c\n", i, i ) ;
    return 0 ;
}
```

(h)
```
# include <stdio.h>
void display( )
{
    printf ( "This does not work\n" ) ;
}
int main( )
{
    display( ) ;
    return 0 ;
}
```

(i)
```
# include <stdio.h>
int main( )
{
    float a = 1.5 ;
    printf ( "%f\n", square ( a ) ) ;
    return 0 ;
}
float square ( float a )
{
    return ( a * a ) ;
}
```

(j)
```
# include <stdio.h>
void g ( int a )
{
    printf ( "a" ) ;
}
int main( )
{
    void g ( void ) ;
    int a ;
    a = g ( 100 ) ;
    return 0 ;
}
```

(k)
```
# include <stdio.h>
int main( )
{
    printf ( "HELLO is it 1 0 0" ) ;
    phonecall( )
    {
        printf ( "Wrong Number" ) ;
    }
    return 0 ;
}
```

[C] Answer the following:

(a) Is this a correctly written function:

```
int sqr ( int a ) ;
{
    return ( a * a ) ;
```

```
}
```

(b) Is this a correctly written function:

```
abs ( int num ) ;
{
    if ( num < 0 )
        num = -num ;
    return ( num ) ;
}
```

(c) State whether the following statements are True or False:

1. The variables commonly used in C functions are available to all the functions in a program.

2. To return the control back to the calling function we must use the keyword **return**.

3. The same variable names can be used in different functions without any conflict.

4. Every called function must contain a **return** statement.

5. A function may contain more than one **return** statements.

6. Each **return** statement in a function may return a different value.

7. A function can still be useful even if you don't pass any arguments to it and the function doesn't return any value back.

8. Same names can be used for different functions without any conflict.

9. A function may be called more than once from any other function.

10. It is necessary for a function to return some value.

11. A function can be defined within another function.

12. Two functions having same name but different number and types of arguments, can exist in a program.

[D] Answer the following:

(a) Write a function to calculate the factorial value of any integer entered through the keyboard.

(b) Write a function **power (a, b)**, to calculate the value of **a** raised to **b**.

(c) Write a general-purpose function to convert any given year into its roman equivalent. The following table shows the roman equivalents of decimal numbers:

Decimal	Roman	Decimal	Roman
1	i	100	c
5	v	500	d
10	x	1000	m
50	l		

Example:

Roman equivalent of 1988 is mdcccclxxxviii
Roman equivalent of 1525 is mdxxv

(d) Any year is entered through the keyboard. Write a function to determine whether the year is a leap year or not.

(e) A positive integer is entered through the keyboard. Write a function to obtain the prime factors of this number.

For example, prime factors of 24 are 2, 2, 2 and 3, whereas prime factors of 35 are 5 and 7.

Function Prototypes, Call by Value/Reference, Pointers

[E] What will be the output of the following programs:

(a)
```
# include <stdio.h>
float circle ( int ) ;
int main( )
{
    float area ;
    int radius = 1 ;
    area = circle ( radius ) ;
    printf ( "%f\n", area ) ;
    return 0 ;
```

```
}
float circle ( int r )
{
    float a ;
    a = 3.14 * r * r ;
    return ( a ) ;
}
```

(b)
```
#include <stdio.h>
int main( )
{
    void slogan( ) ;
    int c = 5 ;
    c = slogan( ) ;
    printf ( "%d\n", c ) ;
    return 0 ;
}
void slogan( )
{
    printf ( "Only He men use C!\n" ) ;
}
```

[F] Answer the following:

(a) Write a function which receives a **float** and an **int** from **main( )**, finds the product of these two and returns the product which is printed through **main( )**.

(b) Write a function that receives 5 integers and returns the sum, average and standard deviation of these numbers. Call this function from **main( )** and print the results in **main( )**.

(c) Write a function that receives marks received by a student in 3 subjects and returns the average and percentage of these marks. Call this function from **main( )** and print the results in **main( )**.

(d) Write a prototype for a function **fool( )**. This function when called receives two values of type **float** and **int** and on performing some calculations returns a **double** value.

(e) How would you send back 3 values from a function simultaneously?

(f) Complete the following program:

```
int main( )
{
    int sum, pro, a = 2, b = 2 ;
    fu ( a, b, &sum, &pro ) ;
    printf ( "%d %d\n", sum, pro ) ;
    fu ( &a, &b, &sum, &pro ) ;
    printf ( "%d %d\n", sum, pro ) ;
    return 0 ;
}
```

(g) Write a prototype of a function which accepts an integer and returns an integer pointer.

[G] What will be the output of the following programs:

(a)
```
# include <stdio.h>
void fun ( int, int ) ;
int main( )
{
    int i = 5, j = 2 ;
    fun ( i, j ) ;
    printf ( "%d %d\n", i, j ) ;
    return 0 ;
}
void fun ( int i, int j )
{
    i = i * i ;
    j = j * j ;
}
```

(b)
```
# include <stdio.h>
void fun ( int *, int * ) ;
int main( )
{
    int i = 5, j = 2 ;
    fun ( &i, &j ) ;
    printf ( "%d %d\n", i, j ) ;
    return 0 ;
}
void fun ( int *i, int *j )
{
    *i = *i * *i ;
    *j = *j * *j ;
}
```

(c)
```
# include <stdio.h>
void fun ( int *x, int y )
int main( )
{
    int i = 4, j = 2 ;
    fun ( &i, j ) ;
    printf ( "%d %d\n", i, j ) ;
    return 0 ;
}
void fun ( int *i, int j )
{
    *i = *i * *i ;
    j = j * j ;
}
```

(d)
```
# include <stdio.h>
int main( )
{
    float a = 13.5 ;
    float *b, *c ;
    b = &a ; /* suppose address of a is 1006 */
    c = b ;
    printf ( "%u %u %u\n", &a, b, c ) ;
    printf ( "%f %f %f %f %f\n", a, *(&a), *&a, *b, *c ) ;
    return 0 ;
}
```

[H] Point out the errors, if any, in the following programs:

(a)
```
# include <stdio.h>
void pass ( int, int ) ;
int main( )
{
    int i = 135, a = 135, k ;
    k = pass ( i, a ) ;
    printf ( "%d\n", k ) ;
    return 0 ;
}
void pass ( int j, int b )
int c ;
{
    c = j + b ;
    return ( c ) ;
```

```
}
```

(b)
```
# include <stdio.h>
void jiaayjo ( int , int  )
int main( )
{
    int  p = 23, f = 24 ;
    jiaayjo ( &p, &f ) ;
    printf ( "%d %d\n", p, f ) ;
    return 0 ;
}
void jiaayjo ( int  q, int  g )
{
    q = q + q ;
    g = g + g ;
}
```

(c)
```
# include <stdio.h>
void check ( int ) ;
int main( )
{
    int  k = 35, z ;
    z = check ( k ) ;
    printf ( "%d\n", z ) ;
    return 0 ;
}
void check ( m )
{
    int  m ;
    if ( m > 40 )
        return ( 1 ) ;
    else
        return ( 0 ) ;
}
```

(d)
```
# include <stdio.h>
void function ( int  * ) ;
int main( )
{
    int  i = 35, *z ;
    z = function ( &i ) ;
    printf ( "%d\n", z ) ;
    return 0 ;
}
```

```
void function ( int *m )
{
    return ( m + 2 ) ;
}
```

[I] What will be the output of the following programs:

(a)
```
# include <stdio.h>
int main( )
{
    int i = 0 ;
    i++ ;
    if ( i <= 5 )
    {
        printf ( "C adds wings to your thoughts\n" ) ;
        exit( ) ;
        main( ) ;
    }
    return 0 ;
}
```

(b)
```
# include <stdio.h>
int main( )
{
    static int i = 0 ;
    i++ ;
    if ( i <= 5 )
    {
        printf ( "%d\n", i ) ;
        main( ) ;
    }
    else
        exit( ) ;
    return 0 ;
}
```

[J] Attempt the following:

(a) A 5-digit positive integer is entered through the keyboard, write a function to calculate sum of digits of the 5-digit number:

(1) Without using recursion
(2) Using recursion

(b) A positive integer is entered through the keyboard, write a program to obtain the prime factors of the number. Modify the function suitably to obtain the prime factors recursively.

(c) Write a recursive function to obtain the first 25 numbers of a Fibonacci sequence. In a Fibonacci sequence the sum of two successive terms gives the third term. Following are the first few terms of the Fibonacci sequence:

1 1 2 3 5 8 13 21 34 55 89...

(d) A positive integer is entered through the keyboard, write a function to find the binary equivalent of this number using recursion.

(e) Write a recursive function to obtain the running sum of first 25 natural numbers.

(f) Write a C function to evaluate the series

$$\sin(x) = x - (x^3/3!) + (x^5/5!) - (x^7/7!) + \cdots$$

to five significant digits.

(g) Given three variables **x, y, z** write a function to circularly shift their values to right. In other words if x = 5, y = 8, z = 10 after circular shift y = 5, z = 8, x =10 after circular shift y = 5, z = 8 and x = 10. Call the function with variables **a, b, c** to circularly shift values.

(h) Write a function to find the binary equivalent of a given decimal integer and display it.

(i) If the lengths of the sides of a triangle are denoted by **a**, **b**, and **c**, then area of triangle is given by

$$area = \sqrt{S(S-a)(S-b)(S-c)}$$

where, S = (a + b + c) / 2

(j) Write a function to compute the distance between two points and use it to develop another function that will compute the area of the triangle whose vertices are **A(x1, y1)**, **B(x2, y2)**, and **C(x3, y3)**. Use these functions to develop a function which returns a value 1 if the point **(x, y)** lines inside the triangle ABC, otherwise a value 0.

(k) Write a function to compute the greatest common divisor given by Euclid's algorithm, exemplified for J = 1980, K = 1617 as follows:

1980 / 1617 = 1 1980 – 1 * 1617 = 363

1617 / 363 = 4   1617 – 4 * 363 = 165
363 / 165 = 2   363 – 2 * 165 = 33
5 / 33 = 5   165 – 5 * 33 = 0

Thus, the greatest common divisor is 33.

(l) A program is to be written to obtain the sum of the following series upto 10 terms. RECURSION should be used.

$$\frac{x}{1!} - \frac{x^3}{3!} + \frac{x^5}{5!} - \frac{x^7}{7!} + \frac{x^9}{9!} \ldots.$$

(m) A 'perfect' number is a number for which the sum of all its divisors is equal to the number itself. For example, 6 is a perfect number because the sum of its divisors 1, 2 and 3 is 6 itself. Similarly, a number whose sum of divisors is greater than the number itself is known as an 'abundant' number. For example, 12 is an abundant number since (1 + 2 + 3 + 4 + 6) > 12. Likewise, 9 is a 'deficient' number since the sum of its divisors (1 + 3) is less than 9 itself. Write a function which receives a number and passes back information whether the number is perfect, abundant or deficient.

(n) Write a program using recursion to convert a base 10 number to a base 2 number.

(o) Find the sum of the following series upto 10 terms.

$$x/((x+1)^2 (x+2)^3) - x^2/((x+2)^3 (x+3)^4) + x^3/((x+3)^4 (x+4)^5) - \ldots\ldots \text{upto10terms.}$$

8 Data Types Revisited

As seen in the first chapter, the primary data types could be of three varieties—**char**, **int**, and **float**. It may seem odd to many, how C programmers manage with such a tiny set of data types. Fact is, the C programmers aren't really deprived. They can derive many data types from these three types. In fact, the number of data types that can be derived in C, is in principle, unlimited. A C programmer can always invent whatever data type he needs, as we would see later in Chapter 10.

Not only this, the primary data types themselves could be of several types. For example, a **char** could be an **unsigned char** or a **signed char**. Or an **int** could be a **short int** or a **long int**. Sufficiently confusing? Well, let us take a closer look at these variations of primary data types in this chapter.

To fully define a variable, one needs to mention not only its type but also its storage class. In this chapter we would be exploring the different storage classes and their relevance in C programming.

Integers, *long* and *short*

We had seen earlier that the range of an Integer constant depends upon the compiler. For a 16-bit compiler like Turbo C or Turbo C++ the range is –32768 to 32767. For a 32-bit compiler the range would be –2147483648 to +2147483647. Here a 16-bit compiler means that when it compiles a C program it generates machine language code that is targeted towards working on a 16-bit microprocessor like Intel 8086/8088. As against this, a 32-bit compiler like VC++ generates machine language code that is targeted towards a 32-bit microprocessor like Intel Pentium. Note that this does not mean that a program compiled using Turbo C would not work on 32-bit processor. It would run successfully but at that time the 32-bit processor would work as if it were a 16-bit processor. This happens because a 32-bit processor provides support for programs compiled using 16-bit compilers. If this backward compatibility support is not provided the 16-bit program would not run on it. This is precisely what happens on the new Intel Itanium processors, which have withdrawn support for 16-bit code.

Remember that out of the two/four bytes used to store an integer, the highest bit ($16^{th}/32^{nd}$ bit) is used to store the sign of the integer. This bit is 1 if the number is negative, and 0 if the number is positive.

C offers a variation of the integer data type that provides what are called **short** and **long** integer values. The intention of providing these variations is to provide integers with different ranges wherever possible. Though not a rule, **short** and **long** integers would usually occupy two and four bytes respectively. Each compiler can decide appropriate sizes depending on the operating system and hardware, for which it is being written, subject to the following rules:

(a) **short**s are at least 2 bytes big
(b) **long**s are at least 4 bytes big
(c) **short**s are never bigger than **int**s
(d) **int**s are never bigger than **long**s

Figure 8.1 shows the sizes of different integers based upon the OS used.

Compiler	short	int	long
16-bit (Turbo C/C++)	2	2	4
32-bit (Visual C++)	2	4	4

Figure 8.1

long variables which hold **long** integers are declared using the keyword **long**, as in,

```
long int i ;
long int abc ;
```

long integers cause the program to run a bit slower, but the range of values that we can use is expanded tremendously. The value of a **long** integer typically can vary from -2147483648 to +2147483647. More than this you should not need unless you are taking a world census.

If there are such things as **long**s, symmetry requires **short**s as well—integers that need less space in memory and thus help speed up program execution. **short** integer variables are declared as,

```
short int j ;
short int height ;
```

C allows the abbreviation of **short int** to **short** and of **long int** to **long**. So the declarations made above can be written as,

```
long i ;
long abc ;
short j ;
short height ;
```

Naturally, most C programmers prefer this short-cut.

Sometimes, we come across situations where the constant is small enough to be an **int**, but still we want to give it as much storage as a **long**. In such cases, we add the suffix 'L' or 'l' at the end of the number, as in 23L.

Integers, *signed* and *unsigned*

Sometimes, we know in advance that the value stored in a given integer variable will always be positive—when it is being used to only count things, for example. In such a case we can declare the variable to be **unsigned**, as in,

```
unsigned int num_students ;
```

With such a declaration, the range of permissible integer values (for a 16-bit OS) will shift from the range -32768 to +32767 to the range 0 to 65535. Thus, declaring an integer as **unsigned** almost doubles the size of the largest possible value that it can otherwise take. This so happens because on declaring the integer as **unsigned**, the left-most bit is now free and is not used to store the sign of the number. Note that an **unsigned** integer still occupies two bytes. This is how an **unsigned** integer can be declared:

```
unsigned int i ;
unsigned i ;
```

Like an **unsigned int**, there also exists a **short unsigned int** and a **long unsigned int**. By default, a **short int** is a **signed short int** and a **long int** is a **signed long int**.

Chars, *signed* and *unsigned*

Parallel to **signed** and **unsigned int**s (either **short** or **long**), there also exist **signed** and **unsigned char**s, both occupying one byte each, but having different ranges. To begin with, it might appear strange as to how a **char** can have a sign. Consider the statement

```
char ch = 'A' ;
```

Here what gets stored in **ch** is the binary equivalent of the ASCII value of 'A' (i.e. binary of 65). And if 65's binary can be stored, then -54's binary can also be stored (in a **signed char**).

A **signed char** is same as an ordinary **char** and has a range from -128 to +127; whereas, an **unsigned char** has a range from 0 to 255. Let us now see a program that illustrates this range:

```
# include <stdio.h>
int main( )
{
    char ch = 291 ;
    printf ( "\n%d %c\n", ch, ch ) ;
    return 0 ;
}
```

What output do you expect from this program? Possibly, 291 and the character corresponding to it. Well, not really. Surprised? The reason is that **ch** has been defined as a **char**, and a **char** cannot take a value bigger than +127. Hence when value of **ch** exceeds +127, an appropriate value from the other side of the range is picked up and stored in **ch**. This value in our case happens to be 35, hence 35 and its corresponding character #, gets printed out.

Here is another program that would make the concept clearer.

```
# include <stdio.h>
int main( )
{
    char ch ;

    for ( ch = 0 ; ch <= 255 ; ch++ )
        printf ( "%d %c\n", ch, ch ) ;
    return 0 ;
}
```

This program should output ASCII values and their corresponding characters. Well, No! This is an indefinite loop. The reason is that **ch** has been defined as a **char**, and a **char** cannot take values bigger than +127. Hence when value of **ch** is +127 and we perform **ch++** it becomes -128 instead of +128. -128 is less than 255, hence the condition is still satisfied. Here onwards **ch** would take values like -127, -126, -125, ... -2, -1, 0, +1, +2, ... +127, -128, -127, etc. Thus the value of **ch** would keep oscillating between -128 to +127, thereby ensuring that the loop never gets terminated. How do you overcome this difficulty? Would declaring **ch** as an **unsigned char** solve the problem? Even this would not serve the purpose since when **ch** reaches a value 255, **ch++** would try to make it 256 which cannot be stored in an **unsigned char**. Thus the only alternative is to declare **ch** as an **int**. However, if we are bent upon writing the program using **unsigned char**, it can be done as shown below. The program is definitely less elegant, but workable all the same.

```
# include <stdio.h>
int main( )
{
    unsigned char  ch ;

    for ( ch = 0 ; ch <= 254 ; ch++ )
        printf ( "%d %c\n", ch, ch ) ;

    printf ( "%d %c\n", ch, ch ) ;
    return 0 ;
}
```

Floats and Doubles

A **float** occupies four bytes in memory and can range from -3.4e38 to +3.4e38. If this is insufficient, then C offers a **double** data type that occupies 8 bytes in memory and has a range from -1.7e308 to +1.7e308. A variable of type **double** can be declared as,

```
double  a, population ;
```

If the situation demands usage of real numbers that lie even beyond the range offered by **double** data type, then there exists a **long double** that can range from -1.7e4932 to +1.7e4932. A **long double** occupies 10 bytes in memory.

You would see that most of the times in C programming, one is required to use either **char**s or **int**s and cases where **float**s, **double**s or **long double**s would be used are indeed rare.

Let us now write a program that puts to use all the data types that we have learnt in this chapter. Go through the following program carefully, which shows how to use these different data types. Note the format specifiers used to input and output these data types.

```
# include <stdio.h>
int main( )
{
    char  c ;
    unsigned char  d ;
    int  i ;
    unsigned int  j ;
```

```
    short int k ;
    unsigned short int l ;
    long int m ;
    unsigned long int n ;
    float x ;
    double y ;
    long double z ;

    /* char */
    scanf ( "%c %c", &c, &d ) ;
    printf ( "%c %c\n", c, d ) ;

    /* int */
    scanf ( "%d %u", &i, &j ) ;
    printf ( "%d %u\n", i, j ) ;

    /* short int */
    scanf ( "%d %u", &k, &l ) ;
    printf ( "%d %u\n", k, l ) ;

    /* long int */
    scanf ( "%ld %lu", &m, &n ) ;
    printf ( "%ld %lu\n", m, n ) ;

    /* float, double, long double */
    scanf ( "%f %lf %Lf", &x, &y, &z ) ;
    printf ( "%f %lf %Lf\n", x, y, z ) ;
}
```

The essence of all the data types that we have learnt so far has been captured in Figure 8.2.

Data Type	Range	Bytes	Format
signed char	-128 to + 127	1	%c
unsigned char	0 to 255	1	%c
short signed int	-32768 to +32767	2	%d
short unsigned int	0 to 65535	2	%u
signed int	-32768 to +32767	2	%d
unsigned int	0 to 65535	2	%u
long signed int	-2147483648 to +2147483647	4	%ld
long unsigned int	0 to 4294967295	4	%lu
float	-3.4e38 to +3.4e38	4	%f
double	-1.7e308 to +1.7e308	8	%lf
long double	-1.7e4932 to +1.7e4932	10	%Lf
Note: The sizes and ranges of int, short and long are compiler dependent. Sizes in this figure are for 16-bit compiler.			

Figure 8.2

A Few More Issues...

Having seen all the variations of the primary types let us take a look at some more related issues.

(a) We saw earlier that size of an integer is compiler dependent. This is even true in case of **char**s and **float**s. Also, depending upon the microprocessor for which the compiler targets its code the accuracy of floating point calculations may change. For example, the result of 22.0/7.0 would be reported more accurately by VC++ compiler as compared to TC/TC++ compilers. This is because TC/TC++ targets its compiled code to 8088/8086 (16-bit) microprocessors. Since these microprocessors do not offer floating point support, TC/TC++ performs all float operations using a software piece called Floating Point Emulator. This emulator has limitations and hence produces less accurate results. Also, this emulator becomes part of the EXE file, thereby increasing its size. In addition to this increased size there is a performance penalty since this bigger code would take more time to execute.

(b) If you look at ranges of **char**s and **int**s there seems to be one extra number on the negative side. This is because a negative number is always stored as 2's compliment of its binary. For example, let us see how -128 is stored. Firstly, binary of 128 is calculated (10000000), then its 1's compliment is obtained (01111111). A 1's compliment is obtained by changing all 0s to 1s and 1s to 0s. Finally, 2's compliment of this number, i.e. 10000000, gets stored. A 2's compliment is obtained by adding 1 to the 1's compliment. Thus, for -128, 10000000 gets stored. This is an 8-bit number and it can be easily accommodated in a **char**. As against this, +128 cannot be stored in a **char** because its binary 010000000 (left-most 0 is for positive sign) is a 9-bit number. However +127 can be stored as its binary 01111111 turns out to be a 8-bit number.

(c) What happens when we attempt to store +128 in a **char**? The first number on the negative side, i.e. -128 gets stored. This is because from the 9-bit binary of +128, 010000000, only the right-most 8 bits get stored. But when 10000000 is stored the left-most bit is 1 and it is treated as a sign bit. Thus the value of the number becomes -128 since it is indeed the binary of -128, as can be understood from (b) above. Similarly, you can verify that an attempt to store +129 in a **char** results in storing -127 in it. In general, if we exceed the range from positive side we end up on the negative side. Vice versa is also true. If we exceed the range from negative side we end up on positive side.

Storage Classes in C

We have already said all that needs to be said about constants, but we are not finished with variables. To fully define a variable, one needs to mention not only its 'type' but also its 'storage class'. In other words, not only do all variables have a data type, they also have a 'storage class'.

We have not mentioned storage classes yet, though we have written several programs in C. We were able to get away with this because storage classes have defaults. If we don't specify the storage class of a variable in its declaration, the compiler will assume a storage class depending on the context in which the variable is used. Thus, variables have certain default storage classes.

From C compiler's point of view, a variable name identifies some physical location within the computer where the string of bits representing the variable's value is stored. There are basically two kinds of locations in a computer where such a value may be kept— Memory and CPU registers. It is the variable's storage class that determines in which of these two types of locations, the value is stored.

Moreover, a variable's storage class tells us:

(a) Where the variable would be stored.

(b) What will be the initial value of the variable, if initial value is not specifically assigned.(i.e. the default initial value).
(c) What is the scope of the variable; i.e. in which functions the value of the variable would be available.
(d) What is the life of the variable; i.e. how long would the variable exist.

There are four storage classes in C:
(a) Automatic storage class
(b) Register storage class
(c) Static storage class
(d) External storage class

Let us examine these storage classes one by one.

Automatic Storage Class

The features of a variable defined to have an automatic storage class are as under:

Storage	–	Memory.
Default initial value	–	An unpredictable value, which is often called a garbage value.
Scope	–	Local to the block in which the variable is defined.
Life	–	Till the control remains within the block in which the variable is defined.

Following program shows how an automatic storage class variable is declared, and the fact that if the variable is not initialized, it contains a garbage value.

```
# include <stdio.h>
int main( )
{
    auto int i, j ;
    printf ( "%d %d\n", i, j ) ;
    return 0 ;
}
```

The output of the above program could be...

```
1211 221
```

where, 1211 and 221 are garbage values of **i** and **j**. When you run this program, you may get different values, since garbage values are unpredictable. So always make it a point that you initialize the automatic variables properly, otherwise you are likely to get unexpected results. Note that the keyword for this storage class is **auto**, and not automatic.

Scope and life of an automatic variable is illustrated in the following program.

```
# include <stdio.h>
int main( )
{
    auto int i = 1 ;
    {
        {
            {
                printf ( "%d ", i ) ;
            }
            printf ( "%d ", i ) ;
        }
        printf ( "%d\n", i ) ;
    }
    return 0 ;
}
```

The output of the above program is:

```
1 1 1
```

This is because, all **printf( )** statements occur within the outermost block (a block is all statements enclosed within a pair of braces) in which **i** has been defined. It means the scope of **i** is local to the block in which it is defined. The moment the control comes out of the block in which the variable is defined, the variable and its value is irretrievably lost. To catch my point, go through the following program.

```
# include <stdio.h>
int main( )
{
    auto int i = 1 ;
    {
        auto int i = 2 ;
        {
            auto int i = 3 ;
            printf ( "%d ", i ) ;
        }
        printf ( "%d ", i ) ;
```

```
    }
    printf ( "%d\n", i ) ;
    return 0 ;
}
```

The output of the above program would be:

```
3 2 1
```

Note that the Compiler treats the three **i**'s as totally different variables, since they are defined in different blocks. Once the control comes out of the innermost block, the variable **i** with value 3 is lost, and hence the **i** in the second **printf( )** refers to **i** with value 2. Similarly, when the control comes out of the next innermost block, the third **printf( )** refers to the **i** with value 1.

Understand the concept of life and scope of an automatic storage class variable thoroughly before proceeding with the next storage class.

Register Storage Class

The features of a variable defined to be of **register** storage class are as under:

Storage	-	CPU registers.
Default initial value	-	Garbage value.
Scope	-	Local to the block in which the variable is defined.
Life	-	Till the control remains within the block in which the variable is defined.

A value stored in a CPU register can always be accessed faster than the one that is stored in memory. Therefore, if a variable is used at many places in a program, it is better to declare its storage class as **register**. A good example of frequently used variables is loop counters. We can name their storage class as **register**.

```
# include <stdio.h>
int main( )
{
    register int  i ;

    for ( i = 1 ; i <= 10 ; i++ )
        printf ( "%d\n", i ) ;
    return 0 ;
```

```
}
```

Here, even though we have declared the storage class of **i** as **register**, we cannot say for sure that the value of **i** would be stored in a CPU register. Why? Because the number of CPU registers are limited, and they may be busy doing some other task. What happens in such an event... the variable works as if its storage class is **auto**.

Not every type of variable can be stored in a CPU register. For example, if the microprocessor has 16-bit registers then they cannot hold a **float** value or a **double** value, which require 4 and 8 bytes respectively. However, if you use the **register** storage class for a **float** or a **double** variable, you won't get any error messages. All that would happen is the compiler would treat the variables to be of **auto** storage class.

Static Storage Class

The features of a variable defined to have a **static** storage class are as under:

Storage	–	Memory.
Default initial value	–	Zero.
Scope	–	Local to the block in which the variable is defined.
Life	–	Value of the variable persists between different function calls.

Compare the two programs and their output given in Figure 8.3 to understand the difference between the **automatic** and **static** storage classes.

The programs in Figure 8.3 consist of two functions **main( )** and **increment( )**. The function **increment( )** gets called from **main( )** thrice. Each time it prints the value of **i** and then increments it. The only difference in the two programs is that one uses an **auto** storage class for variable **i**, whereas the other uses **static** storage class.

Like **auto** variables, **static** variables are also local to the block in which they are declared. The difference between them is that **static** variables don't disappear when the function is no longer active. Their values persist. If the control comes back to the same function again, the **static** variables have the same values they had last time around.

```
# include <stdio.h>                    # include <stdio.h>
void increment( ) ;                    void increment( ) ;
void main( )                           void main( )
{                                      {
    increment( ) ;                         increment( ) ;
    increment( ) ;                         increment( ) ;
    increment( ) ;                         increment( ) ;
}                                      }
void increment( )                      void increment( )
{                                      {
    auto int i = 1 ;                       static int i = 1 ;
    printf ( "%d\n", i ) ;                 printf ( "%d\n", i ) ;
    i = i + 1 ;                            i = i + 1 ;
}                                      }
```

The output of the above programs would be:

```
1                                      1
1                                      2
1                                      3
```

Figure 8.3

In the above example, when variable **i** is **auto**, each time **increment( )** is called, it is re-initialized to one. When the function terminates, **i** vanishes and its new value of 2 is lost. The result: no matter how many times we call **increment( ), i** is initialized to 1 every time.

On the other hand, if **i** is **static**, it is initialized to 1 only once. It is never initialized again. During the first call to **increment( )**, **i** is incremented to 2. Because **i** is static, this value persists. The next time **increment( )** is called, **i** is not re-initialized to 1; on the contrary, its old value 2 is still available. This current value of **i** (i.e. 2) gets printed and then **i = i + 1** adds 1 to **i** to get a value of 3. When **increment( )** is called the third time, the current value of **i** (i.e. 3) gets printed and once again **i** is incremented. In short, if the storage class is **static**, then the statement **static int i = 1** is executed only once, irrespective of how many times the same function is called.

Consider one more program.

```
# include <stdio.h>

int * fun( ) ;
int main( )
{
    int *j ;
    j = fun( ) ;
    printf ( "%d\n", *j ) ;
    return 0 ;
}
int *fun( )
{
    int k = 35 ;
    return ( &k ) ;
}
```

Here we are returning an address of **k** from **fun( )** and collecting it in **j**. Thus **j** becomes pointer to **k**. Then using this pointer we are printing the value of **k**. This correctly prints out 35. Now try calling any function (even **printf( )**) immediately after the call to **fun( )**. This time **printf( )** prints a garbage value. Why does this happen? In the first case, when the control returned from **fun( )** though **k** went dead it was still left on the stack. We then accessed this value using its address that was collected in **j**. But when we precede the call to **printf( )** by a call to any other function, the stack is now changed, hence we get the garbage value. If we want to get the correct value each time then we must declare **k** as **static**. By doing this when the control returns from **fun( )**, **k** would not die.

All this having been said, a word of advice—avoid using **static** variables unless you really need them. Because their values are kept in memory when the variables are not active, which means they take up space in memory that could otherwise be used by other variables.

External Storage Class

The features of a variable whose storage class has been defined as external are as follows:

Storage	–	Memory.
Default initial value	–	Zero.
Scope	–	Global.
Life	–	As long as the program's execution doesn't come to an end.

External variables differ from those we have already discussed in that their scope is global, not local. External variables are declared outside all functions, yet are available to all functions that care to use them. Here is an example to illustrate this fact.

```
# include <stdio.h>

int i ;
void increment( ) ;
void decrement( ) ;

int main( )
{
    printf ( "\ni = %d", i ) ;
    increment( ) ;
    increment( ) ;
    decrement( ) ;
    decrement( ) ;
    return 0 ;
}
void increment( )
{
    i = i + 1 ;
    printf ( "on incrementing i = %d\n", i ) ;
}
void decrement( )
{
    i = i - 1 ;
    printf ( "on decrementing i = %d\n", i ) ;
}
```

The output would be:

```
i = 0
on incrementing i = 1
on incrementing i = 2
on decrementing i = 1
on decrementing i = 0
```

As is obvious from the above output, the value of **i** is available to the functions **increment( )** and **decrement( )** since **i** has been declared outside all functions.

Look at the following program.

```
# include <stdio.h>
int x = 21 ;

int main( )
{
    extern int y ;
    printf ( "%d %d\n", x, y ) ;
    return 0 ;
}
int y = 31 ;
```

Here, **x** and **y** both are global variables. Since both of them have been defined outside all the functions both enjoy external storage class. Note the difference between the following:

```
extern int y ;
int y = 31 ;
```

Here the first statement is a declaration, whereas the second is the definition. When we declare a variable no space is reserved for it, whereas, when we define it space gets reserved for it in memory. We had to declare **y** since it is being used in **printf( )** before it's definition is encountered. There was no need to declare **x** since its definition is done before its usage. Also remember that a variable can be declared several times but can be defined only once.

Another small issue—what will be the output of the following program?

```
# include <stdio.h>
int x = 10 ;
void display( ) ;
int main( )
{
    int x = 20 ;
    printf ( "%d\n", x ) ;
    display( ) ;
    return 0 ;
}

void display( )
{
    printf ( "%d\n", x ) ;
}
```

Here **x** is defined at two places, once outside **main( )** and once inside it. When the control reaches the **printf( )** in **main( )** which **x** gets printed? Whenever such a conflict arises, it's the local variable that gets preference over the global variable. Hence the **printf( )** outputs 20. When **display( )** is called and control reaches the **printf( )** there is no such conflict. Hence, this time, the value of the global **x**, i.e. 10 gets printed.

One last thing—a **static** variable can also be declared outside all the functions. For all practical purposes it will be treated as an **extern** variable. However, the scope of this variable is limited to the same file in which it is declared. This means that the variable would not be available to any function that is defined in a file other than the file in which the variable is defined.

A Few Subtle Issues

Let us now look at some subtle issues about storage classes.

(a) All variables that are defined inside a function are normally created on the stack each time the function is called. These variables die as soon as control goes back from the function. However, if the variables inside the function are defined as **static** then they *do not* get created on the stack. Instead they are created in a place in memory called 'Data Segment'. Such variables die only when program execution comes to an end.

(b) If a variable is defined outside all functions, then not only is it available to all other functions in the file in which it is defined, but is also available to functions defined in other files. In the other files the variable should be declared as **extern**. This is shown in the following program:

```
/* PR1.C */
# include <stdio.h>
# include <functions.c>

int i = 35 ;
int fun1( ) ;
int fun2( ) ;

int main( )
{
    printf ( "%d\n", I ) ;
    fun1( ) ;
    fun2( ) ;
    return 0 ;
}
```

```
/* FUNCTIONS.C */
extern int i ;
int fun1( )
{
    i++ ;
    printf ( "%d\n", i ) ;
    return 0 ;
}
int fun2( )
{
    i-- ;
    printf ( "%d\n", i ) ;
    return 0 ;
}
```

The output of the program would be

```
35
36
35
```

However, if we place the word **static** in front of an external variable (**i** in our case) it makes the variable private and not accessible to use in any other file.

(c) In the following statements the first three are definitions, whereas, the last one is a declaration.

```
auto int i ;
static int j ;
register int k ;
extern int l ;
```

Which to Use When

Dennis Ritchie has made available to the C programmer a number of storage classes with varying features, believing that the programmer is in a best position to decide which one of these storage classes is to be used when. We can make a few ground rules for usage of different storage classes in different programming situations with a view to:

(a) economise the memory space consumed by the variables
(b) improve the speed of execution of the program

The rules are as under:

- Use **static** storage class only if you want the value of a variable to persist between different function calls.
- Use **register** storage class for only those variables that are being used very often in a program. Reason is, there are very few CPU registers at our disposal and many of them might be busy doing something else. Make careful utilization of the scarce resources. A typical application of **register** storage class is loop counters, which get used a number of times in a program.
- Use **extern** storage class for only those variables that are being used by almost all the functions in the program. This would avoid unnecessary passing of these variables as arguments when making a function call. Declaring all the variables as **extern** would amount to a lot of wastage of memory space because these variables would remain active throughout the life of the program.
- If you don't have any of the express needs mentioned above, then use the **auto** storage class. In fact, most of the times, we end up using the **auto** variables, because often it so happens that once we have used the variables in a function, we don't mind losing them.

Summary

(a) We can use different variations of the primary data types, namely **signed** and **unsigned char**, **long** and **short int**, **float**, **double** and **long double**. There are different format specifications for all these data types when they are used in **scanf( )** and **printf( )** functions.

(b) The maximum value a variable can hold depends upon the number of bytes it occupies in memory.

(c) By default all the variables are **signed**. We can declare a variable as **unsigned** to accommodate greater value without increasing the bytes occupied.

(d) We can make use of proper storage classes like **auto**, **register**, **static** and **extern** to control four properties of the variable—storage, default initial value, scope and life.

Exercise

[A] What will be the output of the following programs:

(a)
```
# include <stdio.h>
int main( )
{
    int i ;
```

```
    for ( i = 0 ; i <= 50000 ; i++ )
        printf ( "%d\n", i ) ;
    return 0 ;
}
```

(a)
```
# include <stdio.h>
int main( )
{
    float  a = 13.5 ;
    double  b = 13.5 ;
    printf ( "%f %lf\n", a, b ) ;
    return 0 ;
}
```

(b)
```
# include <stdio.h>
int  i = 0 ;
void val( ) ;
int main( )
{
    printf ( "main's i = %d\n", i ) ;
    i++ ;
    val( ) ;
    printf ( "main's i = %d\n", i ) ;
    val( ) ;
    return 0 ;
}
void val( )
{
    i = 100 ;
    printf ( "val's i = %d\n", i ) ;
    i++ ;
}
```

(c)
```
# include <stdio.h>
int f ( int ) ;
int g ( int ) ;
int main( )
{
    int  x, y, s = 2 ;
    s *= 3 ;
    y = f ( s ) ;
    x = g ( s ) ;
```

```
    printf ( "%d %d %d\n", s, y, x ) ;
    return 0 ;
}
int t = 8 ;

int f ( int a )
{
    a += -5 ;
    t -= 4 ;
    return ( a + t ) ;
}

int g ( int a )
{
    a = 1 ;
    t += a ;
    return ( a + t ) ;
}
```

(d)
```
# include <stdio.h>
int main( )
{
    static int count = 5 ;
    printf ( "count = %d\n", count-- ) ;
    if ( count != 0 )
        main( ) ;
    return 0 ;
}
```

(e)
```
# include <stdio.h>
int g ( int ) ;
int main( )
{
    int i, j ;
    for ( i = 1 ; i < 5 ; i++ )
    {
        j = g ( i ) ;
        printf ( "%d\n", j ) ;
    }
    return 0 ;
}
int g ( int x )
{
    static int v = 1 ;
```

```
    int b = 3 ;
    v += x ;
    return ( v + x + b ) ;
}
```

(f)
```
# include <stdio.h>
float x = 4.5 ;
float f ( float ) ;
int main( )
{
    float y, float f ( float ) ;
    x *= 2.0 ;
    y = f ( x ) ;
    printf ( "%f %f\n", x, y ) ;
    return 0 ;
}
float f ( float a )
{
    a += 1.3 ;
    x -= 4.5 ;
    return ( a + x ) ;
}
```

(g)
```
# include <stdio.h>
int main( )
{
    func( ) ;
    func( ) ;
    return 0 ;
}
void func( )
{
    auto int i = 0 ;
    register int j = 0 ;
    static int k = 0 ;
    i++ ; j++ ; k++ ;
    printf ( "%d % d %d\n", i, j, k ) ;
}
```

(h)
```
# include <stdio.h>
int x = 10 ;
int main( )
{
    int x = 20 ;
```

```
    {
        int x  = 30 ;
        printf ( "%d\n", x ) ;
    }
    printf ( "%d\n", x ) ;
    return 0 ;
}
```

(i)
```
# include <stdio.h>
int main( )
{
    static int a, b, c ;
    printf ( "%d %d %d\n", a, b, c ) ;
    return 0 ;
}
```

(j)
```
# include <stdio.h>
int main( )
{
    int bs = 200 ;
    float gs ;
    gs = 10 / 100 * bs + bs ;
    printf ( "%f\n", gs ) ;
    return 0 ;
}
```

(k)
```
int i = 5, j = 2 ;
void change( ) ;
int main( )
{
    change( ) ;
    printf ( "i = %d j = %d\n", i, j ) ;
    return 0 ;
}
void change( )
{
    int j ;
    j = 10 ;
    i += 5 ;
}
```

(l)
```
# include <stdio.h>
int main( )
```

```
{
    int i = 4 ;
    printf ( "%d\n", ++i * ++i ) ;
    return 0 ;
}
```

(m)
```
# include <stdio.h>
int g = 321 ;
int main( )
{
    int g ;
    printf ( "%d\n", g ) ;
    return 0 ;
}
```

(n)
```
# include <stdio.h>
int main( )
{
    int a = 'A' ;
    {
        int a = 'a' ;
        {
            int a = 12 ;
            printf ( "%d ", a ) ;
        }
        printf ( "%d ", a ) ;
    }
    printf ( "%d ", a ) ;
    return 0 ;
}
```

(o)
```
# include <stdio.h>
int i ;
void f( ) ;
int main( )
{
    f( ) ;
    f( ) ;
    return 0 ;
}
void f( )
{
```

```
        int m ;
        int j = 0 ;
        static int k ;
        register int l = 0 ;
        printf ( "%d %d %d %d %d\n", ++i, ++j, ++k, ++l, m++ ) ;
    }
    int m ;
```

[B] Point out the errors, if any, in the following programs:

(a)
```
    # include <stdio.h>
    int main( )
    {
        long  num ;
        num = 2 ;
        printf ( "%ld\n", num ) ;
        return 0 ;
    }
```

(b)
```
    # include <stdio.h>
    int main( )
    {
        char  ch = 200 ;
        printf ( "%d\n", ch ) ;
        return 0 ;
    }
```

(c)
```
    # include <stdio.h>
    int main( )
    {
        unsigned  a = 25 ;
        long unsigned  b = 25l ;
        printf ( "%lu %u\n", a, b ) ;
        return 0 ;
    }
```

(d)
```
    # include <stdio.h>
    int main( )
    {
        long float  a = 25.345e454 ;
        unsigned double  b = 25 ;
        printf ( "%lf %d\n", a, b ) ;
        return 0 ;
    }
```

(e)
```
# include <stdio.h>
int main( )
{
    float  a = 25.345 ;
    float  *b ;
    b = &a ;
    printf ( "%f %u\n", a, b ) ;
    return 0 ;
}
```

(f)
```
# include <stdio.h>
static int y ;
int main( )
{
    static int z ;
    printf ( "%d %d\n", y, z ) ;
    return 0 ;
}
```

(g)
```
# include <stdio.h>
int main( )
{
    printf ( "%d\n", x ) ;
    return 0 ;
}
int x = 3 ;
```

(h)
```
# include <stdio.h>
int i ;
int main( )
{
    f( ) ;
    return 0 ;
}
void f( )
{
    int j = 0 ;
    static int k ;
    register int l = 0 ;
    printf ( "%d %d %d %d %d\n", i, j, k, l, m++ ) ;
}
int m ;
```

[C] State whether the following statements are True or False:

(a) Storage for a register storage class variable is allocated each time the control reaches the block in which it is present.

(b) An extern storage class variable is not available to the functions that precede its definition, unless the variable is explicitly declared in these functions.

(c) The value of an automatic storage class variable persists between various function invocations.

(d) If the CPU registers are not available, the register storage class variables are treated as static storage class variables.

(e) The register storage class variables cannot hold float values.

(f) If we try to use register storage class for a **float** variable the compiler will flash an error message.

(g) If the variable **x** is defined outside all functions and a variable **x** is also defined as a local variable of some function, then the global variable gets preference over the local variable.

(h) The default value for automatic variable is zero.

(i) The life of static variable is till the control remains within the block in which it is defined.

(j) If a global variable is to be defined, then the **extern** keyword is necessary in its declaration.

(k) The address of register variable is not accessible.

(l) A variable that is defined outside all functions can also have a static **storage** class.

(m) One variable can have multiple storage classes.

(n) A pointer **p** pointing to a float variable can be defined as **float **p**.

(o) Scope of **static** storage class is the function in which it is defined and life is till program execution doesn't come to an end.

[D] Following program calculates the sum of digits of the number 12345. Go through it and find out why is it necessary to declare the storage class of the variable **sum** as **static**.

```
# include <stdio.h>
int main( )
{
    int a ;
    a = sumdig ( 12345 ) ;
    printf ( "%d\n", a ) ;
    return 0 ;
}

int sumdig ( int num )
{
    static int sum ;
    int a, b ;
    a = num % 10 ;
    b = ( num - a ) / 10 ;
    sum = sum + a ;
    if ( b != 0 )
        sumdig ( b ) ;
    else
        return ( sum ) ;
}
```

[E] Out of the following two programs which one would run faster and why?

```
/* Program 1 */
#include <stdio.h>
int main( )
{
    register int i ;
    for ( i = 1 ; i <= 20 ; i++ )
        printf ( "%d\n", i ) ;
    return 0 ;
}

/* Program 2 */
#include <stdio.h>
int main( )
{
```

```
    auto int i ;
    for ( i = 1 ; i <= 20 ; i++ )
        printf ( "%d\n", i ) ;
    return 0 ;
}
```

[F] What are the sizes of an **int** pointer, a **float** pointer, a **char** pointer and a **long int** pointer?

9 The C Preprocessor

- Features of C Preprocessor
- Macro Expansion
    - Macros with Arguments
    - Macros versus Functions
- File Inclusion
- Conditional Compilation
- *#if* and *#elif* Directives
- Miscellaneous Directives
    - *#undef* Directive
    - *#pragma* Directive
- Summary
- Exercise

The C preprocessor is exactly what its name implies. It is a program that processes our source program before it is passed to the compiler. Preprocessor commands (often known as directives) form what can almost be considered a language within C language. We can certainly write C programs without knowing anything about the preprocessor or its facilities. But preprocessor is such a great convenience that virtually all C programmers rely on it. This chapter explores the preprocessor directives and discusses the pros and cons of using them in programs.

Features of C Preprocessor

There are several steps involved from the stage of writing a C program to the stage of getting it executed. The combination of these steps is known as the 'Build Process'. The detailed build process is discussed in the last section of this chapter. At this stage it would be sufficient to note that before a C program is compiled it is passed through another program called 'Preprocessor'. The C program is often known as 'Source Code'. The Preprocessor works on the source code and creates 'Expanded Source Code'. If the source code is stored in a file PR1.C, then the expanded source code gets stored in a file PR1.I. It is this expanded source code that is sent to the compiler for compilation.

The preprocessor offers several features called preprocessor directives. Each of these preprocessor directives begins with a # symbol. The directives can be placed anywhere in a program but are most often placed at the beginning of a program, before the first function definition. We would learn the following preprocessor directives here:

(a) Macro expansion
(b) File inclusion
(c) Conditional Compilation
(d) Miscellaneous directives

Let us understand these features of preprocessor one by one.

Macro Expansion

Have a look at the following program.

```
# include <stdio.h>
# define UPPER 25
int main( )
{
    int i ;
    for ( i = 1 ; i <= UPPER ; i++ )
        printf ( "%d\n", i ) ;
```

```
    return 0 ;
}
```

In this program, instead of writing 25 in the **for** loop we are writing it in the form of UPPER, which has already been defined before **main( )** through the statement,

```
# define UPPER 25
```

This statement is called 'macro definition' or more commonly, just a 'macro'. What purpose does it serve? During preprocessing, the preprocessor replaces every occurrence of UPPER in the program with 25. Here is another example of macro definition.

```
# include <stdio.h>
# define PI  3.1415
int main( )
{
    float  r = 6.25 ;
    float  area ;

    area = PI * r * r ;
    printf ( "Area of circle = %f\n", area ) ;
    return 0 ;
}
```

UPPER and PI in the above programs are often called 'macro templates', whereas, 25 and 3.1415 are called their corresponding 'macro expansions'.

When we compile the program, before the source code passes to the compiler, it is examined by the C preprocessor for any macro definitions. When it sees the **#define** directive, it goes through the entire program in search of the macro templates; wherever it finds one, it replaces the macro template with the appropriate macro expansion. Only after this procedure has been completed, is the program handed over to the compiler.

In C programming, it is customary to use capital letters for macro template. This makes it easy for programmers to pick out all the macro templates when reading through the program.

Note that a macro template and its macro expansion are separated by blanks or tabs. A space between # and **define** is optional. Remember that a macro definition is never to be terminated by a semicolon.

And now a million dollar question... why use **#define** in the above programs? What have we gained by substituting PI for 3.1415 in our program? Probably, we have made the program easier to read. Even though 3.1415 is such a common constant that it is easily recognizable, there are many instances where a constant doesn't reveal its purpose so readily. For example, if the phrase "\x1B[2J" causes the screen to clear. But which would you find easier to understand in the middle of your program "\x1B[2J" or "CLEARSCREEN"? Thus, we would use the macro definition

```
# define CLEARSCREEN "\x1B[2J"
```

Then wherever CLEARSCREEN appears in the program, it would automatically be replaced by "\x1B[2J" before compilation begins.

There is perhaps a more important reason for using macro definition than mere readability. Suppose a constant like 3.1415 appears many times in your program. This value may have to be changed some day to 3.141592. Ordinarily, you would need to go through the program and manually change each occurrence of the constant. However, if you have defined PI in a **#define** directive, you only need to make one change, in the **#define** directive itself:

```
# define PI 3.141592
```

Beyond this, the change will be made automatically to all occurrences of PI before the beginning of compilation.

In short, it is nice to know that you would be able to change values of a constant at all the places in the program by just making a change in the **#define** directive. This convenience may not matter for small programs shown above, but with large programs, macro definitions are almost indispensable.

But the same purpose could have been served had we used a variable **pi** instead of a macro template **PI**. A variable could also have provided a meaningful name for a constant and permitted one change to effect many occurrences of the constant. It's true that a variable can be used in this way. Then, why not use it? For three reasons it's a bad idea.

Firstly, it is inefficient, since the compiler can generate faster and more compact code for constants than it can for variables. Secondly, using a variable for what is really a constant encourages sloppy thinking and makes the program more difficult to understand: if something never changes, it is hard to imagine it as a variable. And thirdly, there is always a danger that the variable may inadvertently get altered somewhere in the program. So it's no longer a constant that you think it is.

Thus, using **#define** can produce more efficient and more easily understandable programs. This directive is used extensively by C programmers, as you will see in many programs in this book.

Following three examples show places where a **#define** directive is popularly used by C programmers.

A **#define** directive is many a time used to define operators as shown below.

```
# include <stdio.h>
# define AND &&
# define OR ||
int main( )
{
    int f = 1, x = 4, y = 90 ;

    if ( ( f < 5 ) AND ( x <= 20 OR y <= 45 ) )
        printf ( "Your PC will always work fine...\n" ) ;
    else
        printf ( "In front of the maintenance man\n" ) ;
    return 0 ;
}
```

A **#define** directive could be used even to replace a condition, as shown below.

```
# include <stdio.h>
# define AND &&
# define ARANGE ( a > 25 AND a < 50 )

int main( )
{
    int a = 30 ;

    if ( ARANGE )
        printf ( "within range\n" ) ;
    else
        printf ( "out of range\n" ) ;
    return 0 ;
}
```

A **#define** directive could be used to replace even an entire C statement. This is shown below.

```
# include <stdio.h>
# define FOUND printf ( "The Yankee Doodle Virus\n" ) ;

int main( )
{
    char  signature ;

    if ( signature == 'Y' )
        FOUND
    else
        printf ( "Safe... as yet !\n" ) ;
    return 0 ;
}
```

Macros with Arguments

The macros that we have used so far are called simple macros. Macros can have arguments, just as functions can. Here is an example that illustrates this fact.

```
# include <stdio.h>
# define AREA(x) ( 3.14 * x * x )

int main( )
{
    float  r1 = 6.25, r2 = 2.5, a ;

    a = AREA ( r1 ) ;
    printf ( "Area of circle = %f\n", a ) ;
    a = AREA ( r2 ) ;
    printf ( "Area of circle = %f\n", a ) ;
    return 0 ;
}
```

Here's the output of the program...

```
Area of circle = 122.656250
Area of circle = 19.625000
```

In this program, wherever the preprocessor finds the phrase **AREA(x)** it expands it into the statement **(3.14 * x * x)**. However, that's not all that it does. The **x** in the macro template **AREA(x)** is an argument that matches the **x** in the macro expansion **(3.14 * x ***

x). The statement **AREA(r1)** in the program causes the variable **r1** to be substituted for **x**. Thus the statement **AREA(r1)** is equivalent to:

```
( 3.14 * r1 * r1 )
```

After the above source code has passed through the preprocessor, what the compiler gets to work on will be this:

```
# include <stdio.h>
int main( )
{
    float r1 = 6.25, r2 = 2.5, a ;

    a = 3.14 * r1 *r1 ;
    printf ( "Area of circle = %f\n", a ) ;
    a = 3.14 *r2 * r2 ;
    printf ( "Area of circle = %f\n", a ) ;
    return 0 ;
}
```

Here is another example of macros with arguments:

```
# include <stdio.h>
# define ISDIGIT(y) ( y >= 48 && y <= 57 )

int main( )
{
    char ch ;

    printf ( "Enter any digit " ) ;
    scanf ( "%c", &ch ) ;

    if ( ISDIGIT ( ch ) )
        printf ( "You entered a digit\n" ) ;
    else
        printf ( "Illegal input\n" ) ;
    return 0 ;
}
```

Here are some important points to remember while writing macros with arguments:

(a) Be careful not to leave a blank between the macro template and its argument while defining the macro. For example, there should be no blank between **AREA** and **(x)** in the definition, #define AREA(x) (3.14 * x * x)

If we were to write **AREA (x)** instead of **AREA(x)**, the **(x)** would become a part of macro expansion, which we certainly don't want. What would happen is, the template would be expanded to

```
( r1 ) ( 3.14 * r1 * r1 )
```

which won't run. Not at all what we wanted.

(b) The entire macro expansion should be enclosed within parentheses. Here is an example of what would happen if we fail to enclose the macro expansion within parentheses.

```
# include <stdio.h>
# define SQUARE(n) n * n

int main( )
{
    int j ;

    j = 64 / SQUARE ( 4 ) ;
    printf ( "j = %d\n", j ) ;
    return 0 ;
}
```

The output of the above program would be:

```
j = 64
```

whereas, what we expected was j = 4.

What went wrong? The macro was expanded into

```
j = 64 / 4 * 4 ;
```

which yielded 64.

(c) Macros can be split into multiple lines, with a '\' (back slash) present at the end of each line. Following program shows how we can define and use multiple line macros.

```
# include <stdio.h>
# define HLINE  for ( i = 0 ; i < 79 ; i++ ) \
                    printf ( "%c", 196 ) ;
# define VLINE( X, Y ) { \
                        gotoxy ( X, Y ) ; \
                        printf ( "%c", 179 ) ; \
                    }

int main( )
{
    int i, y ;
    clrscr( ) ;

    gotoxy ( 1, 12 ) ; /* positions cursor in row x and column y */
    HLINE

    for ( y = 1 ; y < 25 ; y++ )
        VLINE ( 39, y ) ;
    return 0 ;
}
```

This program draws a vertical and a horizontal line in the center of the screen.

(d) If for any reason, you are unable to debug a macro, then you should view the expanded code of the program to see how the macros are getting expanded. If your source code is present in the file PR1.C then the expanded source code would be stored in PR1.I. You need to generate this file at the command prompt by saying:

```
cpp pr1.c
```

Here CPP stands for C PreProcessor. It generates the expanded source code and stores it in a file called PR1.I. You can now open this file and see the expanded source code. Note that the file PR1.I gets generated in C:\TC\BIN directory. The procedure for generating expanded source code for compilers other than Turbo C/C++ might be a little different.

Macros versus Functions

In the above example, a macro was used to calculate the area of the circle. As we know, even a function can be written to calculate the area of the circle. Though macro calls are 'like' function calls, they are not really the same things. Then what is the difference between the two?

In a macro call, the preprocessor replaces the macro template with its macro expansion, in a stupid, unthinking, literal way. As against this, in a function call the control is passed to a function along with certain arguments, some calculations are performed in the function and a useful value is returned back from the function.

This brings us to a question: when is it best to use macros with arguments and when is it better to use a function? Usually macros make the program run faster but increase the program size, whereas functions make the program smaller and compact.

If we use a macro hundred times in a program, the macro expansion goes into our source code at hundred different places, thus increasing the program size. On the other hand, if a function is used, then even if it is called from hundred different places in the program, it would take the same amount of space in the program.

But passing arguments to a function and getting back the returned value does take time and would therefore slow down the program. This gets avoided with macros since they have already been expanded and placed in the source code before compilation. Thus the trade-off is between memory space and time.

Moral of the story is—if the macro is simple and sweet like in our examples, it makes nice shorthand and avoids the overheads associated with function calls. On the other hand, if we have a fairly large macro and it is used fairly often, perhaps we ought to replace it with a function.

If memory space in the machine in which the program is being executed is less (like a mobile phone or a PDA), then it may make sense to use functions instead of macros. By doing so, the program may run slower, but will need less memory space.

File Inclusion

The second preprocessor directive we'll explore in this chapter is file inclusion. This directive causes one file to be included in another. The preprocessor command for file inclusion looks like this:

```
# include "filename"
```

and it simply causes the entire contents of **filename** to be inserted into the source code at that point in the program. Of course, this presumes that the file being included exists. When and why this feature is used? It can be used in two cases:

(a) If we have a very large program, the code is best divided into several different files, each containing a set of related functions. It is a good programming practice to keep different sections of a large program separate. These files are **#included** at the beginning of main program file.

(b) There are some functions and some macro definitions that we need almost in all programs that we write. These commonly needed functions and macro definitions can be stored in a file, and that file can be included in every program we write, which would add all the statements in this file to our program as if we have typed them in.

It is common for the files that are to be included to have a .h extension. This extension stands for 'header file', possibly because it contains statements which when included go to the head of your program. The prototypes of all the library functions are grouped into different categories and then stored in different header files. For example, prototypes of all mathematics related functions are stored in the header file 'math.h', prototypes of console input/output functions are stored in the header file 'conio.h', and so on.

Actually there exist two ways to write **#include** statement. These are:

```
# include "filename"
# include <filename>
```

The meaning of each of these forms is given below:

`# include "goto.h"` This command would look for the file **goto.h** in the current directory as well as the specified list of directories as mentioned in the include search path that might have been set up.

`# include <goto.h>` This command would look for the file **goto.h** in the specified list of directories only.

The include search path is nothing but a list of directories that would be searched for the file being included. Different C compilers let you set the search path in different manners. If you are using Turbo C/C++ compiler, then the search path can be set up by selecting

'Directories' from the 'Options' menu. On doing this, a dialog box appears. In this dialog box against 'Include Directories', we can specify the search path. We can also specify multiple include paths separated by ';' (semicolon) as shown below:

```
c:\tc\lib ; c:\mylib ; d:\libfiles
```

The path can contain maximum of 127 characters. Both relative and absolute paths are valid. For example '..\dir\incfiles' is a valid path.

Conditional Compilation

We can, if we want, have the compiler skip over part of a source code by inserting the preprocessing commands **#ifdef** and **#endif**, which have the general form:

```
# ifdef  macroname
     statement 1 ;
     statement 2 ;
     statement 3 ;
# endif
```

If **macroname** has been **#defined**, the block of code will be processed as usual; otherwise not.

Where would **#ifdef** be useful? When would you like to compile only a part of your program? In three cases:

(a) To "comment out" obsolete lines of code. It often happens that a program is changed at the last minute to satisfy a client. This involves rewriting some part of source code to the client's satisfaction and deleting the old code. But veteran programmers are familiar with the clients who change their mind and want the old code back again just the way it was. Now you would definitely not like to retype the deleted code again.

One solution in such a situation is to put the old code within a pair of /* */ combination. But we might have already written a comment in the code that we are about to "comment out". This would mean we end up with nested comments. Obviously, this solution won't work since we can't nest comments in C.

Therefore, the solution is to use conditional compilation as shown below.

```
int main( )
{
    # ifdef OKAY
        statement 1 ;
```

```
        statement 2 ;  /* detects virus */
        statement 3 ;
        statement 4 ;  /* specific to stone virus */
    # endif

    statement 5 ;
    statement 6 ;
    statement 7 ;
}
```

Here, statements 1, 2, 3 and 4 would get compiled only if the macro OKAY has been defined, and we have purposefully omitted the definition of the macro OKAY. At a later date, if we want that these statements should also get compiled, all that we are required to do is to delete the **#ifdef** and **#endif** statements.

(b) A more sophisticated use of **#ifdef** has to do with making the programs portable, i.e. to make them work on two totally different computers. Suppose an organization has two different types of computers and you are expected to write a program that works on both the machines. You can do so by isolating the lines of code that must be different for each machine by marking them off with **#ifdef**. For example:

```
int main( )
{
    # ifdef INTEL
        code suitable for an Intel PC
    # else
        code suitable for a Motorola PC
    # endif
    code common to both the computers
}
```

When you compile this program, it would compile only the code suitable for Mototola PC and the common code. This is because the macro INTEL has not been defined. Note that, the working of **#ifdef - #else - #endif** is similar to the ordinary **if - else** control instruction of C.

If you want to run your program on a Motorola PC, just add a statement at the top saying,

```
# define INTEL
```

Sometimes, instead of **#ifdef**, the **#ifndef** directive is used. The **#ifndef** (which means 'if not defined') works exactly opposite to **#ifdef**. The above example, if written using **#ifndef**, would look like this:

```
int main( )
{
    # ifndef INTEL
        code suitable for a Intel PC
    # else
        code suitable for a Motorola PC
    # endif
    code common to both the computers
}
```

(c) Suppose a function **myfunc( )** is defined in a file 'myfile.h' which is **#included** in a file 'myfile1.h'. Now in your program file, if you **#include** both 'myfile.h' and 'myfile1.h', the compiler flashes an error 'Multiple declaration for **myfunc**'. This is because the same file 'myfile.h' gets included twice. To avoid this, we can write following code in the 'myfile.h' header file.

```
/* myfile.h */
# ifndef __myfile_h
    # define __myfile_h

    myfunc( )
    {
        /* some code */
    }
# endif
```

First time the file 'myfile.h' gets included, the preprocessor checks whether a macro called **__myfile_h** has been defined or not. If it has not been, then it gets defined and the rest of the code gets included. Next time we attempt to include the same file, the inclusion is prevented since **__myfile_h** already stands defined. Note that there is nothing special about **__myfile_h**. In its place, we can use any other macro as well.

#if and *#elif* Directives

The **#if** directive can be used to test whether an expression evaluates to a nonzero value or not. If the result of the expression is nonzero, then subsequent lines upto a **#else**, **#elif** or **#endif** are compiled, otherwise they are skipped.

A simple example of **#if** directive is shown below:

```
int main( )
{
    # if TEST <= 5
        statement 1 ;
        statement 2 ;
        statement 3 ;
    # else
        statement 4 ;
        statement 5 ;
        statement 6 ;
    # endif
}
```

If the expression, **TEST <= 5** evaluates to true, then statements 1, 2 and 3 are compiled, otherwise statements 4, 5 and 6 are compiled. In place of the expression **TEST <= 5**, other expressions like **(LEVEL == HIGH || LEVEL == LOW)** or **ADAPTER == VGA** can also be used.

If we so desire, we can have nested conditional compilation directives. An example that uses such directives is shown below.

```
# if ADAPTER == VGA
    code for video graphics array
# else
    # if ADAPTER == SVGA
        code for super video graphics array
    # else
        code for extended graphics adapter
    # endif
# endif
```

The above program segment can be made more compact by using another conditional compilation directive called **#elif**. The same program using this directive can be rewritten as shown below. Observe that by using the **#elif** directives, the number of #**endif**s used in the program get reduced.

```
# if ADAPTER == VGA
    code for video graphics array
# elif ADAPTER == SVGA
    code for super video graphics array
# else
```

```
    code for extended graphics adapter
# endif
```

Miscellaneous Directives

There are two more preprocessor directives available, though they are not very commonly used. They are:

(a) #undef
(b) #pragma

#undef Directive

On some occasions, it may be desirable to cause a defined name to become 'undefined'. This can be accomplished by means of the **#undef** directive. In order to undefine a macro that has been earlier **#defined**, the directive,

```
# undef macro template
```

can be used. Thus the statement,

```
# undef PENTIUM
```

would cause the definition of PENTIUM to be removed from the system. All subsequent **#ifdef PENTIUM** statements would evaluate to false. In practice, seldom are you required to undefine a macro, but for some reason if you are required to, then you know that there is something to fall back upon.

#pragma Directive

This directive is another special-purpose directive that you can use to turn on or off certain features. Pragmas vary from one compiler to another. There are certain pragmas available with Microsoft C compiler that deal with formatting source listings and placing comments in the object file generated by the compiler. Turbo C/C++ compiler has got a pragma that allows you to suppress warnings generated by the compiler. Some of these pragmas are discussed below.

(a) **#pragma startup** and **#pragma exit**: These directives allow us to specify functions that are called upon program startup (before **main( )**) or program exit (just before the program terminates). Their usage is as follows:

```
# include <stdio.h>
void fun1( ) ;
void fun2( ) ;

# pragma startup fun1
# pragma exit fun2

int main( )
{
    printf ( "Inside main\n" ) ;
    return 0 ;
}

void fun1( )
{
    printf ( "Inside fun1\n" ) ;
}

void fun2( )
{
    printf ( "Inside fun2\n" ) ;
}
```

And here is the output of the program.

```
Inside fun1
Inside main
Inside fun2
```

Note that the functions **fun1( )** and **fun2( )** should neither receive nor return any value. If we want two functions to get executed at startup then their pragmas should be defined in the reverse order in which you want to get them called.

(b) **#pragma warn**: On compilation the compiler reports Errors and Warnings in the program, if any. Errors provide the programmer with no options, apart from correcting them. Warnings, on the other hand, offer the programmer a hint or suggestion that something may be *wrong* with a particular piece of code. Two most common situations when warnings are displayed are as under:

- If you have written code that the compiler's designers (or the ANSI-C specification) consider bad C programming practice. For example, if a function does not return a value then it should be declared as **void**.

– If you have written code that might cause run-time errors, such as assigning a value to an uninitialised pointer.

The **#pragma warn** directive tells the compiler whether or not we want to suppress a specific warning. Usage of this pragma is shown below.

```
# include <stdio.h>
# pragma warn –rvl   /* return value */
# pragma warn –par  /* parameter not used */
# pragma warn –rch  /* unreachable code */

int f1( )
{
    int a = 5 ;
}

void f2 ( int x )
{
    printf ( "Inside f2" ) ;
}

int f3( )
{
    int x = 6 ;
    return x ;
    x++ ;
}

int main( )
{
    f1( ) ;
    f2 ( 7 ) ;
    f3( ) ;
    return 0 ;
}
```

If you go through the program, you can notice three problems immediately. These are:

(a) Though promised, **f1( )** doesn't return a value.

(b) The parameter **x** that is passed to **f2( )** is not being used anywhere in **f2( )**.

(c) The control can never reach **x++** in **f3( )**.

If we compile the program, we should expect warnings indicating the above problems. However, this does not happen since we have suppressed the warnings using the **#pragma** directives. If we replace the '–' sign with a '+', then these warnings would be flashed on compilation. Though it is a bad practice to suppress warnings, at times, it becomes useful to suppress them. For example, if you have written a huge program and are trying to compile it, then to begin with, you are more interested in locating the errors, rather than the warnings. At such times, you may suppress the warnings. Once you have located all errors, then you may turn on the warnings and sort them out.

The Build Process

There are many steps involved in converting a C program into an executable form. Figure 9.1 shows these different steps along with the files created during each stage.

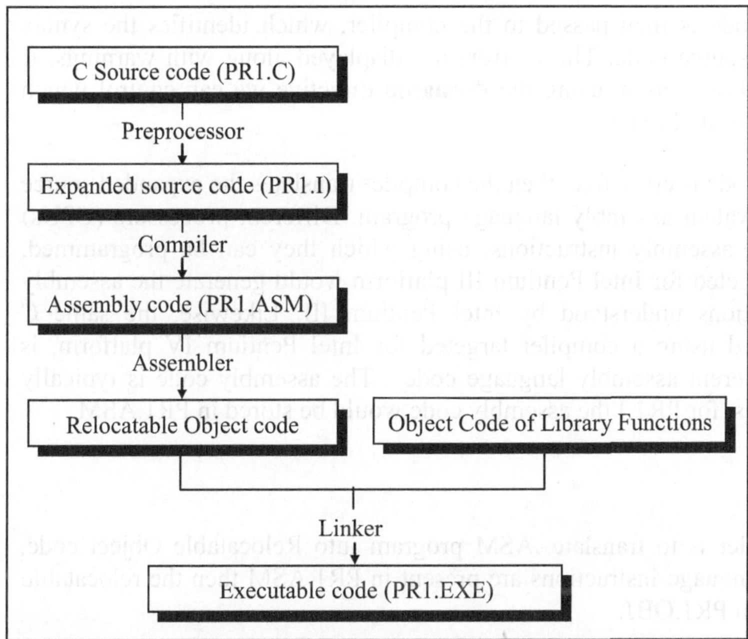

Figure 9.1

Many software development tools, like say TC++ and VC++, hide many of the steps shown in Figure 9.1 from us. However, it is important to understand these steps for two reasons:

(a) It would help you understand the process much better, than just believing that, some kind of 'magic' generates the executable code.
(b) If you are to alter any of these steps, then you would know how to do it.

Let us now understand the steps mentioned in Figure 9.1 in detail.

Preprocessing

During this step, the C source code is expanded based on the preprocessor directives like **#define**, **#include**, **#ifdef**, etc. The expanded source code is stored in an intermediate file with **.i** extension. Thus, if our source code is stored in PR1.C then the expanded source code is stored in PR1.I. The expanded source code is also in C language. Note that the '.I' extension may vary from one compiler to another.

Compilation

The expanded source code is then passed to the compiler, which identifies the syntax errors in the expanded source code. These errors are displayed along with warnings, if any. As we saw in the last section, using the **#pragma** directive we can control which warnings are to be displayed / hidden.

If the expanded source code is error-free, then the compiler translates the expanded source code in C, into an equivalent assembly language program. Different processors (CPUs) support different set of assembly instructions, using which they can be programmed. Hence, the compiler targeted for Intel Pentium III platform would generate the assembly code using the instructions understood by Intel Pentium III. Likewise, the same C program, when compiled using a compiler targeted for Intel Pentium IV platform, is likely to generate a different assembly language code. The assembly code is typically stored in .ASM file. Thus, for PR1.I the assembly code would be stored in PR1.ASM.

Assembling

The job of the Assembler is to translate .ASM program into Relocatable Object code. Thus, if the assembly language instructions are present in PR1.ASM then the relocatable object code gets stored in PR1.OBJ.

Here the word 'Relocatable' means that the program is complete except for one thing—no specific memory addresses have yet been assigned to the code and data sections in the relocatable code. All the addresses are relative offsets.

The .OBJ file that gets created is a specially formatted binary file. The object file contains a header and several sections. The header describes the sections that follow it. These sections are:

(a) Text section – This section contains machine language code equivalent to the expanded source code.

(b) Data Section – This section contains global variables and their initial values.

(c) Bss (Block Started by Symbol) section – This section contains uninitialized global variables.

(d) Symbol Table – This section contains information about symbols found during assembling of the program. Typical information present in the symbol table includes:

- Names, types and sizes of global variables
- Names and addresses of functions defined in the source code
- Names of external functions like **printf( )** and **scanf( )**

Although there are machine language instructions in the .OBJ file it cannot be executed directly. This is because of following reasons:

(a) The external functions like **printf( )** are not present in the .OBJ file.

(b) The .OBJ file may use some global variables defined in another .OBJ file. For example, PR1.OBJ may use a global variable **count2** which is defined in the file PR2.OBJ.

(c) The .OBJ file may use a function defined in another .OBJ file. For example, PR2.OBJ may use a function **display( )** defined in the file PR1.OBJ.

Note that parts of the symbol table may be incomplete because all the variables and functions may not be defined in the same file. The references to such variables and functions (symbols) that are defined in other source files are later on resolved by the linker.

Linking

Linking is the final stage in creating an executable program. It has to do the following important things:

(a) Find definition of all external functions—those which are defined in other .OBJ files, and those which are defined in Libraries (like **printf( )**).

(b) Find definition of all global variables—those which are defined in other .OBJ files, and those which are defined in Libraries (like 'errno' which is a commonly used global variable that is defined in Standard C Library).

(c) Combine Data Sections of different .OBJ files into a single Data Section.
(d) Combine Code Sections of different .OBJ files into a single Code Section.

While combining different .OBJ files the linker has to address one problem. Addresses of all variables and functions in the Symbol Table of the .OBJ file are Relative addresses. This means that address of a Symbol (variable or function), is in fact only an offset from start of the Section (Data or Code Section) to which it belongs. For example, if there are two 4-byte wide global integer variables **count1** and **index1** in PR1.OBJ, then the Symbol Table will have addresses 0 and 4 for them. Similarly, if PR2.OBJ has two similar variables **count2** and **index2** then Symbol Table in PR2.OBJ will have addresses 0 and 4 for these variables. Same addressing scheme is used with functions present in each .OBJ file.

When linker combines the two .OBJ files, it has to re-adjust the addresses of global variables and functions. Thus, the variables **count1**, **index1**, **count2** and **index2** will now enjoy addresses 0, 4, 8 and 12 respectively. Similar re-adjustment of addresses will be done for functions. Even after re-adjustment the addresses of variables and functions are still 'relative' in the combined Data and Code sections of the .EXE file.

In the .EXE file machine language code from all of the input object files will be in the Text section. Similarly, all initialized and uninitialized variables will reside in the new Data and Bss sections, respectively.

During linking if the linker detects errors such as mis-spelling the name of a library function in the source code, or using the incorrect number or type of parameters for a function, it stops the linking process and doesn't create the binary executable file.

Loading

Once the .EXE file is created and stored on the disk, it is ready for execution. When we execute it, it is first brought from the disk into the memory (RAM) by an Operating System component called Program Loader. Program Loader can place the .EXE anywhere in memory depending on its availability. Since all the addresses in the .EXE file are 'relative' addresses, exact 'position' where .EXE is loaded in memory doesn't matter. No further adjustment of addresses is necessary. Thus, the Code and Data in .EXE file are 'Position Independent'. Once the loading process is completed, the execution begins from the first instruction in Code section of the file loaded in memory.

Modern Operating Systems like Windows and Linux permit loading and execution of multiple programs in memory. One final word before we end this topic. Like a .OBJ file, a .EXE file is also a formatted binary file. The format of these binary file differs from one Operating System to another. For example, Windows Operating System use Portable Executable (PE) file format, whereas, Linux uses Executable and Linking Format (ELF). Hence an .OBJ or .EXE file created for Windows cannot be used on Linux and vice-versa.

Figure 9.2 summarizes the role played by each processor program during the build process.

Processor	**Input**	**Output**
Editor	Program typed from keyboard	C source code containing program and preprocessor commands
Prepro-cessor	C source code file	Source code file with the preprocessing commands properly sorted out
Compiler	Source code file with preprocessing commands sorted out	Assembly language code
Assembler	Assembly language code	Relocatable Object code in machine language
Linker	Object code of our program and object code of library functions	Executable code in machine language
Loader	Executable file	

Figure 9.2

Summary

(a) The preprocessor directives enable the programmer to write programs that are easy to develop, read, modify and transport to a different computer system.

(b) We can make use of various preprocessor directives such as **#define**, **#include**, **#ifdef** - **#else** - **#endif**, **#if** and **#elif** in our program.

(c) The directives like **#undef** and **#pragma** are also useful although they are seldom used.

Exercise

[A] Answer the following:

(a) What is a preprocessor directive

1. a message from compiler to the programmer
2. a message from compiler to the linker
3. a message from programmer to the preprocessor
4. a message from programmer to the microprocessor

(b) Which of the following are correctly formed **#define** statements:

```
#define INCH PER FEET 12
#define SQR (X) ( X * X )
#define SQR(X) X * X
#define SQR(X) ( X * X )
```

(c) State True or False:

1. A macro must always be written in capital letters.
2. A macro should always be accommodated in a single line.
3. After preprocessing when the program is sent for compilation the macros are removed from the expanded source code.
4. Macros with arguments are not allowed.
5. Nested macros are allowed.
6. In a macro call the control is passed to the macro.

(d) How many **#include** directives can be there in a given program file?

(e) What is the difference between the following two **#include** directives:

```
#include "conio.h"
#include <conio.h>
```

(f) A header file is:

1. A file that contains standard library functions
2. A file that contains definitions and macros
3. A file that contains user-defined functions
4. A file that is present in current working directory

(g) Which of the following is not a preprocessor directive

1. #if
2. #elseif
3. #undef
4. #pragma

(h) All macro substitutions in a program are done

1. Before compilation of the program
2. After compilation
3. During execution
4. None of the above

(i) In a program the statement:

#include "filename"

is replaced by the contents of the file "filename"

1. Before compilation
2. After Compilation
3. During execution
4. None of the above

[B] What will be the output of the following program:

(a)
```
# include <stdio.h>
int main( )
{
    int i = 2 ;
    # ifdef DEF
        i *= i ;
    # else
        printf ( "%d", i ) ;
    # endif
    return 0 ;
}
```

(b)
```
# include <stdio.h>
# define PRODUCT(x) ( x * x )
int main( )
{
    int i = 3, j ;
    j = PRODUCT( i + 1 ) ;
    printf ( "%d\n", j ) ;
    return 0 ;
}
```

(c)
```
# include <stdio.h>
# define PRODUCT(x) ( x * x )
int main( )
{
    int i = 3, j, k ;
    j = PRODUCT( i++ ) ;
    k = PRODUCT ( ++i ) ;

    printf ( "%d %d\n", j, k ) ;
    return 0 ;
}
```

(d)
```
# include <stdio.h>
# define SEMI ;
int main( )
{
    int p = 3 SEMI ;
    printf ( "%d\n", p ) SEMI
    return 0 ;
}
```

(e)
```
# include <stdio.h>
# define PI 3.14
# define AREA( x, y, z )  ( PI * x * x + y * z ) ;

int main( )
{
    float a = AREA ( 1, 5, 8 ) ;
    float b = AREA ( AREA ( 1, 5, 8 ), 4, 5 ) ;
    printf ( " a = %f\n", a ) ;
    printf ( " b = %f\n", b ) ;
    return 0 ;
}
```

(f)
```
# include <stdio.h>
#define PI 3.14
int main( )
{
    int i = 2, a ;
    #ifdef AREA
        a = PI * i * i ;
    #else
        a = i * i ;
    #endif
```

```
        printf ( "%d\n", a ) ;
        return 0 ;
    }
```

(g)
```
# include <stdio.h>
#define THIS(n)    n * n
int main( )
{
    int i ;
    i = 64 / THIS(4) ;
    printf ( "%d\n", i ) ;
    return 0 ;
}
```

(h)
```
# include <stdio.h>
#define PRODUCT(x)    x * x
int main( )
{
    int i = 3, j = 2, p ;
    p = PRODUCT ( i + j ) ;
    printf ( "%d\n", p ) ;
    return 0 ;
}
```

(i)
```
# include <stdio.h>
#define COMMONSENSE(j,i)  int main( ) { int i ; i = 64 ; printf ( "%d", j ) ; return 0 ; }
COMMONSENSE ( 9, j ) ;
```

(j)
```
# include <stdio.h>
#define CINCINNATI(MSSJS)  printf ( "MSSJS\n" )
#define SUNCITY(MSSJS)  printf ( MSSJS )
int main( )
{
    CINCINNATI ( "20000 leagues under the sea" ) ;
    SUNCITY ( "See C at sea in cicily" ) ;
    return 0 ;
}
```

(k)
```
# include <stdio.h>
#define M
int main( )
{
    #ifdef M
        #ifndef N
            printf ( "Boot the computer" ) ;
        #else
```

```
            printf ( "Wear a boot" ) ;
        #endif
    #endif
    return 0 ;
}
```

[C] Attempt the following:

(a) If a macro is not getting expanded as per your expectation, how will you find out how is it being expanded by the preprocessor.

(b) Write down macro definitions for the following:

1. To test whether a character is a small case letter or not.
2. To test whether a character is a upper case letter or not.
3. To test whether a character is an alphabet or not. Make use of the macros you defined in 1 and 2 above.
4. To obtain the bigger of two numbers.

(c) Write macro definitions with arguments for calculation of area and perimeter of a triangle, a square and a circle. Store these macro definitions in a file called "areaperi.h". Include this file in your program, and call the macro definitions for calculating area and perimeter for different squares, triangles and circles.

(d) Write down macro definitions for the following:

1. To find arithmetic mean of two numbers.
2. To find absolute value of a number.
3. To convert a uppercase alphabet to lowercase.
4. To obtain the bigger of two numbers.

(e) Write macro definitions with arguments for calculation of Simple Interest and Amount. Store these macro definitions in a file called "interest.h". Include this file in your program, and use the macro definitions for calculating simple interest and amount.

(f) In the following statement what are the technical names for EXP and 2.71828.

```
#define EXP 2.71828
```

(g) What is the difference between merging two files while typing the program and #including one file within another.

(h) Where would the include file be searched if we use < > while including a file?

(i) What would be the value of **a** in the following code.

```
#define clock(t) t/t
a = clock ( 10 * 5 * 10 ) ;
```

[D] Out of the following two programs which one would run faster and why?

```
/* Program 1 */
#include <stdio.h>
#define SQR(x)  (x * x)
int main( )
{
    int i = 3, a ;
    a = SQR(i) ;
    printf ( "%d\n", a ) ;
    return 0 ;
}

/* Program 2 */
#include <stdio.h>
int sqr ( int ) ;
int main( )
{
    auto int i = 3 ;
    int a ;
    a = sqr ( i ) ;
    printf ( "%d\n", a ) ;
    return 0 ;
}
int sqr ( int j )
{
    return ( j * j ) ;
}
```

[E] Point out the errors, if any in the following programs:

(a)
```
# include <stdio.h>
#define COND  if ( a > b )
int main( )
{
    int a = 40, b = 50 ;
    COND
```

```
        printf ( "%d\n", a ) ;
    else
        printf ( "%d\n", b ) ;
    return 0 ;
}
```

(b)
```
# include <stdio.h>
int main( )
{
    cls( ) ;
    gotorc ( 12, 30 ) ;
    printf ( "This works\n" ) ;
    return 0 ;
}
#include "goto.c"
```

(c)
```
# include <stdio.h>
#define Correct "Hello friends"
int main( )
{
    printf ( "Correct" ) ;
    return 0 ;
}
```

(d)
```
# include <stdio.h>
#define printf( "m" )
int main( )
{
    printf ( "Old programmers just lose their memory" ) ;
    return 0 ;
}
```

(e)
```
# include <stdio.h>
#define C(j,i) int main( ){ int i ; i = 64 ; printf ( "%d", j ) ; return 0 ; }
C ( j, 9 ) ;
```

10 Arrays

The C language provides a capability that enables the user to design a set of similar data types, called array. This chapter describes how arrays can be created and manipulated in C.

We should note that, in many C books and courses, arrays and pointers are taught separately. I feel it is worthwhile to deal with these topics together. This is because pointers and arrays are so closely related that discussing arrays without discussing pointers would make the discussion incomplete and wanting. In fact, all arrays make use of pointers internally. Hence, it is all too relevant to study them together rather than as isolated topics.

What are Arrays

For understanding the arrays properly, let us consider the following program:

```
# include <stdio.h>
int main( )
{
    int x ;
    x = 5 ;
    x = 10 ;
    printf ( "x = %d\n", x ) ;
    return 0 ;
}
```

No doubt, this program will print the value of **x** as 10. Why so? Because, when a value 10 is assigned to **x**, the earlier value of **x**, i.e. 5, is lost. Thus, ordinary variables (the ones which we have used so far) are capable of holding only one value at a time (as in this example). However, there are situations in which we would want to store more than one value at a time in a single variable.

For example, suppose we wish to arrange the percentage marks obtained by 100 students in ascending order. In such a case, we have two options to store these marks in memory:

(a) Construct 100 variables to store percentage marks obtained by 100 different students, i.e. each variable containing one student's marks.

(b) Construct one variable (called array or subscripted variable) capable of storing or holding all the hundred values.

Obviously, the second alternative is better. A simple reason for this is, it would be much easier to handle one variable than handling 100 different variables. Moreover, there are certain logics that cannot be dealt with, without the use of an array. Now a formal definition of an array—An array is a collective name given to a group of 'similar quantities'. These similar quantities could be percentage marks of 100 students, or salaries of 300 employees, or ages of 50 employees. What is important is that the quantities must be 'similar'. Each member in the group is referred to by its position in the group. For example, assume the following group of numbers, which represent percentage marks obtained by five students.

```
per = { 48, 88, 34, 23, 96 }
```

If we want to refer to the second number of the group, the usual notation used is per_2. Similarly, the fourth number of the group is referred as per_4. However, in C, the fourth number is referred as **per[3].** This is because, in C, the counting of elements begins with 0 and not with 1. Thus, in this example **per[3]** refers to 23 and **per[4]** refers to 96. In general, the notation would be **per[i]**, where, **i** can take a value 0, 1, 2, 3, or 4, depending on the position of the element being referred. Here **per** is the subscripted variable (array), whereas **i** is its subscript.

Thus, an array is a collection of similar elements. These similar elements could be all **int**s, or all **float**s, or all **char**s, etc. Usually, the array of characters is called a 'string', whereas an array of **int**s or **float**s is called simply an array. Remember that all elements of any given array must be of the same type. i.e. we cannot have an array of 10 numbers, of which 5 are **int**s and 5 are **float**s.

A Simple Program Using Array

Let us try to write a program to find average marks obtained by a class of 30 students in a test.

```
# include <stdio.h>
int main( )
{
    int avg, sum = 0 ;
    int i ;
    int marks[30] ; /* array declaration */

    for ( i = 0 ; i <= 29 ; i++ )
    {
        printf ( "Enter marks " ) ;
        scanf ( "%d", &marks[i] ) ; /* store data in array */
    }
```

```
    for ( i = 0 ; i <= 29 ; i++ )
        sum = sum + marks[i] ;  /* read data from an array*/

    avg = sum / 30 ;
    printf ( "Average marks = %d\n", avg ) ;
    return 0 ;
}
```

There is a lot of new material in this program, so let us take it apart slowly.

Array Declaration

To begin with, like other variables, an array needs to be declared so that the compiler will know what kind of an array and how large an array we want. In our program, we have done this with the statement:

```
int marks[30] ;
```

Here, **int** specifies the type of the variable, just as it does with ordinary variables and the word **marks** specifies the name of the variable. The **[30]** however is new. The number 30 tells how many elements of the type **int** will be in our array. This number is often called the 'dimension' of the array. The bracket ([ ]) tells the compiler that we are dealing with an array.

Accessing Elements of an Array

Once an array is declared, let us see how individual elements in the array can be referred. This is done with subscript, the number in the brackets following the array name. This number specifies the element's position in the array. All the array elements are numbered, starting with 0. Thus, **marks[2]** is not the second element of the array, but the third. In our program, we are using the variable **i** as a subscript to refer to various elements of the array. This variable can take different values and hence can refer to the different elements in the array in turn. This ability to use variables to represent subscripts is what makes arrays so useful.

Entering Data into an Array

Here is the section of code that places data into an array:

```
for ( i = 0 ; i <= 29 ; i++ )
{
    printf ( "Enter marks " ) ;
```

```
    scanf ( "%d", &marks[i] ) ;
}
```

The **for** loop causes the process of asking for and receiving a student's marks from the user to be repeated 30 times. The first time through the loop, **i** has a value 0, so the **scanf( )** function will cause the value typed to be stored in the array element **marks[0],** the first element of the array. This process will be repeated until **i** becomes 29. This is last time through the loop, which is a good thing, because there is no array element like **marks[30]**.

In **scanf( )** function, we have used the "address of" operator (&) on the element **marks[i]** of the array, just as we have used it earlier on other variables (**&rate**, for example). In so doing, we are passing the address of this particular array element to the **scanf( )** function, rather than its value; which is what **scanf( )** requires.

Reading Data from an Array

The balance of the program reads the data back out of the array and uses it to calculate the average. The **for** loop is much the same, but now the body of the loop causes each student's marks to be added to a running total stored in a variable called **sum**. When all the marks have been added up, the result is divided by 30, the number of students, to get the average.

```
for ( i = 0 ; i <= 29 ; i++ )
    sum = sum + marks[i] ;

avg = sum / 30 ;
printf ( "Average marks = %d\n", avg ) ;
```

To fix our ideas, let us revise whatever we have learnt about arrays:

(a) An array is a collection of similar elements.
(b) The first element in the array is numbered 0, so the last element is 1 less than the size of the array.
(c) An array is also known as a subscripted variable.
(d) Before using an array, its type and dimension must be declared.
(e) However big an array, its elements are always stored in contiguous memory locations. This is a very important point which we would discuss in more detail later on.

More on Arrays

Array is a very popular data type with C programmers. This is because of the convenience with which arrays lend themselves to programming. The features which make arrays so convenient to program would be discussed below, along with the possible pitfalls in using them.

Array Initialisation

So far we have used arrays that did not have any values in them to begin with. We managed to store values in them during program execution. Let us now see how to initialize an array while declaring it. Following are a few examples that demonstrate this.

```
int num[6] = { 2, 4, 12, 5, 45, 5 } ;
int n[ ] = { 2, 4, 12, 5, 45, 5 } ;
float press[ ] = { 12.3, 34.2 -23.4, -11.3 } ;
```

Note the following points carefully:

(a) Till the array elements are not given any specific values, they are supposed to contain garbage values.

(b) If the array is initialised where it is declared, mentioning the dimension of the array is optional as in the 2nd and 3rd example above.

Array Elements in Memory

Consider the following array declaration:

```
int arr[8] ;
```

What happens in memory when we make this declaration? 16 bytes get immediately reserved in memory, 2 bytes each for the 8 integers (under Windows/Linux, the array would occupy 32 bytes as each integer would occupy 4 bytes). And since the array is not being initialized, all eight values present in it would be garbage values. This so happens because the storage class of this array is assumed to be **auto**. If the storage class is declared to be **static**, then all the array elements would have a default initial value as zero. Whatever be the initial values, all the array elements would always be present in contiguous memory locations. This arrangement of array elements in memory is shown in Figure 10.1.

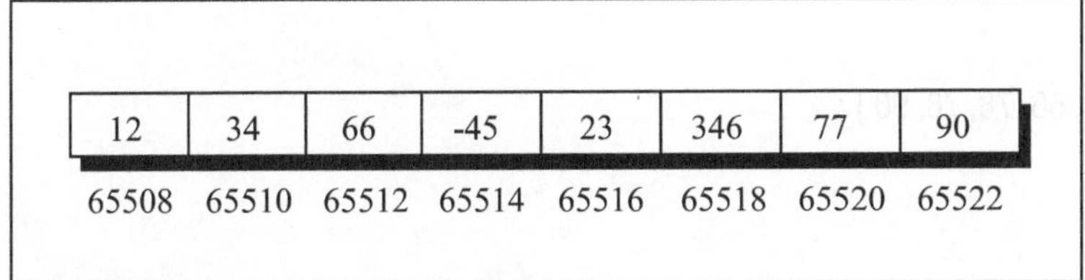

Figure 10.1

Bounds Checking

In C, there is no check to see if the subscript used for an array exceeds the size of the array. Data entered with a subscript exceeding the array size will simply be placed in memory outside the array; probably on top of other data, or on the program itself. This will lead to unpredictable results, to say the least, and there will be no error message to warn you that you are going beyond the array size. In some cases, the computer may just hang. Thus, the following program may turn out to be suicidal.

```
# include <stdio.h>
int main( )
{
    int num[40], i ;

    for ( i = 0 ; i <= 100 ; i++ )
        num[i] = i ;
    return 0 ;
}
```

Thus, to see to it that we do not reach beyond the array size, is entirely the programmer's botheration and not the compiler's.

Passing Array Elements to a Function

Array elements can be passed to a function by calling the function by value, or by reference. In the call by value, we pass values of array elements to the function, whereas in the call by reference, we pass addresses of array elements to the function. These two calls are illustrated below:

```
/* Demonstration of call by value */
# include <stdio.h>
void display ( int ) ;
```

```
int main( )
{
    int i ;
    int marks[ ] = { 55, 65, 75, 56, 78, 78, 90 } ;
    for ( i = 0 ; i <= 6 ; i++ )
        display ( marks[i] ) ;
    return 0 ;
}
void display ( int m )
{
    printf ( "%d ", m ) ;
}
```

And here's the output...

```
55 65 75 56 78 78 90
```

Here, we are passing an individual array element at a time to the function **display( )** and getting it printed in the function **display( ).** Note that, since at a time only one element is being passed, this element is collected in an ordinary integer variable **m**, in the function **display( )**.

And now the call by reference.

```
/* Demonstration of call by reference */
# include <stdio.h>
void disp ( int * ) ;
int main( )
{
    int i ;
    int marks[ ] = { 55, 65, 75, 56, 78, 78, 90 } ;
    for ( i = 0 ; i <= 6 ; i++ )
        disp ( &marks[i] ) ;
    return 0 ;
}
void disp ( int *n )
{
    printf ( "%d ", *n ) ;
}
```

And here's the output...

```
55 65 75 56 78 78 90
```

Here, we are passing addresses of individual array elements to the function **display( )**. Hence, the variable in which this address is collected (**n**), is declared as a pointer variable. And since **n** contains the address of array element, to print out the array element, we are using the 'value at address' operator (*).

Read the following program carefully. The purpose of the function **disp( )** is just to display the array elements on the screen. The program is only partly complete. You are required to write the function **show( )** on your own. Try your hand at it.

```
# include <stdio.h>
void disp ( int * ) ;
int main( )
{
    int i ;
    int marks[ ] = { 55, 65, 75, 56, 78, 78, 90 } ;
    for ( i = 0 ; i <= 6 ; i++ )
        disp ( &marks[i] ) ;
    return 0 ;
}
void disp ( int *n )
{
    show ( &n ) ;
}
```

Pointers and Arrays

To be able to see what pointers have got to do with arrays, let us first learn some pointer arithmetic. Consider the following example:

```
# include <stdio.h>
int main( )
{
    int i = 3, *x ;
    float j = 1.5, *y ;
    char k = 'c', *z ;
    printf ( "Value of i = %d\n", i ) ;
    printf ( "Value of j = %f\n", j ) ;
    printf ( "Value of k = %c\n", k ) ;
    x = &i ;
    y = &j ;
    z = &k ;
```

```
    printf ( "Original address in x = %u\n", x ) ;
    printf ( "Original address in y = %u\n", y ) ;
    printf ( "Original address in z = %u\n", z ) ;
    x++ ;
    y++ ;
    z++ ;
    printf ( "New address in x = %u\n", x ) ;
    printf ( "New address in y = %u\n", y ) ;
    printf ( "New address in z = %u\n", z ) ;
    return 0 ;
}
```

Here is the output of the program.

```
Value of i = 3
Value of j = 1.500000
Value of k = c
Original address in x = 65524
Original address in y = 65520
Original address in z = 65519
New address in x = 65526
New address in y = 65524
New address in z = 65520
```

Observe the last three lines of the output. 65526 is original value in **x** plus 2, 65524 is original value in **y** plus 4, and 65520 is original value in **z** plus 1. This so happens because every time a pointer is incremented, it points to the immediately next location of its type. That is why, when the integer pointer **x** is incremented, it points to an address two locations after the current location, since an **int** is always 2 bytes long (under Windows/Linux, since **int** is 4 bytes long, new value of **x** would be 65528). Similarly, **y** points to an address 4 locations after the current location and **z** points 1 location after the current location. This is a very important result and can be effectively used while passing the entire array to a function.

The way a pointer can be incremented, it can be decremented as well, to point to earlier locations. Thus, the following operations can be performed on a pointer:

(a) Addition of a number to a pointer. For example,

```
int i = 4, *j, *k ;
j = &i ;
j = j + 1 ;
```

```
j = j + 9 ;
k = j + 3 ;
```

(b) Subtraction of a number from a pointer. For example,

```
int i = 4, *j, *k ;
j = &i ;
j = j - 2 ;
j = j - 5 ;
k = j - 6 ;
```

(c) Subtraction of one pointer from another.

One pointer variable can be subtracted from another provided both variables point to elements of the same array. The resulting value indicates the number of elements separating the corresponding array elements. This is illustrated in the following program.

```
# include <stdio.h>
int main( )
{
    int arr[ ] = { 10, 20, 30, 45, 67, 56, 74 } ;
    int *i, *j ;

    i = &arr[1] ;
    j = &arr[5] ;
    printf ( "%d %d\n", j - i, *j - *i ) ;
    return 0 ;
}
```

Here **i** and **j** have been declared as integer pointers holding addresses of first and fifth element of the array respectively.

Suppose the array begins at location 65502, then the elements **arr[1]** and **arr[5]** would be present at locations 65504 and 65512 respectively, since each integer in the array occupies two bytes in memory. The expression **j - i** would print a value 4 and not 8. This is because **j** and **i** are pointing to locations that are 4 integers apart. What will be the result of the expression ***j - *i**? 36, since ***j** and ***i** return the values present at addresses contained in the pointers **j** and **i**.

(d) Comparison of two pointer variables

Pointer variables can be compared provided both variables point to objects of the same data type. Such comparisons can be useful when both pointer variables point to elements of the same array. The comparison can test for either equality or inequality. Moreover, a pointer variable can be compared with zero (usually expressed as NULL). The following program illustrates how the comparison is carried out.

```
# include <stdio..h>
int main( )
{
    int arr[ ] = { 10, 20, 36, 72, 45, 36 } ;
    int *j, *k ;

    j = &arr [ 4 ] ;
    k = ( arr + 4 ) ;
    if ( j == k )
        printf ( "The two pointers point to the same location\n" ) ;
    else
        printf ( "The two pointers do not point to the same location\n" ) ;

    return 0 ;
}
```

A word of caution! Do not attempt the following operations on pointers... they would never work out.

(a) Addition of two pointers
(b) Multiplication of a pointer with a constant
(c) Division of a pointer with a constant

Now we will try to correlate the following two facts, which we have learnt above:

(a) Array elements are always stored in contiguous memory locations.
(b) A pointer when incremented always points to an immediately next location of its type.

Suppose we have an array **num[ ]** = { 24, 34, 12, 44, 56, 17 }. The following figure shows how this array is located in memory.

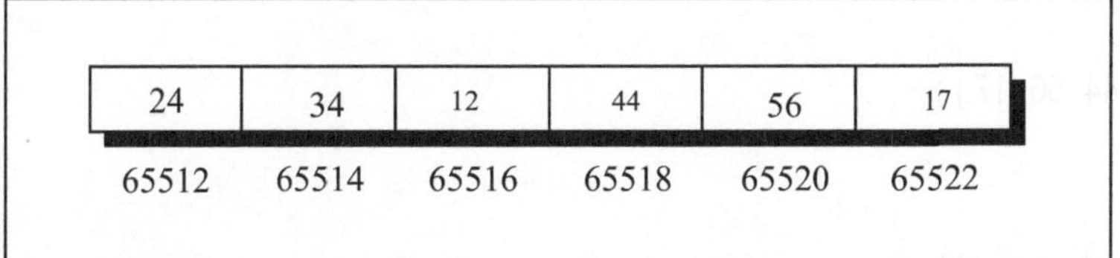

Figure 10.2

Here is a program that prints out the memory locations in which the elements of this array are stored.

```
# include <stdio.h>
int main( )
{
    int num[ ] = { 24, 34, 12, 44, 56, 17 } ;
    int i ;
    for ( i = 0 ; i <= 5 ; i++ )
    {
        printf ( "element no. %d ", i ) ;
        printf ( "address = %u\n", &num[i] ) ;
    }
    return 0 ;
}
```

The output of this program would look like this:

```
element no. 0 address = 65512
element no. 1 address = 65514
element no. 2 address = 65516
element no. 3 address = 65518
element no. 4 address = 65520
element no. 5 address = 65522
```

Note that the array elements are stored in contiguous memory locations, each element occupying two bytes, since it is an integer array. When you run this program, you may get different addresses, but what is certain is that each subsequent address would be 2 bytes (4 bytes under Windows/Linux) greater than its immediate predecessor.

Our next two programs show ways in which we can access the elements of this array.

```
# include <stdio.h>
int main( )
{
    int num[ ] = { 24, 34, 12, 44, 56, 17 } ;
    int i ;
    for ( i = 0 ; i <= 5 ; i++ )
    {
        printf ( "address = %u ", &num[i] ) ;
        printf ( "element = %d\n", num[i] ) ;
    }
    return 0 ;
}
```

The output of this program would be:

```
address = 65512 element = 24
address = 65514 element = 34
address = 65516 element = 12
address = 65518 element = 44
address = 65520 element = 56
address = 65522 element = 17
```

This method of accessing array elements by using subscripted variables is already known to us. This method has in fact been given here for easy comparison with the next method, which accesses the array elements using pointers.

```
# include <stdio.h>
int main( )
{
    int num[ ] = { 24, 34, 12, 44, 56, 17 } ;
    int i, *j ;

    j = &num[0] ; /* assign address of zeroth element */
    for ( i = 0 ; i <= 5 ; i++ )
    {
        printf ( "address = %u ", j ) ;
        printf ( "element = %d\n", *j ) ;
        j++ ; /* increment pointer to point to next location */
    }
    return 0 ;
}
```

The output of this program would be:

```
address = 65512 element = 24
address = 65514 element = 34
address = 65516 element = 12
address = 65518 element = 44
address = 65520 element = 56
address = 65522 element = 17
```

In this program, to begin with, we have collected the base address of the array (address of the 0th element) in the variable **j** using the statement,

```
j = &num[0] ; /* assigns address 65512 to j */
```

When we are inside the loop for the first time, **j** contains the address 65512, and the value at this address is 24. These are printed using the statements,

```
printf ( "address = %u ", j ) ;
printf ( "element = %d\n", *j ) ;
```

On incrementing **j**, it points to the next memory location of its type (that is location no. 65514). But location no. 65514 contains the second element of the array, therefore when the **printf( )** statements are executed for the second time, they print out the second element of the array and its address (i.e. 34 and 65514)... and so on till the last element of the array has been printed.

Obviously, a question arises as to which of the above two methods should be used when? Accessing array elements by pointers is **always** faster than accessing them by subscripts. However, from the point of view of convenience in programming, we should observe the following:

Array elements should be accessed using pointers, if the elements are to be accessed in a fixed order, say from beginning to end, or from end to beginning, or every alternate element or any such definite logic.

Instead, it would be easier to access the elements using a subscript if there is no fixed logic in accessing the elements. However, in this case also, accessing the elements by pointers would work faster than subscripts.

Passing an Entire Array to a Function

In the previous section, we saw two programs—one in which we passed individual elements of an array to a function, and another in which we passed addresses of individual elements to a function. Let us now see how to pass an entire array to a function rather than its individual elements. Consider the following example:

```
/* Demonstration of passing an entire array to a function */
# include <stdio.h>
void display ( int *, int ) ;
int main( )
{
    int num[ ] = { 24, 34, 12, 44, 56, 17 } ;
    dislpay ( &num[0], 6 ) ;
    return 0 ;
}
void display ( int *j, int n )
{
    int i ;
    for ( i = 0 ; i <= n - 1 ; i++ )
    {
        printf ( "element = %d\n", *j ) ;
        j++ ; /* increment pointer to point to next element */
    }
}
```

Here, the **display( )** function is used to print out the array elements. Note that the address of the zeroth element is being passed to the **display( )** function. The **for** loop is same as the one used in the earlier program to access the array elements using pointers. Thus, just passing the address of the zeroth element of the array to a function is as good as passing the entire array to the function. It is also necessary to pass the total number of elements in the array, otherwise the **display( )** function would not know when to terminate the **for** loop. Note that the address of the zeroth element (many a time called the base address) can also be passed by just passing the name of the array. Thus, the following two function calls are same:

```
display ( &num[0], 6 ) ;
display ( num, 6 ) ;
```

The Real Thing

If you have grasped the concept of storage of array elements in memory and the arithmetic of pointers, here is some real food for thought. Once again consider the following array.

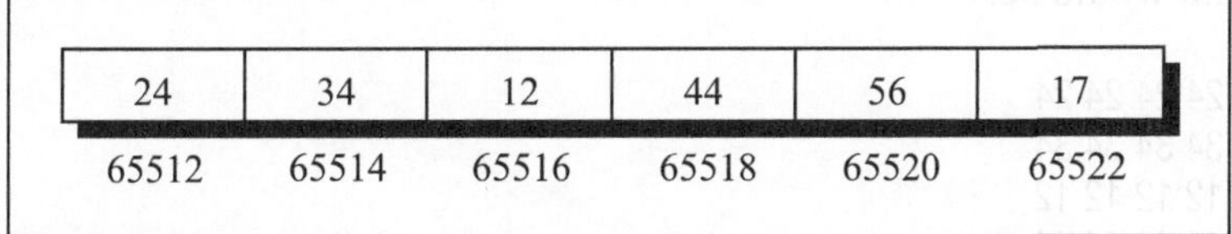

Figure 10.3

This is how we would declare the above array in C,

```
int num[ ] = { 24, 34, 12, 44, 56, 17 } ;
```

We also know, that on mentioning the name of the array, we get its base address. Thus, by saying ***num**, we would be able to refer to the zeroth element of the array, that is, 24. One can easily see that ***num** and *(**num + 0**) both refer to 24.

Similarly, by saying *(**num + 1**), we can refer the first element of the array, that is, 34. In fact, this is what the C compiler does internally. When we say, **num[i]**, the C compiler internally converts it to *(**num + i**). This means that all the following notations are same:

```
num[i]
*( num + i )
*( i + num )
i[num]
```

And here is a program to prove my point.

```
/* Accessing array elements in different ways */
# include <stdio.h>
int main( )
{
    int num[ ] = { 24, 34, 12, 44, 56, 17 } ;
    int i ;
    for ( i = 0 ; i <= 5 ; i++ )
    {
        printf ( "address = %u ", &num[i] ) ;
        printf ( "element = %d %d ", num[i], *( num + i ) ) ;
        printf ( "%d %d\n", *( i + num ), i[num] ) ;
    }
    return 0 ;
}
```

The output of this program would be:

```
address = 65512 element = 24 24 24 24
address = 65514 element = 34 34 34 34
address = 65516 element = 12 12 12 12
address = 65518 element = 44 44 44 44
address = 65520 element = 56 56 56 56
address = 65522 element = 17 17 17 17
```

Two Dimensional Arrays

So far, we have explored arrays with only one dimension. It is also possible for arrays to have two or more dimensions. The two-dimensional array is also called a matrix.

Here is a sample program that stores roll number and marks obtained by a student side by side in a matrix.

```
# include <stdio.h>
int main( )
{
    int stud[4][2] ;
    int i, j ;
    for ( i = 0 ; i <= 3 ; i++ )
    {
        printf ( "Enter roll no. and marks" ) ;
        scanf ( "%d %d", &stud[i][0], &stud[i][1] ) ;
    }
    for ( i = 0 ; i <= 3 ; i++ )
        printf ( "%d %d\n", stud[i][0], stud[i][1] ) ;
    return 0 ;
}
```

There are two parts to the program—in the first part, through a **for** loop, we read in the values of roll no. and marks, whereas, in the second part through another **for** loop, we print out these values.

Look at the **scanf( )** statement used in the first **for** loop:

```
scanf ( "%d %d", &stud[i][0], &stud[i][1] ) ;
```

In **stud[i][0]** and **stud[i][1]**, the first subscript of the variable **stud**, is row number which changes for every student. The second subscript tells which of the two columns are we talking about—the zeroth column which contains the roll no. or the first column which contains the marks. Remember the counting of rows and columns begin with zero. The complete array arrangement is shown below.

	col. no. 0	col. no. 1
row no. 0	1234	56
row no. 1	1212	33
row no. 2	1434	80
row no. 3	1312	78

Figure 10.4

Thus, 1234 is stored in **stud[0][0]**, 56 is stored in **stud[0][1]** and so on. The above arrangement highlights the fact that a two- dimensional array is nothing but a collection of a number of one- dimensional arrays placed one below the other.

In our sample program, the array elements have been stored row-wise and accessed row-wise. However, you can access the array elements column-wise as well. Traditionally, the array elements are being stored and accessed row-wise; therefore we would also stick to the same strategy.

Initialising a 2-Dimensional Array

How do we initialize a two-dimensional array? As simple as this...

```
int stud[4][2] = {
                    { 1234, 56 },
                    { 1212, 33 },
                    { 1434, 80 },
                    { 1312, 78 }
                 } ;
```

or even this would work...

```
int stud[4][2] = { 1234, 56, 1212, 33, 1434, 80, 1312, 78 } ;
```

of course, with a corresponding loss in readability.

It is important to remember that, while initializing a 2-D array, it is necessary to mention the second (column) dimension, whereas the first dimension (row) is optional.

Thus the declarations,

```
int arr[2][3] = { 12, 34, 23, 45, 56, 45 } ;
int arr[ ][3] = { 12, 34, 23, 45, 56, 45 } ;
```

are perfectly acceptable,

whereas,

```
int arr[2][ ] = { 12, 34, 23, 45, 56, 45 } ;
int arr[ ][ ] = { 12, 34, 23, 45, 56, 45 } ;
```

would never work.

Memory Map of a 2-Dimensional Array

Let us reiterate the arrangement of array elements in a two-dimensional array of students, which contains roll nos. in one column and the marks in the other.

The array arrangement shown in Figure 10.4 is only conceptually true. This is because memory doesn't contain rows and columns. In memory, whether it is a one-dimensional or a two-dimensional array, the array elements are stored in one continuous chain. The arrangement of array elements of a two-dimensional array in memory is shown below:

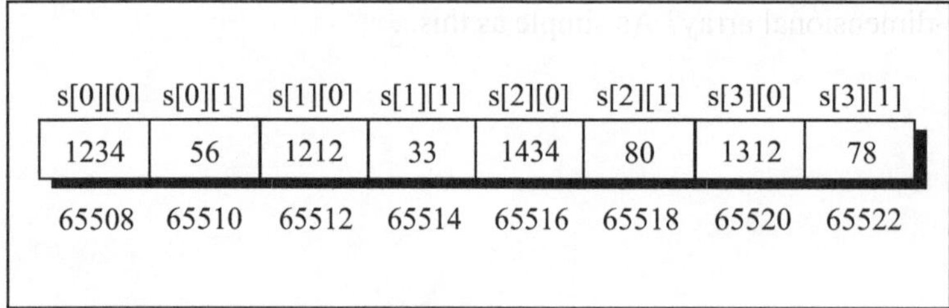

Figure 10.5

We can easily refer to the marks obtained by the third student using the subscript notation as shown below:

```
printf ( "Marks of third student = %d", stud[2][1] ) ;
```

Can we not refer to the same element using pointer notation, the way we did in one-dimensional arrays? Answer is yes. Only the procedure is slightly difficult to understand. So, read on...

Pointers and 2-Dimensional Arrays

The C language embodies an unusual but powerful capability—it can treat parts of arrays as arrays. More specifically, each row of a two-dimensional array can be thought of as a one-dimensional array. This is a very important fact if we wish to access array elements of a two-dimensional array using pointers.

Thus, the declaration,

```
int s[5][2] ;
```

can be thought of as setting up an array of 5 elements, each of which is a one-dimensional array containing 2 integers. We refer to an element of a one-dimensional array using a single subscript. Similarly, if we can imagine **s** to be a one-dimensional array, then we can refer to its zeroth element as **s[0]**, the next element as **s[1]** and so on. More specifically, **s[0]** gives the address of the zeroth one-dimensional array, **s[1]** gives the address of the first one-dimensional array and so on. This fact can be demonstrated by the following program.

```
/* Demo: 2-D array is an array of arrays */
# include <stdio.h>
int main( )
{
    int s[4][2] = {
                        { 1234, 56 },
                        { 1212, 33 },
                        { 1434, 80 },
                        { 1312, 78 }
                    } ;
    int i ;
    for ( i = 0 ; i <= 3 ; i++ )
        printf ( "Address of %d th 1-D array = %u\n", i, s[i] ) ;
    return 0 ;
}
```

And here is the output...

```
Address of 0 th 1-D array = 65508
Address of 1 th 1-D array = 65512
Address of 2 th 1-D array = 65516
Address of 3 th 1-D array = 65520
```

Let's figure out how the program works. The compiler knows that **s** is an array containing 4 one-dimensional arrays, each containing 2 integers. Each one-dimensional array occupies 4 bytes (two bytes for each integer). These one-dimensional arrays are placed linearly (zeroth 1-D array followed by first 1-D array, etc.). Hence, each one-dimensional array starts 4 bytes further along than the last one, as can be seen in the memory map of the array shown in Figure 10.6.

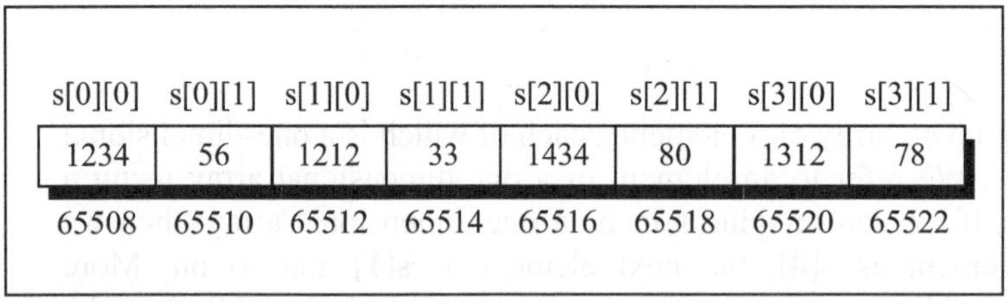

s[0][0]	s[0][1]	s[1][0]	s[1][1]	s[2][0]	s[2][1]	s[3][0]	s[3][1]
1234	56	1212	33	1434	80	1312	78
65508	65510	65512	65514	65516	65518	65520	65522

Figure 10.6

We know that the expressions **s[0]** and **s[1]** would yield the addresses of the zeroth and first one-dimensional array respectively. From Figure 10.6 these addresses turn out to be 65508 and 65512.

Now, we have been able to reach each one-dimensional array. What remains is to be able to refer to individual elements of a one-dimensional array. Suppose we want to refer to the element **s[2][1]** using pointers. We know (from the above program) that **s[2]** would give the address 65516, the address of the second one-dimensional array. Obviously (65516 + 1) would give the address 65518. Or (**s[2] + 1**) would give the address 65518. And the value at this address can be obtained by using the value at address operator, saying *(**s[2] + 1**). But, we have already studied while learning one-dimensional arrays that **num[i]** is same as *(**num + i**). Similarly, *(**s[2] + 1**) is same as, *(*(**s + 2**) **+ 1**). Thus, all the following expressions refer to the same element,

```
s[2][1]
* ( s[2] + 1 )
* ( * ( s + 2 ) + 1 )
```

Using these concepts, the following program prints out each element of a two-dimensional array using pointer notation.

```
/* Pointer notation to access 2-D array elements */
# include <stdio.h>
int main( )
{
    int s[4][2] = {
                    { 1234, 56 },
                    { 1212, 33 },
                    { 1434, 80 },
                    { 1312, 78 }
                  } ;
    int i, j ;

    for ( i = 0 ; i <= 3 ; i++ )
    {
        for ( j = 0 ; j <= 1 ; j++ )
            printf ( "%d ", *( *( s + i ) + j ) ) ;
        printf ( "\n" ) ;
    }
    return 0 ;
}
```

And here is the output...

```
1234 56
1212 33
1434 80
1312 78
```

Pointer to an Array

If we can have a pointer to an integer, a pointer to a float, a pointer to a char, then can we not have a pointer to an array? We certainly can. The following program shows how to build and use it.

```
/* Usage of pointer to an array */
# include <stdio.h>
int main( )
{
    int s[4][2] = {
```

```
                    { 1234, 56 },
                    { 1212, 33 },
                    { 1434, 80 },
                    { 1312, 78 }
                } ;
    int ( *p )[2] ;
    int i, j, *pint ;
    for ( i = 0 ; i <= 3 ; i++ )
    {
        p = &s[i] ;
        pint = ( int * ) p ;
        printf ( "\n" ) ;
        for ( j = 0 ; j <= 1 ; j++ )
            printf ( "%d ", *( pint + j ) ) ;
    }
    return 0 ;
}
```

And here is the output...

```
1234 56
1212 33
1434 80
1312 78
```

Here **p** is a pointer to an array of two integers. Note that the parentheses in the declaration of **p** are necessary. Absence of them would make **p** an array of 2 integer pointers. Array of pointers is covered in a later section in this chapter. In the outer **for** loop, each time we store the address of a new one-dimensional array. Thus first time through this loop, **p** would contain the address of the zeroth 1-D array. This address is then assigned to an integer pointer **pint**. Lastly, in the inner **for** loop using the pointer **pint**, we have printed the individual elements of the 1-D array to which **p** is pointing.

But why should we use a pointer to an array to print elements of a 2-D array. Is there any situation where we can appreciate its usage better? The entity pointer to an array is immensely useful when we need to pass a 2-D array to a function. This is discussed in the next section.

Passing 2-D Array to a Function

There are three ways in which we can pass a 2-D array to a function. These are illustrated in the following program.

```
/* Three ways of accessing a 2-D array */
# include <stdio.h>
void display ( int *q, int , int ) ;
void show ( int ( *q )[4], int, int ) ;
void print ( int q[ ][4], int , int ) ;
int main( )
{
    int a[3][4] = {
                        1, 2, 3, 4,
                        5, 6, 7, 8,
                        9, 0, 1, 6
                    } ;
    display ( a, 3, 4 ) ;
    show ( a, 3, 4 ) ;
    print ( a, 3, 4 ) ;
    return 0 ;
}
void display ( int *q, int row, int col )
{
    int i, j ;
    for ( i = 0 ; i < row ; i++ )
    {
        for ( j = 0 ; j < col ; j++ )
            printf ( "%d ", * ( q + i * col + j ) ) ;
        printf ( "\n" ) ;
    }
    printf ("\n" ) ;
}

void show ( int ( *q )[4], int row, int col )
{
    int i, j ;
    int *p ;

    for ( i = 0 ; i < row ; i++ )
    {
        p = q + i ;
        for ( j = 0 ; j < col ; j++ )
            printf ( "%d ", * ( p + j ) ) ;

        printf ( "\n" ) ;
    }
    printf ( "\n" ) ;
```

```
}

void print ( int q[ ][4], int row, int col )
{
    int i, j ;

    for ( i = 0 ; i < row ; i++ )
    {
        for ( j = 0 ; j < col ; j++ )
            printf ( "%d ", q[i][j] ) ;
        printf ( "\n" ) ;
    }
    printf ( "\n" ) ;
}
```

And here is the output...

```
1 2 3 4
5 6 7 8
9 0 1 6

1 2 3 4
5 6 7 8
9 0 1 6

1 2 3 4
5 6 7 8
9 0 1 6
```

In the **display( )** function, we have collected the base address of the 2-D array being passed to it in an ordinary **int** pointer. Then, through the two **for** loops using the expression * **(q + i * col + j)**, we have reached the appropriate element in the array. Suppose **i** is equal to 2 and **j** is equal to 3, then we wish to reach the element **a[2][3]**. Let us see whether the expression * **(q + i * col + j)** does give this element or not. Refer Figure 10.7 to understand this.

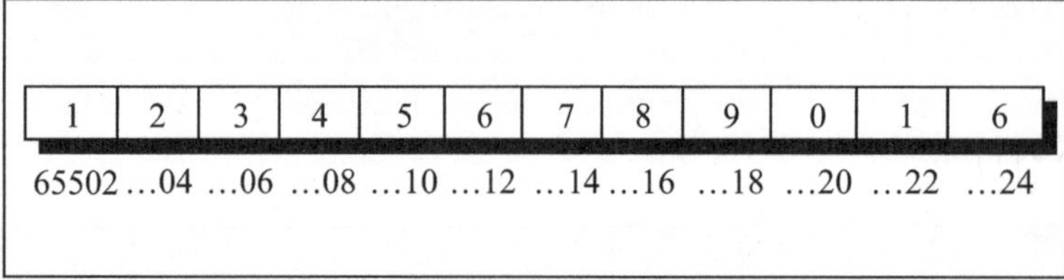

Figure 10.7

The expression * (**q + i * col + j**) becomes * (**65502 + 2 * 4 + 3**). This turns out to be * **(65502 + 11).** Since **65502** is the address of an integer, * (**65502 + 11**) turns out to be * **(65524)**. Value at this address is 6. This is indeed same as **a[2][3]**. A more general formula for accessing each array element would be:

```
* ( base address + row no. * no. of columns + column no. )
```

In the **show( )** function, we have defined **q** to be a pointer to an array of 4 integers through the declaration:

```
int ( *q )[4] ;
```

To begin with, **q** holds the base address of the zeroth 1-D array, i.e. 4001 (refer Figure 10.7). This address is then assigned to **p**, an **int** pointer, and then using this pointer, all elements of the zeroth 1-D array are accessed. Next time through the loop, when **i** takes a value 1, the expression **q + i** fetches the address of the first 1-D array. This is because, **q** is a pointer to zeroth 1-D array and adding 1 to it would give us the address of the next 1-D array. This address is once again assigned to **p**, and using it all elements of the next 1-D array are accessed.

In the third function **print(**), the declaration of **q** looks like this:

```
int q[ ][4] ;
```

This is same as **int (*q)[4]**, where **q** is pointer to an array of 4 integers. The only advantage is that, we can now use the more familiar expression **q[i][j]** to access array elements. We could have used the same expression in **show(**) as well.

Array of Pointers

The way there can be an array of **int**s or an array of **float**s, similarly, there can be an array of pointers. Since a pointer variable always contains an address, an array of pointers would be nothing but a collection of addresses. The addresses present in the array of pointers can be addresses of isolated variables or addresses of array elements or any other addresses. All rules that apply to an ordinary array apply to the array of pointers as well. I think a program would clarify the concept.

```
# include <stdio.h>
int main( )
{
    int *arr[4] ; /* array of integer pointers */
```

```
    int i = 31, j = 5, k = 19, l = 71, m ;

    arr[0] = &i ;
    arr[1] = &j ;
    arr[2] = &k ;
    arr[3] = &l ;

    for ( m = 0 ; m  <= 3 ; m++ )
        printf ( "%d\n", * ( arr[m] ) ) ;
    return 0 ;
}
```

Figure 10.8 shows the contents and the arrangement of the array of pointers in memory. As you can observe, **arr** contains addresses of isolated **int** variables **i, j, k** and **l**. The **for** loop in the program picks up the addresses present in **arr** and prints the values present at these addresses.

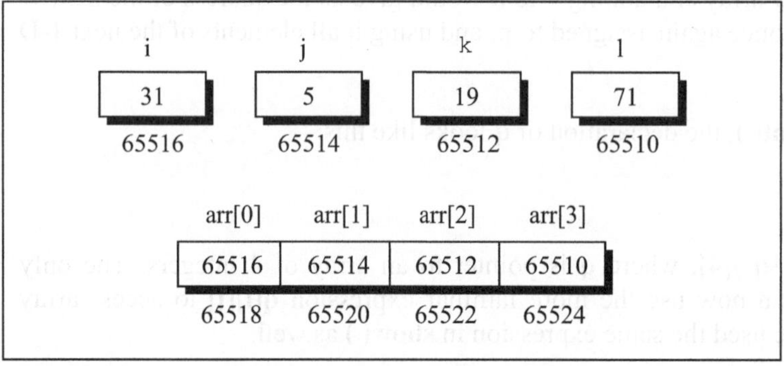

Figure 10.8

An array of pointers can even contain the addresses of other arrays. The following program would justify this.

```
# include <stdio.h>
int main( )
{
    static int a[ ] = { 0, 1, 2, 3, 4 } ;
    int *p[ ] = { a, a + 1, a + 2, a + 3, a + 4 } ;

    printf ( "%u %u %d\n", p, *p, * ( *p ) ) ;
    return 0 ;
}
```

I would leave it for you to figure out the output of this program.

Three-Dimensional Array

We aren't going to show a programming example that uses a three-dimensional array. This is because, in practice, one rarely uses this array. However, an example of initializing a three-dimensional array will consolidate your understanding of subscripts:

```
int arr[3][4][2] = {
                     {
                        { 2, 4 },
                        { 7, 8 },
                        { 3, 4 },
                        { 5, 6 }
                     },
                     {
                        { 7, 6 },
                        { 3, 4 },
                        { 5, 3 },
                        { 2, 3 }
                     },
                     {
                        { 8, 9 },
                        { 7, 2 },
                        { 3, 4 },
                        { 5, 1 },
                     }
                  };
```

A 3-D array can be thought of as an array of arrays of arrays. The outer array has three elements, each of which is a 2-D array of four 1-D arrays, each of which contains two integers. In other words, a 1-D array of two elements is constructed first. Then four such 1-D arrays are placed one below the other to give a 2-D array containing four rows. Then, three such 2-D arrays are placed one behind the other to yield a 3-D array containing three 2-D arrays. In the array declaration, note how the commas have been given. Figure 10.9 would possibly help you in visualizing the situation better.

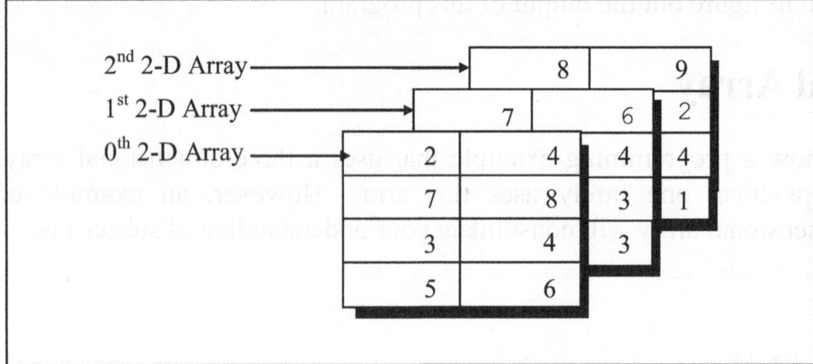

Figure 10.9

Again remember that the arrangement shown above is only conceptually true. In memory, the same array elements are stored linearly as shown in Figure 10.10.

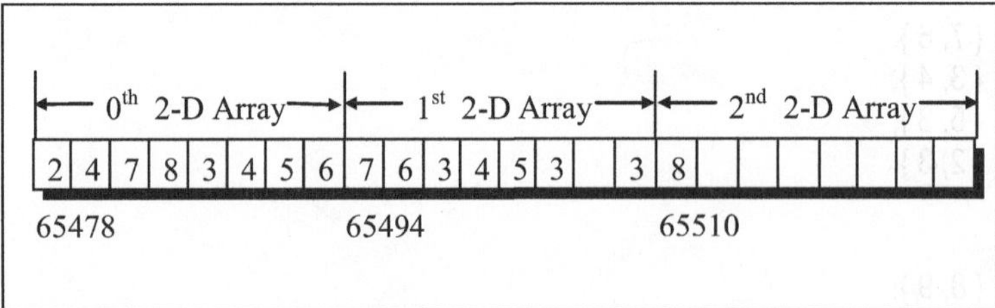

Figure 10.10

How would you refer to the array element 1 in the above array? The first subscript should be [2], since the element is in third two-dimensional array; the second subscript should be [3] since the element is in fourth row of the two-dimensional array; and the third subscript should be [1] since the element is in second position in the one-dimensional array. We can, therefore, say that the element 1 can be referred as **arr[2][3][1]**. It may be noted here that the counting of array elements even for a 3-D array begins with zero. Can we not refer to this element using pointer notation? Of course, yes. For example, the following two expressions refer to the same element in the 3-D array:

```
arr[2][3][1]
*( *( *( arr + 2 ) + 3 ) + 1 )
```

Summary

(a) An array is similar to an ordinary variable except that it can store multiple elements of similar type.
(b) Compiler doesn't perform bounds checking on an array.
(c) The array variable acts as a pointer to the zeroth element of the array. In a 1-D array, zeroth element is a single value, whereas, in a 2-D array this element is a 1-D array.
(d) On incrementing a pointer it points to the next location of its type.
(e) Array elements are stored in contiguous memory locations and so they can be accessed using pointers.
(f) Only limited arithmetic can be done on pointers.

Exercise

Simple arrays

[A] What will be the output of the following programs:

(a)
```
# include <stdio.h>
int main( )
{
    int  num[26], temp ;
    num[0] = 100 ;
    num[25] = 200 ;
    temp = num[25] ;
    num[25] = num[0] ;
    num[0] = temp ;
    printf ( "%d %d\n", num[0], num[25] ) ;
    return 0 ;
}
```

(b)
```
# include <stdio.h>
int main( )
{
    int  array[26], i ;
    for ( i = 0 ; i <= 25 ; i++ )
    {
        array[i] = 'A' + i ;
        printf ( "%d %c\n", array[i], array[i] ) ;
    }
    return 0 ;
}
```

(c)
```
# include <stdio.h>
```

```
int main( )
{
    int sub[50], i ;
    for ( i = 0 ; i <= 48 ; i++ ) ;
    {
        sub[i] = i ;
        printf ( "%d\n", sub[i] ) ;
    }
    return 0 ;
}
```

(d)
```
# include <stdio.h>
int main( )
{
    int a[10], i = 0 ;
    static int b[10] ;

    for ( b[0] ; b[0] < 10 ; b[0]++ )
        printf ( "%d ", a[i++] = b[0] ) ;
    return 0 ;
}
```

[B] Point out the errors, if any, in the following program segments:

(a)
```
/* mixed has some char and some int values */
# include <stdio.h>
int char mixed[100] ;
int main( )
{
    int a[10], i ;
    for ( i = 1 ; i <= 10 ; i++ )
    {
        scanf ( "%d", a[i] ) ;
        printf ( "%d\n", a[i] ) ;
    }
    return 0 ;
}
```

(b)
```
# include <stdio.h>
int main( )
```

```
    {
        int size ;
        scanf ( "%d", &size ) ;
        int arr[size] ;
        for ( i = 1 ; i <= size ; i++ )
        {
            scanf ( "%d", arr[i] ) ;
            printf ( "%d\n", arr[i] ) ;
        }
        return 0 ;
    }
```

(c)
```
    # include <stdio.h>
    int main( )
    {
        int i, a = 2, b = 3 ;
        int arr[ 2 + 3 ] ;
        for ( i = 0 ; i < a+b ; i++ )
        {
            scanf ( "%d", &arr[i] ) ;
            printf ( "%d\n", arr[i] ) ;
        }
        return 0 ;
    }
```

(d)
```
    # include <stdio.h>
    int main( )
    {
        int a[ ] = { 1, 5, 11 } ;
        int i ;
        for ( i = 0 ; i <= 2 ; i++ )
        {
            printf ( "%d\n", *a ) ;
            a++ ;
        }
        return 0 ;
    }
```

[C] Answer the following:

(a) An array is a collection of

1. different data types scattered throughout memory

2. the same data type scattered throughout memory
3. the same data type placed next to each other in memory
4. different data types placed next to each other in memory

(b) Are the following array declarations correct?

```
int a (25) ;
int size = 10, b[size] ;
int c = { 0, 1, 2 } ;
```

(c) Which element of the array does this expression reference?

```
num[4]
```

(d) What is the difference between the 5's in these two expressions? (Select the correct answer)

```
int num[5] ;
num[5] = 11 ;
```

1. first is particular element, second is type
2. first is array size, second is particular element
3. first is particular element, second is array size
4. both specify array size

(e) State whether the following statements are True or False:

1. The array **int num[26]** has twenty-six elements.
2. The expression **num[1]** designates the first element in the array
3. It is necessary to initialize the array at the time of declaration.
4. The expression **num[27]** designates the twenty-eighth element in the array.

(f) Write in clear words what is the meaning of the following declarations:

```
float *modify ( char *, int * ) ;
long *Long ;
```

(g) Write only one statement which performs the task of the three statements given below.

```
int **k, *j, i ;
j = &i ;
k = &j ;
```

(h) Write the function **p( )** which would scan the values of the array **a** from the keyboard.

```
#include <stdio.h>
int main( )
{
    int a[3][2], i, j ;
    p ( a, 3, 2 ) ;
    for ( i = 0 ; i < 3 ; i++ )
    {
        for ( j = 0 ; j < 2 ; j++ )
            printf ( " %d", a[i][j] ) ;
        printf ( "\n" ) ;
    }
    return 0 ;
}
```

(i) Which is the correct way to refer the variable **i**?

1. &i
2. *i
3. &*i
4. *&i

(j) Suppose we call a function with the statement

```
agree ( i, &j ) ;
```

which is the correct way to define the function, if **i** and **j** are integer variables?

1. agree (int x, int y) ;
2. agree (int x, float *y) ;
3. agree (int *x, int *y) ;
4. agree (int x, int *y) ;

(k) Assuming that the address of a variable **vac** has been assigned to the pointer variable **vaccine**, which of the following conditions will evaluate to true?

1. if (vac != *vaccine)
2. if (&vac != vaccine)
3. if (*vaccine != *&vac)
4. if (&vaccine != *&vac)

(l) Assuming that we want to read the value of **j**, does the following program look all right?

```
#include <stdio.h>
int main( )
{
    int j, p = &j ;
    scanf ( "%d", p ) ;
    return 0 ;
}
```

(m) Given the following array declaration,

```
int arr[2][2][3] = {
                       {
                           { 1, 2, 3 },
                           { 4, 5, 6 }
                       },
                       {
                           { 7, 8, 9 },
                           { 10, 11, 12 }
                       }
                   };
```

using pointers how will you print the element 9?

(n) Write in clear words the meaning of the following declarations:

```
float *fp ;
float * modify( ) ;
```

(o) An integer variable **i** contains a value 10. Using pointer operators write at least 3 ways to print the value of **i**.

(p) How many pointers can we associate at a time with

1. a character array
2. a numeric array
3. an array of pointers

(q) Which are the correct ways to refer to the variable **ch** assuming that the address of **ch** has been assigned to the pointer **fingerch**?

1. *fingerch
2. *finger
3. ch

4. *ch

(r) If we call a function with the statement

```
fun ( &b, &w ) ;
```

what do **&b** and **&w** signify?

1. They are integer values we are passing to the function.
2. They are addresses of the function and the calling program.
3. They are addresses of variables where we want values returned or modified in the calling program to be stored.
4. None of the above.

(s) Assuming that the address of a variable **vac** has been assigned to the pointer variable **vaccine**, which of the following conditions would evaluate to true?

1. if (vac == &vaccine)
2. if (vac == *vaccine)
3. if (vaccine == *vac)
4. if (vaccine == &vac)

(t) Assuming that **yankee[ ]** is a one dimensional array of type **int**, which of the following refers to the value of the third element in the array?

1. * (yankee + 2)
2. * (yankee + 4)
3. yankee + 2
4. yankee + 4

(u) Assuming that we want to read in a value of **x**, and the address of **x** has been assigned to **ppx**, does the following statement look all right?

```
scanf ( "%d", *ppx ) ;
```

(v) Given the following array declaration,

```
int arr[2][3] = {
                    { 10, 11, 12 },
                    { 13, 14, 15 }
               } ;
```

Using pointers how will you print the element 14?

[D] Attempt the following:

(a) Twenty-five numbers are entered from the keyboard into an array. The number to be searched is entered through the keyboard by the user. Write a program to find if the number to be searched is present in the array and if it is present, display the number of times it appears in the array.

(b) Implement the Selection Sort, Bubble Sort and Insertion sort algorithms on a set of 25 numbers. (Refer Figure 10.11 for the logic of the algorithms)

- Selection sort
- Bubble Sort
- Insertion Sort

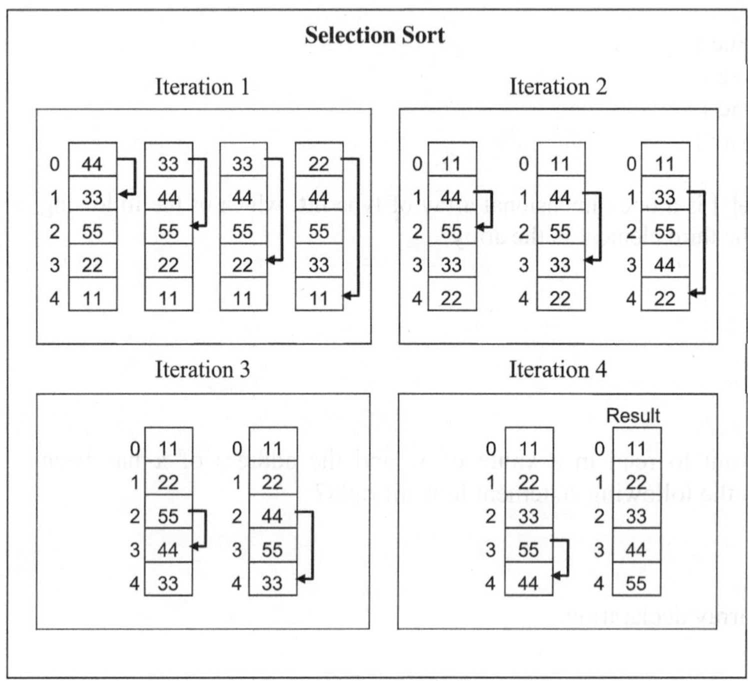

Figure 10.11 (a)

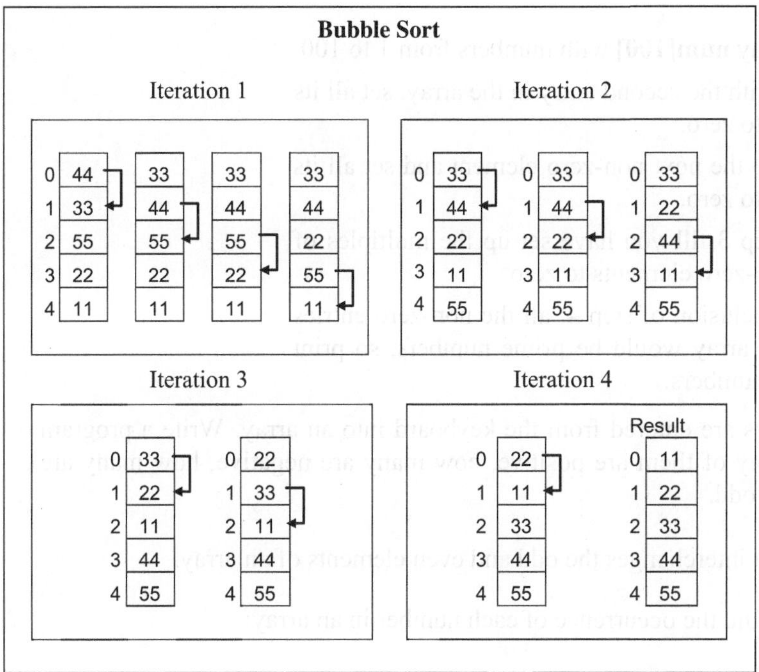

Figure 10.11 (b)

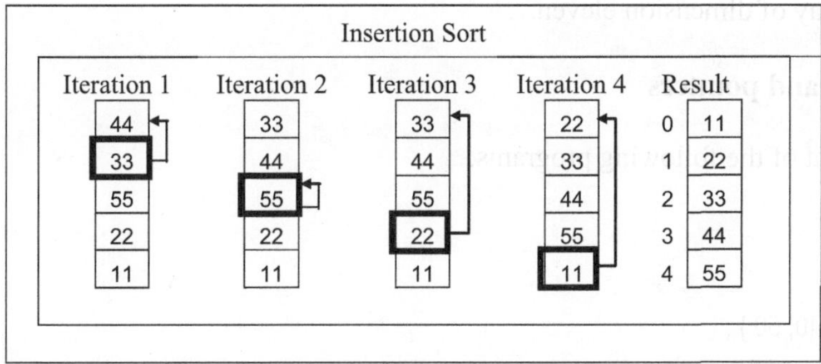

Figure 10.11 (c)

(c) Implement the following procedure to generate prime numbers from 1 to 100 into a program. This procedure is called sieve of Eratosthenes.

step 1 Fill an array **num[100]** with numbers from 1 to 100

step 2 Starting with the second entry in the array, set all its multiples to zero.

step 3 Proceed to the next non-zero element and set all its multiples to zero.

step 4 Repeat step 3 till you have set up the multiples of all the non-zero elements to zero

step 5 At the conclusion of step 4, all the non-zero entries left in the array would be prime numbers, so print out these numbers.

(d) Twenty-five numbers are entered from the keyboard into an array. Write a program to find out how many of them are positive, how many are negative, how many are even and how many odd.

(e) Write a program that interchanges the odd and even elements of an array.

(f) Write a function to find the occurrence of each number in an array:

```
int a[ ] = { 4, 7, 4, 3, 2, 4, 1, 9, 6, 5, 8, 3, 7, 5, 2, 0, 1, 6 } ;
```

The output should be in the form **count[1] = 2** as 1 occurs twice, in the array **a[ ]**, **count** is an integer array of dimension eleven.

More on arrays, Arrays and pointers

[E] What will be the output of the following programs:

(a)
```
# include <stdio.h>
int main( )
{
    int b[ ] = { 10, 20, 30, 40, 50 } ;
    int i ;
    for ( i = 0 ; i <= 4 ; i++ )
        printf ( "%d\n" *( b + i ) ) ;
    return 0 ;
}
```

(b)
```
# include <stdio.h>
int main( )
```

```
{
    int b[ ] = { 0, 20, 0, 40, 5 } ;
    int i, *k ;
    k = b ;
    for ( i = 0 ; i <= 4 ; i++ )
    {
        printf ( "%d\n" *k ) ;
        k++ ;
    }
    return 0 ;
}
```

(c)
```
# include <stdio.h>
void change ( int *, int ) ;
int main( )
{
    int a[ ] = { 2, 4, 6, 8, 10 } ;
    int i ;
    change ( a, 5 ) ;
    for ( i = 0 ; i <= 4 ; i++ )
        printf ( "%d\n", a[i] ) ;
    return 0 ;
}
void change ( int *b, int n )
{
    int i ;
    for ( i = 0 ; i < n ; i++ )
        *( b + i ) = *( b + i ) + 5 ;
}
```

(d)
```
# include <stdio.h>
void f ( int *, int ) ;
int main( )
{
    int a[5], i, b = 16 ;
    for ( i = 0 ; i < 5 ; i++ )
        a[i] = 2 * i ;
    f ( a, b ) ;
    for ( i = 0 ; i < 5 ; i++ )
        printf ( "%d", a[i] ) ;
    printf ( "\n%d", b ) ;
    return 0 ;
}
```

```
void f ( int *x, int y )
{
    int i ;
    for ( i = 0 ; i < 5 ; i++ )
        *( x + i ) += 2 ;
    y += 2 ;
}
```

(e)
```
# include <stdio.h>
int main( )
{
    static int a[5] ;
    int i ;
    for ( i = 0 ; i <= 4 ; i++ )
        printf ( "%d\n", a[i] ) ;
    return 0 ;
}
```

(f)
```
# include <stdio.h>
int main( )
{
    int a[5] = { 5, 1, 15, 20, 25 } ;
    int i, j, k = 1, m ;
    i = ++a[1] ;
    j = a[1]++ ;
    m = a[i++] ;
    printf ( "%d %d %d\n", i, j, m ) ;
}
```

[F] Point out the errors, if any, in the following programs:

(a)
```
# include <stdio.h>
int main( )
{
    int array[6] = { 1, 2, 3, 4, 5, 6 } ;
    int i ;
    for ( i = 0 ; i <= 25 ; i++ )
        printf ( "%d\n", array[i] ) ;
    return 0 ;
}
```

(b)
```
# include <stdio.h>
int main( )
```

```
{
    int sub[50], i ;
    for ( i = 1 ; i <= 50 ; i++ )
    {
        sub[i] = i ;
        printf ( "%d\n" , sub[i] ) ;
    }
    return 0 ;
}
```

(c)
```
# include <stdio.h>
int main( )
{
    int a[ ] = { 10, 20, 30, 40, 50 } ;
    int j ;
    j = a ; /* store the address of zeroth element */
    j = j + 3 ;
    printf ( "%d\n" *j ) ;
    return 0 ;
}
```

(d)
```
# include <stdio.h>
int main( )
{
    float a[ ] = { 13.24, 1.5, 1.5, 5.4, 3.5 } ;
    float *j ;
    j = a ;
    j = j + 4 ;
    printf ( "%d %d %d\n", j, *j, a[4] ) ;
    return 0 ;
}
```

(e)
```
# include <stdio.h>
int main( )
{
    float a[ ] = { 13.24, 1.5, 1.5, 5.4, 3.5 } ;
    float *j, *k ;
    j = a ;
    k = a + 4 ;
    j = j * 2 ;
    k = k / 2 ;
    printf ( "%d %d\n", *j, *k ) ;
    return 0 ;
```

```
}
```

(f)
```
# include <stdio.h>
int main( )
{
    int max = 5 ;
    float arr[max] ;
    for ( i = 0 ; i < max ; i++ )
        scanf ( "%f", &arr[i] ) ;
    return 0 ;
}
```

[G] Answer the following:

(a) What will happen if you try to put so many values into an array when you initialize it that the size of the array is exceeded?

1. nothing
2. possible system malfunction
3. error message from the compiler
4. other data may be overwritten

(b) In an array **int arr[12]** the word **arr** represents the a_________ of the array.

(c) What will happen if you put too few elements in an array when you initialize it?

1. nothing
2. possible system malfunction
3. error message from the compiler
4. unused elements will be filled with 0's or garbage

(d) What will happen if you assign a value to an element of an array whose subscript exceeds the size of the array?

1. the element will be set to 0
2. nothing, it's done all the time
3. other data may be overwritten
4. error message from the compiler

(e) When you pass an array as an argument to a function, what actually gets passed?

1. address of the array
2. values of the elements of the array

3. address of the first element of the array
4. number of elements of the array

(f) Which of these are reasons for using pointers?

1. To manipulate parts of an array
2. To refer to keywords such as **for** and **if**
3. To return more than one value from a function
4. To refer to particular programs more conveniently

(g) If you don't initialize a static array, What will be the elements set to?

1. 0
2. an undetermined value
3. a floating point number
4. the character constant '\0'

[H] State True or False:

(a) Address of a floating-point variable is always a whole number.

(b) Which of the following is the correct way of declaring a float pointer:

1. float ptr ;
2. float *ptr ;
3. *float ptr ;
4. None of the above

(c) Add the missing statement for the following program to print 35.

```
# include <stdio.h>
int main( )
{
    int j, *ptr ;
    *ptr = 35 ;
    printf ( "%d\n", j ) ;
    return 0 ;
}
```

(d) if **int s[5]** is a one-dimensional array of integers, which of the following refers to the third element in the array?

1. *(s + 2)
2. *(s + 3)

3. s + 3
4. s + 2

[I] Attempt the following:

(a) Write a program to copy the contents of one array into another in the reverse order.

(b) If an array **arr** contains **n** elements, then write a program to check if **arr[0] = arr[n-1], arr[1] = arr[n-2]** and so on.

(c) Find the smallest number in an array using pointers.

(d) Write a program which performs the following tasks:

- initialize an integer array of 10 elements in **main( )**
- pass the entire array to a function **modify( )**
- in **modify( )** multiply each element of array by 3
- return the control to **main( )** and print the new array elements in **main( )**

More than one dimension

[J] What will be the output of the following programs:

(a)
```
# include <stdio.h>
int main( )
{
    int n[3][3] = {
                    2, 4, 3,
                    6, 8, 5,
                    3, 5, 1
                  } ;
    printf ( "%d %d %d\n", *n, n[3][3], n[2][2] ) ;
    return 0 ;
}
```

(b)
```
# include <stdio.h>
int main( )
{
    int n[3][3] = {
                    2, 4, 3,
                    6, 8, 5,
                    3, 5, 1
                  } ;
```

```
    int i, *ptr ;
    ptr = n ;
    for ( i = 0 ; i <= 8 ; i++ )
        printf ( "%d\n", *( ptr + i ) ) ;
    return 0 ;
}
```

(c)
```
# include <stdio.h>
int main( )
{
    int n[3][3] = {
                    2, 4, 3,
                    6, 8, 5,
                    3, 5, 1
                  } ;
    int i, j ;
    for ( i = 0 ; i <= 2 ; i++ )
        for ( j = 0 ; j <= 2 ; j++ )
            printf ( "%d %d\n", n[i][j], *( *( n + i ) + j ) ) ;
    return 0 ;
}
```

[K] Point out the errors, if any, in the following programs:

(a)
```
# include <stdio.h>
int main( )
{
    int twod[ ][ ] = {
                       2, 4,
                       6, 8
                     } ;
    printf ( "%d\n", twod ) ;
    return 0 ;
}
```

(b)
```
# include <stdio.h>
int main( )
{
    int three[3][ ] = {
                        2, 4, 3,
                        6, 8, 2,
                        2, 3 ,1
                      } ;
```

```
    printf ( "%d\n", three[1][1] ) ;
    return 0 ;
}
```

[L] Attempt the following:

(a) How will you initialize a three-dimensional array **threed[3][2][3]**? How will you refer the first and last element in this array?

(b) Write a program to pick up the largest number from any 5 row by 5 column matrix.

(c) Write a program to obtain transpose of a 4 x 4 matrix. The transpose of a matrix is obtained by exchanging the elements of each row with the elements of the corresponding column.

(d) Very often in fairs we come across a puzzle that contains 15 numbered square pieces mounted on a frame. These pieces can be moved horizontally or vertically. A possible arrangement of these pieces is shown below:

1	4	15	7
8	10	2	11
14	3	6	13
12	9	5	

Figure 10.12

As you can see there is a blank at bottom right corner. Implement the following procedure through a program:

Draw the boxes as shown above. Display the numbers in the above order. Allow the user to hit any of the arrow keys (up, down, left, or right).

If user hits say, right arrow key then the piece with a number 5 should move to the right and blank should replace the original position of 5. Similarly, if down arrow key is hit, then 13 should move down and blank should replace the original position of 13. If left arrow key or up arrow key is hit then no action should be taken.

The user would continue hitting the arrow keys till the numbers aren't arranged in ascending order.

Keep track of the number of moves in which the user manages to arrange the numbers in ascending order. The user who manages it in minimum number of moves is the one who wins.

How do we tackle the arrow keys? We cannot receive them using **scanf( )** function. Arrow keys are special keys which are identified by their 'scan codes'. Use the following function in your program. It would return the scan code of the arrow key being hit. Don't worry about how this function is written. We are going to deal with it later. The scan codes for the arrow keys are:

up arrow key – 72 down arrow key – 80
left arrow key – 75 right arrow key – 77

```
/* Returns scan code of the key that has been hit */
#include "dos.h"
getkey( )
{
    union REGS i, o ;

    while ( !kbhit( ) )
        ;
    i.h.ah = 0 ;
    int86 ( 22, &i, &o ) ;
    return ( o.h.ah ) ;
}
```

(e) Match the following with reference to the following program segment:

```
int i, j, = 25;
int *pi, *pj = & j;
.......
....... /* more lines of program */
.......
*pj = j + 5;
j = *pj + 5 ;
pj = pj ;
*pi = i + j
```

Each integer quantity occupies 2 bytes of memory. The value assigned to **i** begin at (hexadecimal) address F9C and the value assigned to j begins at address F9E. Match the value represented by left hand side quantities with the right.

1.	&i	a.	30
2.	&j	b.	F9E
3.	pj	c.	35
4.	*pj	d.	FA2
5.	i	e.	F9C
6.	pi	f.	67
7.	*pi	g.	unspecified
8.	(pi + 2)	h.	65
9.	(*pi + 2)	i.	F9E
10.	* (pi + 2)	j.	F9E
		k.	FAO
		l.	F9D

(f) Match the following with reference to the following program segment:

```
int x[3][5] = {
                { 1, 2, 3, 4, 5 },
                { 6, 7, 8, 9, 10 },
                { 11, 12, 13, 14, 15 }
            }, *n = &x ;
```

1.	*(*(x + 2) + 1)	a.	9
2.	*(*x + 2) + 5	b.	13
3.	*(*(x + 1))	c.	4
4.	*(*(x) + 2) + 1	d.	3
5.	* (*(x + 1) + 3)	e.	2
6.	*n	f.	12
7.	*(n +2)	g.	14
8.	(*(n + 3) + 1	h.	7
9.	*(n + 5)+1	i.	1
10.	++*n	j.	8
		k.	5
		l.	10
		m.	6

(g) Match the following with reference to the following program segment:

```
unsigned int arr[3][3] = {
                    2, 4, 6,
                    9, 1, 10,
```

```
                16, 64, 5
            };
```

1.	**arr	a.	64
2.	**arr < *(*arr + 2)	b.	18
3.	*(arr + 2) / (*(*arr + 1) > **arr)	c.	6
4.	*(arr[1] + 1) | arr[1][2]	d.	3
5.	*(arr[0]) | *(arr[2])	e.	0
6.	arr[1][1] < arr[0][1]	f.	16
7.	arr[2][[1] & arr[2][0]	g.	1
8.	arr[2][2] | arr[0][1]	h.	11
9.	arr[0][1] ^ arr[0][2]	i.	20
10.	++**arr + --arr[1][1]	j.	2
		k.	5
		l.	4

(h) Write a program to find if a square matrix is symmetric.

(i) Write a program to add two 6 x 6 matrices.

(j) Write a program to multiply any two 3 x 3 matrices.

(k) Given an array **p[5]**, write a function to shift it circularly left by two positions. Thus, if p[0] = 15, p[1]= 30, p[2] = 28, p[3]= 19 and p[4] = 61 then after the shift p[0] = 28, p[1] = 19, p[2] = 61, p[3] = 15 and p[4] = 30. Call this function for a (4 x 5) matrix and get its rows left shifted.

(l) A 6 x 6 matrix is entered through the keyboard. Write a program to obtain the Determinant value of this matrix.

(m) For the following set of sample data, compute the standard deviation and the mean.

-6, -12, 8, 13, 11, 6, 7, 2, -6, -9, -10, 11, 10, 9, 2

The formula for standard deviation is

$$\frac{\sqrt{(x_i - \bar{x})^2}}{n}$$

where $\mathbf{x_i}$ is the data item and $\bar{\mathbf{x}}$ is the mean.

(n) The area of a triangle can be computed by the sine law when 2 sides of the triangle and the angle between them are known.

Area = (1 / 2) ab sin (angle)

Given the following 6 triangular pieces of land, write a program to find their area and determine which is largest.

Plot No.	a	b	angle
1	137.4	80.9	0.78
2	155.2	92.62	0.89
3	149.3	97.93	1.35
4	160.0	100.25	9.00
5	155.6	68.95	1.25
6	149.7	120.0	1.75

(o) For the following set of n data points (x, y), compute the correlation coefficient r, given by

$$r = \frac{\sum xy - \sum x \sum y}{\sqrt{[n\sum x^2 - (\sum x)^2][n\sum y^2 - (\sum y)^2]}}$$

x	y
34.22	102.43
39.87	100.93
41.85	97.43
43.23	97.81
40.06	98.32
53.29	98.32
53.29	100.07
54.14	97.08
49.12	91.59
40.71	94.85
55.15	94.65

(p) For the following set of point given by **(x, y)** fit a straight line given by

y = a + bx

where,

$a = \overline{y} - b\overline{x}$ and

$$b = \frac{n\sum yx - \sum x \sum y}{[n\sum x^2 - (\sum x)^2]}$$

X	Y
3.0	1.5
4.5	2.0
5.5	3.5
6.5	5.0
7.5	6.0
8.5	7.5
8.0	9.0
9.0	10.5
9.5	12.0
10.0	14.0

(q) The **X** and **Y** coordinates of 10 different points are entered through the keyboard. Write a program to find the distance of last point from the first point (sum of distances between consecutive points).

(r) A dequeue is an ordered set of elements in which elements may be inserted or retrieved from either end. Using an array simulate a dequeue of characters and the operations retrieve left, retrieve right, insert left, insert right. Exceptional conditions such as dequeue full or empty should be indicated. Two pointers (namely, left and right) are needed in this simulation.

11 Puppetting On Strings

- What are Strings
- More about Strings
- Pointers and Strings
- Standard Library String Functions
    - *strlen( )*
    - *strcpy( )*
    - *strcat( )*
    - *strcmp( )*
- Two-Dimensional Array of Characters
- Array of Pointers to Strings
- Limitation of Array of Pointers to Strings
    - Solution
- Summary
- Exercise

In the last chapter, you learnt how to define arrays of various sizes and dimensions, how to initialize arrays, how to pass arrays to a function, etc. With this knowledge under your belt, you should be ready to handle strings, which are, simply put, a special kind of array. And strings, the ways to manipulate them, and how pointers are related to strings are going to be the topics of discussion in this chapter.

What are Strings

The way a group of integers can be stored in an integer array, similarly a group of characters can be stored in a character array. Character arrays are many a time also called strings. Many languages internally treat strings as character arrays, but somehow conceal this fact from the programmer. Character arrays or strings are used by programming languages to manipulate text such as words and sentences.

A string constant is a one-dimensional array of characters terminated by a null ('\0'). For example,

```
char name[ ] = { 'H', 'A', 'E', 'S', 'L', 'E', 'R', '\0' } ;
```

Each character in the array occupies one byte of memory and the last character is always '\0'. What character is this? It looks like two characters, but it is actually only one character, with the \ indicating that what follows it is something special. '\0' is called null character. Note that '\0' and '0' are not same. ASCII value of '\0' is 0, whereas ASCII value of '0' is 48. Figure 11.1 shows the way a character array is stored in memory. Note that the elements of the character array are stored in contiguous memory locations.

The terminating null ('\0') is important, because it is the only way the functions that work with a string can know where the string ends. In fact, a string not terminated by a '\0' is not really a string, but merely a collection of characters.

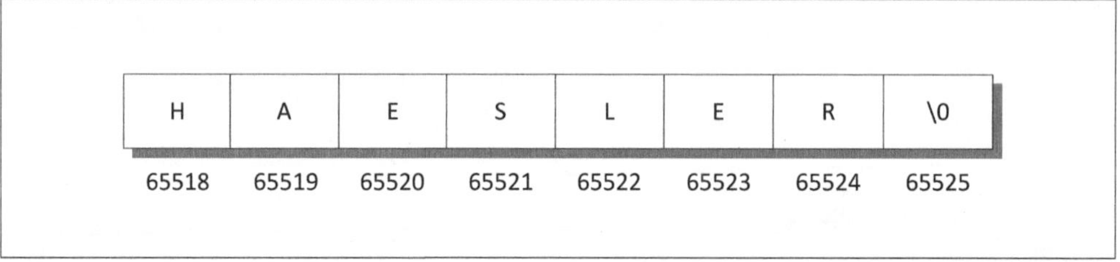

Figure 11.1

C concedes the fact that you would use strings very often and hence provides a shortcut for initializing strings. For example, the string used above can also be initialized as,

```
char name[ ] = "HAESLER" ;
```

Note that, in this declaration '\0' is not necessary. C inserts the null character automatically.

More about Strings

In what way are character arrays different from numeric arrays? Can elements in a character array be accessed in the same way as the elements of a numeric array? Do I need to take any special care of '\0'? Why numeric arrays don't end with a '\0'? Declaring strings is okay, but how do I manipulate them? Questions galore!! Well, let us settle some of these issues right away with the help of sample programs.

```
/* Program to demonstrate printing of a string */
# include <stdio.h>
int main( )
{
    char name[ ] = "Klinsman" ;
    int i = 0 ;

    while ( i <= 7 )
    {
        printf ( "%c", name[i] ) ;
        i++ ;
    }
    printf ( "\n" ) ;
    return 0 ;
}
```

And here is the output...

```
Klinsman
```

No big deal. We have initialized a character array, and then printed out the elements of this array within a **while** loop. Can we write the **while** loop without using the final value

7? We can; because we know that each character array always ends with a '\0'. Following program illustrates this.

```
# include <stdio.h>
int main( )
{
    char name[ ] = "Klinsman" ;
    int i = 0 ;
    while ( name[i] != '\0' )
    {
        printf ( "%c", name[i] ) ;
        i++ ;
    }
    printf ( "\n" ) ;
    return 0 ;
}
```

And here is the output...

```
Klinsman
```

This program doesn't rely on the length of the string (number of characters in it) to print out its contents and hence is definitely more general than the earlier one. Here is another version of the same program; this one uses a pointer to access the array elements.

```
# include <stdio.h>
int main( )
{
    char name[ ] = "Klinsman" ;
    char *ptr ;
    ptr = name ; /* store base address of string */
    while ( *ptr != '\0' )
    {
        printf ( "%c", *ptr ) ;
        ptr++ ;
    }
    printf ( "\n" ) ;
    return 0 ;
}
```

As with the integer array, by mentioning the name of the array, we get the base address (address of the zeroth element) of the array. This base address is stored in the variable **ptr** using,

```
ptr = name ;
```

Once the base address is obtained in **ptr**, ***ptr** would yield the value at this address, which gets printed promptly through,

```
printf ( "%c", *ptr ) ;
```

Then, **ptr** is incremented to point to the next character in the string. This derives from two facts: array elements are stored in contiguous memory locations and on incrementing a pointer, it points to the immediately next location of its type. This process is carried out until **ptr** points to the last character in the string, that is, '\0'.

In fact, the character array elements can be accessed exactly in the same way as the elements of an integer array. Thus, all the following notations refer to the same element:

```
name[i]
*( name + i )
*( i + name )
i[name]
```

Even though there are so many ways (as shown above) to refer to the elements of a character array, rarely is any one of them used. This is because **printf( )** function has got a sweet and simple way of doing it, as shown below. Note that **printf( )** doesn't print the '\0'.

```
# include <stdio.h>
int main( )
{
    char name[ ] = "Klinsman" ;
    printf ( "%s", name ) ;
}
```

The **%s** used in **printf( )** is a format specification for printing out a string. The same specification can be used to receive a string from the keyboard, as shown below.

```
# include <stdio.h>
int main( )
{
    char  name[25] ;

    printf ( "Enter your name " ) ;
    scanf ( "%s", name ) ;
    printf ( "Hello %s!\n", name ) ;
    return 0 ;
}
```

And here is a sample run of the program...

```
Enter your name Debashish
Hello Debashish!
```

Note that the declaration **char name[25]** sets aside 25 bytes under the array **name[ ],** whereas the **scanf( )** function fills in the characters typed at keyboard into this array until the enter key is hit. Once enter is hit, **scanf( )** places a '\0' in the array. Naturally, we should pass the base address of the array to the **scanf( )** function.

While entering the string using **scanf( )**, we must be cautious about two things:

(a) The length of the string should not exceed the dimension of the character array. This is because the C compiler doesn't perform bounds checking on character arrays. Hence, if you carelessly exceed the bounds, there is always a danger of overwriting something important, and in that event, you would have nobody to blame but yourselves.

(b) **scanf( )** is not capable of receiving multi-word strings. Therefore, names such as 'Debashish Roy' would be unacceptable. The way to get around this limitation is by using the function **gets( )**. The usage of functions **gets( )** and its counterpart **puts( )** is shown below.

```
# include <stdio.h>
int main( )
{
    char  name[25] ;
    printf ( "Enter your full name: " ) ;
```

```
    gets ( name ) ;
    puts ( "Hello!" ) ;
    puts ( name ) ;
    return 0 ;
}
```

And here is the output...

```
Enter your full name: Debashish Roy
Hello!
Debashish Roy
```

The program and the output are self-explanatory except for the fact that, **puts( )** can display only one string at a time (hence the use of two **puts( )** in the program above). Also, on displaying a string, unlike **printf( )**, **puts( )** places the cursor on the next line. Though **gets( )** is capable of receiving only one string at a time, the plus point with **gets( )** is that it can receive a multi-word string.

If we are prepared to take the trouble, we can make **scanf( )** accept multi-word strings by writing it in this manner:

```
char name[25] ;
printf ( "Enter your full name " ) ;
scanf ( "%[^\n]s", name ) ;
```

Here, **[^\n]** indicates that **scanf( )** will keep receiving characters into **name[ ]** until a \n is encountered. Though workable, this is not the best of the ways to call a function, you would agree.

Pointers and Strings

Suppose we wish to store "Hello". We may either store it in a string or we may ask the C compiler to store it at some location in memory and assign the address of the string in a **char** pointer. This is shown below:

```
char str[ ] = "Hello" ;
char *p = "Hello" ;
```

There is a subtle difference in usage of these two forms. For example, we cannot assign a string to another, whereas, we can assign a **char** pointer to another **char** pointer. This is shown in the following program.

```
int main( )
{
    char str1[ ] = "Hello" ;
    char str2[10] ;
    char *s = "Good Morning" ;
    char *q ;
    str2 = str1 ; /* error */
    q = s ; /* works */
    return 0 ;
}
```

Also, once a string has been defined, it cannot be initialized to another set of characters. Unlike strings, such an operation is perfectly valid with **char** pointers.

```
int main( )
{
    char str1[ ] = "Hello" ;
    char *p = "Hello" ;
    str1 = "Bye" ; /* error */
    p = "Bye" ; /* works */
}
```

Standard Library String Functions

With every C compiler, a large set of useful string handling library functions are provided. Figure 11.2 lists the more commonly used functions along with their purpose.

Function	Use
strlen	Finds length of a string
strlwr	Converts a string to lowercase

strupr	Converts a string to uppercase
strcat	Appends one string at the end of another
strncat	Appends first n characters of a string at the end of another
strcpy	Copies a string into another
strncpy	Copies first n characters of one string into another
strcmp	Compares two strings
strncmp	Compares first n characters of two strings
strcmpi	Compares two strings without regard to case ("i" denotes that this function ignores case)
stricmp	Compares two strings without regard to case (identical to strcmpi)
strnicmp	Compares first n characters of two strings without regard to case
strdup	Duplicates a string
strchr	Finds first occurrence of a given character in a string
strrchr	Finds last occurrence of a given character in a string
strstr	Finds first occurrence of a given string in another string
strset	Sets all characters of string to a given character
strnset	Sets first n characters of a string to a given character
strrev	Reverses string

Figure 11.2

Out of the above list, we shall discuss the functions **strlen( )**, **strcpy( )**, **strcat( )** and **strcmp( )**, since these are the most commonly used functions. This will also illustrate how the library functions in general handle strings. Let us study these functions one by one.

strlen( )

This function counts the number of characters present in a string. Its usage is illustrated in the following program.

```
# include <stdio.h>
# include <string.h>
int main( )
{
    char arr[ ] = "Bamboozled" ;
    int len1, len2 ;

    len1 = strlen ( arr ) ;
    len2 = strlen ( "Humpty Dumpty" ) ;
    printf ( "string = %s length = %d\n", arr, len1 ) ;
    printf ( "string = %s length = %d\n", "Humpty Dumpty", len2 ) ;
```

```
    return 0 ;
}
```

The output would be...

```
string = Bamboozled length = 10
string = Humpty Dumpty length = 13
```

Note that, in the first call to the function **strlen( )**, we are passing the base address of the string, and the function, in turn, returns the length of the string. While calculating the length it doesn't count '\0'. Even in the second call,

```
len2 = strlen ( "Humpty Dumpty" ) ;
```

what gets passed to **strlen( )** is the address of the string and not the string itself. Can we not write a function **xstrlen( )**, which imitates the standard library function **strlen( )**? Let us give it a try...

```
/* A look-alike of the function strlen( ) */
# include <stdio.h>
int xstrlen ( char * ) ;
int main( )
{
    char arr[ ] = "Bamboozled" ;
    int len1, len2 ;

    len1 = xstrlen ( arr ) ;
    len2 = xstrlen ( "Humpty Dumpty" ) ;
    printf ( "string = %s length = %d\n", arr, len1 ) ;
    printf ( "string = %s length = %d\n", "Humpty Dumpty", len2 ) ;
    return 0 ;
}

int xstrlen ( char *s )
{
    int length = 0 ;

    while ( *s != '\0' )
    {
        length++ ;
        s++ ;
```

```
    }

    return ( length ) ;
}
```

The output would be...

```
string = Bamboozled length = 10
string = Humpty Dumpty length = 13
```

The function **xstrlen( )** is fairly simple. All that it does is to keep counting the characters till the end of string is met. Or in other words, keep counting characters till the pointer **s** points to '\0'.

strcpy( )

This function copies the contents of one string into another. The base addresses of the source and target strings should be supplied to this function. Here is an example of **strcpy( )** in action...

```
# include <stdio.h>
# include <string.h>
int main( )
{
    char source[ ] = "Sayonara" ;
    char target[20] ;
    strcpy ( target, source ) ;
    printf ( "source string = %s\n", source ) ;
    printf ( "target string = %s\n", target ) ;
    return 0 ;
}
```

And here is the output...

```
source string = Sayonara
target string = Sayonara
```

On supplying the base addresses, **strcpy( )** goes on copying the characters in source string into the target string till it encounters the end of source string ('\0'). It is our responsibility to see to it that the target string's dimension is big enough to hold the string being copied into it. Thus, a string gets copied into another, piece-meal, character by character. There is no short cut for this. Let us now attempt to mimic **strcpy( )**, via our own string copy function, which we will call **xstrcpy( ).**

```
# include <stdio.h>
void xstrcpy ( char *, char * ) ;
int main( )
{
    char  source[ ] = "Sayonara" ;
    char  target[20] ;
    xstrcpy ( target, source ) ;
    printf ( "source string = %s\n", source ) ;
    printf ( "target string = %s\n", target ) ;
    return 0 ;
}
void xstrcpy ( char  *t, char  *s )
{
    while ( *s != '\0' )
    {
        *t = *s ;
        s++ ;
        t++ ;
    }
    *t = '\0' ;
}
```

The output of the program would be...

```
source string = Sayonara
target string = Sayonara
```

Note that having copied the entire source string into the target string, it is necessary to place a '\0' into the target string, to mark its end.

If you look at the prototype of **strcpy( )** standard library function, it looks like this…

```
strcpy ( char *t, const char *s ) ;
```

We didn't use the keyword **const** in our version of **xstrcpy( )** and still our function worked correctly. So what is the need of the **const** qualifier?

What would happen if we add the following lines beyond the last statement of **xstrcpy( )**?.

```
s = s - 8 ;
*s = 'K' ;
```

This would change the source string to “Kayonara”. Can we not ensure that the source string doesn’t change even accidentally in **xstrcpy( )**? We can, by changing the definition as follows:

```
void xstrcpy ( char *t, const char *s )
{
    while ( *s != '\0' )
    {
        *t = *s ;
        s++ ;
        t++ ;
    }
    *t = '\0' ;
}
```

By declaring **char *s** as **const**, we are declaring that the source string should remain constant (should not change). Thus the **const** qualifier ensures that your program does not inadvertently alter a variable that you intended to be a constant. It also reminds anybody reading the program listing that the variable is not intended to change.

We can use **const** in several situations. The following code fragment would help you to fix your ideas about **const** further.

```
char *p = "Hello" ;  /* pointer is variable, so is string */
*p = 'M' ;  /* works */
p = "Bye" ;  /* works */

const char *q = "Hello" ;  /* string is fixed, pointer is not */
*q = 'M' ;  /* error */
q = "Bye" ;  /* works */

char const *s = "Hello" ;  /* string is fixed, pointer is not */
*s = 'M' ;  /* error */
s = "Bye" ;  /* works */

char * const t = "Hello" ;  /* pointer is fixed, string is not */
*t = 'M' ;  /* works */
t = "Bye" ;  /* error */
```

```
const char * const u = "Hello" ; /* string is fixed, so is pointer */
*u = 'M' ; /* error */
u = "Bye" ; /* error */
```

The keyword **const** can also be used in context of ordinary variables like **int**, **float**, etc. The following program shows how this can be done.

```
# include <stdio.h>
int main( )
{
    float r, a ;
    const float pi = 3.14 ;
    printf ( "Enter radius of circle " ) ;
    scanf ( "%f", &r ) ;
    a = pi * r * r ;
    printf ( "Area of circle = %f\n", a ) ;
    return 0 ;
}
```

strcat( )

This function concatenates the source string at the end of the target string. For example, "Bombay" and "Nagpur" on concatenation would result into a string "BombayNagpur". Here is an example of **strcat**( ) at work.

```
# include <stdio.h>
# include <string.h>
int main( )
{
    char source[ ] = "Folks!" ;
    char target[30] = "Hello" ;
    strcat ( target, source ) ;
    printf ( "source string = %s\n", source ) ;
    printf ( "target string = %s\n", target ) ;
    return 0 ;
}
```

And here is the output...

```
source string = Folks!
```

target string = HelloFolks!

Note that the target string has been made big enough to hold the final string. I leave it to you to develop your own **xstrcat( )** on lines of **xstrlen( )** and **xstrcpy( ).**

strcmp( )

This is a function which compares two strings to find out whether they are same or different. The two strings are compared character by character until there is a mismatch or end of one of the strings is reached, whichever occurs first. If the two strings are identical, **strcmp( )** returns a value zero. If they're not, it returns the numeric difference between the ASCII values of the first non-matching pair of characters. Here is a program which puts **strcmp( )** in action.

```
# include <stdio.h>
# include <string.h>
int main( )
{
    char string1[ ] = "Jerry" ;
    char string2[ ] = "Ferry" ;
    int i, j, k ;
    i = strcmp ( string1, "Jerry" ) ;
    j = strcmp ( string1, string2 ) ;
    k = strcmp ( string1, "Jerry boy" ) ;
    printf ( "%d %d %d\n", i, j, k ) ;
    return 0 ;
}
```

And here is the output...

```
0 4 -32
```

In the first call to **strcmp( )**, the two strings are identical—“Jerry” and “Jerry”—and the value returned by **strcmp( )** is zero. In the second call, the first character of “Jerry” doesn't match with the first character of “Ferry” and the result is 4, which is the numeric difference between ASCII value of 'J' and ASCII value of 'F'. In the third call to **strcmp( )**, “Jerry” doesn’t match with “Jerry boy”, because the null character at the end of “Jerry” doesn’t match the blank in “Jerry boy”. The value returned is -32, which is the value of null character minus the ASCII value of space, i.e., '\0' minus ' ', which is equal to -32.

The exact value of mismatch will rarely concern us. All we usually want to know is whether or not the first string is alphabetically before the second string. If it is, a negative value is returned; if it isn't, a positive value is returned. Any non-zero value means there is a mismatch. Try to implement this procedure into a function **xstrcmp( )**.

Two-Dimensional Array of Characters

In the last chapter, we saw several examples of 2-dimensional integer arrays. Let's now look at a similar entity, but one dealing with characters. Our example program asks you to type your name. When you do so, it checks your name against a master list to see if you are worthy of entry to the palace. Here's the program...

```
# include <stdio.h>
# include <string.h>
# define FOUND 1
# define NOTFOUND 0
int main( )
{
    char masterlist[6][10] = {
                                "akshay",
                                "parag",
                                "raman",
                                "srinivas",
                                "gopal",
                                "rajesh"
                             } ;
    int i, flag, a ;
    char yourname[10] ;

    printf ( "Enter your name " ) ;
    scanf ( "%s", yourname ) ;

    flag = NOTFOUND ;
    for ( i = 0 ; i <= 5 ; i++ )
    {
        a = strcmp ( &masterlist[i][0], yourname ) ;
        if ( a == 0 )
        {
            printf ( "Welcome, you can enter the palace\n" ) ;
            flag = FOUND ;
            break ;
```

```
        }
    }

    if ( flag == NOTFOUND )
        printf ( "Sorry, you are a trespasser\n" ) ;
    return 0 ;
}
```

And here is the output for two sample runs of this program...

```
Enter your name dinesh
Sorry, you are a trespasser
Enter your name raman
Welcome, you can enter the palace
```

Notice how the two-dimensional character array has been initialized. The order of the subscripts in the array declaration is important. The first subscript gives the number of names in the array, while the second subscript gives the length of each item in the array.

Instead of initializing names, had these names been supplied from the keyboard, the program segment would have looked like this...

```
for ( i = 0 ; i <= 5 ; i++ )
    scanf ( "%s", &masterlist[i][0] ) ;
```

While comparing the strings through **strcmp( )**, note that the addresses of the strings are being passed to **strcmp( )**. As seen in the last section, if the two strings match, **strcmp( )** would return a value 0, otherwise it would return a non-zero value.

The variable **flag** is used to keep a record of whether the control did reach inside the **if** or not. To begin with, we set **flag** to NOTFOUND. Later through the loop, if the names match, **flag** is set to FOUND. When the control reaches beyond the **for** loop, if **flag** is still set to NOTFOUND, it means none of the names in the **masterlist[ ][ ]** matched with the one supplied from the keyboard.

The names would be stored in the memory as shown in Figure 11.3. Note that each string ends with a '\0'. The arrangement, as you can appreciate, is similar to that of a two-dimensional numeric array.

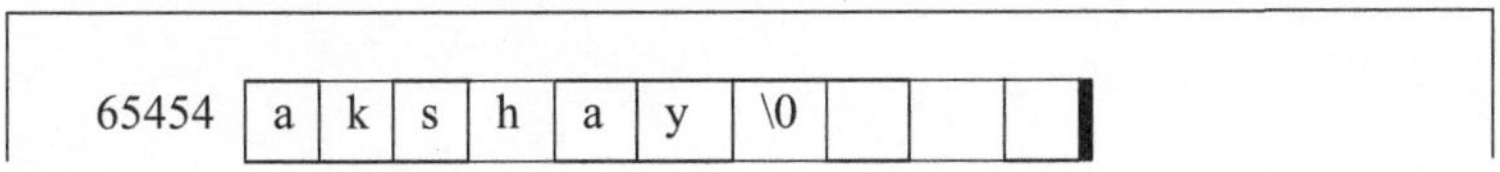

65454	a	k	s	h	a	y	\0			

65464	p	a	r	a	g	\0				
65474	r	a	m	a	n	\0				
65484	s	r	i	n	i	v	a	s	\0	
65494	g	o	p	a	l	\0				
65504	r	a	j	e	s	h	\0			

65513 (last location)

Figure 11.3

Here, 65454, 65464, 65474, etc. are the base addresses of successive names. As seen from the above pattern, some of the names do not occupy all the bytes reserved for them. For example, even though 10 bytes are reserved for storing the name "akshay", it occupies only 7 bytes. Thus, 3 bytes go waste. Similarly, for each name, there is some amount of wastage. In fact, more the number of names, more would be the wastage. Can this not be avoided? Yes, it can be... by using what is called an 'array of pointers', which is our next topic of discussion.

Array of Pointers to Strings

As we know, a pointer variable always contains an address. Therefore, if we construct an array of pointers, it would contain a number of addresses. Let us see how the names in the earlier example can be stored in the array of pointers.

```
char *names[ ] = {
                    "akshay",
                    "parag",
                    "raman",
                    "srinivas",
                    "gopal",
                    "rajesh"
                 } ;
```

In this declaration, **names[ ]** is an array of pointers. It contains base addresses of respective names. That is, base address of "akshay" is stored in **names[0]**, base address of "parag" is stored in **names[1]** and so on. This is depicted in Figure 11.4.

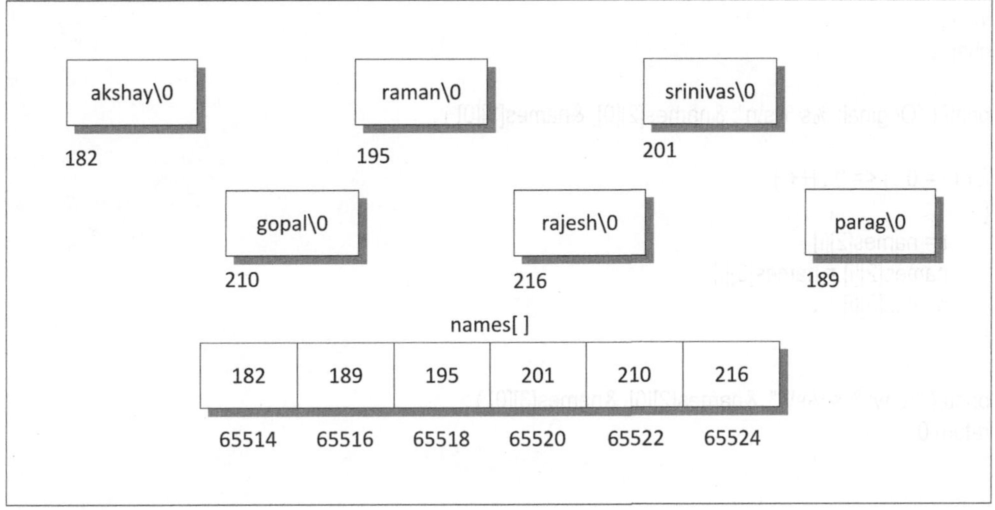

Figure 11.4

In the two-dimensional array of characters, the strings occupied 60 bytes. As against this, in array of pointers, the strings occupy only 41 bytes—a net saving of 19 bytes. A substantial saving, you would agree. But realize that actually 19 bytes are not saved, since 12 bytes are sacrificed for storing the addresses in the array **names[ ]**. Thus, one reason to store strings in an array of pointers is to make a more efficient use of available memory.

Another reason to use an array of pointers to store strings is to obtain greater ease in manipulation of the strings. This is shown by the following programs. The first one uses a two-dimensional array of characters to store the names, whereas the second uses an array of pointers to strings. The purpose of both the programs is very simple. We want to exchange the position of the names "raman" and "srinivas".

```
/* Exchange names using 2-D array of characters */
# include <stdio.h>
int main( )
{
    char names[ ][10] = {
                        "akshay",
                        "parag",
                        "raman",
                        "srinivas",
                        "gopal",
                        "rajesh"
                    } ;
```

```
    int i ;
    char t ;

    printf ( "Original: %s %s\n", &names[2][0], &names[3][0] ) ;

    for ( i = 0 ; i <= 9 ; i++ )
    {
        t = names[2][i] ;
        names[2][i] = names[3][i] ;
        names[3][i] = t ;
    }

    printf ( "New: %s %s\n", &names[2][0], &names[3][0] ) ;
    return 0 ;
}
```

And here is the output...

```
Original: raman srinivas
New: srinivas raman
```

Note that in this program to exchange the names, we are required to exchange corresponding characters of the two names. In effect, 10 exchanges are needed to interchange two names.

Let us see, if the number of exchanges can be reduced by using an array of pointers to strings. Here is the program...

```
# include <stdio.h>
int main( )
{
    char *names[ ] = {
                        "akshay",
                        "parag",
                        "raman",
                        "srinivas",
                        "gopal",
                        "rajesh"
                    } ;
    char *temp ;
    printf ( "Original: %s %s\n", names[2], names[3] ) ;
    temp = names[2] ;
```

```
    names[2] = names[3] ;
    names[3] = temp ;
    printf ( "New: %s %s\n", names[2], names[3] ) ;
    return 0 ;
}
```

And here is the output...

```
Original: raman srinivas
New: srinivas raman
```

The output is same as the earlier program. In this program, all that we are required to do is to exchange the addresses (of the names) stored in the array of pointers, rather than the names themselves. Thus, by effecting just one exchange, we are able to interchange names. This makes handling strings very convenient.

Thus, from the point of view of efficient memory usage and ease of programming, an array of pointers to strings definitely scores over a two-dimensional character array. That is why, even though, in principle, strings can be stored and handled through a two-dimensional array of characters, in actual practice, it is the array of pointers to strings, which is more commonly used.

Limitation of Array of Pointers to Strings

When we are using a two-dimensional array of characters, we are at liberty to either initialize the strings where we are declaring the array, or receive the strings using **scanf( )** function. However, when we are using an array of pointers to strings, we can initialize the strings at the place where we are declaring the array, but we cannot receive the strings from keyboard using **scanf( )**. Thus, the following program would never work out.

```
# include <stdio.h>
int main( )
{
    char *names[6] ;
    int i ;
    for ( i = 0 ; i <= 5 ; i++ )
    {
        printf ( "Enter name " ) ;
        scanf ( "%s", names[i] ) ;
    }
    return 0 ;
```

```
}
```

The program doesn't work because; when we are declaring the array, it is containing garbage values. And it would be definitely wrong to send these garbage values to **scanf( )** as the addresses where it should keep the strings received from the keyboard.

Solution

If we are bent upon receiving the strings from keyboard using **scanf( )** and then storing their addresses in an array of pointers to strings, we can do it in a slightly roundabout manner as shown below.

```
# include <stdio.h>
# include <stdlib.h>
# include <string.h>
int main( )
{
    char *names[6] ;
    char n[50] ;
    int len, i ;
    char *p ;
    for ( i = 0 ; i <= 5 ; i++ )
    {
        printf ( "Enter name " ) ;
        scanf ( "%s", n ) ;
        len = strlen ( n ) ;
        p = ( char * ) malloc ( len + 1 ) ;  /* +1 for accommodating \0 */
        strcpy ( p, n ) ;
        names[i] = p ;
    }
    for ( i = 0 ; i <= 5 ; i++ )
        printf ( "%s\n", names[i] ) ;
    return 0 ;
}
```

Here we have first received a name using **scanf( )** in a string **n[ ]**. Then we have found out its length using **strlen( )** and allocated space for making a copy of this name. This memory allocation has been done using a standard library function called **malloc( )**. This function requires the number of bytes to be allocated and returns the base address of the chunk of memory that it allocates. The address returned by this function is always of the type **void ***. This is because **malloc( )** doesn't know what for did we allocate the memory.

A **void** * means a pointer which is a legal address but it is not address of a **char**, or address of an **int**, or address of any other datatype. Hence it has been converted into **char** * using a C language feature called typecasting. Typecasting is discussed in detail in Chapter 15. The prototype of this function has been declared in the file 'stdlib.h'. Hence we have **#includ**ed this file.

But why did we not use array to allocate memory? This is because, with arrays, we have to commit to the size of the array at the time of writing the program. Moreover, there is no way to increase or decrease the array size during execution of the program. In other words, when we use arrays, static memory allocation takes place. Unlike this, using **malloc( )**, we can allocate memory dynamically, during execution. The argument that we pass to **malloc( )** can be a variable whose value can change during execution.

Once we have allocated the memory using **malloc( )**, we have copied the name received through the keyboard into this allocated space and finally stored the address of the allocated chunk in the appropriate element of **names[ ]**, the array of pointers to strings.

This solution suffers in performance because we need to allocate memory and then do the copying of string for each name received through the keyboard.

Summary

(a) A string is nothing but an array of characters terminated by '\0'.
(b) Being an array, all the characters of a string are stored in contiguous memory locations.
(c) Though **scanf( )** can be used to receive multi-word strings, **gets( )** can do the same job in a cleaner way.
(d) Both **printf( )** and **puts( )** can handle multi-word strings.
(e) Strings can be operated upon using several standard library functions like **strlen( )**, **strcpy( )**, **strcat( )** and **strcmp( )** which can manipulate strings. More importantly we imitated some of these functions to learn how these standard library functions are written.
(f) Though in principle a 2-D array can be used to handle several strings, in practice an array of pointers to strings is preferred since it takes less space and is efficient in processing strings.
(g) **malloc( )** function can be used to allocate space in memory on the fly during execution of the program.

Exercise

Simple strings

[A] What will be the output of the following programs:

(a)
```
# include <stdio.h>
int main( )
{
    char  c[2] = "A" ;
    printf ( "%c\n", c[0] ) ;
    printf ( "%s\n", c ) ;
    return 0 ;
}
```

(b)
```
# include <stdio.h>
int main( )
{
    char  s[ ] = "Get organised! learn C!!" ;
    printf ( "%s\n", &s[2] ) ;
    printf ( "%s\n", s ) ;
    printf ( "%s\n", &s ) ;
    printf ( "%c\n", s[2] ) ;
    return 0 ;
}
```

(c)
```
# include <stdio.h>
int main( )
{
    char  s[ ] = "No two viruses work similarly" ;
    int  i = 0 ;
    while ( s[i] != 0 )
    {
        printf ( "%c %c\n", s[i], *( s + i ) ) ;
        printf ( "%c %c\n", i[s], *( i + s ) ) ;
        i++ ;
    }
    return 0 ;
}
```

(d)
```
# include <stdio.h>
int main( )
{
    char  s[ ] = "Churchgate: no church no gate" ;
    char  t[25] ;
    char  *ss, *tt ;
    ss = s ;
```

```
    while ( *ss != '\0' )
        *ss++ = *tt++ ;
    printf ( "%s\n", t ) ;
    return 0 ;
}
```

(e)
```
# include <stdio.h>
int main( )
{
    char str1[ ] = { 'H', 'e', 'l', 'l', 'o', 0 } ;
    char str2[ ] = "Hello" ;

    printf ( "%s\n", str1 ) ;
    printf ( "%s\n", str2 ) ;
    return 0 ;
}
```

(f)
```
# include <stdio.h>
void main( )
{
    printf ( 5 + "Good Morning " ) ;
    return 0 ;
}
```

(g)
```
# include <stdio.h>
int main( )
{
    printf ( "%c\n",  "abcdefgh"[4] ) ;
    return 0 ;
}
```

(h)
```
# include <stdio.h>
int main( )
{
    printf ( "%d %d  %d\n", sizeof ( '3' ), sizeof ( "3" ), sizeof ( 3 ) ) ;
    return 0 ;
}
```

(i)
```
# include <stdio.h>
int main( )
{
    char str[ ] = "I love to get it so\0I love to give it" ;
    char *a = str ;
    a += strlen ( str ) ;
```

```
        printf ( "%s %s\n", a + 1, str ) ;
        return 0 ;
    }
```

(j)
```
# include <stdio.h>
int main( )
{
    char a[ ] = "hello\0hello" ;
    printf ( "%s", a ) ;
    return 0 ;
}
```

[B] Point out the errors, if any, in the following programs:

(a)
```
# include <stdio.h>
# include <string.h>
int main( )
{
    char *str1 = "United" ;
    char *str2 = "Front" ;
    char *str3 ;
    str3 = strcat ( str1, str2 ) ;
    printf ( "%s\n", str3 ) ;
    return 0 ;
}
```

(b)
```
# include <stdio.h>
int main( )
{
    int arr[ ] = { 'A', 'B', 'C', 'D' } ;
    int i ;
    for ( i = 0 ; i <= 3 ; i++ )
        printf ( "%d", arr[i] ) ;
    printf ( "\n" ) ;
    return 0 ;
}
```

(c)
```
# include <stdio.h>
int main( )
{
    char arr[8] = "Rhombus" ;
    int i ;
    for ( i = 0 ; i <= 7 ; i++ )
```

```
        printf ( "%d", *arr ) ;
        arr++ ;
    return 0 ;
}
```

[C] Fill in the blanks:

(a) "A" is a ___________ whereas 'A' is a ____________.

(b) A string is terminated by a ______ character, which is written as ______.

(c) The array **char name[10]** can consist of a maximum of ______ characters.

(d) The array elements are always stored in _________ memory locations.

[D] Attempt the following:

(a) Which is more appropriate for reading in a multi-word string?

```
gets( )     printf( )     scanf( )     puts( )
```

(b) If the string "Alice in wonder land" is fed to the following **scanf( )** statement, what will be the contents of the arrays **str1**, **str2**, **str3** and **str4**?

```
scanf ( "%s%s%s%s", str1, str2, str3, str4 ) ;
```

(c) Write a program that extracts part of the given string from the specified position. For example, if the sting is "Working with strings is fun", then if from position 4, 4 characters are to be extracted then the program should return string as "king". If the number of characters to be extracted is 0 then the program should extract entire string from the specified position.

(d) Write a program that converts a string like "124" to an integer 124.

(e) This declaration contains an error, correct it.

```
char *s = arr, arr[10] ;
```

(f) What would be the base addresses of the following strings if the base address of the first string is 1000?

```
char *think[ ] =  {
                    "I look before and after",
                    "And find all is right",
```

```
                        "In my deepest sorrows",
                        "There is a soul of light"
                    } ;
```

(g) Write only one statement which performs the task of the three statements within the **while** loop in the following function.

```
void strcpy ( char *s, char *t )
{
    while ( *s != '\0' )
    {
        *t = *s ;
        t++ ;
        s++ ;
    }
}
```

(h) What is the output of the following program and where is the pointer positioned after execution of the **printf( )**.

```
int main( )
{
    char s[ ] = "Rain Rain here again" ;
    char *st ;
    int i ;
    for ( st = s, i = 0 ; i <= 2 ; i++ )
        st++ ;

    printf ( "%c %c ", *st, * ( st + 2 ) ) ;
    return 0 ;
}
```

(i) Write down the function swap( ) which should interchange the positions of the names in the array names[ ] in the following program.

```
int main( )
{
    char *names[ ] = {
                        "Anil",
                        "Santosh"
                    } ;


    swap ( names[0], names[1] ) ;
```

```
    return 0 ;
}
```

Two-dimensional array, Array of pointers to strings

[E] Answer the following:

(a) How many bytes in memory would be occupied by the following array of pointers to strings? How many bytes would be required to store the same strings, if they are stored in a two-dimensional character array?

```
char *mess[ ] = {
                    "Hammer and tongs",
                    "Tooth and nail",
                    "Spit and polish",
                    "You and C"
                } ;
```

(b) Can an array of pointers to strings be used to collect strings from the keyboard? If yes, how? If not, why not?

[F] Attempt the following:

(a) Write a program that uses an array of pointers to strings **str[ ]**. Receive two strings **str1** and **str2** and check if **str1** is embedded in any of the strings in **str[ ]**. If **str1** is found, then replace it with **str2**.

```
char *str[ ] ={
                    "We will teach you how to...",
                    "Move a mountain",
                    "Level a building",
                    "Erase the past",
                    "Make a million",
                    "...all through C!"
            } ;
```

For example if **str1** contains "mountain" and **str2** contains "car", then the second string in **str** should get changed to "Move a car".

(b) Write a program to sort a set of names stored in an array in alphabetical order.

(c) Write a program to reverse the strings stored in the following array of pointers to strings:

```
char *s[ ] = {
```

```
        "To err is human...",
        "But to really mess things up...",
        "One needs to know C!!"
    };
```

(d) Develop a program that receives the month and year from the keyboard as integers and prints the calendar in the following format.

March 2006						
Mon	Tue	Wed	Thu	Fri	Sat	Sun
		1	2	3	4	5
6	7	8	9	10	11	12
13	14	15	16	17	18	19
20	21	22	23	24	25	26
27	28	29	30	31		

Note that according to the Gregorian calendar 01/01/1900 was Monday. With this as the base the calendar should be generated.

(e) A factory has 3 divisions and stocks 4 categories of products. An inventory table is updated for each division and for each product as they are received. There are three independent suppliers of products to the factory:

(a) Design a data format to represent each transaction.
(b) Write a program to take a transaction and update the inventory.
(c) If the cost per item is also given write a program to calculate the total inventory values.

(f) Modify the above program suitably so that once the calendar for a particular month and year has been displayed on the screen, then using arrow keys the user must be able to change the calendar in the following manner:

Up arrow key : Next year, same month
Down arrow key : Previous year, same month
Right arrow key : Same year, next month
Left arrow key : Same year, previous month

If the escape key is hit then the procedure should stop.

Hint: Use the **getkey( )** function discussed in Chapter 8, problem number [L](d).

(g) Write a program to delete all vowels from a sentence. Assume that the sentence is not more than 80 characters long.

(h) Write a program that will read a line and delete from it all occurrences of the word ‘the’.

(i) Write a program that takes a set of names of individuals and abbreviates the first, middle and other names except the last name by their first letter.

(j) Write a program to count the number of occurrences of any two vowels in succession in a line of text. For example, in the sentence

“Please read this application and give me gratuity”

such occurrences are ea, ea, ui.

(k) Write a program that would search a word entered through the keyboard, in an array of pointers to the strings given below.

```
char *strings[ ] =    {
                          "What is this life",
                          "if full of care",
                          "we have no time",
                          "to stand and stare"
                      } ;
```

The program should print the string that contains the word being searched.

(l) Write a program to reverse the following string. You are neither allowed to use any other string nor any standard library functions.

```
str[ ] = "?lla fo tseriaf eht is ohw roriM roriM" ;
```

(m) Write a program to find out the last occurrence of a given character in the following string.

```
char doomsday[ ] = "The fragrance of World-Peace should begin" ;
```

(n) Write a program to test whether given string is a palindrome. For example, the string "ABLE WAS I ERE I SAW ELBA" is a palindrome, since the reverse of this string is same as the string itself.

(o) Following names are stored in an array of pointers.

```
char *names[ ] = {
                      "Santosh",
```

```
        "Amol",
        "John",
        "Kishore",
        "Rahul",
        "Amolkumar",
        "Hemant"
    } ;
```

Write a program to arrange these names in alphabetical order.

(p) Write a function **xstrchr( )** to find the last occurrence of a character in a given string.

For example, if the character whose occurrence is to be searched is 'S' and the string in which it is to be searched is,

"SHE SELLS SEA SHELLS ON THE SEA SHORE"

the answer returned by **xstrchr( )** should be 33, since last S in this string occurs at 33rd position. If the character to be searched is not present, then a zero should be returned.

(q) Complete the following program:

```
int main( )
{
    char str[100], *s ;
    puts ( "Enter any string " ) ;
    gets ( str ) ;
    s = str ;
    /* write statements to take the pointer to the end of the string */

    /* write statement to put the pointer back to first character of the string */

    return 0 ;
}
```

12 Structures

- Why Use Structures
    - Declaring a Structure
    - Accessing Structure Elements
    - How Structure Elements are Stored
- Array of Structures
- Additional Features of Structures
- Uses of Structures
- Summary
- Exercise

Which mechanic is good enough who knows how to repair only one type of vehicle? None. Same thing is true about C language. It wouldn't have been so popular had it been able to handle only all **int**s, or all **float**s or all **char**s at a time. In fact, when we handle real world data, we don't usually deal with little atoms of information by themselves—things like integers, characters and such. Instead, we deal with entities that are collections of things, each thing having its own attributes, just as the entity we call a 'book' is a collection of things such as title, author, call number, publisher, number of pages, date of publication, etc. As you can see, all this data is dissimilar, for example, author is a string, whereas number of pages is an integer. For dealing with such collections, C provides a data type called 'structure'. A structure gathers together, different atoms of information that comprise a given entity. And structure is the topic of this chapter.

Why Use Structures

We have seen earlier how ordinary variables can hold one piece of information and how arrays can hold a number of pieces of information of the same data type. These two data types can handle a great variety of situations. But quite often we deal with entities that are collection of dissimilar data types.

For example, suppose you want to store data about a book. You might want to store its name (a string), its price (a float) and number of pages in it (an int). If data about say 3 such books is to be stored, then we can follow two approaches:

(a) Construct individual arrays, one for storing names, another for storing prices and still another for storing number of pages.

(b) Use a structure variable.

Let us examine these two approaches one by one. For the sake of programming convenience, assume that the names of books would be single character long. Let us begin with a program that uses arrays.

```
# include <stdio.h>
int main( )
{
    char name[3] ;
    float price[3] ;
    int pages[3], i ;

    printf ( "Enter names, prices and no. of pages of 3 books\n" ) ;

    for ( i = 0 ; i <= 2 ; i++ )
```

```
        scanf ( "%c %f %d", &name[i], &price[i], &pages[i] ) ;

    printf ( "\nAnd this is what you entered\n" ) ;
    for ( i = 0 ; i <= 2 ; i++ )
        printf ( "%c %f %d\n", name[i], price[i], pages[i] ) ;
    return 0 ;
}
```

And here is the sample run...

```
Enter names, prices and no. of pages of 3 books
A 100.00 354
C 256.50 682
F 233.70 512

And this is what you entered
A 100.000000 354
C 256.500000 682
F 233.700000 512
```

This approach, no doubt, allows you to store names, prices and number of pages. But as you must have realized, it is an unwieldy approach that obscures the fact that you are dealing with a group of characteristics related to a single entity—the book.

The program becomes more difficult to handle as the number of items relating to the book goes on increasing. For example, we would be required to use a number of arrays, if we also decide to store name of the publisher, date of purchase of book, etc. To solve this problem, C provides a special data type—the structure.

A structure contains a number of data types grouped together. These data types may or may not be of the same type. The following example illustrates the use of this data type.

```
# include <stdio.h>
int main( )
{
    struct book
    {
        char name ;
        float price ;
        int pages ;
    } ;
    struct book b1, b2, b3 ;
```

```
    printf ( "Enter names, prices & no. of pages of 3 books\n" ) ;
    scanf ( "%c %f %d", &b1.name, &b1.price, &b1.pages ) ;
    scanf ( "%c %f %d", &b2.name, &b2.price, &b2.pages ) ;
    scanf ( "%c %f %d", &b3.name, &b3.price, &b3.pages ) ;
    printf ( "And this is what you entered\n" ) ;
    printf ( "%c %f %d\n", b1.name, b1.price, b1.pages ) ;
    printf ( "%c %f %d\n", b2.name, b2.price, b2.pages ) ;
    printf ( "%c %f %d\n", b3.name, b3.price, b3.pages ) ;
    return 0 ;
}
```

And here is the output...

```
Enter names, prices and no. of pages of 3 books
A 100.00 354
C 256.50 682
F 233.70 512
And this is what you entered
A 100.000000 354
C 256.500000 682
F 233.700000 512
```

This program demonstrates two fundamental aspects of structures:

(a) declaration of a structure
(b) accessing of structure elements

Let us now look at these concepts one by one.

Declaring a Structure

In our example program, the following statement declares the structure type:

```
struct book
{
    char name ;
    float price ;
    int pages ;
} ;
```

This statement defines a new data type called **struct book**. Each variable of this data type will consist of a character variable called **name**, a float variable called **price** and an integer variable called **pages**. The general form of a structure declaration statement is given below:

```
struct <structure name>
{
    structure element 1 ;
    structure element 2 ;
    structure element 3 ;
    ......
    ......
} ;
```

Once the new structure data type has been defined, one or more variables can be declared to be of that type. For example, the variables **b1**, **b2**, **b3** can be declared to be of the type **struct book**, as,

```
struct book  b1, b2, b3 ;
```

This statement sets aside space in memory. It makes available space to hold all the elements in the structure—in this case, 7 bytes—one for **name**, four for **price** and two for **pages**. These bytes are always in adjacent memory locations.

If we so desire, we can combine the declaration of the structure type and the structure variables in one statement.

For example,

```
struct book
{
    char  name ;
    float  price ;
    int  pages ;
} ;
struct book  b1, b2, b3 ;
```

is same as...

```
struct book
{
    char  name ;
    float  price ;
    int  pages ;
} b1, b2, b3 ;
```

or even...

```
struct
{
    char name ;
    float price ;
    int pages ;
} b1, b2, b3 ;
```

Like primary variables and arrays, structure variables can also be initialized where they are declared. The format used is quite similar to that used to initialize arrays.

```
struct book
{
    char name[10] ;
    float price ;
    int pages ;
} ;
struct book b1 = { "Basic", 130.00, 550 } ;
struct book b2 = { "Physics", 150.80, 800 } ;
struct book b3 = { 0 } ;
```

Note the following points while declaring a structure type:

(a) The closing brace in the structure type declaration must be followed by a semicolon.

(b) It is important to understand that a structure type declaration does not tell the compiler to reserve any space in memory. All a structure declaration does is, it defines the 'form' of the structure.

(c) Usually structure type declaration appears at the top of the source code file, before any variables or functions are defined. In very large programs they are usually put in a separate header file, and the file is included (using the preprocessor directive #include) in whichever program we want to use this structure type.

(d) If a structure variable is initiated to a value { 0 }, then all its elements are set to value 0, as in **b3** above. This is a handy way of initializing structure variables. In absence of this, we would have been required to initialize each individual element to a value 0.

Accessing Structure Elements

Having declared the structure type and the structure variables, let us see how the elements of the structure can be accessed.

In arrays, we can access individual elements of an array using a subscript. Structures use a different scheme. They use a dot (.) operator. So to refer to **pages** of the structure defined in our sample program, we have to use,

```
b1.pages
```

Similarly, to refer to **price**, we would use,

```
b1.price
```

Note that before the dot, there must always be a structure variable and after the dot, there must always be a structure element.

How Structure Elements are Stored

Whatever be the elements of a structure, they are always stored in contiguous memory locations. The following program would illustrate this:

```
/* Memory map of structure elements */
# include <stdio.h>
int main( )
{
    struct book
    {
        char name ;
        float price ;
        int pages ;
    } ;
    struct book b1 = { 'B', 130.00, 550 } ;

    printf ( "Address of name = %u\n", &b1.name ) ;
    printf ( "Address of price = %u\n", &b1.price ) ;
    printf ( "Address of pages = %u\n", &b1.pages ) ;
    return 0 ;
}
```

Here is the output of the program...

Address of name = 65518
Address of price = 65519
Address of pages = 65523

Actually, the structure elements are stored in memory as shown in the Figure 12.1.

b1.name b1.price b1.pages

'B' 130.00 550

65518 65519 65523

Figure 12.1

Array of Structures

Our sample program showing usage of structure is rather simple minded. All it does is, it receives values into various structure elements and output these values. But that's all we intended to do anyway... show how structure types are created, how structure variables are declared and how individual elements of a structure variable are referenced.

In our sample program, to store data of 100 books, we would be required to use 100 different structure variables from **b1** to **b100**, which is definitely not very convenient. A better approach would be to use an array of structures. Following program shows how to use an array of structures.

```
/* Usage of an array of structures */
# include <stdio.h>
void linkfloat( ) ;
int main( )
{
    struct book
    {
        char name ;
        float price ;
        int pages ;
    } ;

    struct book b[100] ;
    int i ;
```

```
    for ( i = 0 ; i <= 99 ; i++ )
    {
        printf ( "Enter name, price and pages " ) ;
        scanf ( "%c %f %d", &b[i].name, &b[i].price, &b[i].pages ) ;
    }

    for ( i = 0 ; i <= 99 ; i++ )
        printf ( "%c %f %d\n", b[i].name, b[i].price, b[i].pages ) ;

    return 0 ;
}

void linkfloat( )
{
    float a = 0, *b ;
    b = &a ; /* cause emulator to be linked */
    a = *b ;  /* suppress the warning - variable not used */
}
```

Now a few comments about the program:

(a) Notice how the array of structures is declared...

```
struct book b[100] ;
```

This provides space in memory for 100 structures of the type **struct book**.

(b) The syntax we use to reference each element of the array **b** is similar to the syntax used for arrays of **int**s and **char**s. For example, we refer to zeroth book's price as **b[0].price**. Similarly, we refer first book's pages as **b[1].pages**.

(c) It should be appreciated what careful thought Dennis Ritchie has put into C language. He first defined array as a collection of similar elements; then realized that dissimilar data types that are often found in real life cannot be handled using arrays, therefore created a new data type called structure. But even using structures, programming convenience could not be achieved, because a lot of variables (**b1** to **b100** for storing data about hundred books) needed to be handled. Therefore, he allowed us to create an array of structures; an array of similar data types which themselves are a collection of dissimilar data types. Hats off to the genius!

(e) In an array of structures, all elements of the array are stored in adjacent memory locations. Since each element of this array is a structure, and since all structure elements are always stored in adjacent locations, you can very well visualise the arrangement of array of structures in memory. In our example, **b[0]**'s **name**, **price** and **pages** in memory would be immediately followed by **b[1]**'s **name**, **price** and **pages**, and so on.

(f) What is the function **linkfloat( )** doing here? If you don't define it, you are bound to get the error "Floating Point Formats Not Linked" with majority of C Compilers. What causes this error to occur? When parsing our source file, if the compiler encounters a reference to the address of a float, it sets a flag to have the linker link in the floating-point emulator. A floating point emulator is used to manipulate floating point numbers in runtime library functions like **scanf( )** and **atof( )**. There are some cases in which the reference to the **float** is a bit obscure and the compiler does not detect the need for the emulator. The most common is using **scanf( )** to read a **float** in an array of structures as shown in our program.

How can we force the formats to be linked? That's where the **linkfloat( )** function comes in. It forces linking of the floating-point emulator into an application. There is no need to call this function, just define it anywhere in your program.

Additional Features of Structures

Let us now explore the intricacies of structures with a view of programming convenience. We would highlight these intricacies with suitable examples:

(a) The values of a structure variable can be assigned to another structure variable of the same type using the assignment operator. It is not necessary to copy the structure elements piece-meal. Obviously, programmers prefer assignment to piece-meal copying. This is shown in the following example.

```
# include <stdio.h>
# include <string.h>
int main( )
{
    struct employee
    {
        char name[10] ;
        int age ;
        float salary ;
    } ;
    struct employee e1 = { "Sanjay", 30, 5500.50 } ;
    struct employee e2, e3 ;
```

```
    /* piece-meal copying */
    strcpy ( e2.name, e1.name ) ;  /* e2.name = e1. name is wrong */
    e2.age = e1.age ;
    e2.salary = e1.salary ;

    /* copying all elements at one go */
    e3 = e2 ;

    printf ( "%s %d %f\n", e1.name, e1.age, e1.salary ) ;
    printf ( "%s %d %f\n", e2.name, e2.age, e2.salary ) ;
    printf ( "%s %d %f\n", e3.name, e3.age, e3.salary ) ;
    return 0 ;
}
```

The output of the program would be...

```
Sanjay 30 5500.500000
Sanjay 30 5500.500000
Sanjay 30 5500.500000
```

Ability to copy the contents of all structure elements of one variable into the corresponding elements of another structure variable is rather surprising, since C does not allow assigning the contents of one array to another just by equating the two. As we saw earlier, for copying arrays, we have to copy the contents of the array element by element.

This copying of all structure elements at one go has been possible only because the structure elements are stored in contiguous memory locations. Had this not been so, we would have been required to copy structure variables element by element. And who knows, had this been so, structures would not have become popular at all.

(b) One structure can be nested within another structure. Using this facility, complex data types can be created. The following program shows nested structures at work.

```
# include <stdio.h>
int main( )
{
    struct address
    {
        char phone[15] ;
        char city[25] ;
        int pin ;
```

```
    } ;

    struct emp
    {
        char  name[25] ;
        struct address  a ;
    } ;
    struct emp  e = { "jeru", "531046", "nagpur", 10 };

    printf ( "name = %s phone = %s\n", e.name, e.a.phone ) ;
    printf ( "city = %s pin = %d\n", e.a.city, e.a.pin ) ;
    return 0 ;
}
```

And here is the output...

```
name = jeru phone = 531046
city = nagpur pin = 10
```

Notice the method used to access the element of a structure that is part of another structure. For this, the dot operator is used twice, as in the expression,

```
e.a.pin  or  e.a.city
```

Of course, the nesting process need not stop at this level. We can nest a structure within a structure, within another structure, which is in still another structure and so on... till the time we can comprehend the structure ourselves. Such construction, however, gives rise to variable names that can be surprisingly self-descriptive, for example:

```
maruti.engine.bolt.large.qty
```

This clearly signifies that we are referring to the quantity of large sized bolts that fit on an engine of a maruti car.

(c) Like an ordinary variable, a structure variable can also be passed to a function. We may either pass individual structure elements or the entire structure variable at one go. Let us examine both the approaches one by one using suitable programs.

```
/* Passing individual structure elements */
# include <stdio.h>
void display ( char  *, char  *, int ) ;
```

```
int main( )
{
    struct book
    {
        char  name[25] ;
        char  author[25] ;
        int  callno ;
    } ;
    struct book b1 = { "Let us C", "YPK", 101 } ;

    display ( b1.name, b1.author, b1.callno ) ;
    return 0 ;
}

void display ( char  *s, char  *t, int  n )
{
    printf ( "%s %s %d\n", s, t, n ) ;
}
```

And here is the output...

```
Let us C YPK 101
```

Observe that in the declaration of the structure, **name** and **author** have been declared as arrays. Therefore, when we call the function **display( )** using,

```
display ( b1.name, b1.author, b1.callno ) ;
```

we are passing the base addresses of the arrays **name** and **author**, but the value stored in **callno**. Thus, this is a mixed call—a call by reference as well as a call by value.

It can be immediately realized that to pass individual elements would become more tedious as the number of structure elements goes on increasing. A better way would be to pass the entire structure variable at a time. This method is shown in the following program.

```
# include <stdio.h>
struct book
{
    char  name[25] ;
    char  author[25] ;
    int  callno ;
```

```
};
void display ( struct book ) ;

int main( )
{
    struct book  b1 = { "Let us C", "YPK", 101 } ;
    display ( b1 ) ;
    return 0 ;
}

void display ( struct book  b )
{
    printf ( "%s %s %d\n", b.name, b.author, b.callno ) ;
}
```

And here is the output...

```
Let us C YPK 101
```

Note that here the calling of function **display( )** becomes quite compact,

```
display ( b1 ) ;
```

Having collected what is being passed to the **display( )** function, the question comes, how do we define the formal arguments in the function. We cannot say,

```
struct book b1 ;
```

because the data type **struct book** is not known to the function **display( )**. Therefore, it becomes necessary to declare the structure type **struct book** outside **main( )**, so that it becomes known to all functions in the program.

(d) The way we can have a pointer pointing to an **int**, or a pointer pointing to a **char**, similarly we can have a pointer pointing to a **struct**. Such pointers are known as 'structure pointers'.
Let us look at a program that demonstrates the usage of a structure pointer.

```
# include <stdio.h>
int main( )
{
    struct book
    {
```

```
        char name[25] ;
        char author[25] ;
        int callno ;
    } ;
    struct book b1 = { "Let us C", "YPK", 101 } ;
    struct book *ptr ;
    ptr = &b1 ;
    printf ( "%s %s %d\n", b1.name, b1.author, b1.callno ) ;
    printf ( "%s %s %d\n", ptr->name, ptr->author, ptr->callno ) ;
    return 0 ;
}
```

The first **printf( )** is as usual. The second **printf( )** however is peculiar. We can't use **ptr.name** or **ptr.callno** because **ptr** is not a structure variable but a pointer to a structure, and the dot operator requires a structure variable on its left. In such cases C provides an operator **->**, called an arrow operator to refer to the structure elements. Remember that on the left hand side of the '**.**' structure operator, there must always be a structure variable, whereas on the left hand side of the '**->**' operator, there must always be a pointer to a structure. The arrangement of the structure variable and pointer to structure in memory is shown in the Figure 12.2.

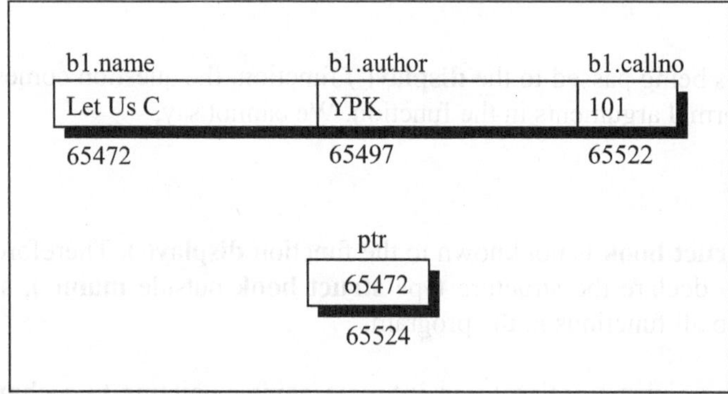

Figure 12.2

Can we not pass the address of a structure variable to a function? We can. The following program demonstrates this.

```
/* Passing address of a structure variable */
# include <stdio.h>
struct book
{
    char name[25] ;
```

```
    char  author[25] ;
    int  callno ;
} ;
void display ( struct book * ) ;

int main( )
{
    struct book  b1 = { "Let us C", "YPK", 101 } ;
    display ( &b1 ) ;
    return 0 ;
}

void display ( struct book *b )
{
    printf ( "%s %s %d\n", b->name, b->author, b->callno ) ;
}
```

And here is the output...

```
Let us C YPK 101
```

Again note that, to access the structure elements using pointer to a structure, we have to use the '->' operator.

Also, the structure **struct book** should be declared outside **main( )** such that this data type is available to **display( )** while declaring pointer to the structure.

(e) Consider the following code snippet:

```
# include <stdio.h>
struct emp
{
    int a ;
    char ch ;
    float s ;
} ;
int main( )
{
    struct emp e ;
    printf ( "%u %u %u\n", &e.a, &e.ch, &e.s ) ;
    return 0 ;
}
```

If we execute this program using TC/TC++ compiler we get the addresses as:

```
65518 65520 65521
```

As expected, in memory the **char** begins immediately after the **int** and **float** begins immediately after the **char**.

However, if we run the same program using VC++ compiler then the output turns out to be:

```
1245044 1245048 1245052
```

It can be observed from this output that the **float** doesn't get stored immediately after the **char**. In fact there is a hole of three bytes after the **char**. Let us understand the reason for this. VC++ is a 32-bit compiler targeted to generate code for a 32-bit microprocessor. The architecture of this microprocessor is such that it is able to fetch the data that is present at an address, which is a multiple of four much faster than the data present at any other address. Hence the VC++ compiler aligns every element of a structure at an address that is multiple of four. That's the reason why there were three holes created between the **char** and the **float**.

However, some programs need to exercise precise control over the memory areas where data is placed. For example, suppose we wish to read the contents of the boot sector (first sector on the floppy/hard disk) into a structure. For this the byte arrangement of the structure elements must match the arrangement of various fields in the boot sector of the disk. The **#pragma pack** directive offers a way to fulfill this requirement. This directive specifies packing alignment for structure members. The pragma takes effect at the first structure declaration after the pragma is seen. Turbo C/C++ compiler doesn't support this feature, VC++ compiler does. The following code shows how to use this directive.

```
# include <stdio.h>
# pragma pack(1)
struct emp
{
    int a ;
    char ch ;
    float s ;
} ;
# pragma pack( )

int main( )
```

```
{
    struct emp e ;
    printf ( "%u %u %u\n", &e.a, &e.ch, &e.s ) ;
    return 0 ;
}
```

Here, **#pragma pack (1)** lets each structure element to begin on a 1-byte boundary as justified by the output of the program given below:

```
1245044 1245048 1245049
```

Uses of Structures

Where are structures useful? The immediate application that comes to the mind is Database Management. That is, to maintain data about employees in an organization, books in a library, items in a store, financial accounting transactions in a company etc. But mind you, use of structures stretches much beyond database management. They can be used for a variety of purposes like:

(a) Changing the size of the cursor
(b) Clearing the contents of the screen
(c) Placing the cursor at an appropriate position on screen
(d) Drawing any graphics shape on the screen
(e) Receiving a key from the keyboard
(f) Checking the memory size of the computer
(g) Finding out the list of equipment attached to the computer
(h) Formatting a floppy
(i) Hiding a file from the directory
(j) Displaying the directory of a disk
(k) Sending the output to printer
(l) Interacting with the mouse

And that is certainly a very impressive list! At least impressive enough to make you realize how important a data type a structure is and to be thorough with it if you intend to program any of the above applications. Some of these applications would be discussed in Chapters 16 to 19.

Summary

(a) A structure is usually used when we wish to store dissimilar data together.
(b) Structure elements can be accessed through a structure variable using a dot (.) operator.
(c) Structure elements can be accessed through a pointer to a structure using the arrow (->) operator.
(d) All elements of one structure variable can be assigned to another structure variable using the assignment (=) operator.
(e) It is possible to pass a structure variable to a function either by value or by address.
(f) It is possible to create an array of structures.

Exercise

[A] What will be the output of the following programs:

(a)
```
# include <stdio.h>
# include <string.h>
int main( )
{
    struct gospel
    {
        int num ;
        char mess1[50] ;
        char mess2[50] ;
    } m ;

    m.num = 1 ;
    strcpy ( m.mess1, "If all that you have is hammer" ) ;
    strcpy ( m.mess2, "Everything looks like a nail" ) ;

    /* assume that the strucure is located at address 1004 */
    printf ( "%u %u %u\n", &m.num, m.mess1, m.mess2 ) ;
    return 0 ;
}
```

(b)
```
# include <stdio.h>
struct gospel
{
    int num ;
    char mess1[50] ;
    char mess2[50] ;
```

```
} m1 = { 2, "If you are driven by success",
            "make sure that it is a quality drive"
        } ;
int main( )
{
    struct gospel  m2, m3 ;
    m2 = m1 ;
    m3 = m2 ;
    printf ( "%d %s %s\n", m1.num, m2.mess1, m3.mess2 ) ;
    return 0 ;
}
```

(c)
```
# include <stdio.h>
int main( )
{
    struct windows
    {
        int a ;
        int *b ;
    } *prog4 ;

    prog4 -> b = &prog4 -> a ;
    prog4 -> a = 0 ;
    printf ( "%d %d\n", prog4 -> a, *prog4 -> b ) ;
    return 0 ;
}
```

(d)
```
# include <stdio.h>
int main( )
{
    struct dtype
    {
        int i ;
        float f ;
        struct dtype *next ;
    } ;
    static struct dtype v = { 10, 3.14, &v } ;
    struct dtype *p ;
    p = &v ;
    while ( p != 0 )
    {
        printf ( "%d %f\n", p -> i, p -> f ) ;
```

```
        p = p -> next ;
    }
    return 0 ;
}
```

(e)
```
# include <stdio.h>
int main( )
{
    struct roses
    {
        int i ;
        char c ;
    } live, love[2] ;

    printf ( "%d %d %d %d\n", sizeof ( live.i ), sizeof ( struct roses ), sizeof ( live ), sizeof ( love ) ) ;
    return 0 ;
}
```

[B] Point out the errors, if any, in the following programs:

(a)
```
# include <stdio.h>
# include <string.h>
int main( )
{
    struct employee
    {
        char  name[25] ;
        int  age ;
        float  bs ;
    } ;
    struct employee  e ;
    strcpy ( e.name, "Hacker" ) ;
    age = 25 ;
    printf ( "%s %d\n", e.name, age ) ;
    return 0 ;
}
```

(b)
```
# include <stdio.h>
int main( )
{
    struct
    {
        char  name[25] ;
        char  language[10] ;
```

```
    } ;
    struct employee  e = { "Hacker", "C" } ;
    printf ( "%s %d\n", e.name, e.language ) ;
    return 0 ;
}
```

(c)
```
# include <stdio.h>
struct virus
{

    char  signature[25] ;
    char  status[20] ;
    int  size ;
} v[2] = {
            "Yankee Doodle", "Deadly", 1813,
            "Dark Avenger",  "Killer", 1795
       } ;
int main( )
{
    int  i ;
    for ( i = 0 ; i <=1 ; i++ )
        printf ( "%s %s\n", v.signature, v.status ) ;
    return 0 ;
}
```

(d)
```
# include <stdio.h>
struct s
{
    char  ch ;
    int  i ;
    float  a ;
} ;
void f ( struct s ) ;
void g ( struct s  * ) ;

int main( )
{
    struct s  var = { 'C', 100, 12.55 } ;
    f ( var ) ;
    g ( &var ) ;
    return 0 ;
}
void f ( struct s  v )
{
```

```
    printf ( "%c %d %f\n", v -> ch, v -> i, v -> a ) ;
}
void g ( struct s  *v )
{
    printf ( "%c %d %f\n", v.ch, v.i, v.a ) ;
}
```

(e)
```
# include <stdio.h>
struct s
{
    int  i ;
    struct s  *p ;
} ;
int main( )
{
    struct s  var1, var2 ;

    var1.i = 100 ;
    var2.i = 200 ;
    var1.p = &var2 ;
    var2.p = &var1 ;
    printf ( "%d %d\n", var1.p -> i, var2.p -> i ) ;
    return 0 ;
}
```

(f)
```
# include <stdio.h>
int main( )
{
    struct dos
    {
        int a ;
        float b ;
    } prog1 = { 45, 4.5 }, prog2 = &prog1 ;
    printf ( "%d %f\n", prog1 -> a, prog2.b ) ;
    return 0 ;
}
```

[C] Answer the following:

(a) Ten floats are to be stored in memory. What would you prefer, an array or a structure?

(b) Given the statement,

```
maruti.engine.bolts = 25 ;
```

which of the following is True?

1. structure bolts is nested within structure engine
2. structure engine is nested within structure maruti
3. structure maruti is nested within structure engine
4. structure maruti is nested within structure bolts

(c) State True or False:

1. All structure elements are stored in contiguous memory locations.
2. An array should be used to store dissimilar elements, and a structure to store similar elements.
3. In an array of structures, not only are all structures stored in contiguous memory locations, but the elements of individual structures are also stored in contiguous locations.

(d)
```
struct time
{
    int hours ;
    int minutes ;
    int seconds ;
}t ;
struct time *tt ;
tt = &t ;
```

With reference to the above declarations which of the following refers to **seconds** correctly:

1. tt.seconds
2. (*tt).seconds
3. time.t
4. tt -> seconds

(e) Match the following with reference to the following program segment:

```
struct
{
    int x, y ;
} s[ ] = { 10, 20, 15, 25, 8, 75, 6, 2 } ;
int *i ;
i = s ;
```

1. *(i + 3) a. 85

2.	s[i[7]].x	b.	2
3.	s[(s + 2)->y / 3[I]].y	c.	6
4.	i[i[1]-i[2]]	d.	7
5.	i[s[3].y]	e.	16
6.	(s + 1)->x + 5	f.	15
7.	*(1 +i)**(i + 4) / *i	g.	25
8.	s[i[0] – i[4]].y + 10	h.	8
9.	(*(s + *(i + 1) / *i)).x + 2	i.	1
10.	++i[i[6]]	j.	100
		k.	10
		l.	20

(f) What is being done in the following statements?

```
struct cop
{
    long unsigned int i ;
} ;
```

1. initialization
2. definition
3. call
4. declaration

[D] Attempt the following:

(a) Create a structure to specify data on students given below:

Roll number, Name, Department, Course, Year of joining

Assume that there are not more than 450 students in the college.

(a) Write a function to print names of all students who joined in a particular year.
(b) Write a function to print the data of a student whose roll number is given.

(b) Create a structure to specify data of customers in a bank. The data to be stored is: Account number, Name, Balance in account. Assume maximum of 200 customers in the bank.

(a) Write a function to print the Account number and name of each customer with balance below Rs. 100.

(b) If a customer requests for withdrawal or deposit, it is given in the form:

Acct. no, amount, code (1 for deposit, 0 for withdrawal)

Write a program to give a message, “The balance is insufficient for the specified withdrawal”.

(c) An automobile company has serial number for engine parts starting from AA0 to FF9. The other characteristics of parts to be specified in a structure are: Year of manufacture, material and quantity manufactured.

(a) Specify a structure to store information corresponding to a part.
(b) Write a program to retrieve information on parts with serial numbers between BB1 and CC6.

(d) A record contains name of cricketer, his age, number of test matches that he has played and the average runs that he has scored in each test match. Create an array of structures to hold records of 20 such cricketers and then write a program to read these records and arrange them in ascending order by average runs. Use the **qsort( )** standard library function.

(e) There is a structure called **employee** that holds information like employee code, name, date of joining. Write a program to create an array of structures and enter some data into it. Then ask the user to enter current date. Display the names of those employees whose tenure is 3 or more than 3 years according to the given current date.

(f) Write a menu driven program that depicts the working of a library. The menu options should be:

1. Add book information
2. Display book information
3. List all books of given author
4. List the title of specified book
5. List the count of books in the library
6. List the books in the order of accession number
7. Exit

Create a structure called **library** to hold accession number, title of the book, author name, price of the book, and flag indicating whether book is issued or not.

(g) Write a program that compares two given dates. To store a date use a structure that contains three members namely date, month and year. If the dates are equal then display message as "Equal" otherwise "Unequal".

(h) Linked list is a very common data structure often used to store similar data in memory. While the elements of an array occupy contiguous memory locations, those of a linked list are not constrained to be stored in adjacent locations. The individual elements are stored "somewhere" in memory, rather like a family dispersed, but still bound together. The order of the elements is maintained by explicit links between them. Thus, a linked list is a collection of elements called nodes, each of which stores two item of information—an element of the list, and a link, i.e., a pointer or an address that indicates explicitly the location of the node containing the successor of this list element.

Write a program to build a linked list by adding new nodes at the beginning, at the end or in the middle of the linked list. Also write a function **display( )** which displays all the nodes present in the linked list.

(i) A stack is a data structure in which addition of new element or deletion of existing element always takes place at the same end. This end is often known as 'top' of stack. This situation can be compared to a stack of plates in a cafeteria where every new plate is added to or taken off from the 'top' of the stack. There are several applications where stack can be put to use. For example, recursion, keeping track of function calls, evaluation of expressions, etc. Write a program to implement a stack using a linked list.

(j) Unlike a stack, in a queue the addition of new element takes place at the end (called 'rear' of queue) whereas deletion takes place at the other end (called 'front' of queue). Write a program to implement a queue using a linked list.

(k) Write a program that should be able to create and delete the nodes in a linked list as specified by the user. The node should be a structure having elements employee code, name, sex, annual income of a person and pointer to the next node. The program should be able to print the information of the nodes when asked to do so.

13 Self Referential Structures and Linked Lists

- What is a Linked List
- Self-referential Structures
- Operations on a Linked List
- Summary
- Exercise

United we stand, divided we fall! This has been proved umpteen numbers of times. More united and connected we are, more is the flexibility and scalability. Same is true with Linked Lists. This is perhaps one data structure that has been used at more number of places in computing than you can count. But, beware, they are not simple. But the flexibility and performance they offer is worth the pain of learning them.

For storing similar data in memory we can use either an array or a linked list. Arrays are simple to understand and elements of an array are easily accessible. But arrays suffer from the following limitations:

- Arrays have a fixed dimension. Once the size of an array is decided it cannot be increased or decreased during execution. For example, if we construct an array of **100** elements and then try to stuff more than **100** elements in it, our program may crash. On the other hand, if we use only **10** elements then the space for balance **90** elements goes waste.
- Array elements are always stored in contiguous memory locations. At times it might so happen that enough contiguous locations might not be available for the array that we are trying to create. Even though the total space requirement of the array can be met through a combination of non-contiguous blocks of memory, we would still not be allowed to create the array.
- Operations like insertion of a new element in an array or deletion of an existing element from the array are pretty tedious. This is because during insertion or deletion each element after the specified position has to be shifted one position to the right (in case of insertion) or one position to the left (in case of deletion). Refer Chapter 2 for more details.

Linked list overcomes all these disadvantages. A linked list can grow and shrink in size during its lifetime. In other words, there is no maximum size of a linked list. The second advantage of linked lists is that, as nodes (elements) are stored at different memory locations it hardly happens that we fall short of memory when required. The third advantage is that, unlike arrays, while inserting or deleting the nodes of the linked list, shifting of nodes is not required.

What is a Linked List

Linked list is a very common data structure often used to store similar data in memory. While the elements of an array occupy contiguous memory locations, those of a linked list are not constrained to be stored in adjacent locations. The individual elements are stored "somewhere" in memory, rather like a family dispersed, but still bound together. The order of the elements is maintained by explicit links between them. For instance, the marks obtained by different students can be stored in a linked list as shown in Figure 13.1.

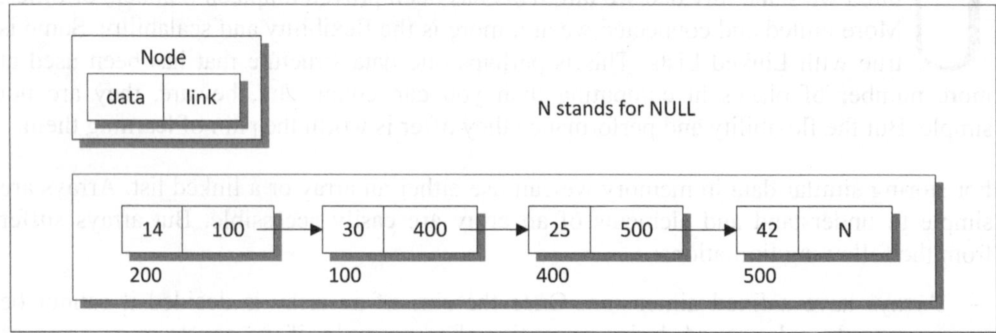

Figure 13.1 Linked list

Observe that the linked list is a collection of elements called nodes, each of which stores two items of information—an element of the list and a link. A link is a pointer or an address that indicates explicitly the location of the node containing the successor of the list element. In Figure 13.1, the arrows represent the links. The **data** part of each node consists of the marks obtained by a student and the **link** part is a pointer to the next node. The **NULL** in the last node indicates that this is the last node in the list.

Self-referential Structures

To represent the nodes shown in Figure 13.1 in a C program we would have to declare a structure. This is because a node is a collection of dissimilar types—in this case—an integer and a pointer to the next node. We can declare this structure as shown below:

```
/* structure containing a data part and link part */
struct node
{
    int data ;
    struct node * link ;
} ;
```

What is special about this structure is that within its declaration (**struct node**) there is a pointer to itself (**struct node** *). Such structures are known as self-referential structures. While implementing any linked list we have to create such self-referential structures.

Operations on a Linked List

There are several operations that we can think of performing on linked lists. The following program shows how to build a linked list by adding new nodes at the beginning, at the end or in the middle of the linked list. It also contains a function **display( )** which displays all the nodes present in the linked list and a function **del( )** which can delete any node in the linked list. Go through the program carefully, a step at a time. I have added suitable comments in the program to help you understand it better.

```
#include <stdio.h>
#include <conio.h>
#include <malloc.h>
#include <windows.h>

/* structure containing a data part and link part */
struct node
{
    int data ;
    struct node * link ;
} ;

void append ( struct node **, int ) ;
void addatbeg ( struct node **, int ) ;
void addafter ( struct node *, int, int ) ;
void display ( struct node * ) ;
int count ( struct node * ) ;
void del ( struct node **, int ) ;

int main( )
{
    struct node *p ;
    p = NULL ;  /* empty linked list */

    printf ( "No. of elements in the Linked List = %d\n", count ( p ) ) ;
    append ( &p, 14 ) ;
    append ( &p, 30 ) ;
    append ( &p, 25 ) ;
    append ( &p, 42 ) ;
    append ( &p, 17 ) ;

    system ( "cls" ) ;
```

```
    display ( p ) ;

    addatbeg ( &p, 999 ) ;
    addatbeg ( &p, 888 ) ;
    addatbeg ( &p, 777 ) ;

    display ( p ) ;

    addafter ( p, 7, 0 ) ;
    addafter ( p, 2, 1 ) ;
    addafter ( p, 5, 99 ) ;

    display ( p ) ;
    printf ( "No. of elements in the Linked List = %d\n", count ( p ) ) ;

    del ( &p, 99 ) ;
    del ( &p, 1 ) ;
    del ( &p, 10 ) ;

    display ( p ) ;
    printf ( "No. of elements in the linked list = %d\n", count ( p ) ) ;
    return 0 ;
}

/* adds a node at the end of a linked list */
void append ( struct node **q, int num )
{
    struct node *temp, *r ;

    if ( *q == NULL )  /* if the list is empty, create first node */
    {
        temp = ( struct node * ) malloc ( sizeof ( struct node ) ) ;
        temp -> data = num ;
        temp -> link = NULL ;
        *q = temp ;
    }
    else
    {
        temp = *q ;

        /* go to last node */
        while ( temp -> link != NULL )
            temp = temp -> link ;
```

```
        /* add node at the end */
        r = ( struct node * ) malloc ( sizeof ( struct node ) ) ;
        r -> data = num ;
        r -> link = NULL ;
        temp -> link = r ;
    }
}

/* adds a new node at the beginning of the linked list */
void addatbeg ( struct node **q, int num )
{
    struct node *temp ;

    /* add new node */
    temp = ( struct node * ) malloc ( sizeof ( struct node ) ) ;

    temp -> data = num ;
    temp -> link = *q ;
    *q = temp ;
}

/* adds a new node after the specified number of nodes */
void addafter ( struct node *q, int loc, int num )
{
    struct node *temp, *r ;
    int i ;

    temp = q ;
    /* skip to desired portion */
    for ( i = 0 ; i < loc ; i++ )
    {
        temp = temp -> link ;

        /* if end of linked list is encountered */
        if ( temp == NULL )
        {
            printf ( "There are less than %d elements in list\n", loc ) ;
            return ;
        }
    }

    /* insert new node */
```

```
        r = ( struct node * ) malloc ( sizeof ( struct node ) ) ;
        r -> data = num ;
        r -> link = temp -> link ;
        temp -> link = r ;
}

/* displays the contents of the linked list */
void display ( struct node *q )
{
        /* traverse the entire linked list */
        while ( q != NULL )
        {
                printf ( "%d ", q -> data ) ;
                q = q -> link ;
        }
        printf ( "\n" ) ;
}

/* counts the number of nodes present in the linked list */
int count ( struct node * q )
{
        int c = 0 ;

        /* traverse the entire linked list */
        while ( q != NULL )
        {
                q = q -> link ;
                c++ ;
        }

        return c ;
}

/* deletes the specified node from the linked list */
void del ( struct node **q, int num )
{
        struct node *old, *temp ;

        temp = *q ;

        while ( temp != NULL )
        {
                if ( temp -> data == num )
```

```
        {
            /* if node to be deleted is the first node in the linked list */
            if ( temp == *q )
                *q = temp -> link ;

            /* deletes the intermediate nodes in the linked list */
            else
                old -> link = temp -> link ;

            /* free the memory occupied by the node */
            free ( temp ) ;
            return ;
        }

        /* traverse the linked list till the last node is reached */
        else
        {
            old = temp ;  /* old points to the previous node */
            temp = temp -> link ;  /* go to the next node */
        }
    }

    printf ( "Element %d not found\n", num ) ;
}
```

On execution of this program it produces the following output:

```
14 30 25 42 17
777 888 999 14 30 25 42 17
777 888 999 1 14 30 99 25 42 17 0
No. of elements in the Linked List = 11
Element 10 not found
777 888 999 14 30 25 42 17 0
No. of elements in the linked list = 9
```

Let us now try to understand this program. To begin with, we have declared a structure for a node. It contains a data part and a link part. The variable **p** has been defined as pointer to a node. We have used this pointer as pointer to the first node in the linked list. No matter how many nodes get added to the linked list, **p** would continue to pointer to the first node in the list. When no node has been added to the list, **p** has been set to **NULL** to indicate that the list is empty.

The **append( )** function has to deal with two situations:

(a) The node is being added to an empty list.
(b) The node is being added at the end of an existing list.

In the first case, the condition

```
if ( *q == NULL )
```

gets satisfied. Hence, space is allocated for the node using **malloc( )**. As **malloc( )** returns a void pointer, it is typecasted into a **struct node** pointer. Next, the data and the link part of this node are set up using the statements

```
temp -> data = num ;
temp -> link = NULL ;
```

Lastly, **p** is made to point to this node, since the first node has been added to the list and **p** must always point to the first node. Note that ***q** is nothing but equal to **p**.

In the other case, when the linked list is not empty, the condition

```
if ( *q == NULL )
```

would fail, since ***q** (i.e. **p** is non-**NULL**). Now **temp** is made to point to the first node in the list through the statement

```
temp = *q ;
```

Then using **temp** we have traversed through the entire linked list using the statements

```
while ( temp -> link != NULL )
    temp = temp -> link ;
```

The position of the pointers before and after traversing the linked list is shown in Figure 13.2.

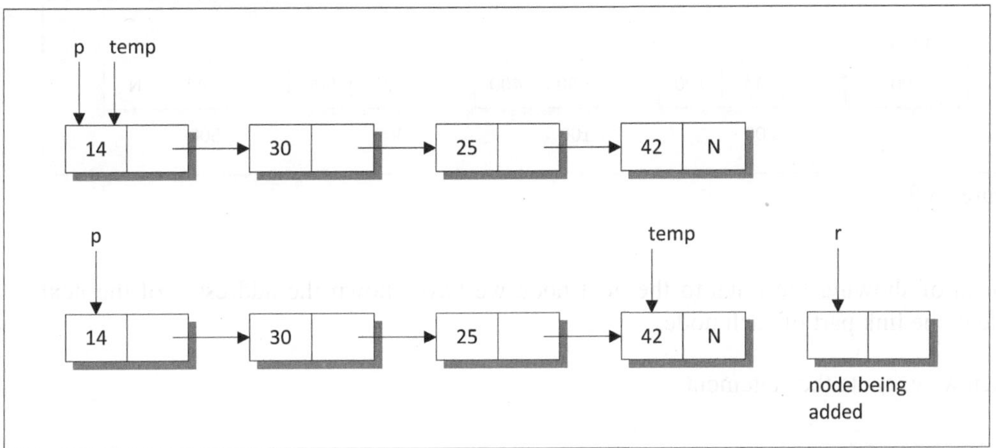

Figure 13.2

Each time through the loop the statement **temp = temp -> link** makes **temp** point to the next node in the list. When **temp** reaches the last node the condition **temp -> link != NULL** would fail. Once outside the loop we allocate space for the new node through the statement

```
r = ( struct node * ) malloc ( sizeof ( struct node ) ) ;
```

Once the space has been allocated for the new node its **data** part is stuffed with **num** and the **link** part with **NULL**. Note that this node is now going to be the last Node in the list.

All that now remains to be done is connecting the previous last node with the new last node. The previous last node is being pointed to by **temp** and the new last node is being pointed to by **r**. They are connected through the statement

```
temp -> link = r ;
```

this link gets established.

There is often a confusion as to how the statement **temp = temp -> link** makes **temp** point to the next node in the list. Let us understand this with the help of an example. Suppose in a linked list containing 4 nodes, **temp** is pointing at the first node. This is shown in Figure 13.3.

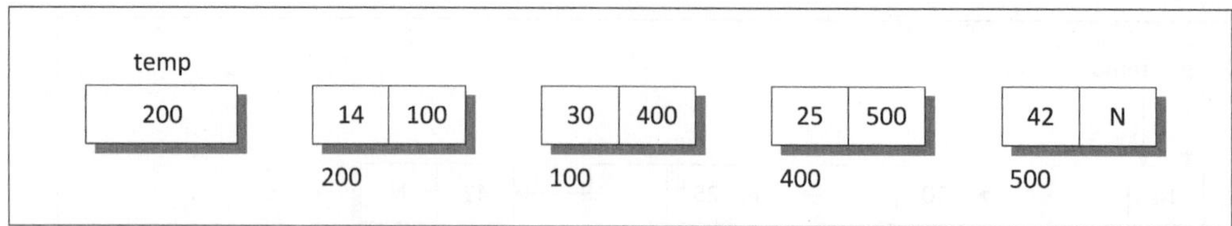

Figure 13.3

Instead of showing the links to the next node we have shown the addresses of the next node in the link part of each node.

When we execute the statement

```
temp = temp -> link ;
```

the right hand side yields **100**. This address is now stored in **temp**. As a result, **temp** starts pointing to the node present at address **100**. In effect the statement has shifted **temp** so that it has started pointing to the next node in the list.

Let us now understand the **addatbeg( )** function. Suppose there are already 5 nodes in the list and we wish to add a new node at the beginning of this existing linked list. This situation is shown in Figure 13.4.

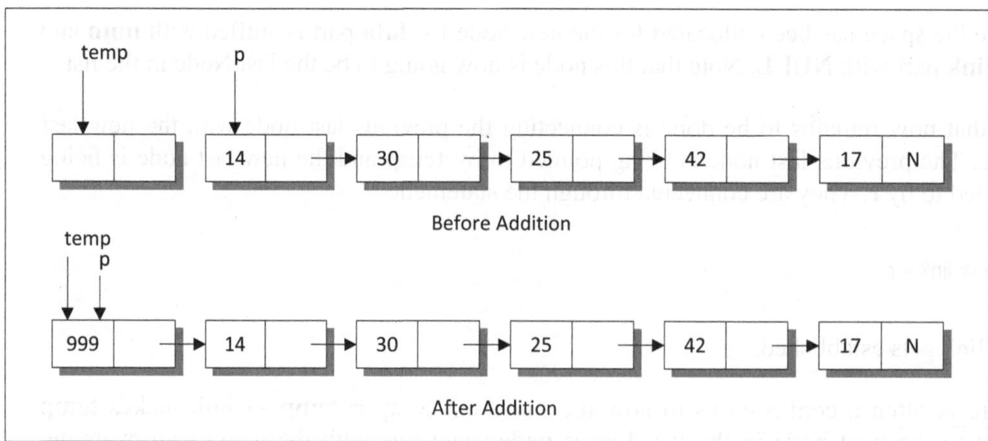

Figure 13.4

For adding a new node at the beginning, firstly space is allocated for this node and data is stored in it through the statement

```
temp -> data = num ;
```

Now we need to make the **link** part of this node point to the existing first node. This has been achieved through the statement

```
temp -> link = *q ;
```

Lastly, this new node must be made the first node in the list. This has been attained through the statement

```
*q = temp ;
```

The **addafter( )** function permits us to add a new node after a specified number of node in the linked list.

To begin with, through a loop we skip the desired number of nodes after which a new node is to be added. Suppose we wish to add a new node containing data as **99** after the 3rd node in the list. The position of pointers once the control reaches outside the **for** loop is shown in Figure 13.5(a). Now space is allocated for the node to be inserted and **99** is stored in the data part of it.

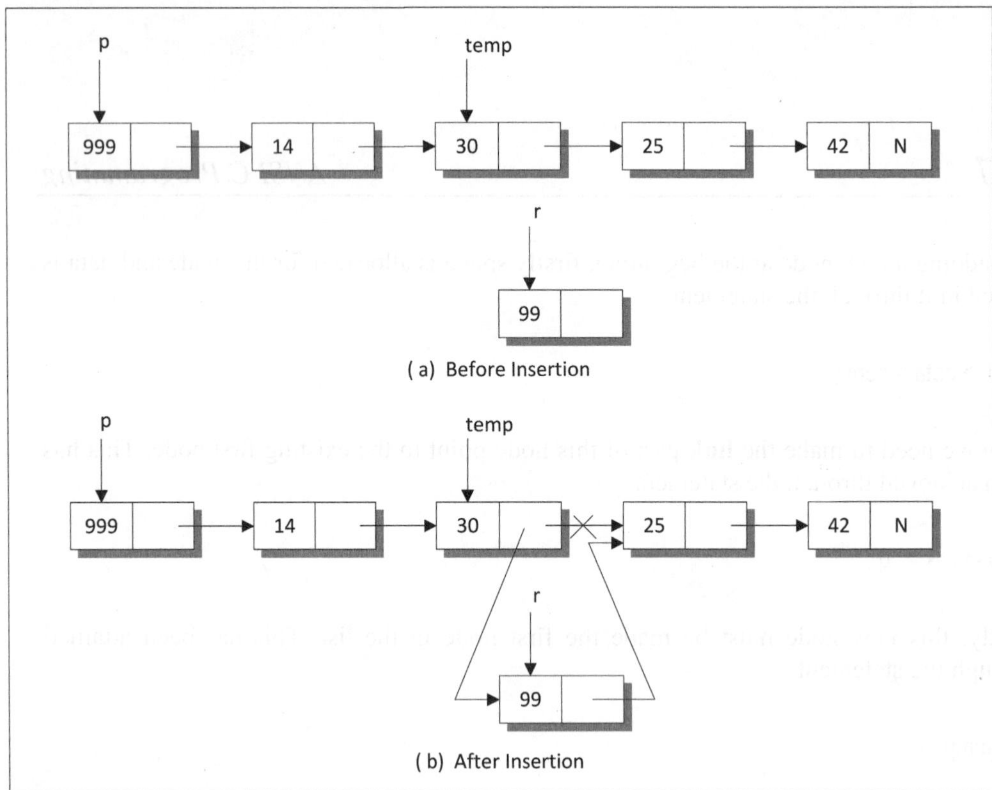

Figure 13.5

All that remains to be done is readjustment of links such that **99** goes in between **30** and **25**. This is achieved through the statements

```
r -> link = temp -> link ;
temp -> link = r ;
```

The first statement makes link part of node containing **99** to point to the node containing **25**. The second statement ensures that the link part of node containing **30** points to the node containing **99**. On execution of the second statement the earlier link between **30** and **25** is severed. So now **30** no longer points to **25**, it points to **99**.

The **display( )** and **count( )** functions are straight forward. We leave them for you to understand.

That brings us to the last function in the program i.e. **del( )**. In this function through the **while** loop, we have traversed through the entire linked list, checking at each node, whether it is the node to be deleted. If so, we have checked if the node being deleted is the first node in the linked list. If it is so, we have simply shifted **p** (which is same as ***q**) to the next node and then deleted the earlier node.

If the node to be deleted is an intermediate node, then the position of various pointers and links before and after the deletion is shown in Figure 13.6.

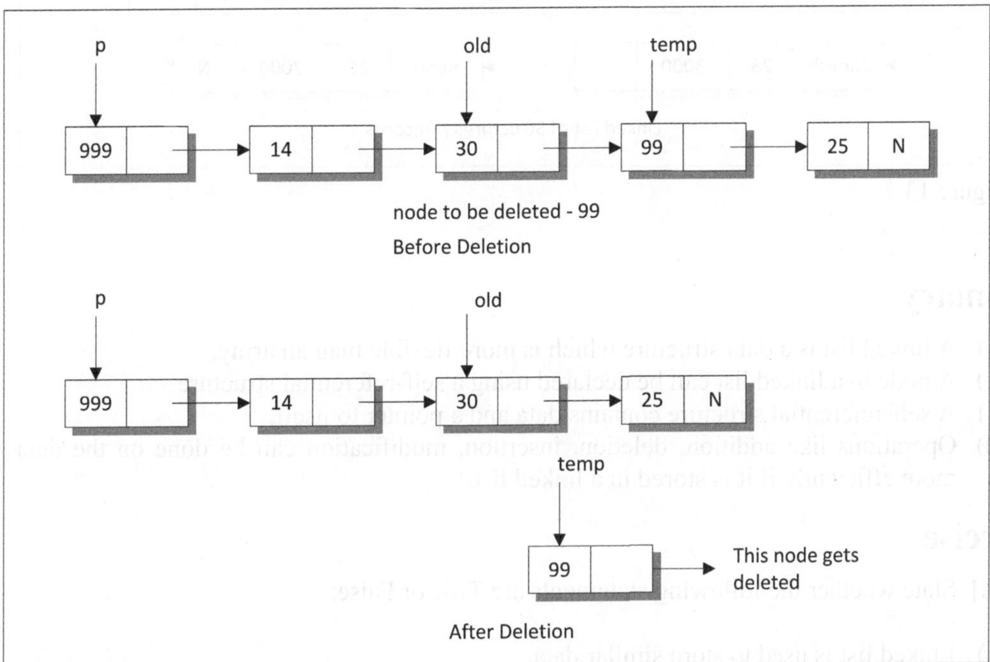

Figure 13.6

A common and a wrong impression that beginners carry is that a linked list is used only for storing integers. However, a linked list can virtually be used for storing any similar data. For example, there can exist a linked list of **float**s, a linked list of names, or even a linked list of records, where each record contains name, age and salary of an employee. These linked lists are shown in Figure 13.7.

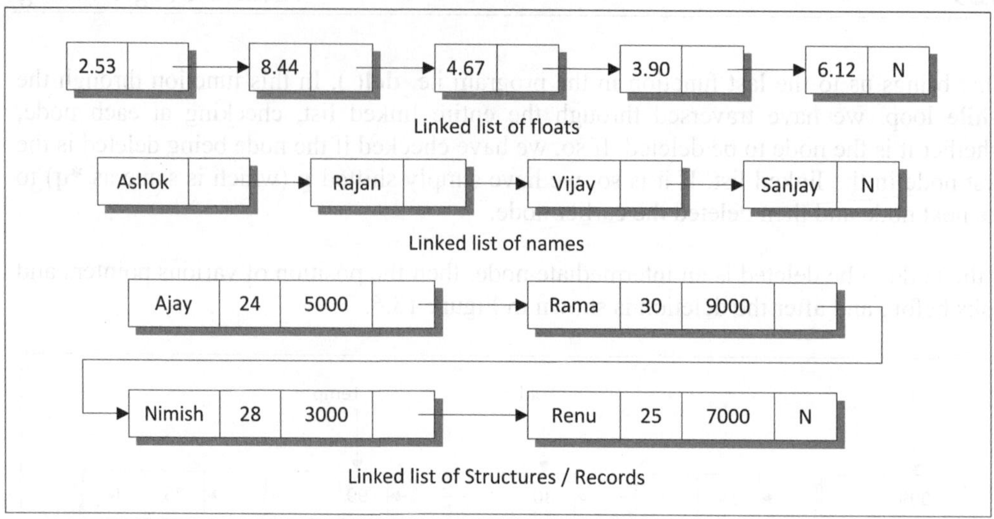

Figure 13.7

Summary

(a) A linked list is a data structure which is more flexible than an array.
(b) A node in a linked list can be declared using a self-referential structure.
(c) A self-referential structure contains data and a pointer to itself.
(d) Operations like addition, deletion, insertion, modification can be done on the data more efficiently if it is stored in a linked list.

Exercise

[A] State whether the following statements are True or False:

(a) Linked list is used to store similar data.

(b) All nodes in the linked list must always be in non-contiguous memory locations.

(c) It is necessary that the link part of the last node in a linked list must contain NULL.

(d) In a linked list, if we lose the location of the first node it is as good as having lost the entire linked list.

(e) A self-referential structure can contain multiple pointers pointing the same structure.

(f) It is not possible to implement a linked list without a self-referential structure.

(g) It is possible to create an array of self-referential structures.

(h) If we use a self-referential structure, then it is mandatory to use **malloc( )** to allocate space for variables of this type.

(i) A self-referential structure may contain any number of data items and any number of self-referring pointers.

[B] Answer the Following:

(j) Write a program that reads the name, age and salary of 10 persons and maintains them in a linked list sorted by name.

(k) Write a program that reverses the nodes in a linked list, i.e. the first node becomes the last node, etc.

(l) Write a program that maintains the nodes added to a linked list in ascending order.

(m) There are two linked lists A and B containing the following data:

A: 3, 7, 10, 15, 16, 9, 22, 17, 32

B: 16, 2, 9, 13, 37, 8, 10, 1, 28

Write a program to create:

- A linked list **C** that contains only those elements that are common in linked list **A** and **B**.
- A linked list **D** which contains all elements of **A** as well as **B** ensuring that there is no repetition of elements.

(n) Assume a singly linked list containing integers. Write a function **move( )** which would move a node forward n positions in the linked list.

(o) There are two linked lists A and B containing the following data:

A: 7, 5, 3, 1, 20

B: 6, 25, 32, 11, 9

Write a function to combine the two lists such that the resulting list contains nodes in the following elements:

7, 6, 5, 25, 3, 32, 1, 11, 20, 9

You are not allowed to create any additional node while writing the function.

(p) A linked list contains some positive numbers and some negative numbers. Using this linked list write a program to create two more linked lists, one containing all positive numbers and the other containing all negative numbers.

(q) Create two linked lists to represent the following polynomials:

$3x^2y + 9xy^3 + 15xy + 3$
$13x^3y^2 + 7x^2y + 22xy + 9y3$

Write a function **add( )** to add these polynomials and print the resulting linked list.

14 Console Input/Output

As mentioned in the first chapter, Dennis Ritchie wanted C to remain compact. In keeping with this intention, he deliberately omitted everything related with Input/Output (I/O) from his definition of the language. Thus, C simply has no provision for receiving data from any of the input devices (like say keyboard, disk, etc.), or for sending data to the output devices (like say VDU, disk, etc.). Then how do we manage I/O, and how is it that we were able to use **printf( )** and **scanf( )** if C has nothing to offer for I/O? This is what we intend to explore in this chapter.

Types of I/O

Though C has no provision for I/O, it, of course, has to be dealt with at some point or the other. There is not much use writing a program that spends all its time telling itself a secret. Each Operating System has its own facility for inputting and outputting data from and to the files and devices. It's a simple matter for a system programmer to write a few small programs that would link the C compiler for a particular Operating system's I/O facilities.

The developers of C Compilers do just that. They write several standard I/O functions and put them in libraries. These libraries are available with all C compilers. Whichever C compiler you are using, it's almost certain that you have access to a library of I/O functions.

Do understand that the I/O facilities with different operating systems would be different. Thus, the way one OS displays output on screen may be different than the way another OS does it. For example, the standard library function **printf( )** for DOS-based C compiler has been written keeping in mind the way DOS outputs characters to screen. Similarly, the **printf( )** function for a Unix-based compiler has been written keeping in mind the way Unix outputs characters to screen. We, as programmers, do not have to bother about which **printf( )** has been written in what manner. We should just use **printf( )** and it would take care of the rest of the details that are OS dependent. Same is true about all other standard library functions available for I/O.

There are numerous library functions available for I/O. These can be classified into two broad categories:

(a) Console I/O functions - Functions to receive input from keyboard and write output to VDU.

(b) File I/O functions - Functions to perform I/O operations on a floppy disk or a hard disk.

In this chapter we would be discussing only Console I/O functions. File I/O functions would be discussed in Chapter 12.

Console I/O Functions

The screen and keyboard together are called a console. Console I/O functions can be further classified into two categories—formatted and unformatted console I/O functions. The basic difference between them is that the formatted functions allow the input read from the keyboard or the output displayed on the VDU to be formatted as per our requirements. For example, if values of average marks and percentage marks are to be displayed on the screen, then the details like where this output would appear on the screen, how many spaces would be present between the two values, the number of places after the decimal points, etc. can be controlled using formatted functions. The functions available under each of these two categories are shown in Figure 14.1. Now let us discuss these console I/O functions in detail.

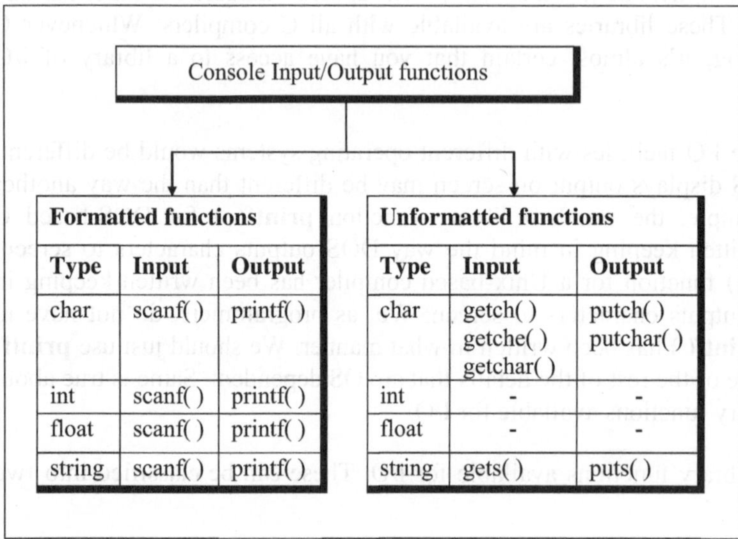

Figure 14.1

Formatted Console I/O Functions

As can be seen from Figure 14.1, the functions **printf( ),** and **scanf( )** fall under the category of formatted console I/O functions. These functions allow us to supply the input in a fixed format and let us obtain the output in the specified form. Let us discuss these functions one by one.

We have talked a lot about **printf( )**, used it regularly, but without having introduced it formally. Well, better late than never. Its general form looks like this...

```
printf ( "format string", list of variables ) ;
```

The format string can contain:

(a) Characters that are simply printed as they are
(b) Conversion specifications that begin with a % sign
(c) Escape sequences that begin with a \ sign

For example, look at the following program:

```
# include <stdio.h>
int main( )
{
    int avg = 346 ;
    float per = 69.2 ;
    printf ( "Average = %d\nPercentage = %f\n", avg, per ) ;
    return 0 ;
}
```

The output of the program would be...

```
Average = 346
Percentage = 69.200000
```

How does **printf( )** function interpret the contents of the format string? For this, it examines the format string from left to right. So long as it doesn't come across either a % or a \, it continues to dump the characters that it encounters, on to the screen. In this example, **Average =** is dumped on the screen. The moment it comes across a conversion specification in the format string, it picks up the first variable in the list of variables and prints its value in the specified format. In this example, the moment **%d** is met, the variable **avg** is picked up and its value is printed. Similarly, when an escape sequence is met, it takes the appropriate action. In this example, the moment **\n** is met, it places the cursor at the beginning of the next line. This process continues till the end of format string is reached.

Format Specifications

The **%d** and **%f** used in the **printf( )** are called format specifiers. They tell **printf( )** to print the value of **avg** as a decimal integer and the value of per as a float. Following is the list of format specifiers that can be used with the **printf( )** function.

Data type		Format specifier
Integer	short signed	%d or %I
	short unsigned	%u
	long singed	%ld
	long unsigned	%lu
	unsigned hexadecimal	%x
	unsigned octal	%o
Real	float	%f
	double	%lf
Character	signed character	%c
	unsigned character	%c
String		%s

Figure 14.2

We can provide following optional specifiers in the format specifications.

Specifier	Description
dd	Digits specifying field width
.	Decimal point separating field width from precision (precision stands for the number of places after the decimal point)
dd	Digits specifying precision.
-	Minus sign for left justifying the output in the specified field width

Figure 14.3

Now a short explanation about these optional format specifiers. The field-width specifier tells **printf( )** how many columns on screen should be used while printing a value. For example, **%10d** says, "print the variable as a decimal integer in a field of 10 columns". If the value to be printed happens not to fill up the entire field, the value is right justified and is padded with blanks on the left. If we include the minus sign in format specifier (as in **%-10d**), this means left justification is desired and the value will be padded with blanks on the right. If the field-width used turns out to be less than what is required to print the number, the field-width is ignored and the complete number is printed. Here is an example that illustrates all this.

```
# include <stdio.h>
int main( )
{
    int weight = 63 ;
    printf ( "weight is %d kg\n", weight ) ;
    printf ( "weight is %2d kg\n", weight ) ;
    printf ( "weight is %4d kg\n", weight ) ;
    printf ( "weight is %6d kg\n", weight ) ;
    printf ( "weight is %-6d kg\n", weight ) ;
    printf ( "weight is %1d kg\n", weight ) ;
    return 0 ;
}
```

The output of the program would look like this ...

```
Columns  0123456789012345678901234567890
         weight is 63 kg
         weight is 63 kg
         weight is   63 kg
         weight is     63 kg
         weight is 63     kg
         weight is 63 kg
```

Specifying the field width can be useful in creating tables of numeric values, as the following program demonstrates.

```
# include <stdio.h>
int main( )
{
    printf ( "%f %f %f\n", 5.0, 13.5, 133.9 ) ;
    printf ( "%f %f %f\n", 305.0, 1200.9, 3005.3 ) ;
    return 0 ;
}
```

And here is the output...

```
5.000000 13.500000 133.900000
305.000000 1200.900000 3005.300000
```

Even though the numbers have been printed, the numbers have not been lined up properly and hence are hard to read. A better way would be something like this...

```
# include <stdio.h>
int main( )
{
    printf ( "%10.1f %10.1f %10.1f\n", 5.0, 13.5, 133.9 ) ;
    printf ( "%10.1f %10.1f %10.1f\n", 305.0, 1200.9, 3005.3 );
    return 0 ;
}
```

This results into a much better output...

```
01234567890123456789012345678901
       5.0       13.5      133.9
     305.0     1200.9     3005.3
```

The format specifiers could be used even while displaying a string of characters. The following program would clarify this point:

```
/* Formatting strings with printf( ) */
# include <stdio.h>
int main( )
{
    char  firstname1[ ] = "Sandy" ;
    char  surname1[ ] = "Malya" ;
    char  firstname2[ ] = "AjayKumar" ;
    char  surname2[ ] = "Gurubaxani" ;

    printf ( "%20s%20s\n", firstname1, surname1 ) ;
    printf ( "%20s%20s\n", firstname2, surname2 ) ;
    return 0 ;
}
```

And here's the output...

```
01234567890123456789012345678901234567890123456789
```

```
               Sandy                         Malya
          AjayKumar                     Gurubaxani
```

The format specifier **%20s** reserves 20 columns for printing a string and then prints the string in these 20 columns with right justification. This helps lining up names of different lengths properly. Obviously, the format **%-20s** would have left justified the string.

Escape Sequences

We saw earlier how the newline character, **\n**, when inserted in a **printf( )**'s format string, takes the cursor to the beginning of the next line. The newline character is an 'escape sequence', so called because the backslash symbol (\) is considered as an 'escape' character—it causes an escape from the normal interpretation of a string, so that the next character is recognized as one having a special meaning.

The following example shows usage of **\n** and a new escape sequence \t, called 'tab'. A **\t** moves the cursor to the next tab stop. A 80-column screen usually has 10 tab stops. In other words, the screen is divided into 10 zones of 8 columns each. Printing a tab takes the cursor to the beginning of next printing zone. For example, if cursor is positioned in column 5, then printing a tab takes it to column 8.

```
# include <stdio.h>
int main( )
{
    printf ( "You\tmust\tbe\tcrazy\nto\thate\tthis\tbook\n" ) ;
    return 0 ;
}
```

And here's the output...

```
          1         2         3         4
01234567890123456789012345678901234567890
You     must    be      crazy
to      hate    this    book
```

The **\n** character causes a new line to begin following 'crazy'. The tab and newline are probably the most commonly used escape sequences, but there are others as well. Figure 14.4 shows a complete list of these escape sequences.

Esc. Seq.	Purpose	Esc. Seq.	Purpose
\n	New line	\t	Tab
\b	Backspace	\r	Carriage return
\f	Form feed	\a	Alert
\’	Single quote	\”	Double quote
\\	Backslash		

Figure 14.4

The first few of these escape sequences are more or less self- explanatory. **\b** moves the cursor one position to the left of its current position. **\r** takes the cursor to the beginning of the line in which it is currently placed. **\a** alerts the user by sounding the speaker inside the computer. Form feed advances the computer stationery attached to the printer to the top of the next page. Characters that are ordinarily used as delimiters... the single quote, double quote, and the backslash can be printed by preceding them with the backslash. Thus, the statement,

```
printf ( "He said, \"Let's do it!\"" ) ;
```

will print...

```
He said, "Let's do it!"
```

So far we have been describing **printf( )**’s specification as if we are forced to use only **%d** for an integer, only **%c** for a char, only **%s** for a string and so on. This is not true at all. In fact, **printf( )** uses the specification that we mention and attempts to perform the specified conversion, and does its best to produce a proper result. Sometimes the result is nonsensical, as in case when we ask it to print a string using **%d**. Sometimes the result is useful, as in the case we ask **printf( )** to print ASCII value of a character using **%d**. Sometimes the result is disastrous and the entire program blows up.

The following program shows a few of these conversions, some sensible, some weird.

```
# include <stdio.h>
int main( )
{
    char ch = 'z' ;
    int i = 125 ;
```

```
    float a = 12.55 ;
    char s[ ] = "hello there !" ;

    printf ( "%c %d %f\n", ch, ch, ch ) ;
    printf ( "%s %d %f\n", s, s, s ) ;
    printf ( "%c %d %f\n",i ,i, i ) ;
    printf ( "%f %d\n", a, a ) ;
    return 0 ;
}
```

And here's the output ...

```
z 122 -9362831782501783000000000000000000000000000.000000
hello there ! 3280 -9362831782501783000000000000000000000000000.000000
} 125 -9362831782501783000000000000000000000000000.000000
12.550000 0
```

I would leave it to you to analyze the results by yourselves. Some of the conversions you would find are quite sensible.

Let us now turn our attention to **scanf( )**. **scanf( )** allows us to enter data from keyboard that will be formatted in a certain way.

The general form of **scanf( )** statement is as follows:

```
scanf ( "format string", list of addresses of variables ) ;
```

For example:

```
scanf ( "%d %f %c", &c, &a, &ch ) ;
```

Note that we are sending addresses of variables (addresses are obtained by using '**&**' the 'address of' operator) to **scanf( )** function. This is necessary because the values received from keyboard must be dropped into variables corresponding to these addresses. The values that are supplied through the keyboard must be separated by either blank(s), tab(s), or newline(s). Do not include these escape sequences in the format string.

All the format specifications that we learnt in **printf( )** function are applicable to **scanf( )** function as well.

sprintf( ) and *sscanf( )* Functions

The **sprintf( )** function works similar to the **printf( )** function except for one small difference. Instead of sending the output to the screen as **printf( )** does, this function writes the output to an array of characters. The following program illustrates this.

```
# include <stdio.h>
int main( )
{
    int i = 10 ;
    char ch = 'A' ;
    float a = 3.14 ;
    char str[20] ;

    printf ( "%d %c %f\n", i, ch, a ) ;
    sprintf ( str, "%d %c %f", i, ch, a ) ;
    printf ( "%s\n", str ) ;
    return 0 ;
}
```

In this program, the **printf( )** prints out the values of **i**, **ch** and **a** on the screen, whereas **sprintf( )** stores these values in the character array **str**. Since the string **str** is present in memory, what is written into str using **sprintf( )** doesn't get displayed on the screen. Once **str** has been built, its contents can be displayed on the screen. In our program this was achieved by the second **printf( )** statement.

The counterpart of **sprintf( )** is the **sscanf( )** function. It allows us to read characters from a string and to convert and store them in C variables according to specified formats. The **sscanf( )** function comes in handy for in-memory conversion of characters to values. You may find it convenient to read in strings from a file and then extract values from a string by using **sscanf( )**. The usage of **sscanf( )** is same as **scanf( )**, except that the first argument is the string from which reading is to take place.

Unformatted Console I/O Functions

There are several standard library functions available under this category—those that can deal with a single character and those that can deal with a string of characters. For openers, let us look at those which handle one character at a time.

So far, for input we have consistently used the **scanf( )** function. However, for some situations, the **scanf( )** function has one glaring weakness... you need to hit the Enter key before the function can digest what you have typed. However, we often want a function that will read a single character the instant it is typed without waiting for the Enter key to be hit. **getch( )** and **getche( )** are two functions which serve this purpose. These functions return the character that has been most recently typed. The 'e' in **getche( )** function means it echoes (displays) the character that you typed to the screen. As against this, **getch( )** just returns the character that you typed without echoing it on the screen. **getchar( )** works similarly and echoes the character that you typed on the screen, but unfortunately requires Enter key to be typed following the character that you typed. The difference between **getchar( )** and **fgetchar( )** is that the former is a macro whereas the latter is a function.

The prototypes of **getch( )** and **getche( )** are present in the header file **conio.h**. The macro **getchar( )** and the prototype of **fgetchar( )** are present in **stdio.h**. Here is a sample program that illustrates the use of these functions and macro.

```
# include <stdio.h>
# include <conio.h>
int main( )
{
    char ch ;

    printf ( "Press any key to continue" ) ;
    getch( ) ; /* will not echo the character */

    printf ( "\nType any character" ) ;
    ch = getche( ) ; /* will echo the character typed */

    printf ( "\nType any character" ) ;
    getchar( ) ; /* will echo character, must be followed by enter key */
    printf ( "\nContinue Y/N" ) ;
    fgetchar( ) ; /* will echo character, must be followed by enter key */
    return 0 ;
}
```

And here is a sample run of this program...

```
Press any key to continue
Type any character B
Type any character W
Continue Y/N Y
```

putch( ) and **putchar( )** form the other side of the coin. They print a character on the screen. As far as the working of **putch( ) putchar( )** and **fputchar( )** is concerned, it's exactly same. The following program illustrates this.

```
# include <stdio.h>
# include <conio.h>
int main( )
{
    char  ch = 'A' ;

    putch ( ch ) ;
    putchar ( ch ) ;
    fputchar ( ch ) ;
    putch ( 'Z' ) ;
    putchar ( 'Z' ) ;
    fputchar ( 'Z' ) ;
    return 0 ;
}
```

And here is the output...

```
AAAZZZ
```

The limitation of **putch( ), putchar( )** and **fputchar( )** is that they can output only one character at a time.

gets( ) and *puts( )*

gets( ) receives a string from the keyboard. Why is it needed? Because **scanf(**) function has some limitations while receiving string of characters, as the following example illustrates...

```
# include <stdio.h>
int main( )
{
    char  name[50] ;

    printf ( "Enter name " ) ;
    scanf ( "%s", name ) ;
    printf ( "%s\n", name ) ;
    return 0 ;
}
```

And here is the output...

```
Enter name Jonty Rhodes
```

Jonty

Surprised? Where did "Rhodes" go? It never got stored in the array **name[ ],** because the moment the blank was typed after "Jonty", **scanf( )** assumed that the name being entered has ended. The result is that there is no way (at least not without a lot of trouble on the programmer's part) to enter a multi-word string into a single variable (**name** in this case) using **scanf( ).** The solution to this problem is to use **gets( )** function. As said earlier, it gets a string from the keyboard. It is terminated when an Enter key is hit. Thus, spaces and tabs are perfectly acceptable as part of the input string. More exactly, **gets( )** gets a newline (**\n**) terminated string of characters from the keyboard and replaces the **\n** with a **\0**.

The **puts( )** function works exactly opposite to **gets( )** function. It outputs a string to the screen.

Here is a program which illustrates the usage of these functions:

```
# include <stdio.h>
int main( )
{
    char  footballer[40] ;

    puts ( "Enter name" ) ;
    gets ( footballer ) ;  /* sends base address of array */
    puts ( "Happy footballing!" ) ;
    puts ( footballer ) ;
    return 0 ;
}
```

Following is the sample output:

```
Enter name
Jonty Rhodes
Happy footballing!
Jonty Rhodes
```

Why did we use two **puts( )** functions to print "Happy footballing!" and "Jonty Rhodes"? Because, unlike **printf( ), puts( )** can output only one string at a time. If we attempt to print two strings using **puts( ),** only the first one gets printed. Similarly, unlike **scanf( ), gets( )** can be used to read only one string at a time.

Summary

(a) There is no keyword available in C for doing input/output.
(b) All I/O in C is done using standard library functions.
(c) There are several functions available for performing console input/output.
(d) The formatted console I/O functions can force the user to receive the input in a fixed format and display the output in a fixed format.
(e) There are several format specifiers and escape sequences available to format input and output.
(f) Unformatted console I/O functions work faster since they do not have the overheads of formatting the input or output.

Exercise

[A] What will be the output of the following programs:

(a)
```
# include <stdio.h>
# include <ctype.h>
int main( )
{
    char ch ;
    ch = getchar( ) ;
    if ( islower ( ch ) )
        putchar ( toupper ( ch ) ) ;
    else
        putchar ( tolower ( ch ) ) ;
    return 0 ;
}
```

(b)
```
# include <stdio.h>
int main( )
{
    int i = 2 ;
    float f = 2.5367 ;
    char str[ ] = "Life is like that" ;

    printf ( "%4d\t%3.3f\t%4s\n", i, f, str ) ;
    return 0 ;
}
```

(c)
```
# include <stdio.h>
int main( )
{
    printf ( "More often than \b\b not \rthe person who \
```

```
                wins is the one who thinks he can!\n" ) ;
    return 0 ;
}
```

(d)
```
# include <conio.h>
char p[ ] = "The sixth sick sheikh's sixth ship is sick" ;
int main( )
{
    int i = 0 ;
    while ( p[i] != '\0' )
    {
        putch ( p[i] ) ;
        i++ ;
    }
    return 0 ;
}
```

(e)
```
# include <conio.h>
int main ( int a, char *b[ ] )
{
    printf ( "%d %s\n", a, *b ) ;
    return 0 ;
}
```

[B] Point out the errors, if any, in the following programs:

(a)
```
# include <stdio.h>
int main( )
{
    int i ;
    char a[ ] = "Hello" ;
    while ( a != '\0' )
    {
        printf ( "%c", *a ) ;
        a++ ;
    }
    return 0 ;
}
```

(b)
```
# include <stdio.h>
int main( )
{
    double dval ;
    scanf ( "%f", &dval ) ;
    printf ( "Double Value = %lf\n", dval ) ;
```

```
    return 0 ;
}
```

(c)
```
# include <stdio.h>
int main( )
{
    int ival ;
    scanf ( "%d\n", &n ) ;
    printf ( "Integer Value = %d\n", ival ) ;
    return 0 ;
}
```

(d)
```
# include <stdio.h>
int main( )
{
    char  *mess[5] ;
    for ( i = 0 ; i < 5 ; i++ )
        scanf ( "%s", mess[i] ) ;
    return 0 ;
}
```

(e)
```
# include <stdio.h>
int main( )
{
    int dd, mm, yy ;
    printf ( "Enter day, month and year\n" ) ;
    scanf ( "%d%*c%d%*c%d", &dd, &mm, &yy ) ;
    printf ( "The date is: %d - %d - %d\n", dd, mm, yy ) ;
    return 0 ;
}
```

(f)
```
# include <stdio.h>
int main( )
{
    char text ;
    sprintf ( text, "%4d\t%2.2f\n%s", 12, 3.452, "Merry Go Round" ) ;
    printf ( "%s\n", text ) ;
    return 0 ;
}
```

(g)
```
# include <stdio.h>
int main( )
{
    char buffer[50] ;
    int no = 97;
```

```
    double val = 2.34174 ;
    char name[10] = "Shweta" ;

    sprintf ( buffer, "%d %lf %s", no, val, name ) ;
    printf ( "%s\n", buffer ) ;
    sscanf ( buffer, "%4d %2.2lf %s", &no, &val, name ) ;
    printf ( "%s\n", buffer ) ;
    printf ( "%d %lf %s\n", no, val, name ) ;
    return 0 ;
}
```

[C] Answer the following:

(a) To receive the string "We have got the guts, you get the glory!!" in an array **char str[100]** which of the following functions would you use?

1. scanf ("%s", str) ;
2. gets (str) ;
3. getche (str) ;
4. fgetchar (str) ;

(b) Which function would you use if a single key were to be received through the keyboard?

1. scanf( )
2. gets( )
3. getche( )
4. getchar( )

(c) If an integer is to be entered through the keyboard, which function would you use?

1. scanf( )
2. gets( )
3. getche( )
4. getchar( )

(d) If a character string is to be received through the keyboard which function would work faster?

1. scanf( )
2. gets( )

(e) What is the difference between **getchar( )**, **fgetchar( )**, **getch( )** and **getche( )**?

(f) What is the difference between the functions **putch( )** and **putc( )** functions?

(g) The format string of a **printf( )** function can contain:

1. Characters, format specifications and escape sequences
2. Character, integers and floats
3. Strings, integers and escape sequences
4. Inverted commas, percentage sign and backslash character

(h) A field-width specifier in a **printf( )** function:

1. Controls the margins of the program listing
2. Specifies the maximum value of a number
3. Controls the size of font used to print numbers
4. Specifies how many columns would be used to print the number

[D] Answer the following:

(a) Write down two functions **xgets( )** and **xputs( )** which work similar to the standard library functions **gets( )** and **puts( )**.

(b) Write down a function **getint( )**, which would receive a numeric string from the keyboard, convert it to an integer number and return the integer to the calling function. A sample usage of **getint( )** is shown below:

```
# include <stdio.h>
int main( )
{
    int a ;
    a = getint( ) ;
    printf ( "you entered %d\n", a ) ;
    return 0 ;
}
```

(c) State the purpose of the functions **printf( )**, **sprintf( )** and **fprintf( )**? Can **sprintf( )** function be used for sending output to the screen. If yes, how?

15 File Input/Output

Often it is not enough to just display the data on the screen. This is because if the data is large, only a limited amount of it can be stored in memory and only a limited amount of it can be displayed on the screen. It would be inappropriate to store this data in memory for one more reason. Memory is volatile and its contents would be lost once the program is terminated. So if we need the same data again it would have to be either entered through the keyboard again or would have to be regenerated programmatically. Obviously both these operations would be tedious. At such times it becomes necessary to store the data in a manner that can be later retrieved and displayed either in part or in whole. This medium is usually a 'file' on the disk. This chapter discusses how file I/O operations can be performed.

Data Organization

Before we start doing file input/output let us first find out how data is organized on the disk. All data stored on the disk is in binary form. How this binary data is stored on the disk varies from one OS to another. However, this does not affect the C programmer since he has to use only the library functions written for the particular OS to be able to perform input/output. It is the compiler vendor's responsibility to correctly implement these library functions by taking the help of OS. This is illustrated in Figure 15.1.

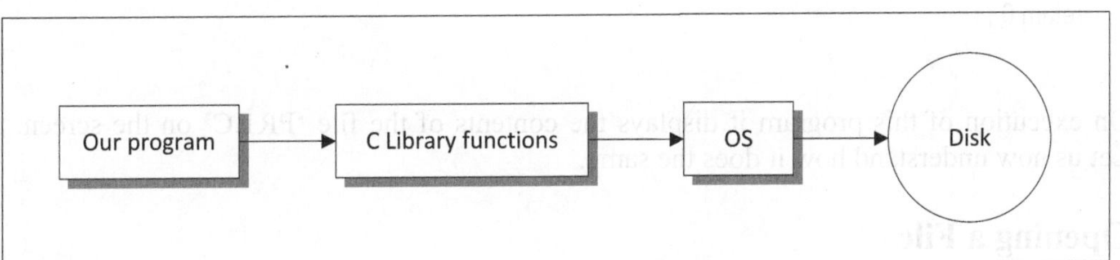

Figure 15.1

File Operations

There are different operations that can be carried out on a file. These are:

(a) Creation of a new file
(b) Opening an existing file
(c) Reading from a file
(d) Writing to a file
(e) Moving to a specific location in a file (seeking)
(f) Closing a file

Let us now write a program to read a file and display its contents on the screen. We will first list the program and show what it does, and then dissect it line by line. Here is the listing…

```
/* Display contents of a file on screen. */
# include <stdio.h>
int main( )
{
    FILE *fp ;
    char ch ;

    fp = fopen ( "PR1.C", "r" ) ;
    while ( 1 )
    {
        ch = fgetc ( fp ) ;
        if ( ch == EOF )
            break ;

        printf ( "%c", ch ) ;
    }
    printf ( "\n" ) ;
    fclose ( fp ) ;
    return 0 ;
}
```

On execution of this program it displays the contents of the file 'PR1.C' on the screen. Let us now understand how it does the same.

Opening a File

Before we can read (or write) information from (to) a file on a disk we must open the file. To open the file we have called the function **fopen( )**. It would open a file "PR1.C" in 'read' mode, which tells the C compiler that we would be reading the contents of the file. Note that "r" is a string and not a character; hence the double quotes and not single quotes. In fact **fopen( )** performs three important tasks when you open the file in "r" mode:

(a) Firstly it searches on the disk the file to be opened.
(b) Then it loads the file from the disk into a place in memory called buffer.
(c) It sets up a character pointer that points to the first character of the buffer.

Why do we need a buffer at all? Imagine how inefficient it would be to actually access the disk every time we want to read a character from it. Every time we read something from a disk, it takes some time for the disk drive to position the read/write head correctly. On a floppy disk system, the drive motor has to actually start rotating the disk from a standstill position every time the disk is accessed. If this were to be done for every character we read from the disk, it would take a long time to complete the reading operation. This is where a buffer comes in. It would be more sensible to read the contents of the file into the buffer while opening the file and then read the file character by character from the buffer rather than from the disk. This is shown in Figure 15.2.

Same argument also applies to writing information in a file. Instead of writing characters in the file on the disk one character at a time it would be more efficient to write characters in a buffer and then finally transfer the contents from the buffer to the disk.

To be able to successfully read from a file information like mode of opening, size of file, place in the file from where the next read operation would be performed, etc. has to be maintained. Since all this information is inter-related, all of it is gathered together by **fopen( )** in a structure called **FILE**. **fopen( )** returns the address of this structure, which we have collected in the structure pointer called **fp**.

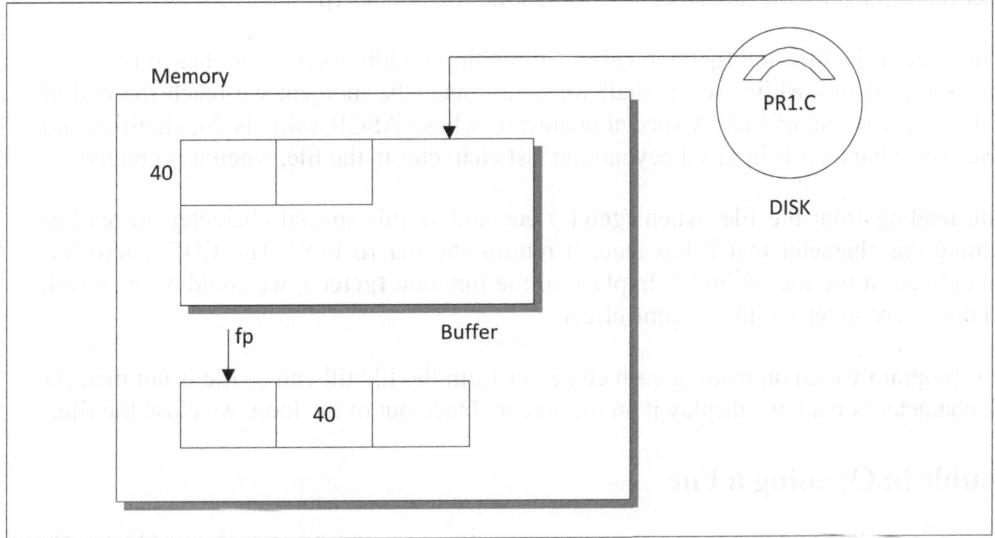

Figure 15.2

We have declared **fp** as

```
FILE *fp ;
```

The **FILE** structure has been defined in the header file "stdio.h" (standing for standard input/output header file). Therefore, it is necessary to **#include** this file.

Reading from a File

Once the file has been opened for reading using **fopen( )**, as we have seen, the file's contents are brought into buffer (partly or wholly) and a pointer is set up that points to the first character in the buffer. This pointer is one of the elements of the structure to which **fp** is pointing (refer Figure 15.2).

To read the file's contents from memory, there exists a function called **fgetc( )**. This has been used in our program as,

```
ch = fgetc ( fp ) ;
```

fgetc( ) reads the character from the current pointer position, advances the pointer position so that it now points to the next character, and returns the character that is read, which we collected in the variable **ch**. Note that once the file has been opened, we no longer refer to the file by its name, but through the file pointer **fp**.

We have used the function **fgetc( )** within an indefinite **while** loop. There has to be a way to break out of this **while**. When shall we break out... the moment we reach the end of file. But what is end of file? A special character, whose ASCII value is 26, signifies end of file. This character is inserted beyond the last character in the file, when it is created.

While reading from the file, when **fgetc( )** encounters this special character, instead of returning the character that it has read, it returns the macro EOF. The EOF macro has been defined in the file "stdio.h". In place of the function **fgetc( )**, we could have as well used the macro **getc( )** with the same effect.

In our program we go on reading each character from the file till end of file is not met. As each character is read, we display it on the screen. Once out of the loop, we close the file.

Trouble in Opening a File

There is a possibility that when we try to open a file using the function **fopen( )**, the file may not be opened. While opening the file in "r" mode, this may happen because the file being opened may not be present on the disk at all. And you obviously cannot read a file that doesn't exist. Similarly, while opening the file for writing, **fopen( )** may fail due to a number of reasons, like, disk space may be insufficient to create a new file, or the disk may be write protected or the disk is damaged and so on.

Crux of the matter is that it is important for any program that accesses disk files to check whether a file has been opened successfully before trying to read or write to the file. If the file opening fails due to any of the several reasons mentioned above, the **fopen( )** function returns a value NULL (defined in "stdio.h" as **#define NULL 0**). Here is how this can be handled in a program...

```
# include <stdio.h>
# include <stdlib.h>
int main( )
{
    FILE *fp ;
    fp = fopen ( "PR1.C", "r" ) ;
    if ( fp == NULL )
    {
        puts ( "cannot open file" ) ;
        exit ( 1 ) ;
    }
    return 0 ;
}
```

The call to the function **exit( )** terminates the execution of the program. Usually, a value 0 is passed to **exit( )** if the program termination is normal. A non-zero value indicates an abnormal termination of the program. If there are multiple exit points in the program, then the value passed to **exit( )** can be used to find out from where the execution of the program got terminated. There are different ways of examining this value in different programming environments. For example, in Turbo C++ environment, this value can be seen through the Compile | Information menu item. The prototype of **exit( )** function is declared in the header file **stdlib.h**.

Closing the File

When we have finished reading from the file, we need to close it. This is done using the function **fclose( )** through the statement,

```
fclose ( fp ) ;
```

Once we close the file, we can no longer read from it using **getc( )** unless we reopen the file. Note that to close the file, we don't use the filename but the file pointer **fp**. On closing the file, the buffer associated with the file is removed from memory.

In this program we have opened the file for reading. Suppose we open a file with an intention to write characters into it. This time too, a buffer would get associated with it.

When we attempt to write characters into this file using **fputc( )** the characters would get written to the buffer. When we close this file using **fclose( )** three operations would be performed:

(a) The characters in the buffer would be written to the file on the disk.
(b) At the end of file a character with ASCII value 26 would get written.
(c) The buffer would be eliminated from memory.

You can imagine a possibility when the buffer may become full before we close the file. In such a case the buffer's contents would be written to the disk the moment it becomes full. All this buffer management is done for us by the library functions.

Counting Characters, Tabs, Spaces, …

Having understood the first file I/O program in detail let us now try our hand at one more. Let us write a program that will read a file and count how many characters, spaces, tabs and newlines are present in it. Here is the program…

```
/* Count chars, spaces, tabs and newlines in a file */
# include <stdio.h>
int main( )
{
    FILE *fp ;
    char ch ;
    int nol = 0, not = 0, nob = 0, noc = 0 ;
    fp = fopen ( "PR1.C", "r" ) ;
    while ( 1 )
    {
        ch = fgetc ( fp ) ;
        if ( ch == EOF )
            break ;
        noc++ ;
        if ( ch == ' ' )
            nob++ ;
        if ( ch == '\n' )
            nol++ ;
        if ( ch == '\t' )
            not++ ;
    }
    fclose ( fp ) ;
    printf ( "Number of characters = %d\n", noc ) ;
    printf ( "Number of blanks = %d\n", nob ) ;
    printf ( "Number of tabs = %d\n", not ) ;
```

```
    printf ( "Number of lines = %d\n", nol ) ;
    return 0 ;
}
```

Here is a sample run...

```
Number of characters = 125
Number of blanks = 25
Number of tabs = 13
Number of lines = 22
```

The above statistics are true for a file "PR1.C", which I had on my disk. You may give any other filename and obtain different results. I believe the program is self-explanatory.

In this program too, we have opened the file for reading and then read it character by character. Let us now try a program that needs to open a file for writing.

A File-copy Program

We have already used the function **fgetc( )** which reads characters from a file. Its counterpart is a function called **fputc( )** which writes characters to a file. As a practical use of these character I/O functions, we can copy the contents of one file into another, as demonstrated in the following program. This program takes the contents of a file and copies them into another file, character by character.

```
# include <stdio.h>
# include <stdlib.h>
int main( )
{
    FILE *fs, *ft ;
    char ch ;

    fs = fopen ( "pr1.c", "r" ) ;
    if ( fs == NULL )
    {
        puts ( "Cannot open source file" ) ;
        exit ( 1 ) ;
    }
    ft = fopen ( "pr2.c", "w" ) ;
    if ( ft == NULL )
    {
        puts ( "Cannot open target file" ) ;
```

```
        fclose ( fs ) ;
        exit ( 2 ) ;
    }
    while ( 1 )
    {
        ch = fgetc ( fs ) ;

        if ( ch == EOF )
            break ;
        else
            fputc ( ch, ft ) ;
    }
    fclose ( fs ) ;
    fclose ( ft ) ;
    return 0 ;
}
```

I hope most of the stuff in the program can be easily understood, since it has already been dealt with in the earlier section. What is new is only the function **fputc( )**. Let us see how it works.

Writing to a File

The **fputc( )** function is similar to the **putch( )** function, in the sense that both output characters. However, **putch( )** function always writes to the VDU, whereas, **fputc( )** writes to the file. Which file? The file signified by **ft**. The writing process continues till all characters from the source file have been written to the target file, following which the **while** loop terminates.

Note that our sample file-copy program is capable of copying only text files. To copy files with extension .EXE or .COM, we need to open the files in binary mode, a topic that would be dealt with in sufficient detail in a later section.

File Opening Modes

In our first program on disk I/O, we have opened the file in read ("r") mode. However, "r" is but one of the several modes in which we can open a file. Following is a list of all possible modes in which a file can be opened. The tasks performed by **fopen( )**, when a file is opened in each of these modes, are also mentioned.

"r" Searches file. If the file is opened successfully **fopen( )** loads it into memory and sets up a pointer which points to the first character in it. If the file cannot be opened, **fopen( )** returns NULL.

Operations possible – reading from the file.

"w" Searches file. If the file exists, its contents are overwritten. If the file doesn't exist, a new file is created. Returns NULL, if unable to open file.

Operations possible – writing to the file.

"a" Searches file. If the file is opened successfully **fopen( )** loads it into memory and sets up a pointer that points to the last character in it. If the file doesn't exist, a new file is created. Returns NULL, if unable to open file.

Operations possible - adding new contents at the end of file.

"r+" Searches file. If is opened successfully **fopen( )** loads it into memory and sets up a pointer which points to the first character in it. Returns NULL, if unable to open the file.

Operations possible - reading existing contents, writing new contents, modifying existing contents of the file.

"w+" Searches file. If the file exists, its contents are overwritten. If the file doesn't exist, a new file is created. Returns NULL, if unable to open file.

Operations possible - writing new contents, reading them back and modifying existing contents of the file.

"a+" Searches file. If the file is opened successfully **fopen( )** loads it into memory and sets up a pointer which points to the first character in it. If the file doesn't exist, a new file is created. Returns NULL, if unable to open file.

Operations possible - reading existing contents, appending new contents to end of file. Cannot modify existing contents.

String (line) I/O in Files

For many purposes, character I/O is just what is needed. However, in some situations, the usage of functions that read or write entire strings might turn out to be more efficient.

Reading or writing strings of characters from and to files is as easy as reading and writing individual characters. Here is a program that writes strings to a file using the function **fputs( )**.

```
/* Receives strings from keyboard and writes them to file */
# include <stdio.h>
# include <stdlib.h>
# include <string.h>
int main( )
{
    FILE *fp ;
    char s[80] ;
    fp = fopen ( "POEM.TXT", "w" ) ;
    if ( fp == NULL )
    {
        puts ( "Cannot open file" ) ;
        exit ( 1 ) ;
    }
    printf ( "\nEnter a few lines of text:\n" ) ;
    while ( strlen ( gets ( s ) ) > 0 )
    {
        fputs ( s, fp ) ;
        fputs ( "\n", fp ) ;
    }
    fclose ( fp ) ;
    return 0 ;
}
```

And here is a sample run of the program...

```
Enter a few lines of text:
Shining and bright, they are forever,
so true about diamonds,
more so of memories,
especially yours !
```

Note that each string is terminated by hitting enter. To terminate the execution of the program, hit enter at the beginning of a line. This creates a string of zero length, which the program recognizes as the signal to close the file and exit.

We have set up a character array to receive the string; the **fputs( )** function then writes the contents of the array to the disk. Since **fputs( )** does not automatically add a newline character to the end of the string, we must do this explicitly to make it easier to read the string back from the file.

Here is a program that reads strings from a disk file.

```
/* Reads strings from the file and displays them on screen */
# include <stdio.h>
# include <stdlib.h>
int main( )
{
    FILE *fp ;
    char s[80] ;

    fp = fopen ( "POEM.TXT", "r" ) ;
    if ( fp == NULL )
    {
        puts ( "Cannot open file" ) ;
        exit ( 1 ) ;
    }

    while ( fgets ( s, 79, fp ) != NULL )
        printf ( "%s" , s ) ;

    printf ( "\n" ) ;
    fclose ( fp ) ;
    return 0 ;
}
```

And here is the output...

```
Shining and bright, they are forever,
so true about diamonds,
more so of memories,
especially yours !
```

The function **fgets( )** takes three arguments. The first is the address where the string is stored, and the second is the maximum length of the string. This argument prevents **fgets( )** from reading in too long a string and overflowing the array. The third argument, as usual, is the pointer to the structure **FILE**. On reading a line from the file, the string **s** would contain the line contents a '\n' followed by a '\0'. Thus the string is terminated by **fgets( )** and we do not have to terminate it specifically. When all the lines from the file have been read, we attempt to read one more line, in which case **fgets( )** returns a **NULL**.

The Awkward Newline

We had earlier written a program that counts the total number of characters present in a file. If we use that program to count the number of characters present in the above poem (stored in the file "POEM.TXT"), it would give us the character count as 101. The same file if seen in the directory, would be reported to contain 105 characters.

This discrepancy occurs because when we attempt to write a "\n" to the file using **fputs( )**, **fputs( )** converts the **\n** to **\r\n** combination. Here **\r** stands for carriage return and **\n** for linefeed. If we read the same line back using **fgets( )** the reverse conversion happens. Thus when we write the first line of the poem and a "\n" using two calls to **fputs( )**, what gets written to the file is

```
Shining and bright, they are forever,\r\n
```

When the same line is read back into the array **s[ ]** using **fgets( )**, the array contains

```
Shining and bright, they are forever,\n\0
```

Thus conversion of **\n** to **\r\n** during writing and **\r\n** conversion to **\n** during reading is a feature of the standard library functions and not that of the OS. Hence the OS counts **\r** and **\n** as separate characters. In our poem there are four lines, therefore there is a discrepancy of four characters (105 - 101).

Record I/O in Files

So far, we have dealt with reading and writing only characters and strings. What if we want to read or write numbers from/to file? Furthermore, what if we desire to read/write a combination of characters, strings and numbers? For this first we would organize this dissimilar data together in a structure and then use **fprintf( )** and **fscanf( )** library functions to read/write data from/to file. Following program illustrates the use of structures for writing records of employees.

```
/* Writes records to a file using structure */
# include <stdio.h>
# include <conio.h>
int main( )
{
    FILE *fp ;
    char another = 'Y' ;
    struct emp
    {
        char name[40] ;
        int age ;
        float bs ;
    } ;
    struct emp e ;

    fp = fopen ( "EMPLOYEE.DAT", "w" ) ;

    if ( fp == NULL )
    {
        puts ( "Cannot open file" ) ;
        exit ( 1 ) ;
    }

    while ( another == 'Y' )
    {
        printf ( "\nEnter name, age and basic salary: " ) ;
        scanf ( "%s %d %f", e.name, &e.age, &e.bs ) ;
        fprintf ( fp, "%s %d %f\n", e.name, e.age, e.bs ) ;

        printf ( "Add another record (Y/N) " ) ;
        fflush ( stdin ) ;
        another = getche( ) ;
    }

    fclose ( fp ) ;
    return 0 ;
}
```

And here is the output of the program...

```
Enter name, age and basic salary: Sunil 34 1250.50
Add another record (Y/N) Y
Enter name, age and basic salary: Sameer 21 1300.50
```

```
Add another record (Y/N) Y
Enter name, age and basic salary: Rahul 34 1400.55
Add another record (Y/N) N
```

In this program we are just reading the data into a structure variable using **scanf( )**, and then dumping it into a disk file using **fprintf( ).** The user can input as many records as he desires. The procedure ends when the user supplies 'N' for the question 'Add another record (Y/N)'.

The key to this program is the function **fprintf( )**, which writes the values in the structure variable to the file. This function is similar to **printf( )**, except that a **FILE** pointer is included as the first argument. As in **printf( )**, we can format the data in a variety of ways, by using **fprintf( ).** In fact, all the format conventions of **printf( )** function work with **fprintf( )** as well.

Perhaps you are wondering what for have we used the function **fflush( )**. The reason is to get rid of a peculiarity of **scanf( )**. After supplying data for one employee, we would hit the enter key. What **scanf( )** does is it assigns name, age and salary to appropriate variables and keeps the enter key unread in the keyboard buffer. So when it's time to supply Y or N for the question 'Another employee (Y/N)', **getch( )** will read the enter key from the buffer thinking that user has entered the enter key. To avoid this problem, we use the function **fflush( )**. It is designed to remove or 'flush out' any data remaining in the buffer. The argument to **fflush( )** must be the buffer which we want to flush out. Here we have used 'stdin', which means buffer related with standard input device—keyboard.

Let us now write a program that reads the employee records created by the above program. Here is how it can be done...

```
/* Read records from a file using structure */
# include <stdio.h>
# include <stdlib.h>
int main( )
{
    FILE *fp ;
    struct emp
    {
        char name[40] ;
        int age ;
        float bs ;
    } ;
    struct emp e ;
```

```
    fp = fopen ( "EMPLOYEE.DAT", "r" ) ;

    if ( fp == NULL )
    {
        puts ( "Cannot open file" ) ;
        exit ( 1 ) ;
    }

    while ( fscanf ( fp, "%s %d %f", e.name, &e.age, &e.bs ) != EOF )
        printf ( "%s %d %f\n", e.name, e.age, e.bs ) ;

    fclose ( fp ) ;
    return 0 ;
}
```

And here is the output of the program...

```
Sunil 34 1250.500000
Sameer 21 1300.500000
Rahul 34 1400.500000
```

Text Files and Binary Files

All the programs that we wrote in this chapter so far worked on text files. Some of them would not work correctly on binary files. A text file contains only textual information like alphabets, digits and special symbols. In actuality the ASCII codes of these characters are stored in text files. A good example of a text file is any C program, say PR1.C.

As against this, a binary file is merely a collection of bytes. This collection might be a compiled version of a C program (say PR1.EXE), or music data stored in a wave file or a picture stored in a graphic file. A very easy way to find out whether a file is a text file or a binary file is to open that file in Turbo C/C++. If on opening the file you can make out what is displayed then it is a text file, otherwise it is a binary file.

As mentioned while explaining the file-copy program, the program cannot copy binary files successfully. We can improve the same program to make it capable of copying text as well as binary files as shown below.

```
# include <stdio.h>
# include <stdlib.h>
int main( )
```

```
{
    FILE *fs, *ft ;
    int ch ;

    fs = fopen ( "pr1.exe", "rb" ) ;
    if ( fs == NULL )
    {
        puts ( "Cannot open source file" ) ;
        exit ( 1 ) ;
    }

    ft = fopen ( "newpr1.exe", "wb" ) ;

    if ( ft == NULL )
    {
        puts ( "Cannot open target file" ) ;
        fclose ( fs ) ;
        exit ( 2 ) ;
    }

    while ( 1 )
    {
        ch = fgetc ( fs ) ;

        if ( ch == EOF )
            break ;
        else
            fputc ( ch, ft ) ;
    }

    fclose ( fs ) ;
    fclose ( ft ) ;
    return 0 ;
}
```

Using this program we can comfortably copy text as well as binary files. Note that here we have opened the source and target files in "rb" and "wb" modes respectively. While opening the file in text mode we can use either "r" or "rt", but since text mode is the default mode we usually drop the 't'.

From the programming angle there are three main areas where text and binary mode files are different. These are:

(a) Handling of newlines
(b) Representation of end of file
(c) Storage of numbers

Let us explore these three differences.

Text versus Binary Mode: Newlines

We have already seen that, in text mode, a newline character is converted into the carriage return-linefeed combination before being written to the disk. Likewise, the carriage return-linefeed combination on the disk is converted back into a newline when the file is read by a C program. However, if a file is opened in binary mode, as opposed to text mode, these conversions will not take place.

Text versus Binary Mode: End of File

The second difference between text and binary modes is in the way the end-of-file is detected. In text mode, a special character, whose ASCII value is 26, is inserted after the last character in the file to mark the end of file. If this character is detected at any point in the file, the read function would return the EOF signal to the program.

As against this, there is no such special character present in the binary mode files to mark the end of file. The binary mode files keep track of the end of file from the number of characters present in the directory entry of the file.

There is a moral to be derived from the end of file marker of text mode files. If a file stores numbers in binary mode, it is important that binary mode only be used for reading the numbers back, since one of the numbers we store might well be the number 26 (hexadecimal 1A). If this number is detected while we are reading the file by opening it in text mode, reading would be terminated prematurely at that point.

Thus the two modes are not compatible. See to it that the file that has been written in text mode is read back only in text mode. Similarly, the file that has been written in binary mode must be read back only in binary mode.

Text versus Binary Mode: Storage of Numbers

The only function that is available for storing numbers in a disk file is the **fprintf( )** function. It is important to understand how numerical data is stored on the disk by **fprintf( ).** Text and characters are stored one character per byte, as we would expect. Are numbers stored as they are in memory, two bytes for an integer, four bytes for a float, and so on? No.

Numbers are stored as strings of characters. Thus, 1234, even though it occupies two bytes in memory, when transferred to the disk using **fprintf( )**, would occupy four bytes, one byte per character. Similarly, the floating-point number 1234.56 would occupy 7 bytes on disk. Thus, numbers with more digits would require more disk space.

Hence if large amount of numerical data is to be stored in a disk file, using text mode may turn out to be inefficient. The solution is to open the file in binary mode and use those functions (**fread( )** and **fwrite( )** which are discussed later) which store the numbers in binary format. It means each number would occupy same number of bytes on disk as it occupies in memory.

Record I/O Revisited

The record I/O program that we did in an earlier section has two disadvantages:

(a) The numbers (basic salary) would occupy more number of bytes, since the file has been opened in text mode. This is because when the file is opened in text mode, each number is stored as a character string.

(b) If the number of fields in the structure increase (say, by adding address, house rent allowance etc.), writing structures using **fprintf( )**, or reading them using **fscanf( ),** becomes quite clumsy.

Let us now see a more efficient way of reading/writing records (structures). This makes use of two functions **fread( )** and **fwrite( )**. We will write two programs, first one would write records to the file and the second would read these records from the file and display them on the screen.

```
/* Receives records from keyboard and writes them to a file in binary mode */
# include <stdio.h>
# include <stdlib.h>
int main( )
{
    FILE *fp ;
    char another = 'Y' ;
    struct emp
    {
        char name[40] ;
        int age ;
        float bs ;
    } ;
    struct emp e ;
```

```
    fp = fopen ( "EMP.DAT", "wb" ) ;

    if ( fp == NULL )
    {
        puts ( "Cannot open file" ) ;
        exit ( 1 ) ;
    }

    while ( another == 'Y' )
    {
        printf ( "\nEnter name, age and basic salary: " ) ;
        scanf ( "%s %d %f", e.name, &e.age, &e.bs ) ;
        fwrite ( &e, sizeof ( e ), 1, fp ) ;

        printf ( "Add another record (Y/N) " ) ;
        fflush ( stdin ) ;
        another = getche( ) ;
    }

    fclose ( fp ) ;
    return 0 ;
}
```

And here is the output...

```
Enter name, age and basic salary: Suresh 24 1250.50
Add another record (Y/N) Y
Enter name, age and basic salary: Ranjan 21 1300.60
Add another record (Y/N) Y
Enter name, age and basic salary: Harish 28 1400.70
Add another record (Y/N) N
```

Most of this program is similar to the one that we wrote earlier, which used **fprintf( )** instead of **fwrite( )**. Note, however, that the file "EMP.DAT" has now been opened in binary mode.

The information obtained from the keyboard about the employee is placed in the structure variable **e**. Then, the following statement writes the structure to the file:

```
fwrite ( &e, sizeof ( e ), 1, fp ) ;
```

Here, the first argument is the address of the structure to be written to the disk.

The second argument is the size of the structure in bytes. Instead of counting the bytes occupied by the structure ourselves, we let the program do it for us by using the **sizeof( )** operator. The **sizeof( )** operator gives the size of the variable in bytes. This keeps the program unchanged in the event of change in the elements of the structure.

The third argument is the number of such structures that we want to write at one time. In this case, we want to write only one structure at a time. Had we had an array of structures, for example, we might have wanted to write the entire array at once.

The last argument is the pointer to the file we want to write to.

Now, let us write a program to read back the records written to the disk by the previous program.

```
/* Reads records from binary file and displays them on VDU */
# include <stdio.h>
# include <stdlib.h>
int main( )
{
    FILE *fp ;
    struct emp
    {
        char name[40] ;
        int age ;
        float bs ;
    } ;
    struct emp e ;

    fp = fopen ( "EMP.DAT", "rb" ) ;

    if ( fp == NULL )
    {
        puts ( "Cannot open file" ) ;
        exit ( 1 ) ;
    }

    while ( fread ( &e, sizeof ( e ), 1, fp ) == 1 )
        printf ( "%s %d %f\n", e.name, e.age, e.bs ) ;

    fclose ( fp ) ;
    return 0 ;
}
```

Here, the **fread( )** function causes the data read from the disk to be placed in the structure variable **e**. The format of **fread( )** is same as that of **fwrite( )**. The function **fread( )** returns the number of records read. Ordinarily, this should correspond to the third argument, the number of records we asked for... 1 in this case. If we have reached the end of file, since **fread( )** cannot read anything, it returns a 0. By testing for this situation, we know when to stop reading.

As you can now appreciate, any database management application in C must make use of **fread( )** and **fwrite( )** functions, since they store numbers more efficiently, and make writing/reading of structures quite easy. Note that even if the number of elements belonging to the structure increases, the format of **fread( )** and **fwrite( )** remains same.

Database Management

So far we have learnt record I/O in bits and pieces. However, in any serious database management application, we will have to combine all that we have learnt in a proper manner to make sense. I have attempted to do this in the following menu driven program. There is a provision to Add, Modify, List and Delete records, the operations that are imperative in any database management. Following comments would help you in understanding the program easily:

- Addition of records must always take place at the end of existing records in the file, much in the same way you would add new records in a register manually.
- Listing records means displaying the existing records on the screen. Naturally, records should be listed from first record to last record.
- While modifying records, first we must ask the user which record he intends to modify. Instead of asking the record number to be modified, it would be more meaningful to ask for the name of the employee whose record is to be modified. On modifying the record, the existing record gets overwritten by the new record.
- In deleting records, except for the record to be deleted, rest of the records must first be written to a temporary file, then the original file must be deleted, and the temporary file must be renamed back to original.
- Observe carefully the way the file has been opened, first for reading & writing, and if this fails (the first time you run this program it would certainly fail, because that time the file is not existing), for writing and reading. It is imperative that the file should be opened in binary mode.
- Note that the file is being opened only once and closed only once, which is quite logical.

– **clrscr( )** function clears the contents of the screen and **gotoxy( )** places the cursor at appropriate position on the screen. The parameters passed to **gotoxy( )** are column number followed by row number.

Given below is the complete listing of the program.

```
/* A menu-driven program for elementary database management */
# include <stdio.h>
# include <stdlib.h>
# include <conio.h>
# include <string.h>
int main( )
{
    FILE *fp, *ft ;
    char another, choice ;
    struct emp
    {
        char name[40] ;
        int age ;
        float bs ;
    } ;
    struct emp e ;
    char empname[40] ;
    long int recsize ;

    fp = fopen ( "EMP.DAT", "rb+" ) ;

    if ( fp == NULL )
    {
        fp = fopen ( "EMP.DAT", "wb+" ) ;

        if ( fp == NULL )
        {
            puts ( "Cannot open file" ) ;
            exit ( 1 ) ;
        }
    }

    recsize = sizeof ( e ) ;

    while ( 1 )
    {
        clrscr( ) ;
```

```
gotoxy ( 30, 10 ) ;
printf ( "1. Add Records" ) ;
gotoxy ( 30, 12 ) ;
printf ( "2. List Records" ) ;
gotoxy ( 30, 14 ) ;
printf ( "3. Modify Records" ) ;
gotoxy ( 30, 16 ) ;
printf ( "4. Delete Records" ) ;
gotoxy ( 30, 18 ) ;
printf ( "0. Exit" ) ;
gotoxy ( 30, 20 ) ;
printf ( "Your choice" ) ;

fflush ( stdin ) ;
choice = getche( ) ;
switch ( choice )
{
    case '1' :

        fseek ( fp, 0 , SEEK_END ) ;
        another = 'Y' ;

        while ( another == 'Y' )
        {
            printf ( "\nEnter name, age and basic salary " ) ;
            scanf ( "%s %d %f", e.name, &e.age, &e.bs ) ;
            fwrite ( &e, recsize, 1, fp ) ;
            printf ( "\nAdd another Record (Y/N) " ) ;
            fflush ( stdin ) ;
            another = getche( ) ;
        }

        break ;

    case '2' :

        rewind ( fp ) ;

        while ( fread ( &e, recsize, 1, fp ) == 1 )
            printf ( "\n%s %d %f", e.name, e.age, e.bs ) ;

        break ;
```

```
case '3' :

    another = 'Y' ;
    while ( another == 'Y' )
    {
        printf ( "\nEnter name of employee to modify " ) ;
        scanf ( "%s", empname ) ;

        rewind ( fp ) ;
        while ( fread ( &e, recsize, 1, fp ) == 1 )
        {
            if ( strcmp ( e.name, empname ) == 0 )
            {
                printf ( "\nEnter new name, age & bs " ) ;
                scanf ( "%s %d %f", e.name, &e.age,
                        &e.bs ) ;
                fseek ( fp, - recsize, SEEK_CUR ) ;
                fwrite ( &e, recsize, 1, fp ) ;
                break ;
            }
        }

        printf ( "\nModify another Record (Y/N) " ) ;
        fflush ( stdin ) ;
        another = getche( ) ;
    }

    break ;

case '4' :

    another = 'Y' ;
    while ( another == 'Y' )
    {
        printf ( "\nEnter name of employee to delete " ) ;
        scanf ( "%s", empname ) ;

        ft = fopen ( "TEMP.DAT", "wb" ) ;

        rewind ( fp ) ;
        while ( fread ( &e, recsize, 1, fp ) == 1 )
        {
```

```
                    if ( strcmp ( e.name, empname ) != 0 )
                        fwrite ( &e, recsize, 1, ft ) ;
                }

                fclose ( fp ) ;
                fclose ( ft ) ;
                remove ( "EMP.DAT" ) ;
                rename ( "TEMP.DAT", "EMP.DAT" ) ;

                fp = fopen ( "EMP.DAT", "rb+" ) ;

                printf ( "Delete another Record (Y/N) " ) ;
                fflush ( stdin ) ;
                another = getche( ) ;
            }
            break ;

        case '0' :
            fclose ( fp ) ;
            exit ( 0 ) ;
        }
    }
    return 0 ;
}
```

To understand how this program works, you need to be familiar with the concept of pointers. A pointer is initiated whenever we open a file. On opening a file, a pointer is set up which points to the first record in the file. To be precise this pointer is present in the structure to which the file pointer returned by **fopen( )** points to. On using the functions **fread( )** or **fwrite( )**, the pointer moves to the beginning of the next record. On closing a file the pointer is deactivated. Note that the pointer movement is of utmost importance since **fread( )** always reads that record where the pointer is currently placed. Similarly, **fwrite( )** always writes the record where the pointer is currently placed.

The **rewind( )** function places the pointer to the beginning of the file, irrespective of where it is present right now.

The **fseek( )** function lets us move the pointer from one record to another. In the program above, to move the pointer to the previous record from its current position, we used the function,

```
fseek ( fp, -recsize, SEEK_CUR ) ;
```

Here, **-recsize** moves the pointer back by **recsize** bytes from the current position. **SEEK_CUR** is a macro defined in "stdio.h".

Similarly, the following **fseek( )** would place the pointer beyond the last record in the file.

```
fseek ( fp, 0, SEEK_END ) ;
```

In fact, **-recsize** or **0** are just the offsets that tell the compiler by how many bytes should the pointer be moved from a particular position. The third argument could be **SEEK_END**, **SEEK_CUR** or **SEEK_SET**. All these act as a reference from which the pointer should be offset. **SEEK_END** means move the pointer from the end of the file, **SEEK_CUR** means move the pointer with reference to its current position and **SEEK_SET** means move the pointer with reference to the beginning of the file.

If we wish to know where the pointer is positioned right now, we can use the function **ftell( )**. It returns this position as a **long int** which is an offset from the beginning of the file. The value returned by **ftell( )** can be used in subsequent calls to **fseek( )**. A sample call to **ftell( )** is shown below:

```
position = ftell ( fp ) ;
```

where **position** is a **long int**.

Low Level Disk I/O

In low level disk I/O, data cannot be written as individual characters, or as strings or as formatted data. There is only one way data can be written or read in low level disk I/O functions—as a buffer full of bytes.

Writing a buffer full of data resembles the **fwrite( )** function. However, unlike **fwrite( )**, the programmer must set up the buffer for the data, place the appropriate values in it before writing, and take them out after writing. Thus, the buffer in the low level I/O functions is very much a part of the program, rather than being invisible as in high level disk I/O functions.

Low level disk I/O functions offer following advantages:

(a) Since these functions parallel the methods that the OS uses to write to the disk, they are more efficient than the high level disk I/O functions.

(b) Since there are fewer layers of routines to go through, low level I/O functions operate faster than their high level counterparts.

Let us now write a program that uses low level disk input/output functions.

A Low Level File-copy Program

Earlier we had written a program to copy the contents of one file to another. In that program we had read the file character by character using **fgetc( )**. Each character that was read was written into the target file using **fputc( )**. Instead of performing the I/O on a character by character basis we can read a chunk of bytes from the source file and then write this chunk into the target file. While doing so the chunk would be read into the buffer and would be written to the file from the buffer. While doing so we would manage the buffer ourselves, rather than relying on the library functions to do so. This is what is low-level about this program. Here is a program which shows how this can be done.

```
/* File-copy program which copies text, .com and .exe files */
# include <fcntl.h>
# include <types.h>  /* if present in sys directory use
                        "c:tc\\include\\sys\\types.h" */
# include <stat.h>  /* if present in sys directory use
                        "c:\\tc\\include\\sys\\stat.h" */
# include <stdlib.h>
# include <stdio.h>
int main ( int argc, char *argv[ ] )
{
    char buffer[ 512 ], source [ 128 ], target [ 128 ] ;
    int inhandle, outhandle, bytes ;

    printf ( "\nEnter source file name" ) ;
    gets ( source ) ;

    inhandle = open ( source, O_RDONLY | O_BINARY ) ;
    if ( inhandle == -1 )
    {
        puts ( "Cannot open file" ) ;
        exit ( 1 ) ;
    }

    printf ( "\nEnter target file name" ) ;
    gets ( target ) ;

    outhandle = open ( target, O_CREAT | O_BINARY | O_WRONLY,
        S_IWRITE ) ;
    if ( outhandle == -1 )
    {
```

```
        puts ( "Cannot open file" ) ;
        close ( inhandle ) ;
        exit ( 2 ) ;
    }

    while ( 1 )
    {
        bytes = read ( inhandle, buffer, 512 ) ;
        if ( bytes > 0 )
            write ( outhandle, buffer, bytes ) ;
        else
            break ;
    }

    close ( inhandle ) ;
    close ( outhandle ) ;
    return 0 ;
}
```

Declaring the Buffer

The first difference that you will notice in this program is that we declare a character buffer,

```
char buffer[512] ;
```

This is the buffer in which the data read from the disk will be placed. The size of this buffer is important for efficient operation. Depending on the operating system, buffers of certain sizes are handled more efficiently than others.

Opening a File

We have opened two files in our program, one is the source file from which we read the information, and the other is the target file into which we write the information read from the source file.

As in high level disk I/O, the file must be opened before we can access it. This is done using the statement,

```
inhandle = open ( source, O_RDONLY | O_BINARY ) ;
```

We open the file for the same reason as we did earlier—to establish communication with operating system about the file. As usual, we have to supply to **open**( ), the filename and the mode in which we want to open the file. The possible file opening modes are given below:

O_APPEND	- Opens a file for appending
O_CREAT	- Creates a new file for writing (has no effect if file already exists)
O_RDONLY	- Opens a new file for reading only
O_RDWR	- Creates a file for both reading and writing
O_WRONLY	- Creates a file for writing only
O_BINARY	- Opens a file in binary mode
O_TEXT	- Opens a file in text mode

These 'O-flags' are defined in the file "fcntl.h". So this file must be included in the program while using low level disk I/O. Note that the file "stdio.h" is not necessary for low level disk I/O. When two or more O-flags are used together, they are combined using the bitwise OR operator (|). Chapter 14 discusses bitwise operators in detail.

The other statement used in our program to open the file is,

```
outhandle = open ( target, O_CREAT | O_BINARY | O_WRONLY,
        S_IWRITE ) ;
```

Note that since the target file doesn't exist when it is being opened, we have used the O_CREAT flag, and since we want to write to the file and not read from it, therefore we have used O_WRONLY. And finally, since we want to open the file in binary mode we have used O_BINARY.

Whenever O_CREAT flag is used, another argument must be added to **open**( ) function to indicate the read/write status of the file to be created. This argument is called 'permission argument'. Permission arguments could be any of the following:

S_IWRITE	- Writing to the file permitted
S_IREAD	- Reading from the file permitted

To use these permissions, both the files "types.h" and "stat.h" must be **#include**d in the program alongwith "fcntl.h".

File Handles

Instead of returning a FILE pointer as **fopen( )** did, in low level disk I/O, **open( )** returns an integer value called 'file handle'. This is a number assigned to a particular file, which is used thereafter to refer to the file. If **open( )** returns a value of -1, it means that the file couldn't be successfully opened.

Interaction between Buffer and File

The following statement reads the file or as much of it as will fit into the buffer:

```
bytes = read ( inhandle, buffer, 512 ) ;
```

The **read( )** function takes three arguments. The first argument is the file handle, the second is the address of the buffer and the third is the maximum number of bytes we want to read.

The **read( )** function returns the number of bytes actually read. This is an important number, since it may very well be less than the buffer size (512 bytes), and we will need to know just how full the buffer is before we can do anything with its contents. In our program we have assigned this number to the variable **bytes**.

For copying the file, we must use both the **read( )** and the **write( )** functions in a **while** loop. The **read( )** function returns the number of bytes actually read. This is assigned to the variable **bytes**. This value will be equal to the buffer size (512 bytes) until the end of file, when the buffer may only be partially full. The variable **bytes** therefore is used to tell **write( )**, as to how many bytes to write from the buffer to the target file.

Note that the buffers are created in the stack, which is of limited size. Hence, when large buffers are used, they must be made global variables, otherwise stack overflow would occur.

I/O Under Windows

As said earlier, I/O in C is carried out using functions present in the library that comes with the C compiler targeted for a specific OS. Windows permits several applications to use the same screen simultaneously. Hence there is a possibility that what is written by one application to the console may get overwritten by the output sent by another application to the console. To avoid such situations, Windows has completely abandoned console I/O functions. It uses a separate mechanism to send output to a window representing an application. The details of this mechanism are discussed in Chapter 17.

Though under Windows, console I/O functions are not used, still functions like **fprintf( )**, **fscanf( )**, **fread( )**, **fwrite( )**, **sprintf( )**, **sscanf( )** work exactly same under Windows as well.

Summary

(a) File I/O can be performed on a character by character basis, a line by line basis, a record by record basis or a chunk by chunk basis.
(b) Different operations that can be performed on a file are—creation of a new file, opening an existing file, reading from a file, writing to a file, moving to a specific location in a file (seeking) and closing a file.
(c) File I/O is done using a buffer to improve the efficiency.
(d) A file can be a text file or a binary file depending upon its contents.
(e) Library functions convert **\n** to **\r\n** or vice versa while writing/reading to/from a file.
(f) Many library functions convert a number to a numeric string before writing it to a file, thereby using more space on disk. This can be avoided using functions **fread( )** and **fwrite( )**.
(g) In low level file I/O we can do the buffer management ourselves.

Exercise

[A] Point out the errors, if any, in the following programs:

(a)
```
# include <stdio.h>
void openfile ( char *, FILE ** ) ;
int main( )
{
    FILE *fp ;
    openfile ( "Myfile.txt", fp ) ;
    if ( fp == NULL )
        printf ( "Unable to open file...\n" ) ;
    return 0 ;
}
void openfile ( char *fn, FILE **f )
{
    *f = fopen ( fn, "r" ) ;
}
```

(b)
```
# include <stdio.h>
# include <stdlib.h>
int main( )
{
    FILE *fp ;
```

```
        char  c ;
        fp = fopen ( "TRY.C", "r") ;
        if ( fp == null )
        {
            puts ( "Cannot open file\n" ) ;
            exit( ) ;
        }
        while ( ( c = getc ( fp ) ) != EOF )
            putch ( c ) ;
        fclose ( fp ) ;
        return 0 ;
    }
```

(c)
```
    # include <stdio.h>
    int main( )
    {
        char fname[ ] = "c:\\students.dat" ;
        FILE *fp ;
        fp = fopen ( fname, "tr" ) ;
        if ( fp == NULL )
            printf ( "Unable to open file...\n" ) ;
        return 0 ;
    }
```

(d)
```
    # include <stdio.h>
    int main( )
    {
        FILE  *fp ;
        char  str[80] ;
        fp = fopen ( "TRY.C", "r" ) ;
        while ( fgets ( str, 80, fp ) != EOF )
            fputs ( str ) ;
        fclose ( fp ) ;
        return 0 ;
    }
```

(e)
```
    # include <stdio.h>
    int main( )
    {
        unsigned char ;
        FILE *fp ;

        fp = fopen ( "trial", 'r' ) ;
        while ( ( ch = getc ( fp ) ) != EOF )
            printf ( "%c", ch ) ;
```

```
    fclose ( *fp ) ;
    return 0 ;
}
```

(f)
```
# include <stdio.h>
int main( )
{
    FILE *fp ;
    char name[25] ;
    int age ;

    fp = fopen ( "YOURS", "r" ) ;
    while ( fscanf ( fp, "%s %d", name, &age ) != NULL )
    fclose ( fp ) ;
    return 0 ;
}
```

(g)
```
# include <stdio.h>
int main( )
{
    FILE *fp ;
    char names[20] ;
    int i ;
    fp = fopen ( "students.dat", "wb" ) ;
    for ( i = 0 ; i <= 10 ; i++ )
    {
        puts ( "\nEnter name " ) ;
        gets ( name ) ;
        fwrite ( name, size of ( name ), 1, fp ) ;
    }
    close ( fp ) ;
    return 0 ;
}
```

(h)
```
# include <stdio.h>
int main( )
{
    FILE *fp ;
    char name[20] = "Ajay" ;
    int i ;
    fp = fopen ( "students.dat", "r" ) ;
    for ( i = 0 ; i <= 10 ; i++ )
        fwrite ( name, sizeof ( name ), 1, fp ) ;
```

```
    close ( fp ) ;
    return 0 ;
}
```

(i)
```
# include <fcntl.h>
# include <stdio.h>
int main( )
{
    int fp ;
    fp = open ( "pr22.c" , "r" ) ;
    if ( fp == -1 )
        puts ( "cannot open file\n" ) ;
    else
        close ( fp ) ;
    return 0 ;
}
```

(j)
```
# include <stdio.h>
int main( )
{
    int fp ;
    fp = fopen ( "students.dat", READ | BINARY ) ;
    if ( fp == -1 )
        puts ( "cannot open file\n" ) ;
    else
        close ( fp ) ;
    return 0 ;
}
```

[B] Answer the following:

(a) The FILE structure is defined in which of the following files:

1. stdlib.h
2. stdio.c
3. io.h
4. stdio.h

(b) If a file contains the line "I am a boy\r\n" then on reading this line into the array **str[ ]** using **fgets( )** what would **str[ ]** contain?

1. I am a boy\r\n\0
2. I am a boy\r\0
3. I am a boy\n\0
4. I am a boy

(c) State True or False:

1. The disadvantage of High Level Disk I/O functions is that the programmer has to manage the buffers.
2. If a file is opened for reading it is necessary that the file must exist.
3. If a file opened for writing already exists its contents would be overwritten.
4. For opening a file in append mode it is necessary that the file should exist.

(d) On opening a file for reading which of the following activities are performed:

1. The disk is searched for existence of the file.
2. The file is brought into memory.
3. A pointer is set up which points to the first character in the file.
4. All the above.

(e) Is it necessary that a file created in text mode must always be opened in text mode for subsequent operations?

(f) While using the statement,

```
fp = fopen ( "myfile.c", "r" ) ;
```

what happens if,

- 'myfile.c' does not exist on the disk
- 'myfile.c' exists on the disk

(g) What is the purpose of the library function **fflush( )**?

(h) While using the statement,

```
fp = fopen ( "myfile.c", "wb" ) ;
```

what happens if,

- 'myfile.c' does not exist on the disk.
- 'myfile.c' exists on the disk

(i) A floating-point array contains percentage marks obtained by students in an examination. To store these marks in a file 'marks.dat', in which mode would you open the file and why?

(j) What will be the output of the following program?

```
#include <stdio.h>
int main( )
{
    FILE *fp ;
    char ch, str[7] ;
```

```
    /* FLINTSTONE.C exists and contains
    "Earth's heart's smiling, Heaven's heart's singing" */

    fp = fopen ( "FLINTSTONE.C", "r" ) ;
    if ( fp == 0 )
    {
        printf ( "Cannot open file\n" ) ;
        exit( ) ;
    }
    fseek ( fp, 9L, SEEK_CUR ) ;
    fgets ( str, 5, fp ) ;
    puts ( str ) ;
    return 0 ;
}
```

(k) The following program is to read the file GOODDAY.C in the text mode and print its contents on the screen. There are several errors in it. Point out these errors.

```
#include <stdlib.h>
int main( )
{
    int *fp ;
    char ch ;
    fp = fopen ( GOODDAY.C, "W" ) ;
    if ( fp == EOF )
    {
        printf ( "Cannot open file\n" ) ;
        exit( ) ;
    }
    while ( ch = getc ( fp ) != NULL )
    puts ( ch ) ;
    close ( fp ) ;
    return 0 ;
}
```

(l) Mention the three tasks performed by the following **fopen( )** statement:

```
FILE *fpt ;
fpt = fopen ( "LIB.DBT", "r" ) ;
```

(m) What is the difference between high level file I/O functions and low level file I/O functions?

[C] Attempt the following:

(a) Write a program to read a file and display its contents along with line numbers before each line.

(b) Write a program to find the size of a text file without traversing it character by character.

(c) Write a program to append the contents of one file at the end of another.

(d) Suppose a file contains student's records with each record containing name and age of a student. Write a program to read these records and display them in sorted order by name.

(e) Write a program to copy one file to another. While doing so replace all lowercase characters to their equivalent uppercase characters.

(f) Write a program that merges lines alternately from two files and writes the results to new file. If one file has less number of lines than the other, the remaining lines from the larger file should be simply copied into the target file.

(g) Write a program to display the contents of a text file on the screen. Make following provisions:

Display the contents inside a box drawn with opposite corner co-ordinates being (0, 1) and (79, 23). Display the name of the file whose contents are being displayed, and the page numbers in the zeroth row. The moment one screenful of file has been displayed, flash a message 'Press any key...' in 24th row. When a key is hit, the next page's contents should be displayed, and so on till the end of file.

(h) Write a program to encrypt/decrypt a file using:

(1) An offset cipher: In an offset cipher each character from the source file is offset with a fixed value and then written to the target file.

For example, if character read from the source file is 'A', then convert this into a new character by offsetting 'A' by a fixed value, say 128, and then writing the new character to the target file.

(2) A substitution cipher: In this each character read from the source file is substituted by a corresponding predetermined character and this character is written to the target file.

For example, if character 'A' is read from the source file, and if we have decided that every 'A' is to be substituted by '!', then a '!' would be written to the target file in place of every 'A'. Similarly, every 'B' would be substituted by '5' and so on.

(i) In the file 'CUSTOMER.DAT' there are 100 records with the following structure:

```
struct customer
{
    int accno ;
    char name[30] ;
    float balance ;
} ;
```

In another file 'TRANSACTIONS.DAT' there are several records with the following structure:

```
struct trans
{
    int accno ;
    char trans_type ;
    float amount ;
} ;
```

The element **trans_type** contains D/W indicating deposit or withdrawal of amount. Write a program to update 'CUSTOMER.DAT' file, i.e. if the **trans_type** is 'D' then update the **balance** of 'CUSTOMER.DAT' by adding **amount** to balance for the corresponding **accno**. Similarly, if **trans_type** is 'W' then subtract the **amount** from **balance.** However, while subtracting the amount make sure that the amount should not get overdrawn, i.e. at least 100 Rs. Should remain in the account.

(j) There are 100 records present in a file with the following structure:

```
struct date
{
    int d, m, y ;
} ;

struct employee
{
    int empcode[6] ;
    char empname[20] ;
    struct date join_date ;
    float salary ;
} ;
```

Write a program to read these records, arrange them in ascending order by **join_date** and write them in to a target file.

(k) A hospital keeps a file of blood donors in which each record has the format:
Name: 20 Columns
Address: 40 Columns
Age: 2 Columns
Blood Type: 1 Column (Type 1, 2, 3 or 4)

Write a program to read the file and print a list of all blood donors whose age is below 25 and blood is type 2.

(l) Given a list of names of students in a class, write a program to store the names in a file on disk. Make a provision to display the **n**th name in the list (**n** is data to be read) and to display all names starting with S.

(m) Assume that a Master file contains two fields, Roll no. and name of the student. At the end of the year, a set of students join the class and another set leaves. A Transaction file contains the roll numbers and an appropriate code to add or delete a student.

Write a program to create another file that contains the updated list of names and roll numbers. Assume that the Master file and the Transaction file are arranged in ascending order by roll numbers. The updated file should also be in ascending order by roll numbers.

(n) In a small firm employee numbers are given in serial numerical order, that is 1, 2, 3, etc.

- Create a file of employee data with following information: employee number, name, sex, gross salary.
- If more employees join, append their data to the file.
- If an employee with serial number 25 (say) leaves, delete the record by making gross salary 0.
- If some employee's gross salary increases, retrieve the record and update the salary.

Write a program to implement the above operations.

(o) Given a text file, write a program to create another text file deleting the words "a", "the", "an" and replacing each one of them with a blank space.

(p) You are given a data file EMPLOYEE.DAT with the following record structure:

```
struct employee {
                    int empno ;
                    char name[30] ;
```

```
        int basic, grade ;
    } ;
```

Every employee has a unique **empno** and there are supposed to be no gaps between employee numbers. Records are entered into the data file in ascending order of employee number. It is intended to check whether there are missing employee numbers. Write a program to read the data file records sequentially and display the list of missing employee numbers.

(q) Write a program to carry out the following:

- To read a text file "TRIAL.TXT" consisting of a maximum of 50 lines of text, each line with a maximum of 80 characters.
- Count and display the number of words contained in the file.
- Display the total number of four letter words in the text file.

Assume that the end of a word may be a space, comma or a full-stop followed by one or more spaces or a newline character.

(r) Write a program to read a list of words, sort the words in alphabetical order and display them one word per line. Also give the total number of words in the list. Output format should be:

Total Number of words in the list is _______
Alphabetical listing of words is:

Assume the end of the list is indicated by **ZZZZZZ** and there are maximum in 25 words in the Text file.

(s) Write a program to carry out the following:

(a) Read a text file 'INPUT.TXT'
(b) Print each word in reverse order

Example:

```
Input: INDIA IS MY COUNTRY
Output: AIDNI SI YM YRTNUOC
```

Assume that each word length is maximum of 10 characters and each word is separated by newline/blank characters.

(t) Write a C program to read a large text file 'NOTES.TXT' and print it on the printer in cut-sheets, introducing page breaks at the end of every 50 lines and a pause message on the screen at the end of every page for the user to change the paper.

(u) Write a program to find the size of a C source file in bytes. You are not allowed to read the file character by character, or line by line or record by record.

(v) Write a function to encrypt a file by changing only those characters specified in the array **str1** to the characters specified in **str2** while the other characters should remain the same. Write another function that should decrypt the encrypted file back to its original form.

```
char str1[ ] = { (a&j74%cbhfkdlsuir#0) } ;
char str2[ ] = { +A7J&$5*;"@!S~IR3)0 } ;
```

(w) There are 10 student records present in a file with the following structure:

```
struct student
{
    char name[12] ;
    int rollno, maxmarks ;
    float percentage ;
    char division[6] ;
}
```

Write a program to read these records, arrange them in ascending order by roll numbers and write them in a target file.

(x) Write a program which prints out only those lines from a file which exceed 80 characters. Also print out the line numbers of these lines.

(y) Write a program to check if there are any nested comments in a C program file.

[D] What will be the output of the following programs:

(a)
```
# include <stdio.h>
int main( )
{
    FILE *fp ;
    char ch ;
    /* HELLO.C exists and contains one line "Hello....Hi" */
    fp = fopen ( "HELLO.C", "r" ) ;
    if ( fp == NULL )
    {
        printf ( "Cannot open file\n" ) ;
        exit( ) ;
    }
```

```
    while ( ( ch = getc ( fp ) ) != NULL )
        putch ( ch ) ;
    fclose ( fp ) ;
    return 0 ;
}
```

(b)
```
# include <stdio.h>
int main( )
{
    FILE *fp ;
    char ch ;
    long count = 0 ;
    fp = fopen ( "ABC.C", "R" ) ;
    if ( fp == NULL )
    {
        printf ( "Cannot open file\n" ) ;
        exit( ) ;
    }
    while ( ( ch = getc ( fp ) ) != EOF )
        count++ ;
    printf ( "Size of file is %ld\n", count ) ;
    return 0 ;
}
```

16 More Issues In Input/Output

- Using *argc* and *argv*
- Detecting Errors in Reading/Writing
- Standard I/O Devices
- I/O Redirection
    - Redirecting the Output
    - Redirecting the Input
    - Both Ways at Once
- Summary
- Exercise

In Chapters 11 and 12 we saw how Console I/O and File I/O are done in C. There are still some more issues related with input/output that remain to be understood. These issues help in making the I/O operations more elegant.

Using *argc* and *argv*

To execute the file-copy programs that we saw in Chapter 12, we are required to first type the program, compile it, and then execute it. This program can be improved in two ways:

(a) There should be no need to compile the program every time to use the file-copy utility. It means the program must be executable at command prompt (A> or C> if you are using MS-DOS, Start | Run dialog if you are using Windows and $ prompt if you are using Unix).

(b) Instead of the program prompting us to enter the source and target filenames, we must be able to supply them at command prompt, in the form:

```
filecopy PR1.C PR2.C
```

where, PR1.C is the source filename and PR2.C is the target filename.

The first improvement is simple. In MS-DOS, the executable file (the one which can be executed at command prompt and has an extension .EXE) can be created in Turbo C/C++ by using the key F9 to compile the program. In VC++ compiler under Windows same can be done by using F7 to compile the program. Under Unix this is not required since in Unix, every time we compile a program, we always get an executable file.

The second improvement is possible by passing the source filename and target filename to the function **main( )**. This is illustrated below:

```
# include <stdio.h>
# include <stdlib.h>
int main ( int argc, char *argv[ ] )
{
    FILE *fs, *ft ;
    char ch ;

    if ( argc != 3 )
    {
        puts ( "Improper number of arguments\n" ) ;
        exit( ) ;
    }
```

```
    fs = fopen ( argv[1], "r" ) ;
    if ( fs == NULL )
    {
        puts ( "Cannot open source file\n" ) ;
        exit( ) ;
    }

    ft = fopen ( argv[2], "w" ) ;
    if ( ft == NULL )
    {
        puts ( "Cannot open target file\n" ) ;
        fclose ( fs ) ;
        exit( ) ;
    }

    while ( 1 )
    {
        ch = fgetc ( fs ) ;

        if ( ch == EOF )
            break ;
        else
            fputc ( ch, ft ) ;
    }

    fclose ( fs ) ;
    fclose ( ft ) ;
    return 0 ;
}
```

The arguments that we pass on to **main( )** at the command prompt are called command line arguments. The function **main( )** can have two arguments, traditionally named as **argc** and **argv**. Out of these, **argv** is an array of pointers to strings and **argc** is an **int** whose value is equal to the number of strings to which **argv** points. When the program is executed, the strings on the command line are passed to **main( )**. More precisely, the strings at the command line are stored in memory and address of the first string is stored in **argv[0]**, address of the second string is stored in **argv[1]** and so on. The argument **argc** is set to the number of strings given on the command line. For example, in our sample program, if at the command prompt we give,

```
filecopy PR1.C PR2.C
```

then,

argc would contain 3
argv[0] would contain base address of the string "filecopy"
argv[1] would contain base address of the string "PR1.C"
argv[2] would contain base address of the string "PR2.C"

Whenever we pass arguments to **main( )**, it is a good habit to check whether the correct number of arguments have been passed on to **main( )** or not. In our program this has been done through,

```
if ( argc != 3 )
{
    puts ( "Improper number of arguments\n" ) ;
    exit( ) ;
}
```

Rest of the program is same as the earlier file-copy program. This program is better than the earlier file-copy program on two counts:

(a) There is no need to recompile the program every time we want to use this utility. It can be executed at command prompt.
(b) We are able to pass source file name and target file name to **main( )**, and utilize them in **main( )**.

One final comment... the **while** loop that we have used in our program can be written in a more compact form, as shown below:

```
while ( ( ch = fgetc ( fs ) ) != EOF )
    fputc ( ch, ft ) ;
```

This avoids the usage of an indefinite loop and a **break** statement to come out of this loop. Here, first **fgetc (fs)** gets the character from the file, assigns it to the variable **ch**, and then **ch** is compared against **EOF**. Remember that it is necessary to put the expression

```
ch = fgetc ( fs )
```

within a pair of parentheses, so that first the character read is assigned to variable **ch** and then it is compared with **EOF**.

There is one more way of writing the **while** loop. It is shown below:

```
while ( !feof ( fs ) )
```

```
{
    ch = fgetc ( fs ) ;
    fputc ( ch, ft ) ;
}
```

Here, **feof( )** is a macro which returns a 0 if end of file is not reached. Hence we use the **!** operator to negate this 0 to the truth value. When the end of file is reached, **feof( )** returns a non-zero value, **!** makes it 0 and since now the condition evaluates to false, the **while** loop gets terminated.

Note that in each one of them, the following three methods for opening a file are same, since in each one of them, essentially a base address of the string (pointer to a string) is being passed to **fopen( )**.

```
fs = fopen ( "PR1.C" , "r" ) ;
fs = fopen ( filename, "r" ) ;
fs = fopen ( argv[1] , "r" ) ;
```

Detecting Errors in Reading/Writing

Not at all times when we perform a read or write operation on a file, are we successful in doing so. Naturally there must be a provision to test whether our attempt to read/write was successful or not.

The standard library function **ferror( )** reports any error that might have occurred during a read/write operation on a file. It returns a zero if the read/write is successful and a non-zero value in case of a failure. The following program illustrates the usage of **ferror( )**.

```
# include <stdio.h>
int main( )
{
    FILE *fp ;
    char ch ;

    fp = fopen ( "TRIAL", "w" ) ;

    while ( !feof ( fp ) )
    {
        ch = fgetc ( fp ) ;
        if ( ferror( ) )
        {
            printf ( "Error in reading file\n" ) ;
```

```
            break ;
        }
        else
            printf ( "%c", ch ) ;
    }

    fclose ( fp ) ;
    return 0 ;
}
```

In this program, the **fgetc( )** function would obviously fail first time around since the file has been opened for writing, whereas **fgetc( )** is attempting to read from the file. The moment the error occurs, **ferror( )** returns a non-zero value and the **if** block gets executed. Instead of printing the error message using **printf( )**, we can use the standard library function **perror( )** which prints the error message specified by the compiler. Thus in the above program the **perror( )** function can be used as shown below.

```
if ( ferror( ) )
{
    perror ( "TRIAL" ) ;
    break ;
}
```

Note that when the error occurs, the error message that is displayed is:

```
TRIAL: Permission denied
```

This means we can precede the system error message with any message of our choice. In our program, we have just displayed the filename in place of the error message.

Standard I/O Devices

To perform reading or writing operations on a file, we need to use the function **fopen( )**, which sets up a file pointer to refer to this file. Most OSs also predefine pointers for three standard files. To access these pointers, we need not use **fopen( )**. These standard file pointers are shown in Figure 16.1

Standard File pointer	Description
Stdin	standard input device (Keyboard)
Stdout	standard output device (VDU)
Stderr	standard error device (VDU)

Figure 16.1

Thus the statement **ch = fgetc (stdin)** would read a character from the keyboard rather than from a file. We can use this statement without any need to use **fopen( )** or **fclose( )** function calls.

Note that under MS-DOS two more standard file pointers are available—**stdprn** and **stdaux**. They stand for standard printing device and standard auxiliary device (serial port). The following program shows how to use the standard file pointers. It reads a file from the disk and prints it on the printer.

```
/* Prints file contents on printer */
# include <stdio.h>
# include <stdlib.h>
int main( )
{
    FILE *fp ;
    char ch ;

    fp = fopen ( "poem.txt", "r" ) ;

    if ( fp == NULL )
    {
        printf ( "Cannot open file\n" ) ;
        exit( ) ;
    }

    while ( ( ch = fgetc ( fp ) ) != EOF )
        fputc ( ch, stdprn ) ;

    fclose ( fp ) ;
    return 0 ;
}
```

The statement **fputc (ch, stdprn)** writes a character read from the file to the printer. Note that although we opened the file on the disk, we didn't open **stdprn**, the printer. Standard files and their use in redirection have been dealt with in more details in the next section.

Note that these standard file pointers have been defined in the file "stdio.h". Therefore, it is necessary to include this file in the program that uses these standard file pointers.

I/O Redirection

Most operating systems incorporate a powerful feature that allows a program to read and write files, even when such a capability has not been incorporated in the program. This is done through a process called 'redirection'.

Normally a C program receives its input from the standard input device, which is assumed to be the keyboard, and sends its output to the standard output device, which is assumed to be the VDU. In other words, the OS makes certain assumptions about where input should come from and where output should go. Redirection permits us to change these assumptions.

For example, using redirection the output of the program that normally goes to the VDU can be sent to the disk or the printer without really making a provision for it in the program. This is often a more convenient and flexible approach than providing a separate function in the program to write to the disk or printer. Similarly, redirection can be used to read information from disk file directly into a program, instead of receiving the input from keyboard.

To use redirection facility is to execute the program from the command prompt, inserting the redirection symbols at appropriate places. Let us understand this process with the help of a program.

Redirecting the Output

Let's see how we can redirect the output of a program, from the screen to a file. We'll start by considering the simple program shown below:

```
/* File name: util.c */
# include <stdio.h>
int main( )
{
    char ch ;
```

```
    while ( ( ch = getc ( stdin ) ) != EOF )
        putc ( ch, stdout ) ;
    return 0 ;
}
```

On compiling this program, we would get an executable file UTIL.EXE. Normally, when we execute this file, the **putc( )** function will cause whatever we type to be printed on screen, until we type Ctrl-Z, at which point the program will terminate, as shown in the following sample run. The Ctrl-Z character is often called end of file character.

```
C>UTIL.EXE
perhaps I had a wicked childhood,
perhaps I had a miserable youth,
but somewhere in my wicked miserable past,
there must have been a moment of truth ^Z
C>
```

Now let's see what happens when we invoke this program from in a different way, using redirection:

```
C>UTIL.EXE > POEM.TXT
C>
```

Here we are causing the output to be redirected to the file POEM.TXT. Can we prove that this output has indeed gone to the file POEM.TXT? Yes, by using the TYPE command as follows:

```
C>TYPE POEM.TXT
perhaps I had a wicked childhood,
perhaps I had a miserable youth,
but somewhere in my wicked miserable past,
there must have been a moment of truth
C>
```

There's the result of our typing sitting in the file. The redirection operator, '>', causes any output intended for the screen to be written to the file whose name follows the operator.

Note that the data to be redirected to a file doesn't need to be typed by a user at the keyboard; the program itself can generate it. Any output normally sent to the screen can be redirected to a disk file. As an example, consider the following program for generating the ASCII table on screen:

```
/* File name: ascii.c*/
# include <stdio.h>
int main( )
{
    int ch ;

    for ( ch = 0 ; ch <= 255 ; ch++ )
        printf ( "%d %c\n", ch, ch ) ;
    return 0 ;
}
```

When this program is compiled and then executed at command prompt using the redirection operator,

```
C>ASCII.EXE > TABLE.TXT
```

the output is written to the file. This can be a useful capability any time you want to capture the output in a file, rather than displaying it on the screen.

DOS predefines a number of filenames for its own use. One of these names is PRN, which stands for the printer. Output can be redirected to the printer by using this filename. For example, if you invoke the "ascii.exe" program this way:

```
C>ASCII.EXE > PRN
```

the ASCII table will be printed on the printer.

Redirecting the Input

We can also redirect input to a program so that, instead of reading a character from the keyboard, a program reads it from a file. Let us now see how this can be done.

To redirect the input, we need to have a file containing something to be displayed. Suppose we use a file called NEWPOEM.TXT containing the following lines:

```
Let's start at the very beginning,
A very good place to start!
```

We'll assume that using some text editor these lines have been placed in the file NEWPOEM.TXT. Now, we use the input redirection operator '<' before the file, as shown below:

```
C>UTIL.EXE < NEWPOEM.TXT
Let's start at the very beginning,
A very good place to start!
C>
```

The lines are printed on the screen with no further effort on our part. Using redirection, we've made our program UTIL.C perform the work of the TYPE command.

Both Ways at Once

Redirection of input and output can be used together; the input for a program can come from a file via redirection, at the same time its output can be redirected to a file. Such a program is called a filter. The following command demonstrates this process.

```
C>UTIL.EXE < NEWPOEM.TXT > POETRY.TXT
```

In this case, our program receives the redirected input from the file NEWPOEM.TXT and instead of sending the output to the screen; it would redirect it to the file POETRY.TXT.

Similarly, to send the contents of the file NEWPOEM.TXT to the printer, we can use the following command:

```
C>UTIL.EXE < NEWPOEM.TXT > PRN
```

While using such multiple redirections, don't try to send output to the same file from which you are receiving input. This is because the output file is erased before it's written to. So by the time we manage to receive the input from a file, it is already erased.

Redirection can be a powerful tool for developing utility programs to examine or alter data in files. Thus, redirection is used to establish a relationship between a program and a file. Another OS operator can be used to relate two programs directly, so that the output of one is fed directly into another, with no files involved. This is called 'piping', and is done using the operator '|', called pipe. We won't pursue this topic, but you can read about it in the OS help/manual.

Summary

(a) We can pass parameters to a program at command line using the concept of 'command line arguments'.
(b) The command line argument **argv** contains values passed to the program, whereas, **argc** contains number of arguments.
(c) We can use the standard file pointer **stdin** to take input from standard input device such as keyboard.
(d) We can use the standard file pointer **stdout** to send output to the standard output device such as a monitor.
(e) We can use the standard file pointers **stdprn** and **stdaux** to interact with printer and auxiliary devices respectively.
(f) Redirection allows a program to read from or write to files at command prompt.
(g) The operators **<** and **>** are called redirection operators.

Exercise

[A] Answer the following:

(a) How will you use the following program to

- Copy the contents of one file into another.
- Print a file on the printer.
- Create a new file and add some text to it.
- Display the contents of an existing file.

```
# include <stdio.h>
int main( )
{
    char ch, str[10] ;
    while ( ( ch = getc ( stdin ) ) != -1 )
        putc ( ch, stdout ) ;
    return 0 ;
}
```

(b) State True or False:

1. We can send arguments at command line even if we define **main( )** function without parameters.
2. To use standard file pointers we don't need to open the file using **fopen( )**.
3. Using **stdaux** we can send output to the printer if printer is attached to the serial port.
4. The zeroth element of the **argv** array is always the name of the executable file.

(c) Point out the errors, if any, in the following program:

```
# include <stdio.h>
int main ( int ac, char ( * ) av[ ] )
{
    printf ( "%d\n", ac ) ;
    printf ( "%s\n", av[0] ) ;
    return 0 ;
}
```

[B] Attempt the following:

(a) Write a program using command line arguments to search for a word in a file and replace it with the specified word. The usage of the program is shown below.

C> change <old word> <new word> <filename>

(b) Write a program that can be used at command prompt as a calculating utility. The usage of the program is shown below.

C> calc <switch> <n> <m>

Where, **n** and **m** are two integer operands. **switch** can be any one of the arithmetic or comparison operators. If arithmetic operator is supplied, the output should be the result of the operation. If comparison operator is supplied then the output should be **True** or **False**.

(c) You have already written a program to change the attributes of a file by changing its directory entry. Using similar logic, write a program to rename a given file on your disk. You must be able to execute the program at command line as shown below:

C> filename <file to be renamed> <new name>

(d) Write a program that will concatenate two files; that is, add the contents of one file at the end of another and write the result into the third file. You must be able to execute the EXE file of the program at the command prompt as follows:

A> CONCAT source1.txt source2.txt result.txt

(e) A particular virus gets attached to the file at its beginning. The size of the virus code is 1600 bytes, of which the first 10 bytes constitutes the signature of the virus. These 10 bytes are 0xE9, 0x20, 0x20, 0xA1, 0x21, 0x20, 0xA1, 0x02, 0x2D, 0xCC. Write a program which accepts the filename as a command line argument, checks whether the first 10 bytes of this file match with the above signature. If it does then the program should copy the contents of the file into a file called TEMP ensuring that the copying begins from byte number 1601 of the source file.

17 Operations On Bits

- Bitwise Operators
    - One's Complement Operator
    - Right Shift Operator
    - Left Shift Operator
    - Bitwise AND Operator
    - Bitwise OR Operator
    - Bitwise XOR Operator
- The *showbits( )* Function
- Hexadecimal Numbering System
- Relationship between Binary and Hex
- Summary
- Exercise

So far we have dealt with characters, integers, floats and their variations. The smallest element in memory on which we are able to operate as yet is a byte; and we operated on it by making use of the data type **char**. However, we haven't attempted to look within these data types to see how they are constructed out of individual bits, and how these bits can be manipulated. Being able to operate on a bit level, can be very important in programming, especially when a program must interact directly with the hardware. This is because, the programming languages are byte oriented, whereas hardware tends to be bit oriented. Let us now delve inside the byte and see how it is constructed and how it can be manipulated effectively. So let us take apart the byte... bit by bit.

Bitwise Operators

One of C's powerful features is a set of bit manipulation operators. These permit the programmer to access and manipulate individual bits within a piece of data. The various Bitwise Operators available in C are shown in Figure 17.1.

<table>
<tr><th>Operator</th><th>Meaning</th></tr>
<tr><td>~</td><td>One's complement</td></tr>
<tr><td>>></td><td>Right shift</td></tr>
<tr><td><<</td><td>Left shift</td></tr>
<tr><td>&</td><td>Bitwise AND</td></tr>
<tr><td>|</td><td>Bitwise OR</td></tr>
<tr><td>^</td><td>Bitwise XOR(Exclusive OR)</td></tr>
</table>

Figure 17.1

These operators can operate upon **int**s and **char**s but not on **float**s and **double**s. Before moving on to the details of the operators, let us first take a look at the bit numbering scheme in integers and characters. Bits are numbered from zero onwards, increasing from right to left as shown below:

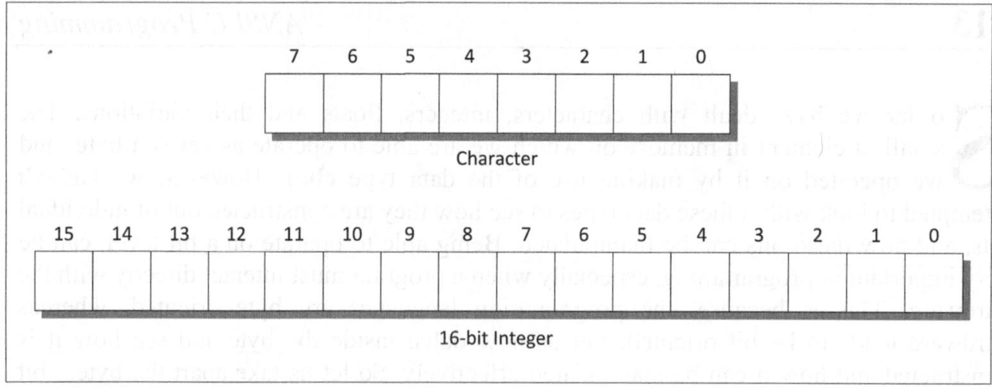

Figure 17.2

Throughout this discussion of bitwise operators, we are going to use a function called **showbits( )**, but we are not going to show you the details of the function immediately. The task of **showbits( )** is to display the binary representation of any integer or character value.

We begin with a plain-jane example with **showbits( )** in action.

```
/* Print binary equivalent of integers using showbits( ) function */
# include <stdio.h>
void showbits ( int ) ;
int main( )
{
    int j ;

    for ( j = 0 ; j <= 5 ; j++ )
    {
        printf ( "Decimal %d is same as binary ", j ) ;
        showbits ( j ) ;
        return 0 ;
    }
}
```

And here is the output...

```
Decimal 0 is same as binary 0000000000000000
Decimal 1 is same as binary 0000000000000001
Decimal 2 is same as binary 0000000000000010
Decimal 3 is same as binary 0000000000000011
```

```
Decimal 4 is same as binary 0000000000000100
Decimal 5 is same as binary 0000000000000101
```

Let us now explore the various bitwise operators one by one.

One's Complement Operator

On taking one's complement of a number, all 1's present in the number are changed to 0's and all 0's are changed to 1's. For example, one's complement of 1010 is 0101. Similarly, one's complement of 1111 is 0000. Note that, here when we talk of a number, we are talking of binary equivalent of the number. Thus, one's complement of 65 means one's complement of 0000 0000 0100 0001, which is binary equivalent of 65. One's complement of 65 therefore would be, 1111 1111 1011 1110. One's complement operator is represented by the symbol ~ (tilde). Following program shows one's complement operator in action.

```
# include <stdio.h>
int main( )
{
    int  j, k ;

    for ( j = 0 ; j <= 3 ; j++ )
    {
        printf ( "Decimal %d is same as binary ", j ) ;
        showbits ( j ) ;

        k = ~j ;
        printf ( "One's complement of %d is ", j ) ;
        showbits ( k ) ;
    }
    return 0 ;
}
```

And here is the output of the above program...

```
Decimal 0 is same as binary 0000000000000000
One's complement of 0 is 1111111111111111
Decimal 1 is same as binary 0000000000000001
One's complement of 1 is 1111111111111110
Decimal 2 is same as binary 0000000000000010
One's complement of 2 is 1111111111111101
Decimal 3 is same as binary 0000000000000011
```

One's complement of 3 is 1111111111111100

In real-world situations, where could the one's complement operator be useful? Since it changes the original number beyond recognition, one potential place where it can be effectively used is in development of a file encryption utility as shown below:

```
/* File encryption utility */
# include <stdio.h>
void encrypt( ) ;
int main( )
{
    encrypt( ) ;
}

void encrypt( )
{
    FILE *fs, *ft ;
    char  ch ;

    fs = fopen ( "SOURCE.C", "r" ) ; /* normal file */
    ft = fopen ( "TARGET.C", "w" ) ; /* encrypted file */

    if ( fs == NULL || ft == NULL )
    {
        printf ( "File opening error!" ) ;
        exit ( 1 ) ;
    }

    while ( ( ch = getc ( fs ) ) != EOF )
        putc ( ~ch, ft ) ;

    fclose ( fs ) ;
    fclose ( ft ) ;
    return 0 ;
}
```

How would you write the corresponding decrypt function? Would there be any problem in tackling the end of file marker? It may be recalled here that the end of file in text files is indicated by a character whose ASCII value is 26.

Right Shift Operator

The right shift operator is represented by >>. It needs two operands. It shifts each bit in its left operand to the right. The number of places the bits are shifted depends on the number following the operator (i.e. its right operand).

Thus, **ch >> 3** would shift all bits in **ch** three places to the right. Similarly, **ch >> 5** would shift all bits 5 places to the right.

For example, if the variable **ch** contains the bit pattern 11010111, then, **ch >> 1** would give 01101011 and **ch >> 2** would give 00110101.

Note that as the bits are shifted to the right, blanks are created on the left. These blanks must be filled somehow. They are always filled with zeros. The following program demonstrates the effect of right shift operator.

```
# include <stdio.h>
void showbits ( int ) ;
int main( )
{
    int i = 5225, j, k ;

    printf ( "Decimal %d is same as binary ", i ) ;
    showbits ( i ) ;

    for ( j = 0 ; j <= 5 ; j++ )
    {
        k = i >> j ;
        printf ( "%d right shift %d gives ", i, j ) ;
        showbits ( k ) ;
    }
    return 0 ;
}
```

The output of the above program would be...

```
Decimal 5225 is same as binary 0001010001101001
5225 right shift 0 gives 0001010001101001
5225 right shift 1 gives 0000101000110100
5225 right shift 2 gives 0000010100011010
5225 right shift 3 gives 0000001010001101
5225 right shift 4 gives 0000000101000110
5225 right shift 5 gives 0000000010100011
```

Note that if the operand is a multiple of 2, then shifting the operand one bit to right is same as dividing it by 2 and ignoring the remainder. Thus,

```
64 >> 1 gives 32
64 >> 2 gives 16
128 >> 2 gives 32
```

but,

```
27 >> 1 is 13
49 >> 1 is 24 .
```

A Word of Caution

In the expression **a >> b** if **b** is negative the result is unpredictable. If **a** is negative then its left most bit (sign bit) would be 1. On some computer right shifting **a** would result in extending the sign bit. For example, if **a** contains -1, its binary representation would be 1111111111111111. Without sign extension, the operation **a >> 4** would be 0000111111111111. However, on the machine on which I executed this expression the result turns out to be 1111111111111111. Thus the sign bit 1 continues to get extended.

Left Shift Operator

This is similar to the right shift operator, the only difference being that the bits are shifted to the left, and for each bit shifted, a 0 is added to the right of the number. The following program should clarify my point.

```
# include <stdio.h>
void showbits ( int ) ;
int main( )
{
    int i = 5225, j, k ;

    printf ( "Decimal %d is same as binary ", i ) ;
    showbits ( i ) ;

    for ( j = 0 ; j <= 4 ; j++ )
    {
        k = i << j ;
        printf ( "%d left shift %d gives ", i, j ) ;
        showbits ( k ) ;
```

```
    }
    return 0 ;
}
```

The output of the above program would be...

```
Decimal 5225 is same as binary 0001010001101001
5225 left shift 0 gives 0001010001101001
5225 left shift 1 gives 0010100011010010
5225 left shift 2 gives 0101000110100100
5225 left shift 3 gives 1010001101001000
5225 left shift 4 gives 0100011010010000
```

Having acquainted ourselves with the left shift and right shift operators, let us now find out the practical utility of these operators.

In DOS/Windows the date on which a file is created (or modified) is stored as a 2-byte entry in the 32 byte directory entry of that file. Similarly, a 2-byte entry is made of the time of creation or modification of the file. Remember that DOS/Windows doesn't store the date (day, month, and year) of file creation as a 8 byte string, but as a codified 2 byte entry, thereby saving 6 bytes for each file entry in the directory. The bitwise distribution of year, month and date in the 2-byte entry is shown in Figure 17.3.

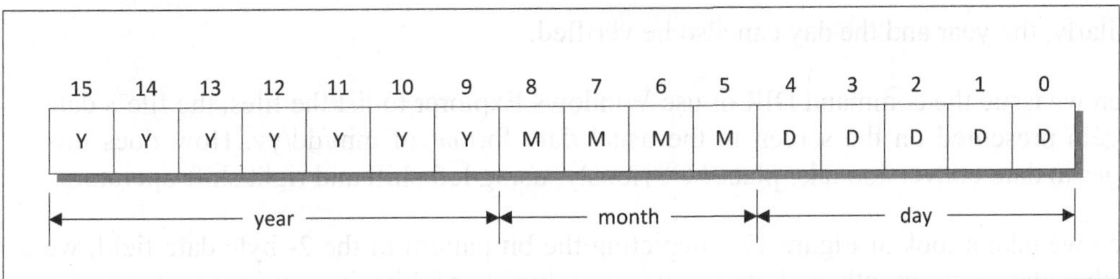

Figure 17.3

DOS/Windows converts the actual date into a 2-byte value using the following formula:

```
date = 512 * ( year - 1980 ) + 32 * month + day
```

Suppose 09/03/1990 is the date, then on conversion the date will be,

```
date = 512 * ( 1990 - 1980 ) + 32 * 3 + 9 = 5225
```

The binary equivalent of 5225 is 0001 0100 0110 1001. This binary value is placed in the date field in the directory entry of the file as shown below.

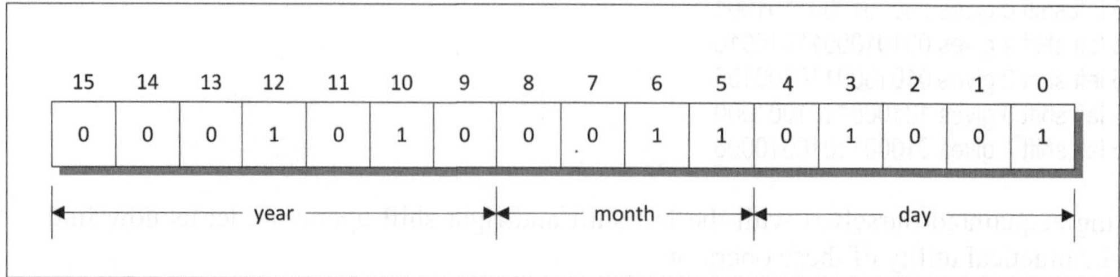

Figure 17.4

Just to verify this bit distribution, let us take the bits representing the month,

```
month = 0011
      = 1 * 2 + 1 * 1
      = 3
```

Similarly, the year and the day can also be verified.

When we issue the command DIR or use Windows Explorer to list the files, the file's date is again presented on the screen in the usual date format of mm/dd/yy. How does this integer to date conversion take place? Obviously, using left shift and right shift operators.

When we take a look at Figure 17.4 depicting the bit pattern of the 2- byte date field, we see that the year, month and day exist as a bunch of bits in contiguous locations. Separating each of them is a matter of applying the bitwise operators.

For example, to get year as a separate entity from the two-byte entry, we right shift the entry by 9. Just see, how...

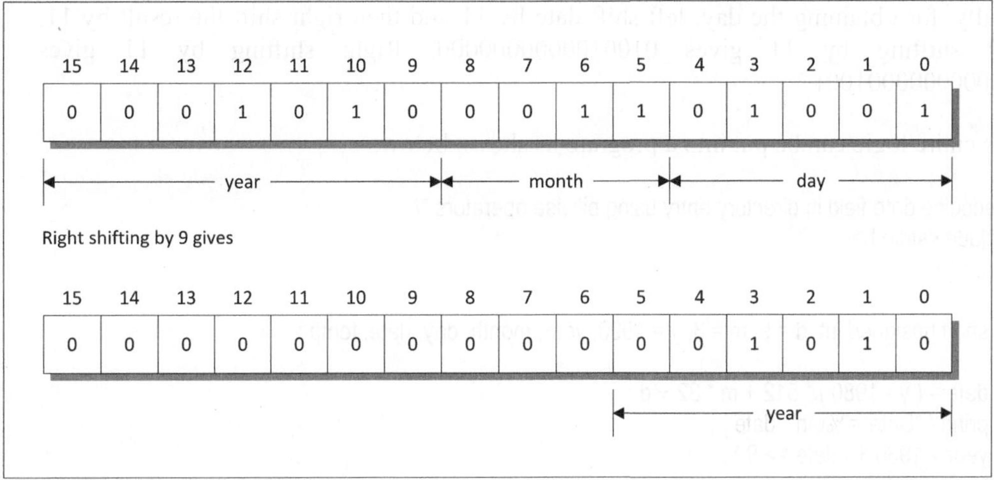

Figure 17.5

On similar lines, left shifting by 7, followed by right shifting by 12 yields month.

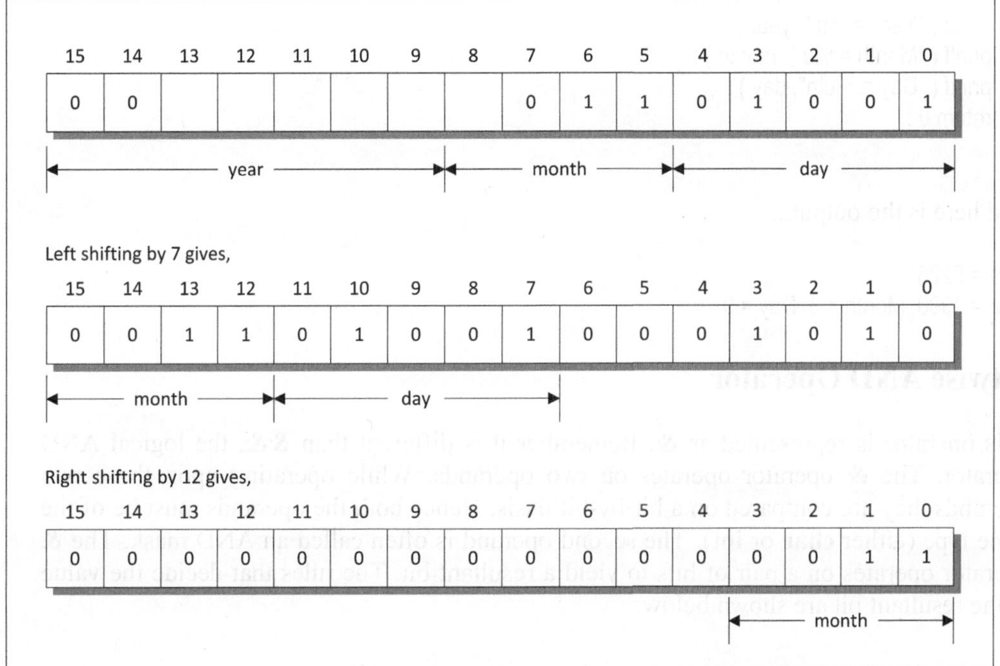

Figure 17.6

Finally, for obtaining the day, left shift date by 11 and then right shift the result by 11. Left shifting by 11 gives 0100100000000000. Right shifting by 11 gives 0000000000001001.

This entire logic can be put into a program as shown below:

```
/* Decoding date field in directory entry using bitwise operators */
# include <stdio.h>
int main( )
{
    short unsigned int  d = 9, m = 3, y = 1990, year, month, day, date, temp ;

    date = ( y - 1980 ) * 512 + m * 32 + d ;
    printf ( "Date = %u\n", date ) ;
    year = 1980 + ( date >> 9 ) ;
    temp = date << 7 ;
    month = temp >> 12 ;
    temp = date << 11 ;
    day = temp >> 11 ;

    printf ( "Year = %u ", year ) ;
    printf ( "Month = %u ", month ) ;
    printf ( "Day = %u\n", day ) ;
    return 0 ;
}
```

And here is the output...

```
Date = 5225
Year = 1990  Month = 3  Day = 9
```

Bitwise AND Operator

This operator is represented as **&**. Remember it is different than **&&**, the logical AND operator. The **&** operator operates on two operands. While operating upon these two operands they are compared on a bit-by-bit basis. Hence both the operands must be of the same type (either **char** or **int**). The second operand is often called an AND mask. The **&** operator operates on a pair of bits to yield a resultant bit. The rules that decide the value of the resultant bit are shown below:

First bit	Second bit	First bit & Second bit
0	0	0
0	1	0
1	0	0
1	1	1

Figure 17.7

This can be represented in a more understandable form as a 'Truth Table' shown in Figure 17.8.

&	0	1
0	0	0
1	0	1

Figure 17.8

The example given below shows more clearly what happens while ANDing one operand with another. The rules given in the Figure 17.8 are applied to each pair of bits one by one.

&	0	1
0	0	0
1	0	1

Figure 17.9

Work through the Truth Table and confirm that the result obtained is really correct.

Thus, it must be clear that the operation is being performed on individual bits, and the operation performed on one pair of bits is completely independent of the operation performed on the other pairs.

Probably, the best use of the AND operator is to check whether a particular bit of an operand is ON or OFF. This is explained in the following example.

Suppose, from the bit pattern 10101101 of an operand, we want to check whether bit number 3 is ON (1) or OFF (0). Since we want to check the bit number 3, the second operand for the AND operation should be 1 * 2^3, which is equal to 8. This operand can be represented bitwise as 00001000.

Then the ANDing operation would be,

```
10101101        Original bit pattern
00001000        AND mask
--------------
00001000        Resulting bit pattern
```

The resulting value we get in this case is 8, i.e the value of the second operand. The result turned out to be 8 since the third bit of the first operand was ON. Had it been OFF, the bit number 3 in the resulting bit pattern would have evaluated to 0 and the complete bit pattern would have been 00000000.

Thus, depending upon the bit number to be checked in the first operand, we decide the second operand, and on ANDing these two operands the result decides whether the bit was ON or OFF. If the bit is ON (1), the resulting value turns out to be a non-zero value, which is equal to the value of second operand. If the bit is OFF (0), the result is zero, as seen above. The following program puts this logic into action.

```
/* To test whether a bit in a number is ON or OFF */
# include <stdio.h>
int main( )
{
    int i = 65, j ;

    printf ( "value of i = %d\n", i ) ;
    j = i & 32 ;

    if ( j == 0 )
        printf ( "and its fifth bit is off\n" ) ;
    else
        printf ( "and its fifth bit is on\n" ) ;

    j = i & 64 ;

    if ( j == 0 )
```

```
        printf ( "whereas its sixth bit is off\n" ) ;
    else
        printf ( "whereas its sixth bit is on\n" ) ;
    return 0 ;
}
```

And here is the output...

```
Value of i = 65
and its fifth bit is off
whereas its sixth bit is on
```

In every file entry present in the directory, there is an attribute byte. The status of a file is governed by the value of individual bits in this attribute byte. The AND operator can be used to check the status of the bits of this attribute byte. The meaning of each bit in the attribute byte is shown in Figure 17.10.

Bit numbers								Meaning
7	6	5	4	3	2	1	0	
.	.	.	.	.	.	.	1	Read only
.	.	.	.	.	.	1	.	Hidden
.	.	.	.	.	1	.	.	System
.	.	.	.	1	.	.	.	Volume label entry
.	.	.	1	.	.	.	.	Sub-directory entry
.	.	1	.	.	.	.	.	Archive bit
.	1	.	.	.	.	.	.	Unused
1	.	.	.	.	.	.	.	Unused

Figure 17.10

Now, suppose we want to check whether a file is a hidden file or not. A hidden file is one, which is never shown in the directory, even though it exists on the disk. From the above bit classification of attribute byte, we only need to check whether bit number 1 is ON or OFF.

So, our first operand in this case becomes the attribute byte of the file in question, whereas the second operand is the $1 * 2^1 = 2$, as discussed earlier. Similarly, it can be checked whether the file is a system file or not, whether the file is read-only file or not, and so on.

The second, and equally important use of the AND operator is in changing the status of the bit, or more precisely, to switch OFF a particular bit.

If the first operand happens to be 00000111, then to switch OFF bit number 1, our AND mask bit pattern should be 11111101. On applying this mask, we get,

```
00000111    Original bit pattern
11111101    AND mask
--------------
00000101    Resulting bit pattern
```

Here in the AND mask we keep the value of all other bits as 1 except the one which is to be switched OFF (which is purposefully kept as 0). Therefore, irrespective of whether the first bit is ON or OFF previously, it is switched OFF. At the same time the value 1 provided in all the other bits of the AND mask (second operand) keeps the bit values of the other bits in the first operand unaltered.

Let's summarize the uses of bitwise AND operator:

(a) It is used to check whether a particular bit in a number is ON or OFF.
(b) It is used to turn OFF a particular bit in a number.

Bitwise OR Operator

Another important bitwise operator is the OR operator which is represented as |. The rules that govern the value of the resulting bit obtained after ORing of two bits is shown in the truth table below.

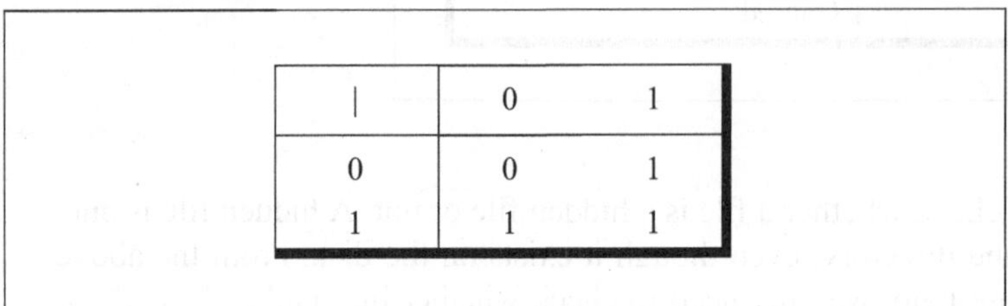

|	0	1
0	0	1
1	1	1

Figure 17.11

Using the Truth table confirm the result obtained on ORing the two operands as shown below.

```
11010000    Original bit pattern
00000111    OR mask
-------------
11010111    Resulting bit pattern
```

Bitwise OR operator is usually used to put ON a particular bit in a number.

Let us consider the bit pattern 11000011. If we want to put ON bit number 3, then the OR mask to be used would be 00001000. Note that all the other bits in the mask are set to 0 and only the bit, which we want to set ON in the resulting value is set to 1.

Bitwise XOR Operator

The XOR operator is represented as ^ and is also called an Exclusive OR Operator. The OR operator returns 1, when any one of the two bits or both the bits are 1, whereas XOR returns 1 only if one of the two bits is 1. The truth table for the XOR operator is given below.

^	0	1
0	0	1
1	1	0

Figure 17.12

XOR operator is used to toggle a bit ON or OFF. A number XORed with another number twice gives the original number. This is shown in the following program.

```
# include <stdio.h>
int main( )
{
    int b = 50 ;

    b = b ^ 12 ;
    printf ( "%d\n", b ) ; /* this will print 62 */

    b = b ^ 12 ;
    printf ( "%d\n", b ) ; /* this will print 50 */
```

```
    return 0 ;
}
```

The *showbits( )* Function

We have used this function quite often in this chapter. Now we have sufficient knowledge of bitwise operators and hence are in a position to understand it. The function is given below followed by a brief explanation.

```
void showbits ( int  n )
{
    int  i, k, andmask ;

    for ( i = 15 ; i >= 0 ; i-- )
    {
        andmask = 1 << i ;
        k = n & andmask ;

        k == 0 ? printf ( "0" ) : printf ( "1" ) ;
    }
    printf ( "\n" ) ;
}
```

All that is being done in this function is, using an AND operator and a variable **andmask**, we are checking the status of individual bits. If the bit is OFF we print a 0, otherwise we print a 1.

First time through the loop, the variable **andmask** will contain the value 1000000000000000, which is obtained by left-shifting 1, fifteen places. If the variable **n**'s most significant bit is 0, then **k** would contain a value 0, otherwise it would contain a non-zero value. If **k** contains 0, then **printf( )** will print out 0, otherwise it will print out 1.

On the second go-around of the loop, the value of **i** is decremented and hence the value of **andmask** changes, which will now be 0100000000000000. This checks whether the next most significant bit is 1 or 0, and prints it out accordingly. The same operation is repeated for all bits in the number.

Hexadecimal Numbering System

When we talk about different numbering systems we are really talking about the base of the numbering system. For example, binary numbering system has base 2 and hexadecimal numbering system has base 16, just the way decimal numbering system has base 10. The base represents number of digits you can use before you run out of digits. For example, in decimal numbering system, when we have used digits from 0 to 9, we run out of digits. That's the time we put a 1 in the column to the left–the ten's column–and again start constructing numbers. This results into numbers from 10 to 99. Once we reach 99, we again run out of digits. That's when we go one column to the left–the hundred's column–and again start constructing numbers like 100, 101, 102, …, etc. up to 999.

Since decimal numbering system is a base 10 numbering system any number in it is constructed using some combination of digits 0 to 9. This seems perfectly natural. However, the choice of 10 as a base is quite arbitrary, having its origin possibly in the fact that man has 10 fingers. It is very easy to use other bases as well. For example, if we wanted to use base 8 or octal numbering system, which uses only eight digits (0 to 7), here's how the counting would look like:

0, 1, 2, 3, 4, 5, 6, 7, 10, 11, 12, .., .., 77, 100, 101, 102, .., .., 777, 1000, ..

Similarly, a hexadecimal numbering system has a base 16. In hex notation, the ten digits 0 through 9 are used to represent the values zero through nine, and the remaining six values, ten through fifteen, are represented by symbols A to F. The hex digits A to F are usually written in capitals, but lowercase letters are also perfectly acceptable. Here is how the counting in hex would look like:

0, 1, 2, 3, 4, 5, 6, 7, 8, 9, A, B, C, D, E, F, 10, 11, 12, .., .., FF, 100, .., .., FFF

The hex numbers are built out of hex digits in much the same way the decimal numbers are built out of decimal digits. For example, when we write the decimal number 342, we mean,

```
  3 times 100 (square of 10)
+ 4 times 10
+ 2 times 1
```

Similarly, if we use number 342 as a hex number, we mean,

```
  3 times 256 (square of 16)
+ 4 times 16
+ 2 times 1
```

Relation between Binary and Hex

In binary numbering system, there are only two digits 0 and 1. Here is how the counting in binary would look like:

0, 1, 10, 11, 100, 101, 110, 111, 1000, 1001, 1010, .., .., 1111, 10000, ..

Binary numbering system is a natural system for computers because each of the thousands of electronic circuits in the computer can be in one of the two states—on or off. Thus, binary numbering system corresponds nicely with the circuits in the computer—0 means off, and 1 means on. 0 and 1 are called bits, a short-form of binary digits.

Hex numbers are used primarily as shorthand for binary numbers that the computers work with. Every hex digit represents four bits of binary information as shown in Figure 17. 13.

Hex	Binary	Hex	Binary
0	0000	8	1000
1	0001	9	1001
2	0010	A	1010
3	0011	B	1011
4	0100	C	1100
5	0101	D	1101
6	0110	E	1110
7	0111	F	1111

Figure 17.13

In binary numbering system 4 bits taken at a time can give rise to sixteen different numbers, so the only way to represent each of these sixteen 4-bit binary numbers in a simple and short way is to use a base sixteen numbering system.

Suppose we want to represent a binary number 11000101 in a short way. One way is to find it decimal equivalent by multiplying each binary digit with an appropriate power of 2 as shown below:

$$1 * 2^7 + 1 * 2^6 + 0 * 2^5 + 0 * 2^4 + 0 * 2^3 + 1 * 2^2 + 0 * 2^1 + 1 * 2^0$$

which is equal to 197.

Another method is much simpler. Just look at Figure 17.13. From it, find out the hex digits for the two four-bit sets (1100 and 0101). These happen to be C and 5. Therefore, the binary number's hex equivalent is C5. You would agree this is an easier way to represent the binary number than to find its decimal equivalent. In this method neither multiplication nor addition is needed. In fact, since there are only 16 hex digits, it's fairly easy to memorize the binary equivalent of each one. Quick now, what's binary 1100 in hex? That's right C. You are already getting the feel of it. With a little practice it is easy to translate even long numbers into hex. Thus, 1100 0101 0011 1010 binary is C53A hex.

As it happens with many unfamiliar subjects, learning hexadecimal requires a little practice. Try your hand at converting some binary numbers and vice versa. Soon you will be talking hexadecimal as if you had known it all your life.

Summary

(a) To help manipulate hardware oriented data—individual bits rather than bytes a set of bitwise operators are used.
(b) The bitwise operators include operators like one's complement, right-shift, left-shift, bitwise AND, OR, and XOR.
(c) The one's complement converts all zeros in its operand to 1s and all 1s to 0s.
(d) The right-shift and left-shift operators are useful in eliminating bits from a number—either from the left or from the right.
(e) The bitwise AND operators is useful in testing whether a bit is on/off and in putting off a particular bit.
(f) The bitwise OR operator is used to turn on a particular bit.
(g) The XOR operator works almost same as the OR operator except one minor variation.
(h) It is convenient to convert binary numbers into their hexadecimal equivalents than converting them to their decimal equivalents.

Exercise

[A] Answer the following:

(a) The information about colors is to be stored in bits of a **char** variable called **color**. The bit number 0 to 6, each represent 7 colors of a rainbow, i.e. bit 0 represents violet, 1 represents indigo, and so on. Write a program that asks the user to enter a number and based on this number it reports which colors in the rainbow does the number represents.

(b) A company planning to launch a new newspaper in market conducts a survey. The various parameters considered in the survey were, the economic status (upper, middle, and lower class) the languages readers prefer (English, Hindi, Regional language) and category of paper (daily, supplement, tabloid). Write a program, which reads data of 10 respondents through keyboard, and stores the information in an array of integers. The bit-wise information to be stored in an integer is given below:

Bit Number	Information
0	Upper class
1	Middle class
2	Lower class
3	English
4	Hindi
5	Regional Language
6	Daily
7	Supplement
8	Tabloid

At the end give the statistical data for number of persons who read English daily, number of Upper class people who read Tabloid and number of Regional Language readers.

(c) In an inter-college competition, various sports like cricket, basketball, football, hockey, lawn tennis, table tennis, carom and chess are played between different colleges. The information regarding the games won by a particular college is stored in bit numbers 0, 1, 2, 3, 4, 5, 6, 7 and 8 respectively of an integer variable called **game**. The college that wins in 5 or more than 5 games is awarded the Champion of Champions trophy. If a number representing the bit pattern mentioned above is entered through the keyboard then write a program to find out whether the college won the Champion of the Champions trophy or not, along with the names of the games won by the college.

(d) An animal could be a canine (dog, wolf, fox, etc.), a feline (cat, lynx, jaguar, etc.), a cetacean (whale, narwhal, etc.) or a marsupial (koala, wombat, etc.). The information whether a particular animal is canine, feline, cetacean, or marsupial is stored in bit number 0, 1, 2 and 3 respectively of a integer variable called **type**. Bit number 4 of the variable **type** stores the information about whether the animal is Carnivore or Herbivore.

For the following animal, complete the program to determine whether the animal is a herbivore or a carnivore. Also determine whether the animal is a canine, feline, cetacean or a marsupial.

```
struct animal
{
```

```
    char name[30] ;
    int type ;
}
struct animal a = { "OCELOT", 18 } ;
```

(e) The time field in the directory entry is 2 bytes long. Distribution of different bits which account for hours, minutes and seconds is given below. Write a function which would receive the two-byte time entry and return to the calling function, the hours, minutes and seconds.

15	14	13	12	11	10	9	8	7	6	5	4	3	2	1	0
H	H	H	H	H	M	M	M	M	M	M	S	S	S	S	S

Figure 17.14

(f) In order to save disk space, information about student is stored in an integer variable. If bit number 0 is on then it indicates Ist year student, bit number 1 to 3 stores IInd year, IIIrd year and IVth year student respectively. Bits 4 to 7 store the stream Mechanical, Chemical, Electronics and IT. Rest of the bits store room number. Based on the given data, write a program that asks for the room number and displays the information about the student, if its data exists in the array. The contents of array are,

```
int data[ ] = { 273, 548, 786, 1096 } ;
```

(g) What will be the output of the following program:

```
# include <stdio.h>
int main( )
{
    int i = 32, j = 65, k, l, m, n, o, p ;
    k = i | 35 ;
    l = ~k ;
    m = i & j ;
    n = j ^ 32 ;
    o = j << 2 ;
    p = i >> 5 ;
    printf ( "k = %d l = %d m = %d\n", k, l, m ) ;
    printf ( "n = %d o = %d p = %d\n", n, o, p ) ;
    return 0 ;
}
```

(h) Write a program to exchange the bits in a byte. Bits to be exchanged are bit 0 and bit 7, bit 1 & bit 6, bit 2 & bit 5, bit 3 & bit 4. For example, if contents of a byte are 10010100 then on exchanging the bits the contents should become 00101001.

(i) Point out and correct the error in the following program:

```
int main( )
{
    char a = 0 ;
    a ~= a ;
    printf ( "%d\n", a ) ;
    return 0 ;
}
```

(j) Suppose a float variable **z** contains a value 3.14. Write a program which would print the individual bits of the four bytes occupied by the variable **z**.

18 Miscellaneous Features

- Enumerated Data Type
    - Uses of Enumerated Data Type
    - Are Enums Necessary
- Renaming Data Types with *typedef*
- Typecasting
- Bit fields
- Pointers to Functions
- Functions Returning Pointers
- Functions with Variable Number of Arguments
- Unions
    - Union of Structures
- Utility of Unions
- The *volatile* Qualifier
- Summary
- Exercise

The topics discussed in this chapter were either too large or far too removed from the mainstream C programming for inclusion in the earlier chapters. These topics provide certain useful programming features, and could prove to be of immense help in certain programming strategies. In this chapter, we would examine enumerated data types, the typedef keyword, typecasting, bit fields, function pointers, functions with variable number of arguments and unions.

Enumerated Data Type

The enumerated data type gives you an opportunity to invent your own data type and define what values the variable of this data type can take. This can help in making the program listings more readable, which can be an advantage when a program gets complicated or when more than one programmer would be working on it. Using enumerated data type can also help you reduce programming errors.

As an example, one could invent a data type called **mar_status** which can have four possible values—single, married, divorced or widowed. Don't confuse these values with variable names; married, for instance, has the same relationship to the variable **mar_status** as the number 15 has with a variable of type **int**.

The format of the **enum** definition is similar to that of a structure. Here's how the example stated above can be implemented:

```
enum mar_status
{
    single, married, divorced, widowed
} ;
enum mar_status  person1, person2 ;
```

Like structures, this declaration has two parts:

(a) The first part declares the data type and specifies its possible values. These values are called 'enumerators'.
(b) The second part declares variables of this data type.

Now we can give values to these variables:

```
person1 = married ;
person2 = divorced ;
```

Remember, we can't use values that aren't in the original declaration.

Thus, the following expression would cause an error:

```
person1 = unknown ;
```

Internally, the compiler treats the enumerators as integers. Each value on the list of permissible values corresponds to an integer, starting with 0. Thus, in our example, single is stored as 0, married is stored as 1, divorced as 2 and widowed as 3.

This way of assigning numbers can be overridden by the programmer by initializing the enumerators to different integer values as shown below.

```
enum mar_status
{
    single = 100, married = 200, divorced = 300, widowed = 400
} ;
enum mar_status  person1, person2 ;
```

Uses of Enumerated Data Type

Enumerated variables are usually used to clarify the operation of a program. For example, if we need to use employee departments in a payroll program, it makes the listing easier to read if we use values like Assembly, Manufacturing, Accounts rather than the integer values 0, 1, 2, etc. The following program illustrates the point I am trying to make.

```
# include <stdio.h>
# include <string.h>
int main( )
{
    enum emp_dept
    {
        assembly, manufacturing, accounts, stores
    } ;
    struct employee
    {
        char  name[30] ;
        int  age ;
        float  bs ;
        enum emp_dept  department ;
    } ;
    struct employee  e ;

    strcpy ( e.name, "Lothar Mattheus" ) ;
```

```
	e.age = 28 ;
	e.bs = 5575.50 ;
	e.department = manufacturing ;

	printf ( "Name = %s\n", e.name ) ;
	printf ( "Age = %d\n", e.age ) ;
	printf ( "Basic salary = %f\n", e.bs ) ;
	printf ( "Dept = %d\n", e.department ) ;

	if ( e.department == accounts )
		printf ( "%s is an accounant\n", e.name ) ;
	else
		printf ( "%s is not an accounant\n", e.name ) ;

	return 0 ;
}
```

And here is the output of the program...

```
Name = Lothar Mattheus
Age = 28
Basic salary = 5575.50
Dept = 1
Lothar Mattheus is not an accountant
```

Let us now dissect the program. We first defined the data type **enum emp_dept** and specified the four possible values, namely, assembly, manufacturing, accounts and stores. Then we defined a variable **department** of the type **enum emp_dept** in a structure. The structure **employee** has three other elements containing employee information.

The program first assigns values to the variables in the structure. The statement,

```
e.department = manufacturing ;
```

assigns the value manufacturing to **e.department** variable. This is much more informative to anyone reading the program than a statement like,

```
e.department = 1 ;
```

The next part of the program shows an important weakness of using **enum** variables... there is no way to use the enumerated values directly in input/output functions like **printf( )** and **scanf( )**.

The **printf( )** function is not smart enough to perform the translation; the department is printed out as 1 and not manufacturing. Of course, we can write a function to print the correct enumerated values, using a **switch** statement, but that would reduce the clarity of the program. Even with this limitation, however, there are many situations in which enumerated variables are god sent!

Are Enums Necessary

Is there a way to achieve what was achieved using Enums in the previous program? Yes, using macros as shown below:

```
# include <string.h>
# define ASSEMBLY 0
# define MANUFACTURING 1
# define ACCCOUNTS 2
# define STORES 3

int main( )
{
    struct employee
    {
        char name[30] ;
        int age ;
        float bs ;
        int department ;
    } ;
    struct employee e ;
    strcpy ( e.name, "Lothar Mattheus" ) ;
    e.age = 28 ;
    e.bs = 5575.50 ;
    e.department = MANUFACTURING ;
    return 0 ;
}
```

If the same effect—convenience and readability can be achieved using macros then why should we prefer enums? Because, macros have a global scope, whereas, scope of enum can either be global (if declared outside all functions) or local (if declared inside a function).

Renaming Data types with *typedef*

There is one more technique, which, in some situations, can help to clarify the source code of a C program. This technique is to make use of the **typedef** declaration. Its purpose is to redefine the name of an existing variable type.

For example, consider the following statement in which the type **unsigned long int** is redefined to be of the type **TWOWORDS**:

```
typedef unsigned long  int TWOWORDS ;
```

Now we can declare variables of the type **unsigned long int** by writing,

```
TWOWORDS  var1, var2 ;
```

instead of

```
unsigned long int  var1, var2 ;
```

Thus, **typedef** provides a short and meaningful way to call a data type. Usually, uppercase letters are used to make it clear that we are dealing with a renamed data type.

While the increase in readability is probably not great in this example, it can be significant when the name of a particular data type is long and unwieldy, as it often is with structure declarations. For example, consider the following structure declaration:

```
struct employee
{
    char  name[30] ;
    int  age ;
    float  bs ;
} ;
struct employee  e ;
```

This structure declaration can be made more handy to use when renamed using **typedef** as shown below:

```
struct employee
{
    char  name[30] ;
    int  age ;
    float  bs ;
```

```
} ;
typedef struct employee EMP ;
EMP e1, e2 ;
```

Thus, by reducing the length and apparent complexity of data types, **typedef** can help to clarify source listing and save time and energy spent in understanding a program.

The above **typedef** can also be written as

```
typedef struct employee
{
    char name[30] ;
    int age ;
    float bs ;
} EMP ;
EMP e1, e2 ;
```

typedef can also be used to rename pointer data types as shown below:

```
struct employee
{
    char name[30] ;
    int age ;
    float bs ;
}
typedef struct employee * PEMP ;
PEMP p ;
p -> age = 32 ;
```

Typecasting

Sometimes we are required to force the compiler to explicitly convert the value of an expression to a particular data type. This would be clear from the following example:

```
# include <stdio.h>
int main( )
{
    float a ;
    int x = 6, y = 4 ;
    a = x / y ;
    printf ( "Value of a = %f\n", a ) ;
    return 0 ;
```

```
}
```

And here is the output...

```
Value of a = 1.000000
```

The answer turns out to be 1.000000 and not 1.5. This is because, 6 and 4 are both integers and hence **6 / 4** yields an integer, 1. This 1 when stored in **a** is converted to 1.000000 . But what if we don't want the quotient to be truncated? One solution is to make either **x** or **y** as **float**. Let us say that other requirements of the program do not permit us to do this. In such a case what do we do? Use type casting. The following program illustrates this.

```
# include <stdio.h>
int main( )
{
    float a ;
    int x = 6, y = 4 ;
    a = ( float ) x / y ;
    printf ( "Value of a = %f\n", a ) ;
    return 0 ;
}
```

And here is the output...

```
Value of a = 1.500000
```

This program uses type casting. This consists of putting a pair of parentheses around the name of the data type. In this program we said,

```
a = ( float ) x / y ;
```

The expression (**float**) causes the variable **x** to be converted from type **int** to type **float** before being used in the division operation.

Here is another example of type casting:

```
# include <stdio.h>
int main( )
{
    float a = 6.35 ;

    printf ( "Value of a on type casting = %d\n", ( int ) a ) ;
```

```
    printf ( "Value of a = %f\n", a ) ;
    return 0 ;
}
```

And here is the output...

```
Value of a on type casting = 6
Value of a = 6.350000
```

Note that the value of **a** doesn't get permanently changed as a result of typecasting. Rather it is the value of the expression that undergoes type conversion whenever the cast appears.

Bit Fields

If in a program a variable is to take only two values 1 and 0, we really need only a single bit to store it. Similarly, if a variable is to take values from 0 to 3, then two bits are sufficient to store these values. And if a variable is to take values from 0 through 7, then three bits will be enough, and so on.

Why waste an entire integer when one or two or three bits will do? Well, for one thing, there aren't any one bit or two bit or three bit data types available in C. However, when there are several variables whose maximum values are small enough to pack into a single memory location, we can use 'bit fields' to store several values in a single integer. To demonstrate how bit fields work, let us consider an example. Suppose we want to store the following data about an employee. Each employee can:

(a) be male or female
(b) be single, married, divorced or widowed
(c) have one of the eight different hobbies
(d) can choose from any of the fifteen different schemes proposed by the company to pursue his/her hobby.

This means we need one bit to store gender, two to store marital status, three for hobby, and four for scheme (with one value used for those who are not desirous of availing any of the schemes). We need ten bits altogether, which means we can pack all this information into a single integer, since an integer is 16 bits long.

To do this using bit fields, we declare the following structure:

```
struct employee
{
```

```
    unsigned  gender  : 1 ;
    unsigned  mar_stat  : 2 ;
    unsigned  hobby  : 3 ;
    unsigned  scheme  : 4 ;
} ;
```

The colon in the above declaration tells the compiler that we are talking about bit fields and the number after it tells how many bits to allot for the field.

Once we have established a bit field, we can reference it just like any other structure element, as shown in the program given below:

```
# include <stdio.h>
# define MALE 0 ;
# define FEMALE 1 ;
# define SINGLE 0 ;
# define MARRIED 1 ;
# define DIVORCED 2 ;
# define WIDOWED 3 ;

int main( )
{
    struct employee
    {
        unsigned  gender : 1 ;
        unsigned  mar_stat : 2 ;
        unsigned  hobby : 3 ;
        unsigned  scheme : 4 ;
    } ;
    struct employee  e ;

    e.gender = MALE ;
    e.mar_status = DIVORCED ;
    e.hobby = 5 ;
    e.scheme = 9 ;

    printf ( "Gender = %d\n", e.gender ) ;
    printf ( "Marital status = %d\n", e.mar_status ) ;
    printf ( "Bytes occupied by e = %d\n", sizeof ( e ) ) ;
    return 0 ;
}
```

And here is the output...

```
Gender = 0
Marital status = 2
Bytes occupied by e = 2
```

Pointers to Functions

Every type of variable that we have discussed so far, with the exception of register, has an address. We have seen how we can reference variables of the type **char, int, float,** etc. through their addresses—that is by using pointers. Pointers can also point to C functions. And why not? C functions have addresses. If we know the function's address, we can point to it, which provides another way to invoke it. Let us see how this can be done.

```
# include <stdio.h>
void display( ) ;
int main( )
{
    printf ( "Address of function display is %u\n", display ) ;
    display( ) ; /* usual way of invoking a function */
    return 0 ;
}

void display( )
{
    puts ( "Long live viruses!!\n" ) ;
}
```

The output of the program would be:

```
Address of function display is 1125
Long live viruses!!
```

Note that, to obtain the address of a function, all that we have to do is mention the name of the function, as has been done in the **printf( )** statement above. This is similar to mentioning the name of the array to get its base address.

Now let us see how using the address of a function, we can manage to invoke it. This is shown in the program given below:

```
/* Invoking a function using a pointer to a function */
# include <stdio.h>
void display( ) ;
int main( )
```

```
{
    void ( *func_ptr )( ) ;

    func_ptr = display ;  /* assign address of function */
    printf ( "Address of function display is %u", func_ptr ) ;
    ( *func_ptr )( ) ;  /* invokes the function display( ) */
    return 0 ;
}
void display( )
{
    puts ( "\nLong live viruses!!" ) ;
}
```

The output of the program would be:

```
Address of function display is 1125
Long live viruses!!
```

In **main( )**, we declare the function **display( )** as a function returning nothing. But what are we to make of the declaration,

```
void ( *func_ptr )( ) ;
```

that comes in the next line? We are obviously declaring something that, like **display( )**, will return nothing, but what is it? And why is ***func_ptr** enclosed in parentheses?

If we glance down a few lines in our program, we see the statement,

```
func_ptr = display ;
```

so we know that **func_ptr** is being assigned the address of **display( )**. Therefore, **func_ptr** must be a pointer to the function **display( )**. Thus, all that the declaration

```
void ( *func_ptr )( ) ;
```

means is, that **func_ptr** is a pointer to a function, which returns nothing. And to invoke the function, we are just required to write the statement,

```
( *func_ptr )( ) ;     /* or simply,  func_ptr( ) ; */
```

Pointers to functions are certainly awkward and off-putting. And why use them at all when we can invoke a function in a much simpler manner? What is the possible gain of using this esoteric feature of C? There are two possible uses:

(a) in implementing callback mechanisms used popularly in Windows programming
(b) in binding functions dynamically, at run-time in C++ programming

The first of these topics is discussed in Chapter 17 briefly. The second topic is beyond the scope of this book. If you want to explore it further you can refer the book "Let Us C++" or "Test Your C++ Skills" by Yashavant Kanetkar.

Functions Returning Pointers

The way functions return an **int**, a **float**, a **double** or any other data type, it can even return a pointer. However, to make a function return a pointer, it has to be explicitly mentioned in the calling function as well as in the function definition. The following program illustrates this.

```
int *fun( ) ;
int main( )
{
    int *p ;
    p = fun( ) ;
    return 0 ;
}

int *fun( )
{
    static int i = 20 ;
    return ( &i ) ;
}
```

This program just indicates how an integer pointer can be returned from a function. Beyond that, it doesn't serve any useful purpose. This concept can be put to use while handling strings. For example, look at the following program which copies one string into another and returns the pointer to the target string.

```
char *copy ( char *, char * ) ;
int main( )
{
    char *str ;
    char *copy ( char *, char * ) ;
    char source[ ] = "Jaded" ;
    char target[10] ;

    str = copy ( target, source ) ;
```

```
	printf ( "%s\n", str ) ;
	return 0 ;
}

char *copy ( char *t, char *s )
{
	char *r ;

	r = t ;

	while ( *s != '\0' )
	{
		*t = *s ;
		t++ ;
		s++ ;
	}

	*t = '\0' ;
	return ( r ) ;
}
```

Here we have sent the base addresses of **source** and **target** strings to **copy( )**. In the **copy( )** function, the **while** loop copies the characters in the source string into the target string. Since during copying **t** is continuously incremented, before entering into the loop, the initial value of **t** is safely stored in the character pointer **r**. Once copying is over, this character pointer **r** is returned to **main( )**.

Functions with Variable Number of Arguments

We have used **printf( )** so often without realizing how it works properly irrespective of how many arguments we pass to it. How do we go about writing such routines that can take variable number of arguments? And what have pointers got to do with it? There are three macros available in the file "stdarg.h" called **va_start**, **va_arg** and **va_list** which allow us to handle this situation. These macros provide a method for accessing the arguments of the function when a function takes a fixed number of arguments followed by a variable number of arguments. The fixed number of arguments are accessed in the normal way, whereas the optional arguments are accessed using the macros **va_start** and **va_arg**. Out of these macros, **va_start** is used to initialize a pointer to the beginning of the list of optional arguments. On the other hand, the macro **va_arg** is used to advance the pointer to the next argument.

Let us put these concepts into action using a program. Suppose we wish to write a function **findmax( )** which would find out the maximum value from a set of values, irrespective of the number of values passed to it. Here is how we can do it…

```
# include <stdio.h>
# include <stdarg.h>
int findmax ( int, ... ) ;
int main( )
{
    int max ;

    max = findmax ( 5, 23, 15, 1, 92, 50 ) ;
    printf ( "maximum = %d\n", max ) ;

    max = findmax ( 3, 100, 300, 29 ) ;
    printf ( "maximum = %d\n", max ) ;
    return 0 ;
}

int findmax ( int tot_num, ... )
{
    int max, count, num ;

    va_list ptr ;

    va_start ( ptr, tot_num ) ;
    max = va_arg ( ptr, int ) ;

    for ( count = 1 ; count < tot_num ; count++ )
    {
        num = va_arg ( ptr, int ) ;
        if ( num > max )
            max = num ;
    }

    return ( max ) ;
}
```

Note how the **findmax( )** function has been declared. The ellipses (…) indicate that the number of arguments after the first argument would be variable.

Here we are making two calls to **findmax( )**, first time to find maximum out of 5 values and second time to find maximum out of 3 values. Note that for each call the first argument is the count of arguments that follow the first argument. The value of the first argument passed to **findmax( )** is collected in the variable **tot_num**. **findmax( )** begins with a declaration of a pointer **ptr** of the type **va_list**. Observe the next statement carefully:

```
va_start ( ptr, tot_num ) ;
```

This statement sets up **ptr** such that it points to the first variable argument in the list. If we are considering the first call to **finndmax( )**, **ptr** would now point to 23. The statement **max = va_arg (ptr, int)** would assign the integer being pointed to by **ptr** to **max**. Thus 23 would be assigned to **max**, and **ptr** would now start pointing to the next argument, i.e 15. The rest of the program is fairly straightforward. We just keep picking up successive numbers in the list and keep comparing them with the latest value in **max**, till all the arguments in the list have been scanned. The final value in **max** is then returned to **main( )**.

How about another program to fix your ideas? This one calls a function **display( )** which is capable of printing any number of arguments of any type.

```
# include <stdio.h>
# include <stdarg.h>
void display ( int, int, ... ) ;
int main( )
{
    display ( 1, 2, 5, 6 ) ;
    display ( 2, 4, 'A', 'a', 'b', 'c' ) ;
    display ( 3, 3, 2.5, 299.3, -1.0 ) ;
    return 0 ;
}

void display ( int type, int num, ... )
{
    int i, j ;
    char c ;
    float f ;
    va_list ptr ;

    va_start ( ptr, num ) ;
    switch ( type )
    {
        case 1 :
            for ( j = 1 ; j <= num ; j++ )
            {
```

```
                i = va_arg ( ptr, int ) ;
                printf ( "%d ", i ) ;
            }
            break ;

        case 2 :
            for ( j = 1 ; j <= num ; j++ )
            {
                c = va_arg ( ptr, char ) ;
                printf ( "%c ", c ) ;
            }
            break ;

        case 3 :
            for ( j = 1 ; j <= num ; j++ )
            {
                f = ( float ) va_arg ( ptr, double ) ;
                printf ( "%f ", f ) ;
            }
    }
    printf ( "\n" ) ;
}
```

Here we pass two fixed arguments to the function **display( )**. The first one indicates the data type of the arguments to be printed and the second indicates the number of such arguments to be printed. Once again, through the statement **va_start (ptr, num)** we set up **ptr** such that it points to the first argument in the variable list of arguments. Then depending upon whether the value of type is 1, 2 or 3, we print out the arguments as **ints**, **chars** or **floats**.

In all calls to **display( )** the second argument indicated how many values are we trying to print. Contrast this with **printf( )**. To it we never pass an argument indicating how many value are we trying to print. Then how does **printf( )** figure this out? Simple. It scans the format string and counts the number of format specifiers that we have used in it to decide how many values are being printed.

Unions

Unions are derived data types, the way structures are. But Unions have the same relationship to structures that you might have with a distant cousin who resembled you but turned out to be smuggling contraband in Mexico. That is, unions and structures look alike, but are engaged in totally different enterprises.

Both structures and unions are used to group a number of different variables together. But while a structure enables us treat a number of different variables stored at different places in memory, a union enables us to treat the same space in memory as a number of different variables. That is, a union offers a way for a section of memory to be treated as a variable of one type on one occasion, and as a different variable of a different type on another occasion.

You might wonder why it would be necessary to do such a thing, but we will be seeing several very practical applications of unions soon. First, let us take a look at a simple example:

```
/* Demo of union at work */
# include <stdio.h>
int main( )
{
    union a
    {
        int i ;
        char ch[2] ;
    } ;
    union a key ;

    key.i = 512 ;
    printf ( "key.i = %d\n", key.i ) ;
    printf ( "key.ch[0] = %d\n", key.ch[0] ) ;
    printf ( "key.ch[1] = %d\n", key.ch[1] ) ;
    return 0 ;
}
```

And here is the output...

```
key.i = 512
key.ch[0] = 0
key.ch[1] = 2
```

As you can see, first we declared a data type of the type **union a**, and then a variable **key** to be of the type **union a**. This is similar to the way we first declare the structure type and then the structure variables. Also, the union elements are accessed exactly the same way in which the structure elements are accessed, using a '**.**' operator. However, the similarity ends here. To illustrate this let us compare the following data types:

```
struct a
{
```

```
    int i ;
    char ch[2] ;
} ;
struct a key ;
```

This data type would occupy 4 bytes in memory, 2 for **key.i** and one each for **key.ch[0]** and **key.ch[1]**, as shown in Figure 18.1.

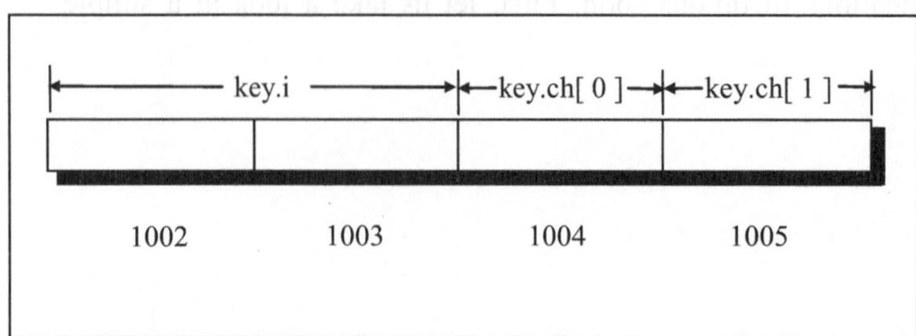

Figure 18.1

Now we declare a similar data type, but instead of using a structure we use a union.

```
union a
{
    int i ;
    char ch[2] ;
} ;
union a key ;
```

Representation of this data type in memory is shown in Figure 18.2.

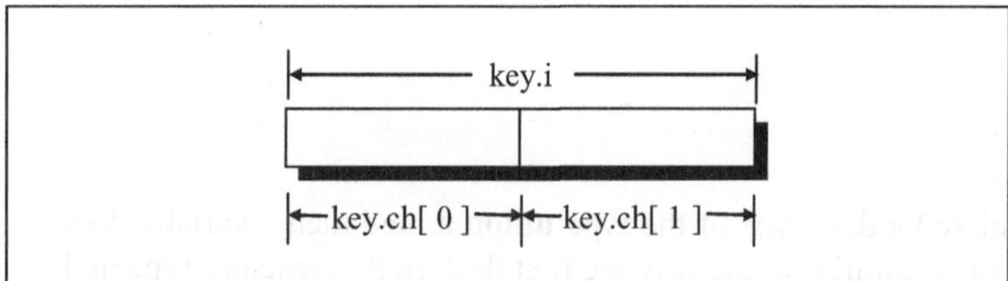

Figure 18.2

As shown in Figure 18.2, the union occupies only 2 bytes in memory. Note that the same memory locations which are used for **key.i** are also being used by **key.ch[0]** and **key.ch[1]**. It means that the memory locations used by **key.i** can also be accessed using **key.ch[0]** and **key.ch[1]**. What purpose does this serve? Well, now we can access the two bytes simultaneously (by using **key.i**) or the same two bytes individually (using **key.ch[0]** and **key.ch[1]**).

This is a frequent requirement while interacting with the hardware. i.e. sometimes we are required to access two bytes simultaneously and sometimes each byte individually. Faced with such a situation, using union is the answer, usually.

Perhaps you would be able to understand the union data type more thoroughly if we take a fresh look at the output of the above program. Here it is...

```
key.i = 512
key.ch[0] = 0
key.ch[1] = 2
```

Let us understand this output in detail. 512 is an integer, a 2 byte number. Its binary equivalent will be 0000 0010 0000 0000. We would expect that this binary number when stored in memory would look as shown below.

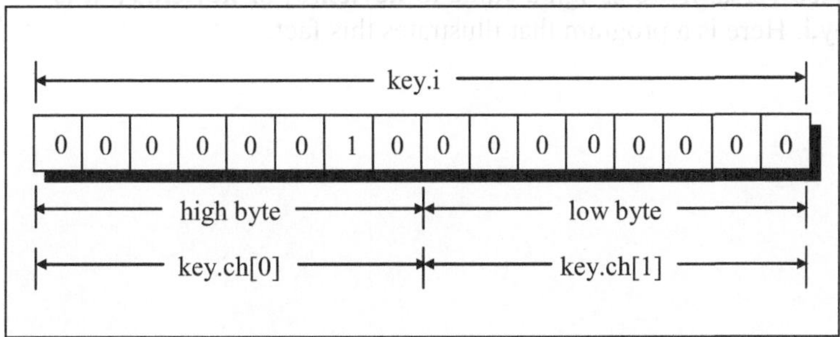

Figure 18.3

If the number is stored in this manner, then the output of **key.ch[0]** and **key.ch[1]** should have been 2 and 0. But, if you look at the output of the program written above, it is exactly the opposite. Why is it so? Because, in CPUs that follow little-endian architecture (Intel CPUs, for example), when a two-byte number is stored in memory, the low byte is stored before the high byte. It means, actually 512 would be stored in memory as shown in Figure 18.4. In CPUs with big-endian architecture this reversal of bytes does not happen.

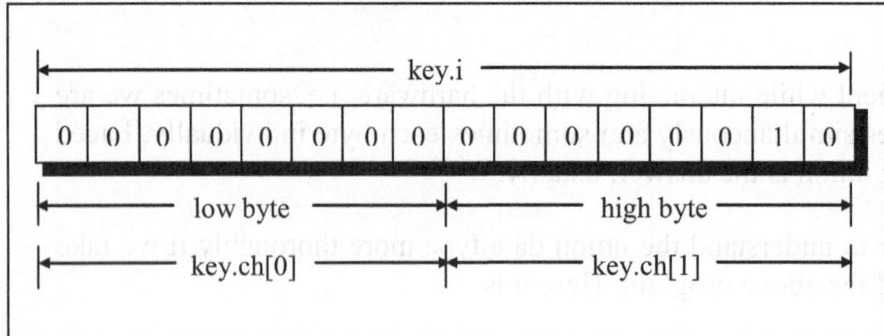

Figure 18.4

Now, we can see why value of **key.ch[0]** is printed as 0 and value of **key.ch[1]** is printed as 2.

One last thing. We can't assign different values to the different union elements at the same time. That is, if we assign a value to **key.i**, it gets automatically assigned to **key.ch[0]** and **key.ch[1]**. Vice versa, if we assign a value to **key.ch[0]** or **key.ch[1]**, it is bound to get assigned to **key.i**. Here is a program that illustrates this fact.

```
# include <stdio.h>
int main( )
{
    union a
    {
        int i ;
        char ch[2] ;
    } ;
    union a key ;

    key.i = 512 ;
    printf ( "key.i = %d\n", key.i ) ;
    printf ( "key.ch[0] = %d\n", key.ch[0] ) ;
    printf ( "key.ch[1] = %d\n", key.ch[1] ) ;

    key.ch[0] = 50 ; /* assign a new value to key.ch[0] */
    printf ( "key.i = %d\n", key.i ) ;
    printf ( "key.ch[0] = %d\n", key.ch[0] ) ;
    printf ( "key.ch[1] = %d\n", key.ch[1] ) ;
    return 0 ;
}
```

And here is the output...

```
key.i = 512
key.ch[0] = 0
key.ch[1] = 2
key.i= 562
key.ch[0] = 50
key.ch[1] = 2
```

Before we move on to the next section, let us reiterate that a union provides a way to look at the same data in several different ways. For example, there can exist a union as shown below.

```
union b
{
    double d ;
    float f[2] ;
    int i[4] ;
    char ch[8] ;
} ;
union b data ;
```

In what different ways can the data be accessed from it? Sometimes, as a complete set of eight bytes (**data.d**), sometimes as two sets of 4 bytes each (**data.f[0]** and **data.f[1]**), sometimes as four sets of 2 bytes each (**data.i[0]**, **data.i[1]**, **data.i[2]** and **data.[3]**) and sometimes as eight individual bytes (**data.ch[0]**, **data.ch[1]... data.ch[7]**).

Also note that, there can exist a union, where each of its elements is of different size. In such a case, the size of the union variable will be equal to the size of the longest element in the union.

Union of Structures

Just as one structure can be nested within another, a union too can be nested in another union. Not only that, there can be a union in a structure, or a structure in a union. Here is an example of stuctures nested in a union.

```
# include <stdio.h>
int main( )
{
    struct a
    {
        int i ;
        char c[2] ;
```

```
    } ;
    struct b
    {
        int j ;
        char d[2] ;
    } ;
    union z
    {
        struct a key ;
        struct b data ;
    } ;
    union z strange ;

    strange.key.i = 512 ;
    strange.data.d[0] = 0 ;
    strange.data.d[1] = 32 ;

    printf ( "%d\n", strange.key.i ) ;
    printf ( "%d\n", strange.data.j ) ;
    printf ( "%d\n", strange.key.c[0] ) ;
    printf ( "%d\n", strange.data.d[0] ) ;
    printf ( "%d\n", strange.key.c[1] ) ;
    printf ( "%d\n", strange.data.d[1] ) ;
    return 0 ;
}
```

And here is the output...

```
512
512
0
0
32
32
```

Just as we do with nested structures, we access the elements of the union in this program using the '**.**' operator twice. Thus,

```
strange.key.i
```

refers to the variable **i** in the structure **key** in the union **strange**. Analysis of the output of the above program is left to the reader.

Utility of Unions

Suppose we wish to store information about employees in an organization. The items of information are as shown below:

```
Name
Grade
Age
If Grade = HSK  (Highly Skilled)
    hobbie name
    credit card no.
If Grade = SSK (Semi Skilled)
    Vehicle no.
    Distance from Co.
```

Since this is dissimilar information we can gather it together using a structure as shown below:

```
struct employee
{
    char n[ 20 ] ;
    char grade[ 4 ] ;
    int age ;
    char hobby[10] ;
    int crcardno ;
    char vehno[10] ;
    int dist ;
} ;
struct employee e ;
```

Though grammatically there is nothing wrong with this structure, it suffers from a disadvantage. For any employee, depending upon his grade either the fields hobby and credit card no. or the fields vehicle number and distance would get used. Both sets of fields would never get used. This would lead to wastage of memory with every structure variable that we create, since every structure variable would have all the four field apart from name, grade and age. This can be avoided by creating a **union** between these sets of fields. This is shown below:

```
sruct info1
{
    char hobby[10] ;
    int crcardno ;
```

```
};
sruct info2
{
    char vehno[10] ;
    int dist ;
};
union info
{
    struct info1 a ;
    struct info2 b ;
};
struct emp
{
    char n[ 20 ] ;
    char grade[ 4 ] ;
    int age ;
    union  info f ;
};
struct employee e ;
```

The *volatile* Qualifier

When we define variables in a function the compiler may optimize the code that uses the variable. That is, the compiler may compile the code in a manner that will run in the most efficient way possible. The compiler achieves this by using a CPU register to store the variable's value rather than storing it in stack.

However, if we declare the variable as volatile, then it serves as a warning to the compiler that it should not *optimize* the code containing this variable. In such a case whenever we use the variable its value would be loaded from memory into register, operations would be performed on it and the result would be written back to the memory location allocated for the variable.

We can declare a volatile variable as:

```
volatile int  j ;
```

Another place where we may want to declare a variable as volatile is when the variable is not within the control of the program and is likely to get altered from outside the program. For example, the variable

```
volatile float temperature ;
```

might get modified through the digital thermometer attached to the computer.

Summary

(a) The enumerated data type and the **typedef** declaration add to the clarity of the program.
(b) Typecasting makes the data type conversions for specific operations.
(c) When the information to be stored can be represented using a few bits of a byte we can use bit fields to pack more information in a byte.
(d) Every C function has an address that can be stored in a pointer to a function. Pointers to functions provide one more way to call functions.
(e) We can write a function that receives a variable number of arguments.
(f) Unions permit access to same memory locations in multiple ways.

Exercise

[A] What will be the output of the following programs:

(a)
```
# include <stdio.h>
int main( )
{
    enum status { pass, fail, atkt } ;
    enum status  stud1, stud2, stud3 ;
    stud1 = pass ;
    stud2 = fail ;
    stud3 = atkt ;
    printf ( "%d %d %d\n", stud1, stud2, stud3 ) ;
    return 0 ;
}
```

(b)
```
# include <stdio.h>
int main( )
{
    printf ( "%f\n", ( float ) ( ( int ) 3.5 / 2 ) ) ;
    return 0 ;
}
```

(c)
```
# include <stdio.h>
int main( )
{
    float  i, j ;
    i = ( float ) 3 / 2 ;
    j = i * 3 ;
```

```
        printf ( "%d\n", ( int ) j ) ;
        return 0 ;
    }
```

(d)
```
    # include <stdio.h>
    int main( )
    {
        union summer
        {
            int i ;
            char c[2] ;
            char c1 ;
        } winter, autumn[2] ;

        winter.i = 1024 ;
        printf ( "%d %d %d %d %d\n", sizeof ( winter ), winter.c[1], winter.c1, sizeof ( autumn ),
    autumn[1].i ) ;
        return 0 ;
    }
```

(e)
```
    # include <stdio.h>
    int main( )
    {
        int ( * message )( ) ;
        print( ) ;
        message = print ;
        ( *message )( ) ;
        return 0 ;
    }
    print( )
    {
        puts ( "Love makes life live, so love somebody\n" ) ;
    }
```

(f)
```
    # include <stdio.h>
    int main( )
    {
        typedef unsigned char SMALL ;
        SMALL b = 0x00, c = 0xAA, d = 0x80 ;
        int i = 7 ;
        for ( ; i >= 0 ; i-- )
            b = ( ( c & ( d >> ( 7 - i ) << ( 7 - i ) ) >> i ) | b ) ;
        printf ( "value of b = %d\n", b ) ;
```

```
        return 0 ;
    }
```

(g)
```
    # include <stdio.h>
    int main( )
    {
        enum cards { heart = 10, diamond = 20, spade = 30 } ;
        enum cards a, b ;
        a = heart + spade ;
        b = heart * diamond ;
        printf ( "%d %d\n", a, b ) ;
        return 0 ;
    }
```

(h)
```
    # include <stdio.h>
    int main( )
    {
        typedef struct emp
        {
            char code[5] ;
            char name[30] ;
            int age ;
        } E ;
        E e ;
        printf ( "%d %d\n", sizeof ( E ), sizeof ( e ) ) ;
        return 0 ;
    }
```

(i)
```
    # include <stdio.h>
    int main( )
    {
        struct a
        {
            unsigned ms : 1 ;
            unsigned dept : 2 ;
            unsigned hobby : 1 ;
        } b ;
        printf ( "%d\n", sizeof ( b ) ) ;
        return 0 ;
    }
```

(j)
```
    # include <stdio.h>
    int main( )
```

```
{
    int a = 10, b = 20 ;
    float c, d = 3.5 ;
    c = ( int ) d * a + b * 2.5 ;
    printf ( "c = %f\n", c ) ;
    return 0 ;
}
```

(k)
```
# include <stdio.h>
int main( )
{
    struct a
    {
        unsigned a : 1 ;
        unsigned b : 2 ;
        unsigned c : 2 ;
    } ;
    struct a *y ;
    int x = 22 ;
    y = &x ;
    printf ( "%d %d %d\n", ( *y ).a, ( *y ).b, y -> c ) ;
    return 0 ;
}
```

[B] Point out the error, if any, in the following programs:

(a)
```
# include <stdio.h>
int main( )
{
    typedef struct patient
    {
        char name[20] ;
        int age ;
        int systolic_bp ;
        int diastolic_bp ;
    } ptt ;
    ptt p1 = { "anil", 23, 110, 220 } ;
    printf ( "%s %d\n", p1.name, p1.age ) ;
    printf ( "%d %d\n", p1.systolic_bp, p1.diastolic_bp ) ;
    return 0 ;
}
```

(b)
```
# include <stdio.h>
```

```
void show( ) ;
int main( )
{
    void ( *s )( ) ;
    s = show ;
    ( *s )( ) ;
    return 0 ;
}
void show( )
{
    printf ( "don't show off. It won't pay in the long run\n" ) ;
}
```

(c)
```
# include <stdio.h>
int show( ) ;
int main( )
{
    int ( *s )( ) ;
    s = show( ) ;
    ( *s )( ) ;
    return 0 ;
}
float show( )
{
    printf ( "Control did reach here\n" ) ;
    return ( 3.33 ) ;
}
```

(d)
```
# include <stdio.h>
void show ( int, float ) ;
int main( )
{
    void ( *s )( int, float ) ;
    s = show ;
    ( *s )( 10, 3.14 ) ;
    return 0 ;
}
void show ( int i, float f )
{
    printf ( "%d %f\n", i, f ) ;
}
```

(e)
```
# include <stdio.h>
```

```
int main( )
{
    void see( ) ;
    void ( *s ) ;
    s = see( ) ;
    ( *s ) ;
    return 0 ;
}
void see( )
{
    printf ( "C unlimited powers of C" ) ;
}
```

[C] Attempt the following:

(a) Create an array of four function pointers. Each pointer should point to a different function. Each of these functions should receive two integers and return a float. Using a loop call each of these functions using the addresses present in the array.

(b) Write a function that receives variable number of arguments, where the arguments are the coordinates of a point. Based on the number of arguments received, the function should display type of shape like a point, line, triangle, etc. that can be drawn.

(c) Write a program, which stores information about a date in a structure containing three members—day, month and year. Using bit fields the day number should get stored in first 5 bits of day, the month number in 4 bits of month and year in 12 bits of year. Write a program to read date of joining of 10 employees and display them in ascending order of year.

(d) Write a program to read and store information about insurance policy holder. The information contains details like gender, whether the holder is minor/major, policy name and duration of the policy. Make use of bit-fields to store this information.

A Precedence Table

Description	Operator	Associativity
Function expression	( )	Left to Right
Array Expression	[ ]	Left to Right
Structure operator	->	Left to Right
Structure operator	.	Left to Right
Unary minus	-	Right to left
Increment/Decrement	++ --	Right to Left
One's compliment	~	Right to left
Negation	!	Right to Left
Address of	&	Right to left
Value of address	*	Right to left
Type cast	(type)	Right to left
Size in bytes	sizeof	Right to left
Multiplication	*	Left to right
Division	/	Left to right
Modulus	%	Left to right
Addition	+	Left to right
Subtraction	-	Left to right
Left shift	<<	Left to right
Right shift	>>	Left to right
Less than	<	Left to right
Less than or equal to	<=	Left to right
Greater than	>	Left to right
Greater than or equal to	>=	Left to right
Equal to	==	Left to right
Not equal to	!=	Left to right

Continued…

Continued...

Description	Operator	Associativity
Bitwise AND	&	Left to right
Bitwise exclusive OR	^	Left to right
Bitwise inclusive OR	|	Left to right
Logical AND	&&	Left to right
Logical OR	||	Left to right
Conditional	? :	Right to left
Assignment	=	Right to left
	*= /= %=	Right to left
	+= -= &=	Right to left
	^= |=	Right to left
	<<= >>=	Right to left
Comma	,	Right to left

Figure A.1

B Chasing The Bugs

C programmers are great innovators of our times. However, there is no shortage of horror stories about programs that took twenty times to 'debug' as they did to 'write'. Many a time programs had to be rewritten all over again because the bugs present in them could not be located. Bugs are C programmer's birthright. But how do we chase them away. No sure-shot way for that. I thought if I make a list of more common programming mistakes, it might be of help. They are not arranged in any particular order. But as you would realize, surely a great help!

[1] Omitting the ampersand before the variables used in **scanf( )**. For example,

```
int choice ;
scanf ( "%d", choice ) ;
```

Here, the **&** before the variable choice is missing. Another common mistake with **scanf( )** is to give blanks either just before the format string or immediately after the format string as in,

```
int choice ;
scanf ( " %d ", &choice ) ;
```

Note that this is not a mistake, but till you don't understand **scanf( )** thoroughly, this is going to cause trouble. Safety is in eliminating the blanks.

[2] Using the operator **=** instead of the operator **= =**. For example, the following **while** loop becomes an infinite loop since every time, instead of checking the value of **i** against 10, it assigns the value 10 to **i**. As 10 is a non-zero value the condition will always be treated as true, forming an infinite loop.

```
int i = 10 ;
while ( i = 10 )
{
    printf ( "got to get out" ) ;
    i++ ;
}
```

[3] Ending a loop with a semicolon. Observe the following program.

```
int j = 1 ;
while ( j <= 100 ) ;
{
    printf ( "\nCompguard" ) ;
    j++ ;
}
```

Here, inadvertently, we have fallen in an indefinite loop. Cause is the semicolon after **while**. This semicolon is treated as a null statement by the compiler as shown below:

```
while ( j <= 100 )
    ;
```

This is an indefinite loop since the null statement keeps getting executed indefinitely as **j** never gets incremented

[4] Omitting the **break** statement at the end of a **case** in a **switch** statement. Remember that, if a **break** is not included at the end of a **case**, then execution will continue into the next **case**.

```
int ch = 1 ;
switch ( ch )
{
    case 1 :
        printf ( "\nGoodbye" ) ;
    case 2 :
        printf ( "\nLieutenant" ) ;
}
```

Here, since the **break** has not been given after the **printf( )** in **case 1**, the control runs into **case 2** and executes the second **printf( )** as well. However, this sometimes turns out to be a blessing in disguise. Especially, in cases when we want same set of statements to get executed for multiple cases.

[5] Using **continue** in a **switch**. It is a common error to believe that the way the keyword **break** is used with loops and a **switch**; similarly the keyword **continue** can also be used with them. Remember that **continue** works only with loops, never with a **switch**.

[6] A mismatch in the number, type and order of actual and formal arguments. Consider the following call:

```
yr = romanise ( year, 1000, 'm' ) ;
```

Here, three arguments in the order **int**, **int** and **char** are being passed to **romanise( )**. When **romanise( )** receives these arguments into formal arguments, they must be received in the same order. A careless mismatch might give strange results.

[7] Omitting provisions for returning a non-integer value from a function. If we make the following function call,

```
area = area_circle ( 1.5 ) ;
```

then, while defining **area_circle( )** function later in the program, care should be taken to make it capable of returning a floating point value. Note that unless otherwise mentioned, the compiler would assume that this function returns a value of the type **int**.

[8] Inserting a semicolon at the end of a macro definition. This might create a problem as shown below.

```
# define UPPER 25 ;
```

would lead to a syntax error if used in an expression such as

```
if ( counter == UPPER )
```

This is because on preprocessing, the **if** statement would take the form

```
if ( counter == 25 ; )
```

[9] Omitting parentheses around a macro expansion. Consider the following macro:

```
# define SQR(x) x * x
```

If we use this macro as

```
int a ;
a = 25 / SQR ( 5 ) ;
```

we expect the value of **a** to be 1, whereas it turns out to be 25. This so happens, because, on preprocessing, the statement takes the following form:

```
a = 25 / 5 * 5 ;
```

[10] Leaving a blank space between the macro template and the macro expansion.

```
# define ABS  (a) ( a = 0  ? a : -a )
```

Here, the space between **ABS** and **(a)** makes the preprocessor believe that you want to expand **ABS** into **(a)**, which is certainly not what you want.

[11] Using an expression that has side effects in a macro. Consider the following macro:

```
# define SUM ( a ) ( a + a )
```

If we use this macro as

```
int  w, b = 5 ;
w = SUM( b++ ) ;
```

On preprocessing, the macro would be expanded to,

```
w = ( b++ ) + ( b++ ) ;
```

Thus, contrary to expectation, **b** will get incremented twice.

[12] Confusing a character constant and a character string. In the statement

```
ch = 'z' ;
```

a single character is assigned to **ch**. In the statement

```
ch = "z" ;
```

a pointer to the character string "z" is assigned to **ch**.

Note that in the first case, the declaration of **ch** would be,

```
char  ch ;
```

whereas in the second case it would be,

```
char  *ch ;
```

[13] Forgetting the bounds of an array.

```
int num[50], i ;
for ( i = 1 ; i <= 50 ; i++ )
    num[i] = i * i ;
```

Here, in the array **num**, there is no such element as **num[50]**, since array counting begins with 0 and not 1. Compiler would not give a warning if our program exceeds the bounds. If not taken care of, in extreme cases, the above code might even hang the computer.

[14] Forgetting to reserve an extra location in a character array for the null terminator. Remember each character array ends with a '\0', therefore its dimension should be declared big enough to hold the normal characters as well as the '\0'. For example, the dimension of the array **word[ ]** should be 9 if a string "Jamboree" is to be stored in it.

[15] Confusing the precedences of the various operators.

```
char ch ;
FILE *fp ;
fp = fopen ( "text.c", "r" ) ;
while ( ch = getc ( fp ) != EOF )
    putch ( ch ) ;
fclose ( fp ) ;
```

Here, the value returned by **getc( )** will be first compared with EOF, since **!=** has a higher priority than **=**. As a result, the value that is assigned to **ch** will be the true/false result of the test—1 if the value returned by **getc( )** is not equal to **EOF**, and 0 otherwise. The correct form of the above **while** would be,

```
while ( ( ch = getc ( fp ) ) != EOF )
    putch ( ch ) ;
```

[16] Confusing the operator **->** with the operator **.** while referring to a structure element. Remember, on the left of operator **.** only a structure variable can occur, whereas, on the left of operator **->** only a pointer to a structure can occur. Following example demonstrates this.

```
struct emp
{
    char name[35] ;
    int age ;
} ;
```

```
struct emp e = { "Dubhashi", 40 } ;
struct emp *ee ;
printf ( "\n%d", e.age ) ;
ee = &e ;
printf ( "\n%d", ee->>age ) ;
```

[17] Exceeding the range of integers and chars. Consider the following code snippet:

```
char  ch ;
for ( ch = 0 ; ch <= 255 ; ch++ )
    printf ( "\n%c %d", ch, ch ) ;
```

This is an indefinite loop. Reason is, **ch** has been declared as a **char** and its valid range is -128 to +127. Hence, the moment **ch** tries to become 128 (through **ch++**), the range is exceeded. As a result, the first number from the negative side of the range, -128, gets assigned to **ch**. Naturally, the condition is satisfied and the control remains within the loop.

C ASCII Chart

There are 256 distinct ASCII characters that can be used in C programming . Their values range from 0 to 255. These can be grouped as under:

Character Type	No. of Characters
Capital letters	26
Small-case Letters	26
Digits	10
Special Symbols	32
Control Character	34
Graphics Character	128
Total	256

Figure C.1

Out of the 256 character set, the first 128 are often called ASCII characters and the next 128 as Extended ASCII characters. Each ASCII character has a unique appearance. The following simple program can generate the ASCII chart:

```
# include <stdio.h>
int main( )
{
    int ch ;

    for ( ch = 0 ; ch <= 255 ; ch++ )
        printf ( "%d %c\n", ch, ch ) ;
    return 0 ;
}
```

This chart is shown at the end of this appendix. Out of the 128 graphic characters (Extended ASCII characters), there are characters that are used for drawing single line and double line boxes in text mode. For convenience these characters are shown in Figure C.2.

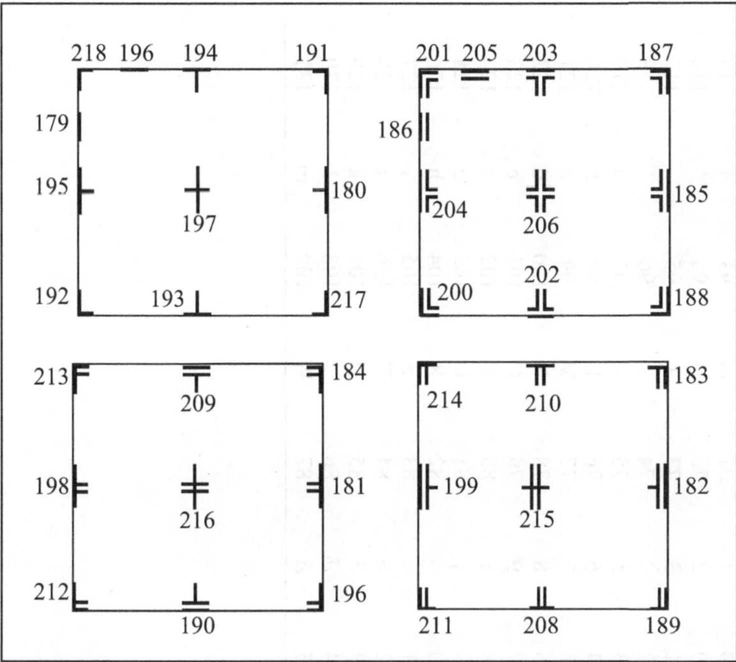

Figure C.2

Value	Char	Value	Char	Value	Char	Value	Char	Value	Char	Value	Char
0		22	▬	44	,	66	B	88	X	110	n
1	☺	23	↨	45	-	67	C	89	Y	111	o
2	☻	24	↑	46	.	68	D	90	Z	112	p
3	♥	25	↓	47	/	69	E	91	[	113	q
4	♦	26	→	48	0	70	F	92	\	114	r
5	♣	27	←	49	1	71	G	93	]	115	s
6	♠	28	⌐	50	2	72	H	94	^	116	t
7	•	29	↔	51	3	73	I	95	_	117	u
8	◘	30	▲	52	4	74	J	96	`	118	v
9	○	31	▼	53	5	75	K	97	a	119	w
10	◙	32		54	6	76	L	98	b	120	x
11	♂	33	!	55	7	77	M	99	c	121	y
12	♀	34	"	56	8	78	N	100	d	122	z
13	♪	35	#	57	9	79	O	101	e	123	{
14	♫	36	$	58	:	80	P	102	f	124	|
15	☼	37	%	59	;	81	Q	103	g	125	}
16	►	38	&	60	<	82	R	104	h	126	~
17	◄	39	'	61	=	83	S	105	i	127	MH
18	↕	40	(	62	>	84	T	106	j	128	Ç
19	‼	41	)	63	?	85	U	107	k	129	ü
20	¶	42	*	64	@	86	V	108	l	130	é
21	§	43	+	65	A	87	W	109	m	131	â

Value	Char	Value	Char	Value	Char	Value	Char	Value	Char	Value	Char
132	ä	154	Ü	176	░	198	╞	220	▄	242	≥
133	à	155	¢	177	▒	199	╟	221	▌	243	<
134	å	156	£	178	▓	200	╚	222	▐	244	⌠
135	c	157	¥	179	│	201	╔	223	▀	245	⌡
136	ê	158	₧	180	┤	202	╩	224	α	246	÷
137	ë	159	ƒ	181	╡	203	╦	225	ß	247	≈
138	è	160	á	182	╢	204	╠	226	Γ	248	°
139	ï	161	í	183	╖	205	═	227	π	249	•
140	î	162	ó	184	╕	206	╬	228	Σ	250	·
141	ì	163	ú	185	╣	207	╧	229	σ	251	√
142	Ä	164	ñ	186	║	208	╨	230	µ	252	η
143	Å	165	Ñ	187	╗	209	╤	231	τ	253	²
144	É	166	ª	188	╝	210	╥	232	Φ	254	■
145	æ	167	º	189	╜	211	╙	233	θ	255	
146	Æ	168	¿	190	╛	212	╘	234	Ω		
147	ô	169	⌐	191	┐	213	╒	235	δ		
148	ö	170	¬	192	└	214	╓	236	∞		
149	ò	171	½	193	┴	215	╫	237	ø		
150	û	172	¼	194	┬	216	╪	238	∈		
151	ù	173	¡	195	├	217	┘	239	∩		
152	ÿ	174	«	196	─	218	┌	240	≡		
153	Ö	175	»	197	┼	219	█	241	±		

Index

Index

!

A

B

C

R

S

T

U

V

W